Getting Naked with Harry Crews

UNIVERSITY PRESS OF FLORIDA

Florida A&M University, Tallahassee
Florida Atlantic University, Boca Raton
Florida Gulf Coast University, Ft. Myers
Florida International University, Miami
Florida State University, Tallahassee
New College of Florida, Sarasota
University of Central Florida, Orlando
University of Florida, Gainesville
University of North Florida, Jacksonville
University of South Florida, Tampa
University of West Florida, Pensacola

University Press of Florida
Gainesville
Tallahassee
Tampa
Boca Raton
Pensacola
Orlando
Miami
Jacksonville
Ft. Myers
Sarasota

GETTING
NAKED
WITH
HARRY

Interviews / Edited by Erik Bledsoe

Copyright 1999 by Erik Bledsoe
All rights reserved
Published in the United States of America

30 29 28 27 26 25   6 5 4 3 2 1

First clothing printing, 1999
First paperback printing, 2025

Library of Congress Cataloging-in-Publication Data
Crews, Harry, 1935–2012
Getting naked with Harry Crews; interviews / edited by Erik Bledsoe.
p. cm.
ISBN 978-0-8130-1709-9 (cloth) | ISBN 978-0-8130-8142-7 (pbk.)
1. Crews, Harry, 1935– . Interviews. 2. Novelists, American—20th century—
interviews. 3. Georgia—In literature. 4. Florida—In literature. 5. Fiction—
Authorship. I. Bledsoe, Erik, 1965– . II. Title.
PS3553.R46Z49   1999
8813'.54—dc21
[B]   99-33902

Cover and title page: Harry Crews in 1983.
Photos by Hank Rowland.

The University Press of Florida is the scholarly publishing agency for the
State University System of Florida, comprising Florida A&M University,
Florida Atlantic University, Florida Gulf Coast University, Florida International University, Florida State University, New College of Florida, University of Central Florida, University of Florida, University of North Florida, University of South Florida, and University of West Florida.

University Press of Florida
2046 NE Waldo Road
Suite 2100
Gainesville, FL 32609
http://upress.ufl.edu

GPSR EU Authorized Representative: Mare Nostrum Group B.V.,
Mauritskade 21D, 1091 GC Amsterdam, The Netherlands,
gpsr@mare-nostrum.co.uk

For Margie
and my parents

CONTENTS

Introduction by Erik Bledsoe 1

Anne Foata
Interview with Harry Crews 26

Sterling Watson
Arguments over an Open Wound:
An Interview with Harry Crews 49

Joe David Bellamy
Harry Crews: An Interview 64

Al Burt
Harry Crews: Working the Kinks Out 81

Steve Oney
Harry Crews Is a Stomp-Down Hard-Core Moralist 91

David K. Jeffrey and Donald R. Noble
Harry Crews: Part of an Interview 99

David K. Jeffrey and Donald R. Noble
Harry Crews: An Interview 104

Al Burt
The Troubles with Harry 121

Tom Graves
Harry Crews 130

Kay Bonetti
An Interview with Harry Crews 156

Rodney Elrod
The Freedom to Act: An Interview with Harry Crews 172

A. B. Crowder
Harry Crews 188

Hank Nuwer
The Writer Who Plays with Pain: Harry Crews 206

Mary T. Schmich
Still in the Game: On the Straight and Narrow
with Writer Harry Crews 219

Mary Voboril
Harry Goes Cruising for a Bruising 228

William Walsh
Harry Crews 236

Rob Michaels
Harry Crews: Pen-Packin' Old Boy 247

Dinty W. Moore
An Interview with Harry Crews 255

Joann Biondi
Still Macho after All These Years 263

David Aronson
Writing Is an Act of Discovery: Harry Crews 268

Tammy Lytal and Richard R. Russell
Some of Us Do It Anyway: An Interview with Harry Crews 273

Ruth Ellen Rasche
Blue-Eyed Boy 291

Susan Ketchin
Interview with Harry Crews 295

Cathi Unsworth
Harry Crews: Literary Terminator 309

Damon Sauve
Everything Is Optimism, Beautiful and Painless:
A Conversation with Harry Crews 315

Erik Bledsoe
An Interview with Harry Crews 331

Credits

Getting Naked with Harry Crews

ERIK BLEDSOE

Introduction

Harry Crews loves a good epigraph. Most of his twenty-three books begin with carefully chosen words, generally quoted from writers he admires. In conversation his speech is liberally sprinkled with favorite comments from Faulkner, Flaubert, and assorted others. One gets the impression that he is always looking for a catchy and insightful quip that will set just the right tone for one of his own stories. For *The Gospel Singer* (1968), his first published novel, he composed his own: "Men to whom God is dead worship one another." *The Gospel Singer* is the story of a honey-throated singer's return to the small Georgia town where he was born. The mostly poor residents of Enigma, Georgia (pop. 600), have little to look forward to except the Gospel Singer's periodic visits and concerts. To them, he has become larger than life, more than a hometown boy who made good. Soon stories begin to circulate that he can heal the sick, and the townspeople gather, seeking cures for their ailments both physical and spiritual. But the Gospel Singer has no such powers and is himself consumed with self-loathing for his sexual appetites. When the townspeople discover that the Gospel Singer cannot offer salvation, that he is only human with human flaws, they turn deadly violent.

The Gospel Singer's epigraph perfectly sets the tone for the book, but although Crews surely could not have realized it at the time he chose it, the line is also an apt introduction to all of his work. Most of Crews's characters are searching for something in which to place their faith, and that search almost always takes place outside the bounds of traditional religions. Often the characters throw themselves into some task with a single-minded devotion, hoping therein to find order and perspective. John Kaimon in *Karate Is a Thing of the Spirit* (1971) finds fulfillment briefly in the discipline of the dojo. In *All We Need of Hell* (1987), Duffy Deeter looks for it in body-punishing physical exercise. Facing a suburban existence that seems hollow, George Gattling takes up the ancient art of austringery in *The Hawk Is Dying* (1973). In *Body* (1990) Russell "Muscle" Morgan places his faith in his bodybuilding protégé, Shereel Dupont, who he believes has the talent to "win the world," a level he never achieved in his own career. In Crews's second novel, *Naked in Garden Hills* (1969), the residents of Garden Hills, an abandoned phosphate mine, look first to industrialist Jack O'Boylan, and when it becomes obvious that he will not return to reopen the mine, they look toward Fat Man, to whom O'Boylan deeded the mine when he closed the operation. When they realize that Fat Man is as unable to direct their lives as he is unable to control his own weight, the people abandon him for former beauty queen Dolly Furgeson, who promises economic and spiritual rejuvenation through go-go dancing for tourists. Inevitably, those characters who place their faith in others have their folly revealed—if not to themselves, then at least to the reader.

Crews's theological interests link him to fellow Georgian Flannery O'Connor, a writer whom he greatly admires and frequently quotes.[1] In fact, when I interviewed Crews at his home in July 1997, his built-in bookshelves were mostly barren as a result of his habit of giving away books, but one of the few books in the house was O'Connor's *The Habit of Being*, which rested on the table beside Crews's chair. Unlike O'Connor, though, whose literary explorations of man's spiritual needs arose from, as she explained, being a devout Catholic "living in a non-Catholic but religious society,"[2] Crews lacks the religious certainty that O'Connor felt, perhaps because he is from a different generation. In 1966, when *Time* published its famous cover that asked "Is God Dead?" O'Connor had been dead for two years, but Crews was still a young man working on *The Gospel Singer*, whose epigraph offers a possible answer to *Time*'s question. O'Connor writes of characters in need of redemption and their responses when it is offered. Crews's characters may seek it, but true redemption is never offered because there is no outside force capable of granting it. Unrequited spiritual longing is a subject that Crews knows well. In his own life Crews continually confronts a particularly postmodern angst, having been raised in a society of believers, inheriting that sense of belief, that need for belief, and yet living in a secular world that at times makes it difficult to believe. The nature of belief and his quest for it is a common topic in the interviews collected in this book.

As is O'Connor, Crews is often identified as writing in the tradition of the Southern Gothic or the Southern Grotesque, a tradition noted for its emphasis on violence, strange behavior, and abnormal characters. But even in a tradition noted for its abnormalities, Crews stands out from the pack. A reviewer once wrote, "A novel by Harry Crews . . . is inevitably a freak show."[3] There are midgets in *The Gospel Singer, Naked in Garden Hills, This Thing Don't Lead to Heaven* (1970), *Karate Is a Thing of the Spirit,* and *The Knockout Artist* (1988). The narrator of *The Gypsy's Curse* (1974) is a deaf mute who straps his withered, useless legs to his buttocks and walks on his hands. The Boss, the multimillionaire of *The Mulching of America* (1996), is proud to have succeeded despite his diminutive size and a cleft palate. In *The Gospel Singer,* Foot owns and operates a traveling freak show and is one of its featured attractions because of his twenty-seven-inch foot. Even those characters without physical deformities behave in freakish ways. In fact, in Crews's world it is often those who appear most normal who are, in actuality, the most abnormal. In *Car* (1972) Herman Mack announces his intention to consume a Ford Maverick piece by piece. Duffy Deeter plays recordings of Hitler and fantasizes about concentration camps during intercourse in *All We Need of Hell.* Oyster Boy, a prominent New Orleans businessman, leads a second life filled with sexual kinkiness and perversion in *The Knockout Artist.*

Because of their recurring presence in Crews's work, freaks come up more frequently than any other subject when interviewers speak to him or critics write about his work. His reputation regarding freaks is at once earned and overemphasized. Many people have attempted to locate Crews's fascination with freaks in an inexplicable childhood illness (eventually and probably mistakenly diagnosed as polio) that caused his legs to draw up beneath him until his heels touched his buttocks, leaving him bedridden for weeks until the affliction went away as mysteriously as it appeared. Crews has bolstered this explanation by writing in *A Childhood* (1978), his memoir of growing up in

Georgia, that as he lay helplessly in bed while family, visitors, and the local physician looked down on him with horrified fascination, he "felt how lonely and savage it was to be a freak."[4]

Critics also frequently point to an essay in which Crews recalled the time he had briefly worked as a carnival caller and shared a trailer with a married couple who performed in the freak show. She was the bearded lady, and he had been born with a disfigured face that made him resemble a Picasso painting. In "Carny" Crews describes waking early one morning to witness a tender moment between his two roommates, a loving kiss as the husband headed to work. The scene epitomized for Crews the underlying humanity beneath the couple's unusual bodies:

> *Their lips brushed briefly and I heard them murmur to each other and he was gone through the door. And I, lying at the back of the trailer, was never the same again.*
>
> *I have never stopped remembering that, as wondrous and special as those two people were, they were only talking about and looking forward to and needing precisely what the rest of us talk about and look forward to and need. He might have been any husband going to any job anywhere. He just happened to have that divided face.*[5]

Accounts such as these underscore Crews's personal experience with so-called freaks and his great empathy for them. Too often, however, readers cannot look beyond the disfigurements of some of the characters and are too eager to accuse Crews of sensationalism. Such readers cannot see that ultimately he is concerned with universal issues of humanity—feelings of alienation, fear, grief, love. The freaks in Crews's novels, as David K. Jeffrey has pointed out, merely help to point to those themes and serve as "normative characters" by which the other characters are evaluated.[6]

If Crews's fascination with deformities places him squarely in the tradition of southern literature whose freakish banner is also carried by the likes of Flannery O'Connor, Erskine Caldwell, Carson McCullers, and the Faulkner of *Sanctuary*, Crews differs from those writers in a very important way. Recent scholarship has emphasized the degree to which literature that traditionally has been considered southern actually represents the perspective of a rather limited number of the area's inhabitants—namely, the white middle-to-upper classes. Harry Crews's roots, though, are poor white. His parents were farmers, sharecroppers for a time. He grew up in a community where, as he writes, "there wasn't enough cash money in the county to close up a dead man's eyes."[7]

Thus Frank W. Shelton could write in 1988, "Crews, to my knowledge, is absolutely unique among Southern writers in that he writes about life from the perspective of the poor white. He writes from *within* the class, not by observing it from without, the traditional perspective of white Southern writers."[8] Although Crew's perspective may have been uncommon up to that point, that same year saw first books by Dorothy Allison (*Trash*) and Larry Brown (*Facing the Music*), perhaps the two best-known younger writers of poor white origins. With the popularity of Allison and Brown and the later emergence of lesser-known writers from similar origins, such as Tim McLaurin, Donald Secreast, and Nancy Peacock, southern literature is undergoing a vogue of the poor and working-class white. Crews is the literary father of these younger writers. Brown and McLaurin in particular cite Crews as an influence.[9] What they and other writers have found in Crews is a voice that more closely matches their own experiences than that presented by Faulkner or O'Connor or even Caldwell, who, though they often wrote sympathetically about poor whites, were themselves from middle-class backgrounds.[10]

But Crews's novels seldom deal with poor whites who live in trailer parks or the run-down shanties of Erskine Caldwell's Jeeter Lester clan. Rather, in Crews's fiction there are characters such as the Kid in *The Knockout Artist* who have left behind the farms of their youth for the big city. Characters such as George Gattling in *The Hawk Is Dying* and Shereel Dupont in *Body*, both born in rural southern Georgia, also have left for the city and become comfortably middle class, economically if not spiritually. Thus, what Crews often records in his novels is a society in transition, a world that is changing from its rural roots to a more urban existence. In their journey from farm to suburbia, Crews's characters mirror their author's own journey from son of a sharecropper to university professor.

★ ★ ★

Harry Eugene Crews was born on June 7, 1935, in Bacon County, Georgia, the youngest child of Ray and Myrtice Crews, whose firstborn had died shortly after birth. Just north of the Okefenokee Swamp, Bacon County is a land of slow rolling hills and sandy soil. In 1935, as now, farmers grew cotton and tobacco, two crops that quickly drain the nutrients from the land. It is a place where residents give directions by telling strangers which church to turn beside. When Ray Crews married Myrtice, he was a sharecropper, but by the time Harry (their second surviving son) was born, the couple were farming their own land and soon would buy a 200-acre farm. A hardworking man given to driving himself to exhaustion, Ray Crews died in his sleep from a massive heart attack as Harry, not yet two, slept beside him. Faced with raising two boys by herself, Myrtice remarried quickly, taking Ray's brother Pascal as her new husband.

Too young at the time of his father's death to retain memories of him, Crews grew up believing his stepfather/uncle was his natural father. He did not learn differently until he was about six years old and his mother was divorcing Pascal, a man prone to drunken violence. Discovering that he never knew his biological father at the same time that the only man he had ever known as father was leaving his life made Crews keenly aware of an absence. He would later write of his biological father: "the worst thing that had happened in my life was his early death, that never having known him, I knew that I would, one way or another, be looking for him the rest of my life."[11] Crews has written eloquently and movingly of that search in *A Childhood: The Biography of a Place*. A memoir that focuses primarily upon his first six years, *A Childhood* is, according to many readers, his best work.

In *A Childhood* Crews vividly describes the poverty in which he grew up, the houses with cracks in the floor large enough to allow a young boy to "fish" for chickens running loose beneath the house. Except for the ever-present Bible, books were virtually unknown, a luxury that few could afford. It seems an unlikely place for a writer to emerge, but it was a place that loved the art of narrative, though in the spoken form rather than the written. With few books in the county, no picture shows, and no money to spend on them even if a theater had existed, people entertained themselves by telling stories. "When I was a boy," Crews wrote, "stories were conversation and conversation was stories. For me it was a time of magic."[12] This magic enabled a young listener to develop a sense of the place being described, its people, its customs, its sounds. Sitting at the feet of his elders as they told stories, Crews also developed a fine sense of narrative. As commonplace as it has become, the adage about the South producing so many writers because it is—or was—a society of storytellers has some truth to it.

When Crews's mother left Pascal, she took the children to the Springfield section of Jacksonville, Florida. Hundreds of immigrants from south Georgia settled in Springfield, lured by the promise of better-paying jobs in the city's factories. New arrivals were certain to find friends or family who had left earlier. Factory work paid precious little, but to farmers who were unaccustomed to seeing cash money, the pay seemed extraordinary. Crews's mother worked at the King Edward Cigar Factory on a piecework basis. It was difficult and monotonous work that barely paid enough to support her family. Early on Crews and his brother were forced to take jobs, selling newspapers, gathering scrap metal to sell, or doing whatever two kids could do to bring in a few dimes and quarters.

While offering amenities such as indoor plumbing, the city also exacted a high emotional price from those accustomed to the manners and independence of the country. As Crews described later, "it seemed dreadfully unnatural to them to stand on their front porch and be able to talk to somebody else standing on *his* front porch. It sometimes happened back in the country that a man could *see* another house from his front porch, but not often. In the city, though, they were forever cheek to jowl. They felt like animals in a pen."[13] Throughout the rest of Crews's childhood, he and his family would move back and forth between Bacon County and Jacksonville, returning home to Georgia when Myrtice had saved some money or could stand the city no longer.

In 1953 Crews became the first in his family to graduate from high school, and then, just shy of his eighteenth birthday, he joined the Marine Corps. His older brother, Hoyet, was already in Korea, but the cease-fire that was signed in July, before Crews completed basic training on Parris Island, South Carolina, kept him from going to war. He signed up partly because it is the habit of young men from Bacon County to respond when Uncle Sam calls, but also because the military represented the most common way for a young man to escape Bacon County and see the world beyond. Crews first tried to join the Army, but the doctor at the recruiting office took one look at his calf, which still showed signs of the mysterious childhood illness, and told him to go home. For whatever reason, the Marine doctor said nothing, and shortly afterward Crews was on a train bound for South Carolina. Not until he arrived at Parris Island did he realize that he and the other recruits "had all truly stepped in shit."[14] He suffered the ire of his drill instructor because of a weak bladder that caused him to wet himself whenever he was physically struck without warning, a not-uncommon occurrence for recruits on Parris Island in the 1950s. He served three years at various bases with, as he says, a rifle in one hand and a book in the other, having discovered that every base had a lending library.

Joining the Marines was an important step for Crews's development as a person and a writer. As he had hoped, he escaped Bacon County. In fact, after his discharge he would never again live in Georgia for an extended time. Most importantly, the Marine Corps demanded discipline. Crews claims, in the interview with Hank Nuwer in this collection, that if he had not joined the Corps he probably would have ended up in prison, too young and too hotheaded to avoid trouble. It also instilled in him a regimented approach to work. Even today, more than forty years after his discharge, he still approaches writing with the seriousness of a recruit going before inspection. As he reveals to interviewers, he rises early and works diligently on a daily basis.

In the military Crews was surrounded for the first time by people who were, as his mother would say, "not our kind of people," meaning essentially almost anyone not from Bacon County. "I left Georgia at seventeen," he later said, "and was thrown into the Marine Corps with a bunch of guys from Jersey and New York, a bunch of Yankees. I was like fuckin' ashamed of where I came from and how I talked."[15] A natural mimic, Crews tried to fit in, to hide his rural upbringing, to lose his Georgia accent. As he says in a typically descriptive phrase, "I carry Georgia in my mouth."[16] Even before he joined the Marines, he knew that he wanted to be a writer, but Bacon County offered no models; writers simply did not come from Bacon County. Just as Faulkner first had to go away to Paris and New Orleans before he discovered the literary value of his own postage stamp of soil in northern Mississippi, Crews also had to reject his native soil before he could later find inspiration from it and its people.

Such an acceptance was years in coming, however, and it would come only when Crews was in despair, frustrated by his inner feeling that he was a writer, yet unable to publish a story. Late one night when he was sitting at the typewriter, surrounded by rejected manuscripts that were "so god-damned bad" that even he could tell they were worthless, he had a revelation that he later described in an essay:

> *For many and complicated reasons, circumstances had collaborated to make me ashamed that I was a tenant farmer's son. As weak and warped as it is, and as difficult as it is even now to admit it, I was so humiliated by the fact that I was from the edge of the Okefenokee Swamp in the worst hookworm and rickets part of Georgia I could not bear to think of it, and worse to believe it. Everything I had written had been out of a fear and loathing for what I was and who I was. It was all out of an effort to pretend otherwise. I believe to this day, and will always believe, that in that moment I literally saved my life, because the next thought—and it was more than a thought, it was a dead-solid conviction—was that all I had going for me in the world or would ever have was that swamp, all those goddamn mules, all those screwworms that I'd dug out of pigs and all the other beautiful and dreadful and sorry circumstances that had made me the Grit I am and will always be. Once I realized that the way I saw the world and man's condition in it would always be exactly and inevitably shaped by everything which up to that moment had only shamed me, once I realized that, I was home free.*[17]

Since this revelation, Crews has consistently drawn upon his roots for his writing, celebrating Bacon County and its proud and tough inhabitants, but such an acceptance was years beyond the maturity of a young Marine recruit. Private Crews wanted nothing more than to hide his poor white origins, to hide the fact that, unlike his new friends, he had never driven a car—he would be twenty-one before he learned how to do so—and that he was more familiar with pig intestines than the engine of a Chevy.

But if he did not fit in with his more worldly companions, he also knew that he was unlike his friends and relatives back home. His love of reading was peculiar in their eyes, but even stranger was his desire to become a writer, an occupation that few had ever imagined and almost none believed could actually earn a man a dollar. Like many of the characters he would later create, Crews found himself stuck between worlds, alienated from both. Discharged in the summer of 1956, he returned briefly to Bacon County, but a few days in the fields with his family and friends only confirmed the distance between himself and his previous life. Recalling that time years later, Crews wrote, "I stood there feeling how much I had left this place and these people, and at the same time knowing that it would be forever impossible to leave them completely. Wherever I might go in the world, they would go with me."[18]

Like millions of others in the post–World War II era, after completing his military service Crews went to college on the GI Bill, choosing the University of Florida, not because he thought he would learn to write there, but because "I thought someone there might teach me how to make a living while I taught myself to write."[19] As a result of frequently skipping school as an adolescent, his academic and test-taking skills were less developed than his reading background would suggest, and early in his freshman year an advisor suggested he should drop out and enroll in a trade school. Nevertheless, he stayed and performed adequately, earning mostly B's and C's, which were more a result of his voracious reading habits than his scholarly acumen.

After two years, though, he had had enough; the academic environment was too stifling. He was, he would later write, "choking and gasping from Truth and Beauty."[20] He headed west on a Triumph 650cc motorcycle with about $100 in his pocket and no clear destination. He roamed, drifting through Colorado and California, up into Canada and down into Mexico, working odd jobs along the way, meeting interesting people, and, as he describes in "The Violence That Finds Us," occasionally getting his ass kicked by one of them in a barroom brawl. He kept a journal of his travels, called "There's Something about Being Straddle of a Thing," which he has never published, although he has on occasion written about his journey in his essays. He returned to Gainesville about eighteen months after he left, ready to finish school.

Upon his return to the campus, Crews had the good fortune to meet Andrew Lytle, who had come to the University of Florida a few years earlier to teach creative writing, a term Lytle deplored. A friend of Crews had taken one of Lytle's classes and convinced a reluctant Crews to sit in on a session. Lytle, a novelist, biographer, essayist, and editor, had been one of the Agrarians, a group of twelve men associated with Vanderbilt University who issued the manifesto *I'll Take My Stand* in 1930 to defend an agrarian and traditionally southern lifestyle opposed to a dehumanizing industrial and, as they saw it, primarily northern way of life that they felt was engulfing America. While the Agrarian movement had a limited effect and had long since disintegrated as a force by the time Lytle arrived at the University of Florida, Lytle would always retain the movement's basic ideals in his personal views. In 1957 he published *The Velvet Horn*, his most widely acclaimed novel. When Crews met him, Lytle was at the peak of his powers, and the line of students who wanted to be one of his chosen was long. But Lytle did not take just any writer under his wing; each candidate had to prove his or her desire and talent.

Lytle was a perfectionist and refused to coddle his students. At times brutally honest, he demanded from them the same dedication to the craft of writing that he himself gave. After reading the first story that Crews showed him, Lytle returned it and advised the aspiring writer to burn it.[21] Lytle was, in short, precisely the type of man Crews could respect—honest, direct, and serious about writing. Like many others, Crews set out to win his approval. Crews knew that Lytle had accepted him as one of his anointed few when the professor showed up at Crews's house one night and invited him to go have a drink. By the time Crews returned home early in the morning, he and Lytle had split a bottle of whiskey, an act as symbolic as it was inebriating. "The man took me to get a drink," Crews thought. "It means I can do it. Do it!"[22]

Lytle became more than a teacher to Crews; he was the mentor and father figure for whom Crews longed. Lytle believed what Crews himself wanted to believe but which no one else had ever told him: that he was a writer—raw, unpolished, undisciplined in his craft, but a writer nonetheless. Even today, nearly forty years after their first meeting, and after drifting apart because of philosophical differences, Crews speaks with respect and admiration for his former mentor, a man whose demanding expectations he feels he never satisfied. Crews's approach to teaching is similar to the way Lytle ran his classes, and Crews has split more than one bottle of whiskey with his own students.

Crews graduated from the University of Florida in 1960 and took a job teaching junior high school in Jacksonville. Teaching, he hoped, would allow him time to write, but Crews did not need an entire school year to realize that the demands of teaching several classes of adolescents five days a week left him precious little time for writing. He was also feeling the strain of a failing marriage.

While in his senior year at the university, Crews had met Sally Ellis, a nineteen-year-old sophomore English major. They met in a Spanish class. Crews made quite an entrance on the first day of class as he came in on crutches with his right leg in a cast, the result of a motorcycle accident. Never having taken Spanish before, he struggled more with the language than with the crutches. Sally, a gifted student, took pity on Crews and helped him with his lessons. Soon study sessions developed into a romance. They married on January 24, 1960, and their son, Patrick, was born in September, shortly after Crews began teaching. Living with a man obsessed with becoming a writer and prone to all-night writing binges proved difficult for Sally, and she divorced Crews the following year, taking Patrick with her to live in Ohio. Crews later convinced her to give their marriage another chance, and they remarried in 1962. They would divorce for a second and final time in the early 1970s. A second son, Byron, was born August 24, 1963.

Like his father before him, Crews was to lose his firstborn. On July 31, 1964, he awoke to the sound of Sally screaming and the yammering of neighborhood children trying to tell her something. He found Patrick face down in a neighbor's pool, where the other children had discovered him. Crews's efforts to revive his son were unsuccessful. The essay that Crews wrote about the experience more than twenty years later remains one of his most poignant. It moves from a vivid description of the mental anguish he felt over Patrick's death to the pride he feels in his surviving son, Byron. The essay is also a perfect example of how Crews is willing to admit his flaws. Part of the charm of Harry Crews is his honesty, often at his own expense. He describes a time when Byron was seven and Crews made him stand outside the house in the rain to make a point. Intending to leave him there only for a minute, Crews, who had been drinking, fell asleep and awoke an hour and a half later to find an angry and determined Byron still standing outside. Discussing the event with his son a few years later, Crews finally apologized and learned an important lesson about the type of man his son would become.[23]

Crews spent only one year teaching junior high school before returning to college to earn a master's degree, which he hoped would enable him to teach at a junior college. He applied for admission to the graduate program in English at the University of Florida, but was rejected. Determined not to return to the junior high school, Crews applied successfully to the university's graduate program in education. He received his M.S.Ed. in 1962 and that fall began teaching English to freshmen at the Junior College of Broward County in Fort Lauderdale, Florida.

In 1963 Crews had his first success as a writer when his mentor Andrew Lytle, now at the University of the South, accepted the short story "The Unattached Smile" for the *Sewanee Review*, which Lytle edited. The story is unlike what readers have come to expect from Crews, as is often the case with writers' early publications. It tells the story of a young sailor on leave in San Juan. When he and a friend pick up a couple of young prostitutes, the youthful body and smile of one of the girls remind him of a sexually charged moment with his sister when they were adolescents. With its crisp, staccato dialogue and Spanish flavor, the story reveals the influence of Hemingway. The only significant element that anticipates Crews's later work is the interest in and sympathy for people who live in the underworld of society. The story's setting in exotic Puerto Rico reveals that he was still not yet comfortable with looking toward his south Georgia roots as a source of inspiration for his fiction.

The following summer Crews published a second story, this time in the *Georgia Review*. Unlike "The Unattached Smile," "A Long Wail" clearly carries the mark of his Georgia background and anticipates many of his later concerns. It tells the story of a widowed farmer, identified only as "the old man," who, the story suggests, is planning to kill himself rather than continue to suffer the effects of mouth cancer and face the surgical removal of his tongue. Over dinner he attempts to make arrangements for his daughter to marry one of his sharecroppers so that she will be provided for after his death. What is remarkable about the story is how faithfully Crews captures the dialect of the characters. They speak with "Georgia in their mouths," but the nonstandard dialect is not meant to be derogatory. Rather, it is an essential part of character development and setting. This gift for dialect would reappear in many of his novels. In two studies of Crews's fiction, linguist Barbara Johnstone has written that "Crews has a good ear for Southern discourse" and that he "gets Southern speech right on all levels."[24] "A Long Wail" also reveals for the first time Crews's fascination with physical deformities. The old man's cancer has eaten through his cheek, and Gaff, the sharecropper, watches with horrified fascination as the old man eats his dinner, exposing his grinding teeth through the gaping hole.

Despite placing two stories in respected literary journals, Crews's writing career was not progressing as well as he would have liked. During the 1960s he wrote hundreds of stories and several novels, which were all roundly rejected. He worked in a frenzy, teaching during the day and writing late into the night, popping speed like M&M's to maintain the pace. In later years his drug abuse would spiral out of control, but for a while it simply allowed him to pursue his dream. When a publisher accepted his manuscript entitled *The Gospel Singer,* Crews was thrilled. When the publisher sat on the project for more than a year, Crews was afraid to demand action lest the book not be published at all. Finally, a friend convinced him to demand the return of the manuscript and helped him place it with the William Morrow publishing company. Early in 1968, at the relatively late age of thirty-two, Harry Crews published his first novel. It was the culmination of more than fifteen years of writing. The reviews were mixed, praising the author's promise while pointing out the shortcomings of a first novel.[25]

With a published novel to his credit, Crews was offered a job teaching creative writing and literature at the University of Florida. Ironically, the Department of English eventually made him a full professor, the same department that eight years earlier had denied him admission to its graduate program.

In 1969 Crews published his second novel, *Naked in Garden Hills,* which he often names as his best. Most reviewers praised it highly. In the *New York Times Book Review* Jean Stafford called it "howlingly funny" and said it "lives up to and beyond the promise of Mr. Crews's first novel."[26] Set in an abandoned phosphate mine, the novel is an attack on modern industrialization. With its bizarre cast of characters—including a 600-pound homosexual Metrecal addict who fled college after his romantic advances were spurned, a jockey who lost his nerve after being thrown from a horse and who now "rides" a chair while watching televised races at full volume, an old man prone to nude romps through the mine, and an entire community who waits for the second coming of an industrialist—the novel firmly established Crews's reputation as a chronicler of freaks. As Stafford more eloquently phrased it in an often-quoted line, the novel is "southern Gothic at its best, a Hieronymus Bosch landscape in Dixie."[27]

Although Crews's third novel, *This Thing Don't Lead to Heaven*, received harsh reviews, through the late 1960s and early 1970s his literary star continued to rise as he published a new novel every year. He became a faculty member at the prestigious Bread Loaf Writers Conference, a summer institute whose faculty and students have included John Ciardi, Joe David Bellamy, Rosellen Brown, Tim O'Brien, and John Irving. In 1972 he received the National Institute for Arts and Letters Award for Fiction, honoring his body of work. In his fiction he turned a satirical eye to new subjects while exploring the major themes that still concerned him. *This Thing Don't Lead to Heaven* focuses on the universal fear of death, while *Karate Is a Thing of the Spirit* explores the need for spiritual structure even as it turns a comic eye upon beauty pageants and crowds. In *Car* Herman Mack sets out to eat—and then defecate—a Ford Maverick piece by piece over several months in front of a paying audience, allowing Crews to satirize both America's obsession with the automobile and its ghoulish voyeurism, a tendency that has only worsened in the ensuing quarter century.

In the mid-1970s Crews began contributing regularly to *Playboy* and *Esquire*. For more than a year (July 1976–August 1977), he wrote a monthly column entitled "Grits" for *Esquire*. In his essays and journalism Crews is indebted to the so-called new journalists, writers such as Tom Wolfe and Hunter S. Thompson, who beginning in the 1960s brought a new style of writing to traditionally conservative journalism. The new journalists, according to Norman Sims, "called attention to their own voices; they self-consciously returned character, motivation, and voice to nonfiction writing."[28] The new journalists essentially bring the techniques of fiction to nonfiction, usually doing away with the reporter's expected objective stance and injecting themselves into the story, where they often "confess to human failings and emotions."[29] In an *Esquire* profile of television evangelist Garner Ted Armstrong, for example, Crews recalls attending a revival when he was twelve and being so scared by the preacher's hell-and-damnation sermon that he defecated in his pants. Later in the piece, after describing one of Brother Armstrong's articles in a ministry magazine, Crews asks, "Is it my own warped and limited religious perception or does that sound like wig city?"[30]

Because of Crews's tendency to share insights like this about himself, his journalism is an excellent place to get a sense of him as a person. In Crews's hands an assignment to write about actor Robert Blake, then starring in the television series *Baretta*, becomes a meditation on coming to terms with one's past and general alienation, feelings that Crews discovered he shares with Blake. A visit to the University of Texas campus, where Charles Whitman climbed into the bell tower in 1966 and began shooting passers-by before turning the gun on himself, finds a drunken Crews sitting late at night on the lawn under the tower and imagining himself in Whitman's position. Whitman's action, Crews realizes, is just a more extreme case of what we are all capable of doing. "All of us have our towers to climb," he concludes. "Some are worse than others, but to deny that you have your tower to climb and that you must resist it or succumb to the temptation to do it, to deny that is done at the peril of your heart and mind."[31]

In his journalism Crews seeks to identify with the people he encounters in order to understand what drives them, whether they are movie stars, carnival workers, gator poachers, evangelists, Klan leaders, or mass murderers. Crews's chameleon changeability serves him well as he moves among these folks. Sometimes his efforts to identify with them cause him to recognize unpleasant aspects of himself. By taking his readers along this path of self-recognition, Crews invites us to take the same journey for themselves. He also asks us to take this journey in his fiction, where, he tells several interviewers, he seeks to turn his readers back in upon themselves. This process is not always an easy or pleasant one, which perhaps accounts for some of the strongly negative reactions Crews's works have generated in the past.

Another image of Crews emerges most clearly from his nonfiction, that of a modern-day Thoreau, railing against the pretensions of the typical American. In "L. L. Bean Has Your Number, America!" Crews visits the L. L. Bean store in Freeport, Maine, and lampoons suburban families decked out in designer outdoor gear to go camping in forty-foot-long Winnebagos. While Thoreau warns his readers to be wary of jobs that require new clothes, Crews warns his to be wary of people who need new clothes to commune with nature. Like Thoreau, Crews disdains many of the niceties of civilization. He absolutely refuses to mow a lawn, and Crews's yard is as natural a spot as one can find in the middle of Gainesville. He also eschews material possessions and prides himself on having completely furnished his sparse home in a single afternoon. The only copies of his own books that he possesses were inherited from his mother; he has given away all the others.

In 1976 Crews published his darkest, most violent book, *A Feast of Snakes*. Like Robert Altman's film *Nashville* (1975) and Martin Scorsese's *Taxi Driver* (1976), this novel presented a bleak vision of the American Dream while the United States was celebrating its bicentennial. Joe Lon Mackey was once the all-star captain of the high school football team, but a college scholarship and promising career were sidelined when Joe Lon could not meet the entrance requirements. He can now only watch as fans cheer the new high school quarterback and his ex-girlfriend comes home from college with a member of the debate team. (Poor Joe Lon cannot fathom what type of ball they use for that sport.) The novel, covering one weekend in Mystic, Georgia, when the town hosts an annual rattlesnake roundup, has a typically Crewsian surreal quality. (Crews has a canny knack for finding the surreal in the real; a small town in south Georgia *does* host an annual snake roundup that draws huge crowds who fan out across the countryside, pouring gasoline into badger holes to drive hidden snakes above ground.) Like *Taxi Driver*, the novel ends with brutal and graphic violence as Joe Lon takes out his pent-up frustration in a shooting spree. While some reviewers hailed the novel as "Crews at his best,"[32] others, such as the critic for the *New York Times Book Review*, claimed the snakes were more interesting than the human characters and deemed the violence "gratuitous," a charge that always angers Crews.[33]

A Feast of Snakes would be the last novel Crews would publish for eleven years. One critic has suggested that with its explosive conclusion the novel "represented a dead end" for the themes that he had been exploring.[34] Whether this is true or not, there is a more practical and simple explanation for the long silence. Crews was drunk. He had always drunk heavily and used a potpourri of drugs, but in the late 1970s and through the 1980s, his indulgences would for the first time significantly interfere with his writing. The decade-long binge was brought on, in part, by Crews's confrontation with the memories of his past. In 1978 he published *A Childhood: The Biography of a Place*, his now classic memoir. It was a project he had been working on for several years. In an interview included in this collection, Crews first mentioned to Sterling Watson in 1973 that he was contemplating writing a memoir. The following year he published a piece in *Shenandoah* that would later be incorporated into *A Childhood*. In interviews following the book's publication, he spoke freely of the spiritual purging he had hoped its writing would accomplish, and how it had failed to do so. Instead, it had exacted a heavy toll that drove Crews further into alcohol and drug abuse in an effort to numb the pain caused by rehashed memories.

For Crews's career the binge could not have come at a worse time. Having established himself as a significant writer, Crews was frequently invited to read on campuses, to appear at literary festivals, and to attend other events expected of a man of letters. He often arrived drunk at these events, and if he was not drunk when he arrived, he soon found a way to remedy the situation. Dozens, perhaps hundreds, of stories circulate about Crews's outrageous drunken behavior, many of them dating from this era. It became almost a game; as the stories spread, those who invited Crews to appear expected a drunken performance and plied him with alcohol to get it. Along with his friend James Dickey, the accomplished poet best known as the author of *Deliverance*, Crews became known as one of the bad boys of American letters.

His well-known love of blood sports, such as boxing, football, and cockfighting, created a myth of machismo around him. Those who had read his works or heard the stories about him sometimes sought him out to see if he was as tough as they believed. Not being one to back down from a fight (at least not in his younger days), he spent more than one night in jail as a result of drunken brawls. His behavior was so out of control that, despite his rank of tenured professor, he was once nearly dismissed from the university. A portrait of Crews during this era is captured by Mary Voboril in her 1987 interview.

In May 1990 Crews went on the wagon, and though he has fallen off a couple of times, he is presently sober and writing. He has published seven novels since 1987, not the pace of his youth but still a significant production. Another collection of his essays is due out, and he has been working, albeit slowly, on a second autobiography. This time, he is careful to set the work aside for long stretches when it becomes too emotionally taxing. Crews's recent novels reflect both a continuation of his previous concerns and an effort to explore new ground. His satiric eye and wit are as keen as ever, focusing upon Disney World, corporate America, exclusive hotels, and sometimes on issues that reflect his own aging process.

In *Celebration* (1997) Crews explores how America shoves aside its elderly to retirement communities, where they are expected to wait patiently for death. *The Knockout Artist* was the first of his novels to be set outside of northern Florida or southern Georgia. It also has the distinction of being the only novel he has written while living outside the region he calls home, having holed up in an isolated cabin in Louisiana to escape the familiar call of his favorite bars. Both *Scar Lover* (1992) and *The Mulching of America* have an unusually surreal quality that by his own admission sets them apart from his typical work. In the hard-to-find *Where Does One Go When There Is No Place Left to Go?* (1998),[35] Crews turns self-reflexive as characters from his previous novels kidnap Harry Crews. He officially retired from the University of Florida in 1997, although his teaching load had been reduced for several years. He continues to live and write in Gainesville, a community that he says gives him "the kind of geographic and emotional distance [from his roots in Georgia] that I need to write."[36]

★ ★ ★

For more than thirty years Harry Crews has given us glimpses into his unique view of the world through his writing. In the interviews collected in this volume, we see glimpses of the man behind the writing. He talks about literary influences on his own work, about the writers he admires and those he does not, about which of his own books he likes and which he does not, about his fascination with so-called freaks, and about his love of blood sports. He also speaks frankly about his failed relationships, the role that writing played in them, and his personal struggles with alcohol and drugs and the impact they have had on his life and work.

Crews is a good interview subject, talkative and forthright, with interesting experiences and stories to tell. Those seeking insights into his work will find them here. Those seeking to be entertained in Crewsian fashion will howl with laughter at some of his comments and be moved to anger by others, just as with his best writing.

The interviews in this book were conducted over a period of three decades and appeared in a variety of places, from small-circulation literary journals to major newspapers. The earliest published interview did not appear until 1972, after Crews had already published several novels and won the American Institute of Arts and Letters Award. The most recent were conducted in 1997. I have not tried to include every interview published. Some have been omitted because they covered no topics not covered at least as well in other interviews. A few that I would have liked to include could not be reprinted because permissions could not be acquired or the cost was prohibitive. I also have omitted interviews conducted with Crews for video documentaries and television appearances because of the difficulty of extracting a coherent print interview from the surrounding media. Nevertheless, the collection represents, I feel, the best print interviews with Crews. The interviews are arranged chronologically by the date of the interview itself rather than by its appearance in print. When the interview date was not given, I have used internal clues to estimate its occurrence.

As with any subject who has been repeatedly interviewed and asked the same questions time and again, Crews has developed stock answers to certain questions. To reduce repetition, I have silently edited the interviews to eliminate redundancies. Such changes were made, however, only when Crews's answer provided no additional information to a previous answer *and* when the cut could be made without damaging the ability of the interview to stand on its own. Occasional minor editing of the interviewers' prose was sometimes necessary, usually in order to smooth transitions over deletions of repetitious material. A few pieces could not be edited as a condition of their appearance in this collection. While some repetition remains, I feel that it is informative in that it both reveals continuity and highlights subtle changes that occur over time in some answers. I have silently corrected a few factual errors made by the interviewers. In interviews with a question-and-answer format, I have standardized the indication of a change in speaker throughout, using his or her initials. I have also standardized the spelling of a few frequently used words for which interviewers used variant spellings.

As might be expected, the interviews are clustered around times when Crews had recently published a new book. This is particularly true of those that appeared in newspapers. Crews's publishing career can be roughly divided into three periods. First, there was the youthful, incredibly productive decade from *The Gospel Singer* of 1968 to *A Childhood* of 1978. Then there was the long binge that interfered with his writing, lasting until the release of *All We Need of Hell* in 1987. Although Crews was not yet sober in 1987, his long silence was over. Admittedly, to call this period a long silence is a bit deceptive. Crews did, in fact, publish several books during this period; however, both *Blood and Grits* (1979) and *Florida Frenzy* (1982) were collections that consisted mostly of previously published essays and excerpts, and *The Enthusiast* (1981) was a limited edition, containing fiction that was eventually incorporated into *All We Need of Hell,* indicating just how long it took Crews to finish the novel that broke the silence. The final period extends to the present.

The interviews can be grouped similarly. The earliest were more likely to have been published in literary journals. On a couple of occasions, the interviewers were friends or former students. These pieces tend to feel relaxed, like recorded conversations. Crews discusses his novels in great detail and, reflecting the more specialized literary audience, talks about his literary influences and writing habits.

The interviews from the second period are as likely to have been published in newspapers or mass-circulation magazines as in literary journals, reflecting his growing popularity. These interviews focus more upon Crews's reputation for hard living and drinking than upon his writing. They are sometimes painfully revealing, as Crews will say in one that he has stopped drinking and hasn't had a drink in a certain number of months, and then in a later interview he will repeat his claim, but will cite fewer months' sobriety than have passed since the earlier interview.

During the third period, the interviews shift in tone. Crews is often treated with a new respect, almost as an elder statesman. It is as though, having survived his destructive habits with his talent intact, he has been elevated to a new status. This is evidenced by the interview conducted by Tammy Lytal and Richard Russell for the *Georgia Review*, a journal that will often publish works by rising artists, as it did with Crews in 1964, but that generally will run interviews only with established and respected writers.

Crews's work has also seen a rise in academic interest in recent years. A special 1998 issue of the *Southern Quarterly* devoted to him, which I edited, attracted several essays of high quality. Two documentary films about him were also produced in the 1990s.

Finally, I should say a few words about the title of this collection. I have taken the phrase "getting naked" from Crews himself. He used the metaphor a few times in these interviews in slightly different contexts. He first told Steve Oney in 1977 that "getting naked" is "that thing in me that wants to get as far on the edge as I can of anything that I can." In 1992 Lytal and Russell recorded his admonition to would-be writers: "for God in heaven's sake try to get naked. Try to write the truth. Try to get underneath all the sham, all the excuses, all the lies that you've been told." "Getting naked," then, is Crews's metaphor for being honest, particularly to one's self, and exposing one's self emotionally and psychologically to experiences from which honest writing can emerge. Given the frankness with which Crews generally approaches interviews, I could think of no more appropriate title for this collection.

But the title also works on another level, for while Crews is usually brutally honest in his comments, taken as a whole these interviews reveal qualities that are often overlooked as stories about his life "far on the edge" continue to circulate. Certainly, he is at times revealed as boisterous, abrasive, and self-destructive, but we also see a Crews who is thoughtful and concerned, on both a social and a human level, a man who can be incredibly tender and charming. In "getting naked" with Harry Crews, we see the writer in his full human complexity.

★ ★ ★

I have incurred numerous debts during the completion of this project. Gary Richards, Michael Kreyling, Jerry Bledsoe, and Margaret Morrison all read versions of this introduction and made helpful suggestions, as did the anonymous reviewers of the manuscript for the press. I thank Margaret Morrison, who assisted with my interview and transcription, and Sharon Antrican, who also assisted with the transcription. The book would not be possible, of course, without the diligent staff at the University Press of Florida, especially Susan Fernandez, Alex Leader, Beth Kent, and my editor, Deidre Bryan, whose persistence and patience were greatly appreciated. I would also like to thank my eagle-eyed copyeditor, Sharon Damoff, whose careful attention to detail saved me from making numerous embarrassing errors. There are, of course, many others whose efforts and names are unknown to me but to whom I extend my thanks.

While more legalistic acknowledgments appear elsewhere in the book, I would like to thank the interviewers whose work made this collection possible. The collection would not have been as thorough without the assistance of Damon Sauve, the staff of interlibrary loan at the John C. Hodges Library, and Gordon Osing.

The Office of Research at the University of Tennessee, Knoxville, provided a generous grant from the Exhibit, Performance, and Publication Fund that helped defray the cost of permissions fees.

Others who provided me with valuable information or less concrete but nevertheless essential support include Freda Ann Taylor, Sally Crews, Don Noble, Stephen Flinn Young, Edwin "Chip" Arnold, Jeanne Leiby, Michael Reynolds, Lucinda MacKethan, Thomas Hester, Vereen Bell, Sam Girgus, and Cecelia Tichi. To all of you, I offer my humble thanks.

A special acknowledgment must be addressed to Harry Crews, who opened his house and his life to a stranger who presumptuously asked if he would do so: Your gift with language is the reason for this book. The friendship you have offered during its completion is my reward. Thank you.

Notes

1. Crews is compared to O'Connor more than to any other writer. In *A Grit's Triumph: Essays on the Works of Harry Crews*, ed. David K. Jeffrey (Port Washington, N.Y.: Associated Faculty Press, 1983), the only book of criticism devoted to Crews, the index records more references to O'Connor than to any person other than Crews himself. Indeed, of the ten essays collected there, four make a comparison between Crews and O'Connor on their first page.

2. "The Catholic Novelist in the Protestant South," in *Mystery and Manners* (New York: Farrar, Straus, and Giroux, 1969), 205.

3. Christopher Lehmann-Haupt, "Books of the Times: A Pugilist's Descent into a Self-Inflicted Hell," *New York Times*, April 18, 1988, sec. C, 21.

4. *A Childhood: The Biography of a Place* (New York: Harper and Row, 1978), 79.

5. "Carny," in *Blood and Grits* (New York: Harper and Row, 1979), 166.

6. "Crews's Freaks," in *A Grit's Triumph*, 77.

7. *A Childhood*, 11.

8. "The Poor Whites' Perspective: Harry Crews among Georgia Writers," *Journal of American Culture* 11.3 (1988): 47.

9. Larry Brown, "Harry Crews: Mentor and Friend," *Southern Quarterly* 37.1 (1998): 8–12. Tim McLaurin, "'Is Your Novel Worth a Damn?': Meeting Harry Crews," *Southern Quarterly* 37.1 (1998): 13–14.

10. In addition to the Shelton essay cited above, for a discussion of how Crews differs from the tradition of Southern writing, also see William M. Moss, "Postmodern Georgia Scene: Harry Crews and the Southern Tradition in Fiction," in *A Grit's Triumph*, 33–45.

11. *A Childhood*, 15.

12. Ibid., 93.

13. Ibid., 129.

14. "Building Men the Marine Corps Way," *Esquire*, September 1976, 22.

15. "On Food," *Antæus* 68 (1992): 128.

16. "A Stubborn Sense of Place: Forum," *Harper's*, August 1986, 39.

17. "Television's Junkyard Dog," in *Blood and Grits*, 145.

18. *A Childhood*, 171.

19. Harry Crews, Introduction to *Classic Crews: A Harry Crews Reader* (New York: Poseidon Press, 1993). The phrase first appears in the author biography Crews wrote for *The Gospel Singer* (New York: William Morrow, 1968), 249.

20. Ibid. This phrase also first appeared in the author biography Crews wrote for *The Gospel Singer*, 249.

21. Erik Hedegaard, with Michael Schrage and David M. Abramson, "Mentors: Students Who Made It and the Teachers Who Made the Difference," *Rolling Stone*, April 15, 1982, 58.

22. Qtd. by Erik Hedegaard, with Michael Schrage and David M. Abramson, in "Mentors: Students Who Made It and the Teachers Who Made the Difference," 58.

23. "Fathers, Sons, Blood," *Playboy*, January 1985, 110+. A more readily available version of this essay appears in *Classic Crews: A Harry Crews Reader;* however, a typographical error in the first line of that reprint gives an incorrect date for Patrick's death.

24. "Violence and Civility in Discourse: Uses of Mitigation by Rural Southern White Men," *SECOL (Southeastern Conference on Linguistics) Review* 16.1 (1992): 4; "'You gone have to learn to talk right': Linguistic Deference and Regional Dialect in Harry Crews's *Body*," in *The Text and Beyond: Essays in Literary Linguistics*, ed. Cynthia Goldin Bernstein (Tuscaloosa: University of Alabama Press, 1994), 291.

25. See, for example, Walter Sullivan, "Fiction in a Dry Season: Some Signs of Hope," *Sewanee Review* 77 (Winter 1969): 159–60.

26. *New York Times Book Review*, April 13, 1969, 4.

27. Ibid.

28. "The Literary Journalists," in *The Literary Journalists*, ed. Norman Sims (New York: Ballantine, 1984), 5.

29. Ibid., 6.

30. "Temple of the Airwaves: A Visit with Garner Ted Armstrong and the World Tomorrow," *Esquire*, December 1976, 176.

31. "Climbing the Tower," in *Blood and Grits*, 213.

32. Michelle M. Leber, review of *A Feast of Snakes*, by Harry Crews, *Library Journal* 101 (June 15, 1976): 1445.

33. Jerome Charyn, review of *A Feast of Snakes*, by Harry Crews, *New York Times Book Review*, September 12, 1976, 43.

34. Frank W. Shelton, "Harry Crews after *A Childhood*," *Southern Literary Journal* 24.2 (1992): 3.

35. In the United States, *Where Does One Go When There Is No Place Left to Go?* was published as a limited edition of 426 copies by Blood and Guts Press, and in England it was included in a paperback reprint of *The Gospel Singer* by Gorse Publications.

36. Harry Crews, "Why I Live Where I Live," in *Florida Frenzy* (Gainesville: University Press of Florida, 1982), 10.

ANNE FOATA

Interview with Harry Crews

Mr. Crews has published five novels: The Gospel Singer, Naked in Garden Hills, This Thing Don't Lead to Heaven, Karate Is a Thing of the Spirit, *and* Car. The Gospel Singer, Naked in Garden Hills, *and* Car *have been adapted for the movies. Crews himself wrote the screenplays of the last two, and* Naked in Garden Hills *is to be filmed by Frank Perry, the director of* David and Lisa *and* The Diary of a Mad Housewife.

Harry Crews will soon be read in France. The first novel to appear here will be Car, *probably in the spring of 1973.*

A.F.: Harry Crews, you have just received the award of the National Institute of Arts and Letters. What does it mean to you and to your career as a writer?

H.C.: Well, it was a big surprise. There are enormous numbers of writers about, and many of them very, very good, and one never expects one's name to come up.

To me, it simply means that men and women I respect in letters have voted to recognize the work that I have done. And probably psychologically, emotionally, in any number of ways, this might sustain me, help me in the work that I'll be doing.

A.F.: You have written five books, five novels . . .

From Recherches Anglaises et Americaines 5 (1972): 207–25.

H.C.: I have published five novels; my sixth is just finished, and Knopf is publishing it. It is called The Hawk Is Dying. In fact, I wrote four novels before I ever published one; my first published novel was actually the fifth novel I had written. I am one of those people who served a long apprenticeship, and wrote an awful lot of copy before anybody anywhere ever mentioned that I might have any talent, or that there was any promise, or potential: literally hundreds of stories, four novels, any number of essays, all kinds of private experiments, simply trying to find my own voice and my own subject.

A.F.: Speaking of subject, all your novels are "southern" novels. They have a southern setting and atmosphere, and they insert themselves into a "southern" literary tradition, made of freaks, illiterate rural communities, etc. What is your reaction at being labeled a "southern" novelist?

H.C.: If somebody told me I was a "southern" novelist, I would not be offended, but I would not be particularly pleased. I write fiction, and I don't think any novelist of any consequence particularly wants to be called a "southern" novelist, or a "Jewish" novelist, or a "black" novelist, or anything: he is a novelist. Period. But I certainly understand that my novels are in the southern tradition.

I myself am from tenant farmers, peasants, in south Georgia. Nobody in my family went to college or to the university, or even finished high school for that matter. But for whatever reason, I wanted to be a writer since I was a little boy. It's the only thing I ever wanted to be. I used to tell stories when I was just a child; I tried to write a detective story when I was eleven. Obviously, whenever I was able to learn enough technically about craft and any other thing one has to learn and know to be able to write narratives, when that time came, obviously the fact that I was raised on the land, in the South, caused my fiction to take a southern flavor. I greatly admire people like Eudora Welty, Katherine Anne Porter, Walker Percy, Faulkner, Robert Penn Warren, Erskine Caldwell . . . But then I admire many other writers too, some of this country, some not. For instance I probably have learned more from Graham Greene than from any other writer that I could name. I particularly like him, because whatever else he does, he always tells you a story.

But a writer doesn't really sit down and say, "Well now, it's time to write another novel here. I have an empty page and what shall I say?" He starts in his head with an image of place, an action, somebody, something, and then he fiddles with it. There is a marvelous thing Einstein said one time. He was at a party, and a lady asked him one of those awful questions. "Doctor," she said, "how do you discover truth?" Apparently this is not apocryphal, it really did happen. Einstein waited a moment, and he finally said: "Madam, I grope." That's what one does in fiction, just fumble about.

Now, you asked a while ago about freaks, or you mentioned them, and people do seem to mention them to me a good deal. My first three novels all have midgets in them. Midgets are very different from each other; they just happen to be very little people, to share that common characteristic: Jefferson Davis Munroe, Jester, and Foot. I have never been particularly close to midgets; I have known one or two, but I never thought of it very much. But here is the thing about midgets, and it may make some comment on the whole kind of deformed and perverted—perverted in the sense of not responding to reason, being strange, to some extent unnatural—characters of my novels. Midgets have to deal with the fact of their bodies every instant of their lives. Whatever compromises they want to make, whatever adjustments they want to make, when they turn the corner, somebody new will look upon them, and there they stand in their tiny body. And if they go into a place to eat, the chairs are not right, and if they go into a clothing store, the clothes are not right. That's true emotionally, spiritually, as well as physically.

You and I can live emotionally anywhere we choose in our heads as long as we function in society, so that nobody notices it; we can believe our right foot's turning into a cocker spaniel if we want to, and nobody is going to bother us about believing that. Thus, in our inner selves, we don't have to react so much and so immediately to whatever we believe or to whatever we are, but midgets in a sense do. What I am trying to suggest is that we are all a mysterious, complex, involved entity that we *pretend* by and large is pretty ordinary. We pretend there is a tremendous commonality. I'm not sure that's true.

A.F.: Flannery O'Connor said that she used freaks as symbols for the alienated condition of men without God in our twentieth-century world. Do you use your freaks, your midgets, your Fat Man in the same sense? And then, what is your conception of this world, your Weltanschauung?

H.C.: It is true Miss O'Connor said that we in the modern world are so accustomed to freakishness and grotesquerie, it has so become the condition of the world, that we see it as normal, and that for the writer writing now, the job is to make the reader see grotesquerie as grotesque, and freakishness as freakish. That's when she made that marvelous statement: "For the hard of hearing you shout, for the very nearly blind you draw large pictures." All right, but you see, Miss O'Connor had something I don't have. She has an essay that begins: "I am no vague believer." She had the whole Catholic faith; I don't. Sometimes I think I am a believer with nothing to believe.

You see, first you have to understand—and this is not modesty on my part—I am not an intellectual. My education has huge holes in it; I've read indiscriminately since I was a little child, but I never had any discipline in formal learning. I am not of any organized church or any organized religion. To tell you the truth, I very often wish that I could be; but I can't. I have tried to be; I can't. On any given day I am a believer or not a believer, just as you might ask me; but always there is a thing in me that desperately would like to be. I feel myself cut off from almost everything. The South that *I* came out of is very different from Faulkner's. Faulkner was out of the aristocracy of the South, or his people, anyway; mine were not.

A.F.: You would rather be from Erskine Caldwell's South then?

H.C.: Yes, except that Caldwell's father was a minister, and they lived pretty well; I mean, they ate, they had a church, and the boy grew up with a good education and a good tight home. My father died when I was eighteen months old; I never had a father the whole time that I was growing up. Very often I didn't have my mother either; she got very sick, and my brother and I had to live with other people, not together, he in one place, I in another. I don't mean that to be a long catalog of my pains; I don't take it that way at all. If it had not happened that way, I would not be what I am.

A.F.: Even if you are no believer of any established church, you must all the same have some kind of conception of the world and of human existence. In *The Gospel Singer* you make a newspaper man comment:

"there is nothing so predictable as the ritual of catastrophe and tragedy." Do you think that human existence is chaos and tragedy, and therefore won't you use midgets and other freaks, the "unfortunate of the world," to quote one of your lines again, as symbols of your specific conception of the world?

H.C.: Well, I don't know . . . The reason I am skirting this, I suppose, is that I am scared to death of the word "symbol." I think of myself as a fairly conscious writer—that is to say, I think of matters of craft, and technique, and point of view, and other things—but I can't really say what I feel you are asking me to say. God knows there are symbols. Everything is a symbol as it becomes involved in any narrative, any sequence of events where human beings are involved and things become infused with meaning larger than themselves.

Take Jefferson Davis Munroe, for instance, in *This Thing Don't Lead to Heaven,* a book nobody liked very much except me. He is a midget, and he says at one point to another character—and when he said this, I was sitting at my typewriter, not knowing exactly what was coming; it just came out—well, he says: "My daddy used to get drunk and come into the house and beg me to grow. He would fall on his knees and embrace me and say 'Son, don't hold it against me: grow', except that he never told me," Jefferson Davis adds, "what I was supposed to be holding against him; he never said, and I never asked." This to me is the awesome mystery of how we become what we are, and how we deal with what we have become, and how everybody around us deals with whatever we become. That's what I am interested in.

Let me say something Flannery O'Connor once said about all of this, and which I very much believe. She said that for the writer, no matter the subject, what he was really interested in was the mystery of that subject, which he could not be expected to solve, but could only be expected to deepen. So, if there are freaks in my novels, if Foot is there with the largest foot in the world, if the Gospel Singer's brother, Gerd, is there with his erupting skin over which he has no control, and all those other people—Fat Man, who weighs six hundred pounds and can't help himself, not even bathe himself—it is only that these people have conditions which are more apparent and more immediate than the people around them. But I am convinced that you and I, all of us, are caught in the same kind of inexplicable, almost blind terror, except that ours is not so apparent.

The Gospel Singer's predicament is more terrible than Foot's, because the Gospel Singer has nothing he can point to; he can't say to the people who have come to listen to him: "See, I have the largest foot in the world and you have to let me be who I am." He can only say: "Don't you know by your own black hearts what mine must be like?" But God knows, if they know that, they will never admit it; they can't admit it, and the only thing they can do is hang him on a tree, which of course they do.

I fear my worldview is a terribly black, awful one. I think sometimes that's why so many of my reviewers have said some of the things they have said about me, why, in *This Thing Don't Lead to Heaven*, they were just outraged by all these old people dying alone. Jeremy Tetley is eighty years old; he is trying to love Molly; he has got a woman and he wants to love her, not just emotionally, but physically, you know, "God touch me!" And he can't. His teeth are falling out, and it is just too horrible. I have only one thing to say to people. As soon as something pleasant and cheerful and confectionery occurs to me, I'll write about it; but I can only write about whatever comes. And what has come thus far has been a kind of blackness. People say that there is no love in much of the stuff that I write. I'm not sure that it is true; I hope it's not true. I think there *is* love; I just don't think there is love the way most people want to use the word.

A.F.: An awful world, a world of blackness: this outlook you have manifested as early as your first novel, *The Gospel Singer*. Since then, you have written book after book on the tragedy of a dehumanizing world, where frustration arises from a loss of meaning, where God is absent, and where man creates his own idols. Your tragedies are Christian tragedies, because we live in a Christian world, even if we deny God.

H.C.: If you are a Westerner, you are a Christian. Period.

A.F.: Yes. And your "Christian" tragedies, you build them carefully around the ancient Aristotelian model—that is, you seem to cling to the rules of unities, for instance. The action, violent death or undoing, takes place in a very short period of time, one day in two of your novels, in one restricted place, Enigma, or the "Senior Club" in Cumseh, Georgia, a phosphate hill in Polk County, or the dilapidated motel of a karateka in Florida. And when the book closes, both protagonists and fictional and real audiences leave purged of their unhealthy emotions; in other words, you have managed a powerful catharsis.

H.C.: I am very pleased to hear you say that. Every writer's effort is to make the reader make the judgment. You see, in the world that we live in, here in this country, the United States, we are drowning, we are drowning in things. I was sitting in my living room the other night; it was late and I was reading a book, and I saw there were about ten lightbulbs burning in the room. I was under one of them, and there were nine others burning with nobody in the room but me. My God, why nine other lightbulbs?

A.F.: The American way of waste, perhaps! Why not burn ten bulbs if you have them? You, Americans, have nothing in common with our European sense of economy, thrift. But, of course, your affluent society leaves a lot of waste, of rubbish . . . Isn't that the subject of your last book, *Car?*

H.C.: Yes, in a way. We are all so virginal here, in the truest sense of the word, in so many ways. We were talking yesterday of our innocent messianic view of things, in large part because this country has never been destroyed, reduced to a rubble. But that's a long way from where I live. I live still in my little—and it is a very little—world, the southern landscape of Georgia, full of hookworms and poverty. It's still fairly much now the way it was then, when I was a boy. Things have not changed that much, for the whites or the blacks. The blacks where I come from are just as exploited and ignorant and hopeless and helpless as they ever were. But that's beyond the point here.

A.F.: No, I don't think so. You said that the southern setting of your novels was a part of your experience. It is what makes your novels so different from the novels of New York, for instance.

H.C.: Let me just say something. In *The Gospel Singer,* Willalee Bookatee Hull, the black preacher, is a man. You must understand that in my books, when I am writing them, and afterwards when I am talking about them, these people are not *archetypal* of something, or symbolic or anything else. They are people, or at least to me they are.

A.F.: People you knew yourself?

H.C.: I knew a guy named Willalee Bookatee once, a black that I grew up with and who was my very dear friend. God knows where he is these days. He is about my age; his last name was not "Hull" though. What I was trying to get to in the book is that Willalee Bookatee does believe in God; he is not trembling and scared. He says, "They are going to kill me either way; they are going to hang me, so it really doesn't matter." What Willalee wants to do is to get right with his God, to know why he killed Mary Bell Carter, why he hit her with his ice pick so many times, which is how the novel opens up. To me, he is just the opposite of the other character; the Gospel Singer knows what his sins are: he trades on love. He traded on Mary Bell's love, which is the worst thing you can trade on. He knows that, but he has nobody to get right with. Mr. Keene, his first manager, knows that he is a son of a bitch, but he does not care. But Willalee does, so there is a kind of balance in the book.

A.F.: The Gospel Singer is a victim too, a victim of the mob who worships him and cannot bear the truth. A sinner, but also a victim.

H.C.: Very much so. But then we are all victims; we are victims of the human condition; we are victims of the little bit we can see, and hear, and know at any given moment. We are all victims of our angle of vision, and that includes spiritual vision, emotional vision, as much as anything else. Take that man in *The Gospel Singer,* whose skin is black with disease, and who left his tobacco crop to ruin in the field, and came to be healed. Well, hell, if you're dying, and your skin is turning black, and somebody even *suggests* that there may be somebody who can do something, why not come, and not just ask, but *demand* to be saved, which is what we are all asking of each other.

A.F.: Considering your tragic outlook on the world and the experience of your childhood and youth in south Georgia, wouldn't the South that you describe be the archetype of a more general world, the world which we live in? It is an archetype, but at the same time it remains "southern," and thus—excuse me please if I insist on that subject—

your novels must be awfully different from the Jewish novels of New York, or the midwestern novels of Wright Morris, etc. Do you think that the southern background is so peculiar that it is bound to produce novels that resemble no other in the United States?

H.C.: I think that the only sense of place in this country is in the South. There is no sense of place anywhere else, sense of place in the way I'm using it—that is, where people *there* have a sense of place, where they know not just what kind of trees there are, but where they are, where the rivers are, and who the people are who are living there, not just now, but were living there last year; the whole thing, you know . . .

A.F.: A sense of community, of family in a certain place?

H.C.: Yes, that sort of thing. If I could not have been a southerner, I think that I would have liked to be a Jew, or a black, maybe a black first, for this simple reason: A Jew can look back over his shoulder all the way to the wailing wall; there is that tremendous thing there if he looks back. The black looks over his shoulder, and he sees blackness, the experience of the black. I don't know what in God's name a man who is born and raised in California, when he looks over his shoulder, sees. Or in a New York high-rise apartment . . .

You know this from reading Faulkner: Southerners are very concerned about their connections, which simply mean blood relatives . . .

A.F.: Kin.

H.C.: Yes, kin. Who is your kin? A sense of family, a sense of land.

A.F.: A sense of history?

H.C.: Yes. I have uncles who live on land our great-grandfathers lived on, in the same houses. It's almost European, in a very limited sense, of course. But to be in a house [like] Mr. Lytle's, for instance, a house that was his grand-daddy's summer home, with his study where the stables used to be—well, you are not going to find that anywhere much but in the South.

A.F.: You have a sense of continuity, but then also an acute sense of change, disruption. The things that made you different, and which you cherish, are going to disappear. Southerners are going to live just like the other Americans.

H.C.: Oh yes!

A.F.: Excuse me if I mention this, but I sometimes wonder, did this old southern style of living really exist? Did the dirt-road farms, the swamps, the very poor illiterate people really exist as they are described over and over in your novels? While reading James Dickey's novel, *Deliverance,* I asked American friends of mine if such characters as the two degenerate woodsmen were really to be encountered; they replied: "Certainly. We met the like of them once we went camping."

H.C.: Very definitely. Eighty miles from where we are sitting now I could take you back to the edges of the Okefenokee Swamp, which is a federal refuge, and where a large number of families exist by poaching, as illegal trappers and moonshiners. And up in the hills of Kentucky, in Tennessee, and parts of Georgia, and other places, similar people live. Oh yes, it's all still there.

Getting back to the South and its sense of continuity, as you said, one doesn't want to make anything out of it, because so much has been made out already, but the fact of the matter is we, in the South, were a defeated people, we were a decimated people, we were a people from whom tribute was demanded and exacted. We had men imposed upon us as leaders during Reconstruction, leaders who were anathema to us. I guess saying such things offends a lot of people. But this time in our history and these circumstances bound us together as a people . . . I count myself as an egalitarian. And I try as much as I possibly can to take men on the basis of how they come to me, and not on the basis of their color or anything else. But the fact of the matter is that I am a southerner raised in the South, and I question whether or not I can ever wash that out of my blood; and the answer is probably that I can't. Intellectually I can, but I suspect somewhere back in here, there is a little cancerous seed growing in the dark about all that, that never can be beaten, no matter how much I try.

A.F.: To come back to southern literature, it seems that it had flourished every time the South was threatened, or had to meet a challenge from the North. I'm referring to all the novels of the 1840s, of the

Reconstruction period, when southerners longed after the old order of things, transforming reality into a myth, the myth of the antebellum South. Then you had the Agrarian and Renascence movement of the 1920s and '30s, when the South was "threatened" by northern industrialism, and by the average American way of living. Would you think that the flourishing of southern literature now, with authors like yourself, Madison Jones, Reynolds Price, Fred Chappell, and all the others, comes from another challenge, which is the civil rights issue and the eventual transformation of southern society? Could that be an incentive?

H.C.: I really don't know. When I heard that Madison Jones had published a novel with a "racial conflict,"[1] I thought: "Oh my God, no, he hasn't tried that too! He's doomed to fail." As it turns out, he has not failed; he has written a fine novel, I think, a very fine novel. I don't think in my own work it will have any influence, because I don't feel any compulsion to deal with blacks as blacks, or whites as whites, or their problems with one another, or how they meet one another, or anything like that. There are other writers who do. It very well might be that that will happen, I just don't know. Take Peter Taylor, who is not all that young: his subject is and has always been the disintegration of the family. I don't think the young writers that I know are preoccupied with that problem. But the fact that this general kind of turmoil exists, not just here in the South, but everywhere in the country, may generate a certain kind of literature.

A.F.: The racial crisis, particularly since 1954, has brought about a whole collection of topical novels, some good, some a little less.[2] There is this essay by Floyd C. Watkins, entitled *The Death of Art: Black and White in the Recent Southern Novel*.[3] It may be true that the racial issue has killed the novel in the South, but among the best writers emerges this concern for the southern society that is changing, just as it had changed after the Civil War, in the "New South."

H.C.: Every time a novel or a story has a point to make, it fails, whether it is a novel by Ayn Rand, who comes in bearing the burden of whatever that philosophy is that she's got, subjectivism, or even the fiction of Sartre. You see, the problem is that I don't believe in good men any more than I believe in evil men. I believe that good men sometimes do evil things, and evil men sometimes do good things. The people who write the kind of fiction you were talking about all want to fix the blame, so there can be a sociological or philosophical point made. If you want social reform, then you ought to stand for public office, and if you want to preach, then take a pulpit, and if you want to send messages, use Western Union. I mean, that's not what Art's about. For the very simple reason that man is a complex, mysterious, unknowable thing, and to reduce that thing to some kind of a simplistic notion of what society ought to be, or economy, I just can't get into that, as a writer. I mean, it's foreign to me to think like that.

A.F.: So, you don't really exploit this topical subject of the race relations, even though *The Gospel Singer* has two barbarous lynchings in it. You use the southern setting because it is part of your experience, as you said, but your real subject is the modern alienating world: the problems of environment as in *Naked in Garden Hills* and *Car*, of old age as in *This Thing Don't Lead to Heaven*, or . . .

H.C.: You know, Mr. Lytle says there are only two subjects: love and the absence of love. I don't know exactly what he means by it, except that I sort of believe it. I know that the people living in Manhattan, or in France, or anywhere else have by and large to deal with the same things that I deal with, obviously, but the land that I know there in Georgia, and the people I know, who are all fond of the land, somehow their struggles with the things that every man must struggle with are simplified, made stark and vivid and immediate.

A man who can buy barbiturates, who can buy warm blankets, and six mistresses and wives, and all the other things, can at least disguise, even to himself, the problems of his own life and his own world. A man who is farming in the South—what Mr. Lytle calls making "man's eternal last stand"—is always making that last stand, because he always has his back to the wall. If you lose your crop, you won't have any seed, and if you don't have any seed . . . So, in such a place, all the archetypal concerns of man are there in such a way that there is no possibility to disguise them, to hide them. Pain is a thing that they have to confront.

Let me say a word about Didymus in *The Gospel Singer*. It isn't often that I can say anything specific and fairly coherent about what somebody is doing in a book. Didymus is stone crazy, insane. But to my mind, Didymus never does anything that is any more essentially insane than the stuff we see a lot of other people in the book do. To my mind, the Gospel Singer, getting into a closed closet, on his knees, and singing the same song over and over again, when in point of fact he is in rebellion with God, is a species of madman. Obviously the climactic scene when the mob kills the two boys not for telling a lie, but for telling the truth, is essentially insane. And Didymus, being absolutely crazy, has found a context for his madness, a place where his madness will work. He is there as a kind of antithesis or counterpoint to the Gospel Singer himself and to the crowd.

A.F.: Didymus has a very crazy, puritanical view of God. His God is a God of wrath, suffering, and death. In a way, don't you think that it's better to have a thwarted image of God and have some thwarted meaning in one's life than have nothing at all, like the Gospel Singer, whose only aim in life is money, Cadillacs, and cheap women?

H.C.: I think generally that I would answer "yes." But I don't know really whether it's better to be Didymus than be the Gospel Singer, because, as you know, Didymus kills Mr. Keene to take his place. The most awful thing, however, that I can imagine is a kind of moral vacuum, in the sense not so much that you are being an evil man—you can be a good man, you try not to hurt people and you try to be decent, and all that—as to be cut loose from the universe, to be cut loose from the fact that rocks fall when you drop them, that stars move in certain patterns, to be cut loose from all that and have no sense that it is all working somehow; this, to my mind, is the scariest thing that I can imagine. I suspect that it may be what much or all of my work comes out of.

A.F.: Do you think that by destroying God, or their gods, men destroy themselves? An atheistic thinker would rather say that by killing their gods, men create themselves.

H.C.: I don't know. The history of belief, as we both know, has been a history of persecution, of blood, of subjection. Man becomes a beast when he gets a god that he believes in with every ounce of his blood, categorically. At the same time that I am aware of this, I am aware of the black kind of vacuum that you have to get up with in the morning if there is no belief. I think of Beckett a lot. I wonder how he gets out of bed in the morning...You see, I can't say that man has destroyed himself by destroying God, or that by inventing God he invented himself, or any of those things. I have to get back to the place where every—I always balk at the word "artist," but I say it—where every artist lives, and every artist lives very much in himself. I only know about my own little thing that I walk around in.

If I could anchor myself irrevocably in belief and order, and put God in his heaven or wherever he is, if I could, I would do that, irrevocably. Some days I can, and some days I can't. It is that kind of... vacillation—floating about, anchored down, not anchored down, not knowing what and where I am—that I struggle with. This all seems so pompous to me somehow, just talking about these things...

A.F.: Let's just say that having lived with a God for twenty centuries, we are a little lost now that we may question him overtly. We shall soon recover, maybe, with a new philosophy...

H.C.: There is a very strange thing. In *The Yale Crosscultural Survey,* done by a very famous anthropologist whose name now slips me, out of three hundred cultures, some dead, some still living, every single one has some idea of an afterlife. It was in fact one of the nine universals found in those three hundred cultures. It is a thing all men have struggled with apparently, either struggled to do or not to do, to believe or not to believe, to make some kind of adjustment with. I think all of literature is about the same thing; it's about a man doing the best he can with what he's got to do with. James Baldwin, in the preface to *Blues for Mr. Charlie,* says a beautiful thing: "No man is a villain in his own heart." We all have our reasons and our blind little justifications, our little cruelties, and, thank God, our little charities, and what little compassion we can manage.

I think literature is very close to somebody walking over the Niagara Falls on a tightrope. We go watching and we say: "My God, there's a man up there, and I am a man myself." It opens up some of the alternatives of what it means to be a human being, perhaps silly, perhaps courageous, perhaps anything. When the Gospel Singer finally goes up on the stage and decides to tell the truth, when he does that, I was—perhaps nobody else was—very moved by that, and I thought that it was a fine thing for a man to have done.

A.F.: You mentioned Andrew Lytle a few times. What has he brought to you, in the field of technique, ideas, worldview? Has he been one of your "masters," if of course you recognize having had any?

H.C.: Mr. Lytle has indeed been my master. The thing that I love about him is that he is a very exacting man in many ways. Certainly where literature is concerned, where writing is concerned, he is almost brutal in his honesty, in his determination to have you do something of merit, or have you do nothing at all. Mr. Lytle did everything for me: fed me, drank with me, talked to me, beat on me in the best sense of the word. And he read my stuff back when I was just awful, back when I was very young.

You see, I went into the Marine Corps when I was seventeen years old, for the good reason that I had no place else to go. I wasn't equipped to do anything, I had no education, and so, I just went down to the Post Office and joined the Marine Corps. I was in there three years and didn't learn anything, and came out, all this time writing and writing and writing. But I had nobody, I didn't know any writers, I didn't know any intellectuals, I didn't know anything. So, I was stumbling around, and I stumbled into Mr. Lytle. Quite by accident.

A.F.: As an undergraduate at the University of Florida, in Gainesville?

H.C.: Yes. So I stumbled into him, and he, for whatever reason, liked the stuff I was doing, and allowed me to enter his life, not just as a teacher, but as a man. He took up an awful lot of time with me that he could have been using otherwise. He did it with a lot of writers. He did it with Madison Jones and Jesse Hill Ford, here at the university, and in other places with writers like Flannery O'Connor and Peter Taylor. There are a great many writers who owe much to Mr. Lytle, and I am one of them.

He wrote me a letter one time—I don't think Mr. Lytle would object to my mentioning this—after I had published, I think, three novels, in which he said: "Son, the reason you cannot end your fiction properly"—"properly" is a big word in Mr. Lytle's vocabulary; it means that something has a certain aesthetic rightness—"the reason you cannot end your fiction properly is that you do not believe in the natural order of things, and you have no sense of the divine." He did say that.

I think what he was really talking about when he said that is that *my* belief and *my* sense of the divine are not as firm and as *consistent* as his. So, maybe his judgment is right, and maybe that will make me write deformed novels. I don't know. It does not really bother me; I work as best as I can.

A.F.: You don't share Andrew Lytle's ideas of agrarian order and tradition. In a way, you don't belong to the tradition of southern literature which he illustrates.

H.C.: No, I don't really share those ideas, and I don't really belong to his tradition of southern literature. I love and revere and believe in tradition of all sorts; I believe in men knowing where they come from and who their people are. But here again we go back to a very simple reason: Mr. Lytle's father was "rich"—"rich," that old word, not just "wealthy," which is the new word. Murfreesboro, in Tennessee, is all land that was given by his ancestors to build that town. I don't share that thing. So, obviously, the South that I see, and my understanding of things must of necessity be tremendously different from his.

I shouldn't say these things, speak for him, but as best I can understand, I think that Mr. Lytle believes that the best world would be a world in which "every man has his man, and God has the king," this tremendously medieval sort of thing. That's the way I read him anyway; I may be wrong. I would not presume to speak for Mr. Lytle.

A.F.: Anyway, you recognize Andrew Lytle as a definite master of yours.

H.C.: A master of mine and a master of fiction. A very fine man and a master of the craft.

A.F.: You also said that in the field of fiction Graham Greene taught you a lot. Do you recognize other influences?

H.C.: Faulkner's rhetoric is the sea around us in whose depth more than one of us has drowned. He is such an overwhelming talent that he has damaged a whole generation of writers, because they all come along and try to be Faulkner and to write about the stuff that to him was a blood-and-bone issue and to them only a kind of romantic nonsense. You see, you can't fake any of this in art. The thing is either in your blood or it isn't. Faulkner has been a tremendous influence in my life.

Erskine Caldwell is a much finer writer than anybody gives him any credit for being. *God's Little Acre* turns out to have been a tremendous conception. You can quarrel with his execution perhaps, but not the conception. His short stories are marvelously written. He is a very fine writer.

And probably, because of Mr. Lytle, Flaubert has been an influence in my work. I try to read—and this will sound like some kind of romantic thing to somebody; well, let it—I try to read *Madame Bovary* once a year, just to read it. It's so incredibly well done.

A.F.: He was a very conscious and conscientious craftsman, rewriting his novels until they were perfect.

H.C.: Yes, we know that from his letters and manuscripts. I'd probably faint if I saw an actual manuscript of his. See, there is another thing you have to understand: I'm still, after all these years—I have been writing with some discipline for seventeen years—in awe of Letters and of writers. If I saw an actual manuscript that Flaubert's actual hand had touched, I don't know what I might do—hell, I might burst into tears. If I didn't have novels to work at, I don't know what I would do in this world, how I would manage to survive. It's a hell of a thing to say, but it's true.

A.F.: Writing is your reason of living?

H.C.: It is; it is right in the center of my life.

A.F.: Do you think that as a writer you have some sort of mission on the earth?

H.C.: No, I can't get into that. I can't think of myself as having a mission. I hope that I am able to do something of merit before I die. I think that for a writer to have a messianic mission, to think he is here to teach people or to save people or to reform them, eventually corrupts him. I don't think that I know anything about the human heart that every other man doesn't know. I just don't believe that the people who go through the world and leave behind them poems, or music, or sculptures are any different from other men; I just believe that they have gone to tremendous trouble to find some way to release whatever they have to release. An illiterate Mississippi farmer can have a mystic experience or revelation; he just can't tell about it, but God knows he can have it.

A.F.: Was it André Gide who said that the only mission of a writer was to write well, and Henry James who declared that if a writer was to write anything, it had to be interesting and entertaining enough to be read? That's about all the responsibility a writer has, according to them.

H.C.: I would subscribe to both of these statements. That's exactly what I think: write well enough for somebody to read what you've written.

A.F.: You mentioned Flaubert and his craftsmanship. What about Katherine Anne Porter, who also is a very conscious craftsman?

H.C.: Katherine Anne Porter's reputation rests, and rests firmly, on her short stories. I don't admire *Ship of Fools;* I think it was a big unread bestseller. But her stories, any number of them, are beautiful. I have also learned a lot from Eudora Welty; she too is a magnificent and very sure craftsman. I believe art is just craft raised to a certain level; other people have said that; I must be quoting somebody. But that's what I believe. There are a lot of writers who consciously don't want to know anything about craft and techniques and so on; they are afraid that it will somehow damage them. I never believed that knowledge will corrupt your art. I always wanted to know as much as possible about how other writers have done things, about the alternatives they had to accomplishing certain effects.

I would like to say one thing since we are on the subject. People have said—and they have said it in a damaging sense—that I write too much, that I write a book a year. Those books were not written that way. It took almost four years for *The Gospel Singer* to find a publisher. One publisher kept it eighteen months, saying that he was going to publish it—World Publishing, a big house in New York—and finally never did.

A.F.: Isn't that the usual fate for a first manuscript?

H.C.: Well, yes. So, anyway, my novels are not written that way. I don't turn them out on mimeograph machines.

A.F.: You have written a novel entitled *Karate Is a Thing of the Spirit*. Are you an adept of karate? In your novel, you seem to show that the karatekas are just another bunch of freaks, "tranquillity freaks." Would karate just be another desperate way of finding some meaning in one's empty life?

H.C.: I think the book is about the nature of belief, how people believe things, and how they come to that belief. I stumbled onto a karate tournament once, in some supermarket where karatekas were giving demonstrations. I looked at it and thought: "My God, what a self-contained, self-justifying madness!" Yes, madness. Then I thought to myself: "Yes, but so many other things are too." Education, as I am exposed to in the university where I teach, and as I had been exposed to as a student, seems to me most often to be that sort of thing, a self-contained, self-justifying madness that men impose upon other men, not because they can justify it, but simply because it is contained within certain borders.

Now, as I was watching these guys kicking each other and uttering their kyais, I wondered if I could use karate as a kind of metaphor in which to inform much of what I see about mid-twentieth-century experience in America. As we all specialize, compartmentalize, and are driven back upon anonymity—once upon a time you knew who made your shoes or baked your bread—we more and more are driven into that self-contained, self-justifying madness.

A.F.: So, karate would be one of the many devices the Americans invent in their longing for something more genuine, less anonymous, like the Earth movement, the do-it-yourself ventures, etc. It's just another kind of escape, isn't it?

H.C.: Yes, obviously, although the Americans did not invent karate. There is a character in the book whose last name used to be "Fyber," but who renamed himself "Belt." He says he is no longer from any country; he is from wherever he finds himself standing. What he has done is, as you said, to escape, though I don't know if he made good his escape.

Also, one of the things that I wanted to get into the book is that a real karateka is not a violent person. He wouldn't hurt anybody, you couldn't insult him, he has a sense of himself, a sense of dignity and peace. I think it was a mistake to bring karate into the Western world; it should have stayed in the East. We, in this country, are the most violent people on the earth. Our traditions are violent, and I think the violence extends far beyond just blood. There is spiritual violence, emotional violence, psychological violence, and unfortunately, this being true, it only remains to be seen whether or not we can succeed in destroying the world as it sometimes seems to me we are determined to do.[4]

A.F.: What about industrial violence? I am thinking of your novel *Naked in Garden Hills,* your favorite book, as you told me yesterday.

H.C.: Yes, in many ways, I suppose, if one has to have a favorite book. I'll tell you exactly how it came about. I was driving from Fort Lauderdale to Tampa, which means that I had to cross the Florida peninsula from the Atlantic to the Gulf of Mexico, and I drove through Polk County, which is the phosphate capital of the world, as they call it. As I was driving along that day, as it so often is in Florida, the sky was a brilliant blue, the air was beautiful, and then way ahead I began to see this awful yellow pall hanging in the sky; then I began to smell it, and the air began to get gritty, and then the landscape became ruined; as far as the eye could see, there were ponds of scummy water, broken tracks, barbed wire . . . It looked like war.

Then I began to see the refineries, some of them abandoned, some of them still working. It depressed me, and I thought: "Oh my God, here we are again right in the middle of man and what he is capable of on the earth." And then another thought occurred to me: this yellow pall hanging in the air is there constantly; people live under that thing . . . If you grow a garden under there and eat the vegetables that come out of it, your teeth will fall out, your bones will soften. Grass grows under that pall, but cattle can stand belly-deep in it and starve to death. So what I thought was, "The men who put that gritty thing in the air don't live under it; they live in Miami Beach, or on the Riviera, or somewhere else. It's Capital that put it up there. And those poor hopeless people who live under it were glad when the factories came in; they thought that it was Progress."

Somebody else would say: "Well, if the factories didn't come, they would be hungry." Well, I think by God that I have some right to say this: I have been hungry, and I have been hungry in the most barren place you can find, south Georgia. And I've got to tell you this: I'd rather be hungry, and I'd rather be cold, and I'd rather not have a roof than have that kind of thing in the sky and that kind of livelihood.

A.F.: You'd rather be poor in a healthy environment.

H.C.: And from that first conception, I thought how absentmindedly we heap injustice and suffering on the heads of people we don't know and never will know, because, as I told you, we are so specialized, compartmentalized. I don't know where my bank has its investments; it probably owns a lot of slum real estate, because slum real estate is very profitable. I don't know if the men who made the shoes on my feet were paid a living wage or not, and on and on and on . . . But finally I did not mean the novel to be a diatribe against big business. I only meant to stress the fact that we are caught, all of us, the rich men as well as the poor, in a world we partially made but did not make, we partially understand and do not understand. And so here we are.

A.F.: And what about Jack O'Boylan? Is he only the absentee owner of the plant, the capitalist, or some symbol perhaps for God, the One we seek and never find, who might not even exist, the One who is responsible for our plight?

H.C.: Well obviously, the title of the novel cannot help but suggest "Naked in the Garden of Eden." Jack O'Boylan is a character everybody talks about, everybody's waiting for, and everybody thinks will save them, and who never appears. He *has* appeared, and left a ruin which they cannot successfully cope with. I think the inference is there. I myself am not willing to say that he is God, or symbolic of God, or anything else, but he certainly represents a power, a condition that men themselves aspire to, a hope of salvation, and something which does not ever materialize. And in order to come to grips with the fact that he is not going to come back, the fact that he has left a ruin, Dolly takes them all into a mindless, exhibitionist, humanless, loveless, violent way of surviving. It's not that I object to the music, the tinsels, or the paint, or anything, what I object to is that in such conditions love is so utterly hopeless, impossible.

A.F.: I have one last question. The most important subjects in life as in fiction are love and death. We have talked about love, or the absence of love; let's now talk about death. It seems to be a deep preoccupation in your fiction; your novel *This Thing Don't Lead to Heaven* is devoted to it.

H.C.: I don't know how to talk about death, which is probably why it so preoccupies me. Death is a black glass wall on which nobody can get a handhold or a foothold. But I would say this: death gives a certain meaning, a certain order, and a certain direction to your life. Somebody said that if your death does not mean anything, then your life did not mean anything. We are all going toward the death that we are preparing ourselves to receive. We have that phrase: "He got what he was looking for," when somebody gets killed. That's obviously true.

I do believe that in order to live in our terribly violent society, we try to successfully disguise the fact that anybody ever dies, or that death is there. We do it from high-altitude bombers or from ships fifteen miles offshore. Our American way of death ... everything is so perfumed, so distant. You talked about this country never having been ruined, reduced to a rubble. I think it would be good if we could see it, face it. I don't want to be hidden from it, I don't want anybody to make death palatable to me. I want to look at it, smell it, feel it, and know it is there. There is a scene in my next novel *The Hawk Is Dying*, a scene in a funeral parlor, where a hawk catches a corpse in the face ... I think about death a great deal.

In *This Thing Don't Lead to Heaven*, it all takes place on a Sunday in a place called Cumseh, Georgia. Jeremy Tetley, who is an old man of eighty and the center of the novel—well, it's his turn to die. This is his day. He gets up in the morning; one of his few—nine, in fact—teeth drops into his mouth from his atrophied gums; he carries that tooth with him all day and he is dead at the end of the book. Now, around that day, which is his, swirl all these other people whose day of death is coming. The sort of conception that I had of the book was to show the beautiful, tragic, ludicrous, macabre dance of life, people trying to make adjustments, trying to handle, relate, understand, make provisions for the fact that they will die, and at the same time trying not to think about it. It's an awful book, and I understand why people didn't like it, why reviewers by and large didn't like it. It's a black thing; but if they don't like it, that's their problem, not mine.

A.F.: Thank you very much, Harry Crews. There are a lot of other things I'd like to discuss with you, but one must end somewhere. Let's make a date for a future interview, after you have finished, let's say, five other novels . . .

H.C.: Good. Let's.

Notes

1. *A Cry of Absence* (New York: Crown Publishers, 1971).
2. For instance, Harper Lee's novel *To Kill a Mockingbird,* Jesse Hill Ford's *The Liberation of Lord Byron Jones,* or Peter Feibleman's *A Place without Twilight.*
3. Mercer University Lamar Memorial Lecture No. 13 (Athens: University of Georgia Press, 1970). Floyd Watkins has read dozens of recent southern novels and his assertion is that they all, or almost all, are highly prejudiced against the white man. Whereas "it may be possible to defend this bias as a historical, political, or social corrective, . . . as fiction the bias fails" (ix).
4. This interview took place during President Nixon's blockade of the North Vietnamese harbors—in fact, on the very morning it became effective. Harry Crews's wife, Sally, had the transistor on that morning to learn whether or not we were going to explode into atomic smoke. Four days later, presidential candidate George Wallace was to be shot and severely injured during his campaigning in Maryland.

STERLING WATSON

Arguments over an Open Wound: An Interview with Harry Crews

Ahead of me he is running, combined of Cherokee color, heaving flanks, and the shambling get-along of a cripple. Again, at the foot of this last hill in his neighborhood, I realize I cannot catch up with him. Somehow, the sudden knowledge that he runs with some anonymous pursuer at his back contributes to my own quitting.

We round a corner, and finish. We have run five miles, our regular course. He is literally steaming in fumy contrast to the dark green backgrounds. I see him pulse like a single organ. Able to talk, he says, "Like to see the birds?"

Of course, the answer is yes, but I can only nod. We move down the sharp slanted driveway. I am glad in all of my muscles for the downgrade. Ahead, I see the garage now converted into a large coop. What surrounds us, this neighborhood, is somebody's dream of life, not Harry's. The hills are good hills but only for running. Look at the rape of this perfectly good two-car garage.

Two-by-four studs run vertically across its mouth. Plywood is nailed to them upward until, at eye level, four feet below the garage ceiling, a long span of chicken wire admits light. I stand on a cinder block and look in. Clearly, the hawks are birds of prey—my eye focuses on talons and the sharp downturned beak like a linoleum knife. They are sullen, indomitable; two big, cruel birds. But they are no more cruel, only different, than the five miles we have just run with varying degrees of success. I ask what kind. He tells me, red tail and red shoulder. I ask when, where. I know enough not to ask why.

Harry Crews was born in Bacon County, Georgia. He is from people who lived on, and worked, but did not often own land. This produced in them a love which holds them in a place and a bitterness which drives them to acts of violence, excessive procreation, music, and sometimes, fiction. One of the things I want to know is how Harry feels about this land.

Harry's enthusiasms are his art: witness the two birds. He "manned" these two hawks in the mode of the austringer, in the manner described by Frederick II in the thirteenth century. The emperor's book, The Art of Falconry, *and a restless suburban discontent are two focal points in the life of George Gattling, the central character in Crews's latest published book,* The Hawk Is Dying.

Harry's enthusiasms are also a paradox; they account for certain visible ruinations (two shattered knees and a withered calf cause the shamble in his running style), and supply a fuel which drives him in his art at a blistering pace.

* * *

On the day we have set aside to talk, I drive east out of Gainesville, Florida, on highway 26, never leaving it until I come to Melrose, where Harry Crews lives in a small lakeside bungalow. What am I expecting? If not affluence, something easy and charming, and probably large enough for him to ramble around in. What I find surprises me. The place is literally a wreck. We meet and he suggests we go out for a beer to wet our throats for "high-tone" talk. Maybe he lives like this because he just doesn't care about surroundings anymore. After all, he has just recently abdicated house and hills, neighborhood and oaks, to take up his running in the piney woods halfway between our university city and the Atlantic Ocean. Or maybe he has thought deeply about the change and it represents a return to something: in the best sense, to roots and a personal reality; in the worst sense, to some romantic ideal of isolation.

He is diminished somewhat, but honed. It is some seven months since we took off daily to go the five miles; and since the hawk book there have been two more. We shake hands, get in my car, and go to a little town further east called Putnam Hall. When we stop I ask, "What's the name of this place?"

"The Blue Pine," he answers. "You can usually get killed in here."

We order two of the coldest drafts I have ever tasted. Little chunks of ice float in the beer. Down at the other end of the bar stand two men wearing *stretched-out body shirts, off-the-ass Levi's; the wet head is not dead in Putnam Hall. We do not occupy the same space easily. On the bar in front of one man is a fancy case containing a pool cue. A one-armed man handles things behind the bar. Beside the cash register sits his holstered .38 special. I ask him, "Can you hit anything with that?"*

He looks at me. "Yes. I can hit anything with that."

I ask, "When's the last time you got robbed?"

"'Forty-one," he says, pointing to a wasted newspaper clipping on the wall above the register. It shows two corpses in front of what was, thirty-two years ago, the Blue Pines.

With the novelist's ability to distill all potential from plot, Harry suggests we play pool. We do, awkwardly. I am aware of an occasional glance from the two at the bar. It is as inadvertent as the sage flick of a hawk's eye. Sharp, the one with the cue sheathed in Samsonite begins, lovingly, to uncase and assemble the long stick. Sharp says, "Two like to play some partners?"

With a grace (mostly in his eyes and big grin) that shows his kinship with these two, with a little ripple of deference all in his face, Harry eases the threat away. He says, "'Spect not. We don't play with anybody real good." Smiles. A laugh. Sharp breaks the cue.

Later, we sit on Harry's bunk out on the screen porch. The house behind us is a dark place. Out front, from the lake, a man's voice comes reedy and petulant from a racy little boat—water-ski instructions. Little rings of oil glimmer in the shoals. Red-winged blackbirds have made their woven, contingent nests among the cattails. We talk.

S.W.: When and how did you get started writing?

H.C.: Truthfully, I can't remember how I got started writing because it was so long ago. I wrote a kind of detective story, a novel, about two hundred pages long, when I was thirteen. And I was writing stories when I was just a child—seven or eight. It sounds like some sort of cliché, but I think I got started because when I was a boy, we had no radio, no television, did not subscribe to newspapers; we were on a farm, and the highlight of every day was when we were by the fire and the work was done and we were all sitting there and my uncles would tell stories to one another. Not really stories; it was out of their own experience, tricks they had played, times they had gotten in fights, been hunting, or whatever. That sort of just rubbed off on me. I repeated what grown-ups were doing.

And also, I was encouraged in this by the kind of mother I had. I remember very distinctly one night, for no reason at all, I looked at my mother and said, "I think I'd like to preach." And I didn't mean preach as a vocation in the future, I meant preach now, and she understood it as such. And she said, "Well, son, just get up there and preach." I made myself a little pulpit, and I got right up there in it, and turned up a chair and put a blanket on top and got up behind it, and preached to my mother and my brother. I began by saying, out of that great Baptist tradition, "Man's made out of spit and dust . . . ," you know, and the whole thing. I was about five years old, hadn't even started school.

S.W.: How do you relate to other writers in the matter of influences?

H.C.: Well, influences! I've said, again and again, that if any novelist has ever influenced me, it's been Graham Greene. I've read Graham Greene very closely with the conscious idea of seeing how in the hell he did things.

There were times when I was writing, beginning all the way back in my teens, when I consciously imitated all manner of people. Graham Greene's seemed closer to my storytelling sense than other people's did. So I took one of his novels and reduced it to numbers: how many characters; how many days did the novel take; how many cities were involved; how far into the novel did I understand the climax to take place; where did the action turn; how many men, women, children, rooms. Then I sat down and tried to write a novel using that skeleton—characters, cities, children, conflicts, all those things. Of course, you've got to understand what I'm describing is a desperate ploy by the rankest kind of amateur who could find no help, no reader, and was just thrashing about trying to learn something.

Needless to say, the novel that resulted from this was an abominable piece of work—arbitrary, mechanical, and uninteresting. At the same time, I think I learned a great deal from that exercise—and it took me damn near a year out of my life. Matters of physical transition, say from room X to room Y across town; how did Greene get 'em over there, did he just do it in a sentence or did they go down and get on a bus? Psychological kinds of transitions; somebody is very angry and you got to take him back to a state of tranquillity or happiness. I tried to see how he did it and then I did it.

S.W.: Did you know at the time that there was a history of this kind of thing being done? For example, that a woman took James Jones and made him type through novels.

H.C.: I heard about that later. I didn't know about it at the time. But I imagine in the back of my head I had the idea that somehow, as an apprentice writer, you had to really get close to a piece of writing. We speak of close reading. If you have to type it, that's a kind of closeness, and if you have to use its skeleton, that's another. I didn't know this then either: when you go into the Metropolitan Museum you see students standing in front of the masterpieces with canvas and easel copying the goddamn things, and they've been sent there by their teachers. So why not? Robert Louis Stevenson said that a writer was a "sedulous ape," and by "ape," he meant copier, but of course that is not to say that he is a copier ultimately. I see nothing wrong with learning from your betters. It does not mean they will always be your betters.

S.W.: Recently George Garrett and William Styron, two southern novelists, have turned to subjects in history with great success; do you anticipate anything of this sort for yourself?

H.C.: Never! Absolutely not! I can't conceive of anything more alien. As a matter of fact, I don't admire Robert Penn Warren's fiction. With the exception of . . . what's the one about the Louisiana politician?

S.W.: *All the King's Men.*

H.C.: I think that's a fine novel. But Robert Penn Warren said that, to him, the idea of going out to deliberately research a novel, in the library or anywhere else, seemed obscene. He said it all very well and anybody's interested can go see what he had to say on the matter—it's in the *Paris Review* interview. I feel the same way about it. To research a thing seems to me to be obscene. I have been involved, with the hawk and with karate, in experiences which I felt, in the back of my head, would somehow cause something to happen from which I would write a novel. But it wasn't as though I were making notes. I've never worked from notes. I don't even work from any kind of outline. No, I'm never going to write an historical novel.

S.W.: Are your works conceived out of traditional principles of craft?

H.C.: I think of myself as a very traditional storyteller. I really do. As a matter of fact, whatever new things may be happening in fiction, I'm just not interested in them.

S.W.: Could you say why?

H.C.: Because the writers I've read who undertake to do these things—Robbe-Grillet, or whatever his name is, the Frenchman—simply seem to me not to render the human situation in a human way. It all becomes too intellectual, too complicated for complication's sake. I don't like to talk about or think about the novel or short story writer's "responsibilities." What I like to think about is that if he's going to write a story, it ought to be a story that doesn't need an index, a special key, an interpreter, a commentator . . .

S.W.: Why do you live in the South?

H.C.: Probably I live in the South because I have a terror of cold weather. It's just that simple. Maybe. Secondly, I live in the South because all my people live in the South. I'm three hours from my Ma up on the farm there in Ashburn, Georgia. I'm five hours from my brother in Atlanta. Over and above that I have to admit that I like to hear the cadences of the voices. I've been up North a few times and stayed up there for a while, and I find the speech alien. I find the manners alien.

S.W.: You wrote an article for *The Writer* magazine ("Getting It Together," 1971) about the "sense of place" in fiction. Care to talk about that?

H.C.: Well, when I start out to write fiction, or write a story, I don't start out to dramatize a message, or a social insight, or an economic imperative. I simply start out to get in touch with another life, another guy somewhere in his circumstances, doing the best he can with what he's got. I think that's what all fiction is about, a guy doing the best he can with what he's got. Now, in order to do that, in order to get in touch with a life, first you have to be in touch with everything that circumscribes that life: what his lawn looks like, what the trees around him look like, what his food looks like, what the place where he shaves himself looks like, his relationship with his wife, and where his wife came from. Everything around him. On the other hand, if you're trying to get in touch with a message or trying to dramatize some sort of thing for the world to live by (God help us), then you don't have to do that.

S.W.: Is there a *new* South? Are you a writer of the new South?

H.C.: Well, I hope I'm not a writer of the new South any more than I'm a writer of the Midwest. I hope I'm just a writer who happens to live in a certain place. Obviously, there is a new South, because there is a new everything. That's a cliché. We know that. The new South comes from the fact of affluence, the television; the cadences of speech are breaking down or have all broken down. Instead of children in Ludowici, Georgia, listening to their grandfather talk and tell stories of their uncle, of their mother, they're listening to the television and, of course, the television has no accent. There are no characteristics inherent to its speech. The guy from California sounds like the guy from Florida sounds like the guy from Texas. So, the speech has broken down. The affluence has caused tremendous mobility. Agriculture has become enormous heavy industry rather than the small farm.

I'm not saying any of these things are bad. I'm just saying that all those things which identified the South—a kind of loyalty to blood, and a suspicion of the outsider, and a nurturing of familiar things, and a rejection of unfamiliar things—have all broken down. Because of mobility, television, and affluence, people simply can't stay alive in the tiny pockets of labor on farms any longer. And so that's all gone by the way, and it's foolish to say or think otherwise.

S.W.: Your character George Gattling, in *The Hawk Is Dying*, is a transplanted man, a man out of the rural into the urban. Some of the things that have happened to him in the transition cause problems in his present life.

H.C.: On one level he's made the transition tremendously well. He's got a business, makes money, lives in a very expensive house, drives a nice car; he's got a lot to eat, you know, all those things. In another way, coming as he does from Bainbridge, Georgia, off the farm to this business he has established, what he's found and what he says in the novel is "I was being continually warned while I was growing up about various things, but I was never warned what I should have been warned about. They told me, 'work hard'. That work would save me. 'Work hard, save money, and you'll be happy'."

He worked hard, and one day turned a corner and found that he was on the edge of some kind of enormous hole, was about to fall in, and didn't understand any of it. He has no real relationships with his job, or his family. He has no real connection with the city in which he lives. He goes to cocktail parties and is a stranger. He goes to his office as a stranger, to his home as a stranger. What he ultimately falls back on is this tremendous attraction to blood.

S.W.: George Gattling comes to some equilibrium in his life through a reassertion of a rural motif—the keeping and subduing of a bird, the hawk. What does this mean?

H.C.: Well now, I can't say what it means. I don't think a novel means anything, any more than a life means anything. I was trying to deal with a man in a place. But what I wanted to deal with was the fact that man, traditionally, controls everything on earth—that's the myth—control over all the things that creep and crawl and fly. I said a while ago, that George has an attraction to blood. This is a return to the most basic of all human actions. To dominate a thing physically. And to dominate yourself, in a kind of metaphor, emotionally and spiritually and every other way. You can't argue about an open wound. I mean, "I am cut. I am bleeding. My arm won't work." And if you are my adversary and you've beaten me, never mind why, then I have to make my adjustments within that defeat. The hawk has to make his adjustment within the defeat by the man, and obviously George Gattling has to make his adjustments, defeated as he is by the society he finds himself in.

S.W.: But it's nothing as simple as going back and calling the hogs? It's not going through the motions of a re-creation of the rural?

H.C.: No, I don't think it's anything as simple as that. But there are certain echoes. Everybody likes to rhapsodize about how beautiful the rural life is. The rural life, as I knew and experienced it in childhood, is, without exception, dreadful. It makes a man brutal to animals, to himself. It makes him callous and unfeeling. It's not that he hates the animals. It's not even that he hates himself. This is just the way the world is: I cut the nuts off hogs. I dig screwworms out of a cow. And the cow is lowing and screaming and frothing at the mouth, but that's all right, you just dig 'em out and put the tar in, and hope she lives. It's the same way with yourself. You get back to that kind of brutal one-to-one view of how the world is. There's no way to talk about it. Those rural people don't sit around and talk about the way the world is. The world is as close to them as their own skins.

S.W.: Do the freaks in your work reflect your own view of yourself? You have a withered leg.

H.C.: Yes, I do have a game leg, it's true . . . They're not me. I'll tell you about as close as I can get to it. One of the reasons they keep cropping up in my fiction—and this is all after the fact, because people keep after me, so I've thought about it. If you have a withered arm or a badly deformed back, or if you're a midget, all the facades that people maintain in their lives to keep people from knowing who they are and what they're like and what they're doing, don't work for you. When a midget walks into a place to get on a stool to get a hamburger, he's got ten problems to solve with people looking at him. He's got to somehow get up on the stool, he's got to somehow negotiate everything that's out of place.

Did you ever stop to think how much we're influenced by the kind of body we inherit? A guy that's five feet two inches tall or a guy that's five ten and weighs four hundred pounds. It's a truism that psychologically, and every other way, we are busily concealing ourselves. Well, it's just infinitely more difficult to conceal yourself if you are walking around in that kind of body. Diane Arbus, a fantastic photographer who killed herself, talks about the fact that we all eventually come to our traumas in life, nobody escapes this. A freak is born with his trauma. And looking back on these things, I think maybe that's the compulsion behind all that stuff in my fiction. Still, I don't think about those things when I'm working.

S.W.: Are you going anywhere that you can foresee?

H.C.: No. Again, it's one of the things I don't think about. It amused me that my new publisher—I got a new publisher with *The Hawk Is Dying*—wrote in his advertising that "Harry Crews, who heretofore has written about freaks and grotesqueries, now has changed all that, and is writing about people you can recognize." It dumbfounded me. And now, the book I've just finished, *The Gypsy's Curse*, is the freakiest thing I've ever written.

You've got to understand, I don't really think of those people as freaky. I really don't. The word "freak" never occurs to me. Except it's what the world calls them. Jesus, Lord knows, if I could get into your head and heart for a while . . . you couldn't tell me what's in yours and I couldn't tell you what's in mine. We'd be embarrassed. You just don't do that. But freaks are human beings who happen to be "enterable." They are human beings who offer a kind of avenue for entrance. And, for that matter, if you look at the first three midgets, Foot in *The Gospel Singer*, Jester in *Naked in Garden Hills*, and Jefferson Davis Munroe in *This Thing Don't Lead to Heaven*, they're three very different people. They're not even remotely alike. They all happen to be tiny people. They're very different human beings with different preoccupations, with different things that they want in the world, with different kinds of drives. And anybody who lumps them all together and calls them midgets and thinks he's now dealt with them—it offends me . . .

S.W.: You once said, "Write looking over your shoulder."

H.C.: I think that's true; I think that if you listen carefully enough to the very language, just in the way you describe a character—a simile, or a metaphor, or an image of any kind—that language will help you discover more about who he is, what he will say in a given circumstance, what he will do in a given situation; and so that's what I meant. I guess I say that because when I start working, I don't know where the hell I'm going.

S.W.: Do you mean also that there is a great deal of craft involved in writing?

H.C.: Yeah, you gotta work at it. Technique is not something you've got up your sleeve. Craft and technique mean, I guess, that you have submerged yourself so totally in your art, you've read what other men and women have done, the way they solved problems, made certain transitions, whatever, and you've worked at this for so long that it is embodied in you. It is something you don't think about much. As a matter of fact, when I'm writing a first draft, I rarely ever think about the problem of point of view or other matters of craft. It is only after I go back and begin to rewrite that I begin to think consciously about the implications of what I've done—the technical implications of the point of view or some other matter of craft.

S.W.: Why do you write so fast?

H.C.: I don't write fast. I write what is given to me to write. It seems to me that writers by definition are people who write. It has nothing to do with publication. It has nothing to do with what the world thinks of you. It has nothing to do, or shouldn't have ultimately to do, with money. There are lots of easier ways to make money. People may not believe that. Of course, you don't make much money writing anyway, so it has nothing to do with that. It is just that certain men are given to be compulsive about golf, writing . . .

S.W.: It goes back to preaching?

H.C.: Well, it's something like that. I'm compulsive about going to the typewriter. There again it has nothing to do with liking to do it. I don't think that compulsive horse players *like* to go to the track particularly. I think they enjoy themselves sometimes, but they do it because it's in them to do it . . . Faulkner published his first novel in 1926, *Soldier's Pay*. He published his fifth novel, *As I Lay Dying*, in 1930. Well, I am not here comparing myself to Faulkner, God knows. But Faulkner wrote those novels because he wrote those novels. It was given to him to write them.

S.W.: What was it like between the time you began to write and the time you began to publish?

H.C.: For me, it was . . . pretty dreadful. I will go on record as saying that I wanted to publish about as badly as any man has wanted to do anything *ever*. Today I lust after an audience. I wish I were widely, widely read. I wish the audience of people who read and like my work were eight times as big as it is. I wrote fifteen years without any approval at all. I was rejected by everybody in the country, and nobody ever mentioned anything about talent in the letters they wrote back to me. In the form rejection slips, nobody ever said a word about talent.

I used to dream when I was as old as twenty-five or twenty-six that one of my novels (of course, I'd written four novels by that time which had been rejected), I used to dream that one of my novels had been published; and dream while I was asleep this tremendous joy and celebration and the rest of it and then wake up literally humiliated, crushed, depressed, stricken that I was still where I was. Let me rush to add that I thought somehow that if I ever published a novel, my life would change. Well, the truth of the matter is, it changed nothing. Now I have six novels and in my personal life it's done nothing. I always somehow assumed that it would. It hasn't.

S.W.: Why are you in the university? Is it a good or a bad place to be?

H.C.: I think it can be good and it can be bad. I've talked to novelists, friends of mine, who say that they would be stifled and overwhelmed and it would hurt them and they couldn't work on a university campus. I think that for such people it would be bad. The university doesn't get in my way at all, not at all. I never planned to be a teacher. I didn't train in school to be a teacher. It was something that happened by accident. I find that I like to teach. I like to talk to students and have them talk to me. And the university has been very kind and generous with me. I've all the time in the world I need to write, more than enough time. And so for me it is very good. I don't ever visualize quitting teaching.

Steinbeck, in talking about the Depression, said that when a man got up in the morning and put his pants on, he needed some place to go. Well, by extension, I need some sort of job to keep me at anchor. It stabilizes my life. If I didn't have a job, I would probably lie around and stay drunk all the time. Just knowing I have to go somewhere at a certain time gives my life a certain order.

Suppose you asked, "Did I think writing could be taught?" Now this has been hashed over time out of mind. And I don't think you ever change anybody's mind about it. I don't know whether writing can be taught or not. Just let me go on record as saying that when

I work with people in the university who think they want to write fiction, I think of myself only as what a very fine editor would be—I'm a reader. I read their work and give my best reaction to it. I say to them, "I believe this, I don't believe this, this seems too quick, this is whatever, the language is garbled, or whatever." I give them my best reaction, and from my reaction, the best reading I can give the piece, the writer is free to go and do whatever he wants to do with this work, including nothing. I have never told anybody, "Go and do this: add another character."

Every writer up to a certain point needs a reader. I don't think John Barth needs a reader. He may. I don't know. While we're on it, my own personal reaction is that John Barth could use a reader, a good one. But that's just my own personal prejudice. Let me cite Ralph Ellison. In an interview in *Harper's*, he said he thought it was important for a writer to be around other writers *particularly* when he was young, because when he was young he was developing that fund of craft out of which he would draw for the rest of his life—almost a direct quotation, and that marvelous "fund of craft"—I love that. I don't think anybody's ever hurt by knowing too much about his art.

S.W.: Your last two books, *Car* and *The Hawk Is Dying,* have characters in them who do significant battle with the encroachment of technology. What is the future of fiction in the face of urban encroachments upon the rural places?

H.C.: Flannery O'Connor talks about rootedness in time and place and, by implication, in manners in her book *Mystery and Manners.* The truth is that a man's environment, a man's living space, the way he uses the world, is going to be there, whether he's lived in one place or fifty places in a very short period of time. Man is such that he, I don't mean all men, but Man with a capital *M*, is such that he makes, whether he wills it or not, an integrated vision of his experiences. Real estate salesmen do it. Jet-setters do it. Everybody does it.

To say that you have to be in one place and deal with characters who have a certain tradition and manners and are rooted in the land and all of that, to have effective characters in fiction and write effective fiction is about like saying you have to experience the experiences you write about in order to write about them well. Stephen Crane wasn't in the Civil War. The Brontës lived on a heath in virtual isolation and wrote tremendously compelling psychological stories, effective fiction about people.

S.W.: Tell me about this trip you're going on and what you mean to do with the results. What questions might it answer?

H.C.: If I knew what questions it was going to answer for me, I wouldn't have to go, would I? The truth is I don't have to do it. It's true that in about a week and a half I intend to go into the woods at Springer Mountain, Georgia, and walk toward Vermont for a couple of months. In terms of denial, on the obvious level you deny sleeping in a bed at night, the comforts of staying dry, you eat strange foods, fight chiggers. On one level it means I can't get any phone calls, and I get away from the typewriter.

Over and above that, for whatever reason, I have always been strongly attracted to physical confrontations with the world. Now, if this is just an outsized ego, or if this is a macho thing, if it is some sort of criticism of me as a human being because I do it, well then, I think I ought to make the best of it. I want to go and see what it's like to have to fall back on myself. And this is the thing that other people have done and talked about. Going on the trail and this desire to fall back on my own resources, just me and the woods and hiking along with a pack on my back for days on end—none of that's new with me and it shouldn't be new with me. People who are continually looking for something that will be "new" or "original" are fools. We're really only going to do what all other men have done.

Thomas Wolfe said that you write about America much better living in Europe than you do living in America; that is to say, you get a certain distance on things. I'll think about beds, food, and cars in a certain different way after having been away from them for a long time.

Also, I'm curious. When I was a boy, nature was always something to get out of, not get into. We have spent millions and millions of dollars to control the environment—air conditioning and all of that. And people lust after the outdoors. You can't even get into the national parks. People are anxious to get bitten by a bug and get dirty again. And one of the things I want is to talk to people walking on the Appalachian Trail and see what they're doing, why they're out there. The first place it occurred to me to do this was on the trail up in Vermont where I saw some terribly strange and freaky things. You know I never make up any freaky things. I modify and reorganize things I see and know and believe, I hope toward some kind of artistic goal or aim. But I never make up anything. I want to get on the trail and talk to these folk and see what it is they're doing.

And I think I might write a nonfiction book about the people I meet, and walking on the trail. I suppose it'll be thinly disguised autobiography. I have to confess that I am to the point in my life (thirty-eight years old on my birthday two days ago) where I want to talk about myself—not in fiction but just straight out, about my childhood, my motorcycle trip when I was gone a year and a half around the country, my education. If I do the book, it will have as much to do with me as with the people on the trail.

JOE DAVID BELLAMY

Harry Crews: An Interview

The photographer circles. She is focusing on, click, Harry Crews, novelist. Harry has just recovered from the flu, and he is telling me about this very bad bug, gesturing and squinting and moving around in his chair, which is his way of telling almost anything. He looks about as healthy as anyone, a lot healthier than most, tanned, wiry, animated as any wildman in his blue work shirt and Levi's and suede track shoes.

We are sitting in green wicker chairs on the porch-balcony of Maple, the faculty residence at Bread Loaf in Vermont. It is mid-morning, a fine, sunny, windy day in late August.

Harry Crews has extremely deep-set eyes under a jutting brow, and he will fix you with the steely-eyed intensity of a drill sergeant, an intimidating scowl, while his hands spin around his ears, and his elbow joints keep jerking in and out as he talks. When he smiles, it is a surprising, broad, toothy grin. His mustache, womb-broom, and hambone sideburns slide back, and his face is transformed by gigantic crow's-feet.

The photographer leaves. Occasionally the light glints from the gold ear-ring in Harry's left ear as he moves and speaks.

J.D.B.: Do you see yourself as part of any literary tradition, part of a southern tradition or an experimental tradition?

H.C.: Well, I'll have to tell you the truth. I've never really been very comfortable with schools of writing or, as you say, the idea of myself as part of some tradition.

From *Fiction International* 6–7 (1976): 83–93.

Obviously I live in the South and I am from the South. Just as obviously, it has not been just southerners who have been influenced by people like Faulkner. Damn near everybody has, to some extent, drowned or not in his rhetoric, and that power and overwhelming sort of primal thing that he was. I don't know anybody who wanted to try to imitate him. As a matter of fact, most people I knew or heard anything about were scared to death of getting caught in that kind of thing. O'Connor said nobody wants to be on the railroad track when the Dixie special comes through. She's talking about Faulkner. Obviously again, I work out of the conditions of the South, primarily Georgia and north Florida—those cadences of speech, that weather, that whole thing. Not many people know it, but north Florida is the same place as Georgia. Now, south Florida's another thing that I don't understand at all.

J.D.B.: What writers would you say *have* influenced you the most?

H.C.: I don't think there is any doubt but what I have been influenced most by, strangely enough, Graham Greene, in England. Graham Greene was my first hero as a writer. The thing I loved about Graham Greene is that no matter what else he did, he always told you a story, and the story had that hard, clean narrative line which I admire very much. It is the thing that is most central to the way I work. Those long, introspective, bemused wanderings over some sort of psychological landscape inside the character are alien to me, although there is some of that in Greene. There is some of that in any writer. Obviously, there are characters who think and wonder about the implications of who they are and what they've done and where they're going and all of that. But you take a book like *The Power and the Glory* and it's got this nice, clean, hard narrative sort of line that I admire.

J.D.B.: Well, it seems to me that, while there are conventional techniques in your books, I see evidence of a kind of experimentation too. I'm thinking of *Naked in Garden Hills,* for instance, and the way you treat time in that book.

H.C.: Well, see now there you are. Yeah, that's true. *Naked in Garden Hills* almost scares me when I go back and look at it. The way time is handled in *Naked in Garden Hills* is that it has been taken out of any sort of chronology and put back together another way, and the way it's been put back together is, in some sense, a manifestation or reflection of the way these individual lives have been taken apart and put back together by the rather extraordinary landscape they live in—this mining company that's come and left a Dante's *Inferno* right there in the middle of Florida, this ruined landscape. The time thing does do that, and that sort of thing fascinates me. More of it's been surfacing in the stuff that I do.

J.D.B.: Frequently, your characters, too, are quite extraordinary, and it's not just the midgets. There are so many other extreme types. It brings to mind the very idea of the grotesque in American literature. I could see somebody putting you right alongside Nathaniel West and . . .

H.C.: Well, of course, I'd be in very good company if anybody did do that, but most people who say anything to me (and this includes people who write anything about what I do) usually seem to be really unhappy that I write about this sort of thing, as though I had somehow just perversely decided one day that I am going to write about grotesque things and all that.

J.D.B.: It's certainly a legitimate way of handling character.

H.C.: Well, I'll tell you. On the one hand, I think of myself as a tremendously conscious writer. Maybe that's a strike against me or a bad thing to say, but if it is, hell, let everybody make the most of it. I'm a very conscious writer, not when I'm doing things initially, not in the first draft business; in the first draft that's just kind of a wingin' thing, that's when you're trying to get through, you're trying to get it down. But in the rewriting after the draft is done, why, I go back and begin to look at it and try to see the implications of what I put down and try to see whether the thing fits together in the best possible way I can make it fit together. Then it becomes all very conscious for me, the way I work, the way I'm thinking about it. But the other part of it, the business of taking a character and deliberately exaggerating some aspect of his body—I don't do that. It's just the way it happens to be.

J.D.B.: It just happens . . .

H.C.: I don't know any writer who knows where all that stuff comes from. It comes from the fact that you're a writer and that's what you do. There it is. I've thought about it a lot and I can't seem to settle it in my own mind. I just finished a book which will be out next year. It's a book about a legless hand balancer who can't talk and can't hear, and it's a first person narrative from his point of view. He tells the story. But he can't talk.

J.D.B.: It's not in his head?

H.C.: Well, yes and no. He can talk with his hands, and he can also write things down on a piece of paper. Anyway, I suppose that the people who've been unhappy that I write about grotesqueries of one kind or another will be very unhappy about this because there's a scene in it where a deaf-mute choir sings, and there's a deaf-mute out front who's leading the thing. They're all standing with their hands down by their sides, and when the choral director raises his baton, like this, and brings it down, all their hands fly up in the chorus and they sing this song to an audience of deaf-mutes who sit and listen to it and then applaud.

J.D.B.: It seems to me that your imagination, in all kinds of ways, with character, with setting, and with your narrative technique, is really striving to get out of a realistic mode, even though you tend to use some realistic conventions. What do you think about the realistic tradition? If you can stomach that kind of a phrase, do you think the realistic novel is dead?

H.C.: No, no, I don't think it's dead, any more than the five-act play is dead. Nobody's writing five-act plays much anymore, you know, in the ordinary sense, but that's not to say somebody won't; but on the level that most people mean it, maybe the realistic novel is dead.

The whole business of the age and time we live in—with media of all sorts, television, newspapers, magazines, movies, and everything (there's so much of it)—we have this incredible sense of time at our backs. Everybody's got a watch on, and everybody's looking at it every five minutes, and there're clocks in stores, and there're clocks all over the street, and we got to go six hundred miles an hour in airplanes. Do you know anybody who *needs* to go six hundred miles an hour in airplanes? I don't. But we all do it; and so it seems to me that this state of affairs, instead of saving time as everybody pretends it does and giving us more of it, it has fragmented and disjointed our conception of time. Of course, when you fragment and disjoint time, you fragment and disjoint what we call reality. The world becomes a little like a Barthelme story, those little fragmented, disjointed, isolated islands of experience.

J.D.B.: How do you feel this idea finds expression in *your* work?

H.C.: One subject that fascinates me and seems to come up again and again is isolation of one sort or another. If you read *Karate Is a Thing of the Spirit,* you'll find that Belt in that book says, "I used to be from Arkansas, but now I'm not from anywhere." He says, "The only place I'm from is wherever I happen to find myself standing, and I'll never defend anything except the five-foot radius around wherever I happen to be standing." In one sense, he's broken from country. He's no longer from America; he's no longer from Arkansas. So, in one sense, he's liberated into the status of a world citizen, but in another way he has isolated himself totally in this tiny little circle with these other people, wherever they happen to be.

It seems to me that it's not so much that I am experimental or that I do things other guys haven't done. It's that I take things other people have done and compress them. I say a human body is less than four feet tall and has got a twenty-two-inch foot. To give a guy a twenty-two-inch foot is in one sense to exaggerate the proportions of a certain part of his anatomy, but in another way it compresses it. It gives you the footiness of the foot, if you can get into that. Often I read people who talk about their work—sometimes it's writing I greatly admire—and they're so lucid and they seem to have such an intellectual command of what they're doing. I don't have that at all, as you can probably see. Rationally, I understand very little of it. I think I understand it absolutely in *some* sort of terms once I get it out there, putting it together in the best possible way.

J.D.B.: You mentioned the other day that you thought it was extremely important to pay attention to what is coming out of your pen *right now*. Well, that seems to me a defensible principle of writing, you know, trying to cultivate spontaneity and inventiveness as you write.

H.C.: Lots of people don't believe me when I say this, but it is true. Of course, I've never consciously thought that I was trying to cultivate spontaneity or that it was a way of inventing things. The truth of the matter is that as I work I discover the story, and as I write about the character I discover who he is. This necessitates finding out some things as we go along.

J.D.B.: As you say: you do a quick first draft. How many times do you go through it and work on the structure after you get the first draft down? How long does it take you to complete your book?

H.C.: Well, usually it depends. For that *Car* book, which is a very small book, I did the first draft in six weeks. It took me about ten months before I sent it off to the publisher. But that varies a lot. Sometimes it takes me two years to write a book.

People always think that I wrote all these books one at a time, the way they appear, but it's just not true at all. I wrote them one at a time, but I didn't write one a year. I wrote *The Gospel Singer* in the middle '60s. About '64 I sent it off to World Publishing Company, God love 'em, and they kept it a year and a half. They wrote me a letter and said we're going to publish your book, and I was so stupid and everything else that I didn't ask for a contract and didn't get one. Anyway, they kept it a year and a half, during which time I worked on *Naked in Garden Hills*. When *The Gospel Singer* came out, I had at that time already finished *Naked in Garden Hills*, the publisher had already bought it, and I had finished two drafts of *This Thing Don't Lead to Heaven*, and the work was almost finished on that. So, in point of fact, when I started publishing there were three books that were already done.

Another thing that pisses me off is that everybody's always yelling about how fast I write. I don't know what that means. If a guy says, "I wrote a book in a year," it may mean he worked an hour a day for a year, or it may mean he worked twelve hours a day for a year, so to say "a year" doesn't mean anything.

J.D.B.: What kind of a schedule do you have? Are you especially disciplined?

H.C.: Well, it's an extraordinary thing. People say to me sometimes, "you must have extraordinary discipline to do that." It doesn't require any discipline at all for me. It's just something I happen to do. I write every day when I'm writing, Sundays, Christmas, except when I come away to places like this. I work first thing in the morning. There's no particular time I have to be there, but I usually work about four hours, four and a half hours. And you know, you just write a little bit and you'd be surprised. The problem is not what to use, the problem is what to throw away. You write two pages a day and, Jesus, in a year, you'll end up with what, nine hundred pages, eight hundred pages of stuff. That's just too much, obviously.

J.D.B.: You teach too, don't you?

H.C.: I teach at the University of Florida, but I come in and do a single Tuesday night and a Thursday night. And I work primarily with graduate students who think they want to write fiction, and I don't have that many students. But a lot of people have wondered how that works—can you work on campus? Some of my friends say that they don't know how I can bear it on a university campus. But the point is, I have to have a job of some kind. Maybe when I get older, maybe when I get fifty, I'll be cool enough not to have a job. But if I didn't have a job now I'd probably end up drunk all the time or something. Some sort of job gives my life a little direction, you know? Thursday night I know I gotta be somewhere. Otherwise, I'd just be all over the landscape.

J.D.B.: When you work do you drink coffee or water or booze or anything to help you work, or do you just sit there . . . ?

H.C.: Well, no. When I first started out writing with some regularity and discipline, when I was seventeen or eighteen years old, I used to always work at night. I never work at night now. I trust nothing I write at night. I can't, you know. For years I thought that I could sip a beer or two. Even three or four beers are not going to do anything to you. Three or four beers is like water. Except now I'm convinced that I can't do that. Even one beer does something, distorts something, makes it not work. I don't drink coffee, whiskey, beer, any of that.

I do get extraordinarily nervous when I'm working, and I do a great deal of jumping up and down and pacing about the room. This sounds awful, but during a session I'll very often do an awful lot of push-ups or sit-ups. I learned how to stand on my hands through the same sort of nervous thing. I get so nervous that if I don't jump up and do something, I just about come apart. It's a strange thing that the better the writing is going, the more nervous I become, and the more angered. I mean, I live in my private life, and at the typewriter I'm in a kind of . . . the only thing I can call it is anger. It's a kind of rage. I don't know why. I don't know what it comes out of, but I do it.

J.D.B.: Directed toward what?

H.C.: Well, directed toward nothing—and toward everything. It does come out in terms of kicking the dog and yelling at the kid and doing other things. But, by and large, I don't do too much of that. It's an undefined rage. It's probably anxiety. That kind of anonymous, directionless anxiety, where you feel this enormous thing on your back. That's probably what it is, but it also feels like anger. I wonder about it, think about it. I don't think it's a very healthy thing, healthy in terms of your nonwriting life.

J.D.B.: We were talking before about Belt in *Karate Is a Thing of the Spirit* and how he was depending on that five feet of land around him, and how he seemed to be cut off from Arkansas or Florida or any sense of possessiveness about country or geography. But it seems to me that in others of your books, in *Car* and particularly in *Naked in Garden Hills*, you are very interested in the effect of "geography" and even in saying something about what America is all about, what venality motivates the average citizen and what really makes American culture tick. Am I right about that?

H.C.: Well, it's an extraordinary thing. I really don't admire social protest fiction. You take a book like *Car*, which is the easiest to talk about in those terms. That book came directly out of my fear of, horror of, and hatred for automobiles. I don't even own a car. It's all rather obvious. *Car* would have been a better book if I had not been so outraged over the subject. I never was quite able to get the distance on the subject that I would have liked, that I should have gotten; and so it becomes a kind of outraged joke in a way. It may be a little better than that, but I don't think of it as in any way my best work. I hope. But anyway, let me say something about the metaphor there. Okay, on the literal level, there's a guy eating a car, but the point is that we have to eat Texaco and Amoco and all those roads we got in this country. Cars shouldn't be allowed in Manhattan; cars shouldn't be allowed in Atlanta. Everybody knows that, but goddamn we got to chaw it in anyway.

So to get back to your original observation, I think that my immediate world triggers the things I write about. Let me give you a for instance: *Karate Is a Thing of the Spirit.* I didn't know a thing about karate. I heard the word and I was in a shopping mall and I saw some karate freaks giving a demonstration and it really turned my head around good. I thought, "God, that's fantastic." As I stood there, I thought of it as a self-contained, self-justifying madness, and so is education. I'm at a university and I know how awful what passes for education is in this country. So here is the gig and it came right out of this. I said to myself, I wonder whether or not I might be able to use karate to inform an action which itself deals with what life in this country has become.

I don't mean just cars and whether or not we have double-knit trousers; I mean the ways people think, the ways they perceive the world they live in—we were talking about time a while ago—the ways people think about time, the ways they think about themselves inside time, the ways they think about their bodies, their muscles and everything. That's what the book came out of. I swear to God I hope my fiction is not made up of little moral lessons or instructions of some nature. My God, the last thing in the world I think I'm qualified to do is instruct anybody on anything, but I do write out of my own immediate loves and hates.

J.D.B.: Well, there's certainly a moral edge to some of these things. You can't get away from it. If you hate cars, that's a moral stance.

H.C.: Yeah, that's right, and this place that *Naked in Garden Hills* takes place in . . .

J.D.B.: Does that really exist, that place?

H.C.: Let me tell you . . . I was going from Fort Lauderdale to Tampa. I had finished *The Gospel Singer,* and I was going over there to leave the book with a writer friend of mine and then I was going to come back in a week. We were just going to talk. We read for each other as writers often do. I drove into Polk County and there's a little town there, Mulberry, Florida, and underneath it on the sign it says, "Phosphate

Capital of the World," and they do mine more phosphate there than they do anywhere else in the world. But it's just like it was in the book. I was driving along in my little Volkswagen—I had a Volkswagen in those days—and I smelled it long before I ever knew what was going on, this thing in my nose, and on both sides of the road just stretching away as far as I could see were these broken pieces of wire and old abandoned equipment. The land was ruined, lakes and scummy ponds, and I thought, "My God!"

The really screwy thing about it is that I don't know the first damn thing about mining phosphate. Do you know I never got close to a mine at all. I never was in one. Everything in that book about how phosphate's mined and everything is made up, which to my way of thinking makes no difference at all. The human truth is there, never mind the mechanical truth. You know, the guy digs an enormous hole and puts a town in the bottom of it. Well, if you dig a damn hole in Florida, you get water, so it's absolutely impossible. But that didn't bother me a bit.

J.D.B.: How about the karate stuff in *Karate Is a Thing of the Spirit*? I see your knuckles are not enlarged.

H.C.: No, I didn't want my hand deformed, thank you very much. It's possible to mess your hand up pretty good. I studied karate for two years with a fourth-degree black belt named Dirk Mosig, a German boy raised in Argentina. He's twenty-seven or twenty-eight, and that is the Kyokū-shin system of karate as opposed to shenaru, or tae kwon do, or some other system.

J.D.B.: One thing that struck me in thinking over your novels is a situation that recurs, a scene where there is some kind of performance going on and there is an audience watching it.

H.C.: The audience is always present, and they are almost always tourists of one kind or another.

J.D.B.: Frequently, they're obnoxious, they're like cattle.

H.C.: If you look at, for instance, the Fourth of July celebration scene in *Karate Is a Thing of the Spirit* or if you look at the swimming pool scenes in the same book, where the people are filing by, or in *Car*, the audience when he's eating the car and the people down in the street—and, well, it goes on in every one. The audiences are a big part of this book I just finished now. For me, tourists or audiences as such are almost like a recurrent dream, if you ever had a dream that came back again and again and again.

My attitude toward, my feeling for, and my experiences with groups of people who have assembled for some reason have been almost uniformly bad, including when I was a boy and I was taken to church a great deal, including congregations at tent meetings, camp meetings, and even the Baptist church house. There's something that happens to men and women as soon as they are brought in cheek and jowl. It's all rather obvious stuff; I didn't think anybody'd take issue with it.

Every crowd takes on a character. The men have individual characters, it's true, and the men have individual minds, inside; but the group takes one and . . . I must admit my audiences really reflect what, I think, has caused this country so much grief. They're almost uniformly violent, and the crowds I know anything about are violent. They're greedy, they're pushy, they're disrespectful of the most human kinds of considerations as well as spiritual or economic considerations, all of them. It's nothing I ever thought about; it's something that just appeared in my fiction.

J.D.B.: One of the techniques you use sometimes, like a carrot before a horse's nose, to propel your reader through your novel, is a typical device but one which you use a little bit differently. It appears as if it's planned out that way. I'm sure there must be some consciousness about it. It's when you leave a question unanswered and part of the process of the novel becomes the answering of the question. For instance, in *Naked in Garden Hills* it's the big question of what in the *hell's* going on out in that barn.

H.C.: I think that the reader ought to be entertained. I see nothing wrong with entertainment. I think the reader ought to be taken out of his own skin for a while and put into someone else's skin, out of his own place and into somebody else's place. And I think he ought to read with great interest. The nicest thing anybody can say to me is, "I read with interest." So, all that stuff is rather a conscious putting together of the story in a way that seems to me to be psychologically and artistically true, but at the same time to be valid as far as motivating a reader to want to go on through the book. Being true in that way.

J.D.B.: Do you think it out in terms of, "I'm going to leave three questions unanswered" and tantalize him in that way?

H.C.: No. I sure don't. The only time I ever begin to look at stuff like that is after I've got the whole draft there in front of me and I begin to look at it then. I do think about it in *this* way, when I'm writing even on the first draft: a chapter sometimes, or a scene or a section, just feels dead. It just doesn't feel alive, and I go back and begin to look at the people in it, the actions in it, the situations, and all the rest of it to see whether or not there aren't some things in there that I can use to make the thing snap a little bit, crackle a little bit. So I do that, but in terms of consciously saying, I will use this and this and this, no.

As a matter of fact, I've looked at the notebooks that many writers have kept, Fitzgerald's notes for some of his books and notes that Dostoyevsky left. I'm pretty often amazed at how, in the most initial stages, those men seemed to have pretty clearly in mind what they wanted to do. I don't have clearly in mind what I want to do until I'm about three-quarters through it; then I begin to see what the thing is. Until then it's just some people somewhere in a narrative, a sequence of events, and they're doing something. Maybe it's not quite as blind or stumbling as I'm trying to pretend.

But let me give you a quick example. *The Gospel Singer* opens up with this black man in jail. Willalee Bookatee is his name. He's in jail for killing a white woman with an ice pick, killing her and raping her. We're in Willalee's head in that chapter. He says he didn't rape her; he says that's white talk. And he didn't rape her. He killed her; he knows he killed her. He doesn't know why he killed her, but he knows he killed her. He also says he did not rape her, he knows that. Now when I wrote that thing I didn't know why he killed her either. I had no idea why he killed her. I believed him when he said that he didn't rape her, that that was white talk. He said he did kill her, and I believed that because he said he did; it just makes sense.

And the Gospel Singer was on the way home at the time because his brother'd come in and said he was on the way home. So before the novel is over, you see the Gospel Singer, although he was miles and miles and miles away, killed that girl as much as Willalee did because it was his actions and his basic corruption that brought Willalee to do what he did and brought the girl to do what she did. So although he was a long ways away, he had killed her as much as Willalee.

But my point is that when something like this comes up in a piece of fiction that I'm working on, I have a choice to believe it or not to believe it, to believe he did rape her or to believe he did not rape her. Once you make the commitment for one side or the other, believing it or not believing it, then you simply work it out; you work out the consequences of your believing it or not believing it. I don't know if that makes any sense to you, but it does to me.

J.D.B.: Have you ever gone back and changed something like that if it came to you spontaneously?

H.C.: Oh, yeah, there're lots of times when things that you do simply won't work. Also lots of times when you get into a piece and you find it just isn't viable; you can't go on with it; there's nothing there that is developable—in which case you either abandon it or you go back and try to see where you went wrong.

J.D.B.: What books of yours do you like best?

H.C.: I think the best book of mine, the one I like best and think is my best book is *Naked in Garden Hills*. When I finished it, I thought, "There's a good chance you may never do anything better than that as long as you live." We've all got this great Puritan ethic on our backs, and I get so sick of it. People always think that a writer has to outstrip himself every time out. He's got to get better or he's dead, which is silly and stupid. Everything J. D. Salinger does, all the critics say, "Yes, but it's not *Catcher in the Rye*." Well, of course, it's not *Catcher in the Rye*. It's another thing. And writers get caught in it. It's a deadly thing to get caught in though.

J.D.B.: The other morning Vance Bourjaily was saying he thinks that we're at a watershed point in the history of fiction and that maybe the sort of fiction that's been written for the last hundred to a hundred-and-fifty years is now going out of fashion. What's coming into fashion, he's afraid—and he uses Vonnegut as an example—is a kind of didactic writing or moralizing in a very didactic way. I don't agree with him, but I wonder what you think. Does that worry you, or is there a case to be made that you're that kind of a writer too?

H.C.: Well, see, some people have made the case that I'm that kind of writer, and it hurts my heart that they have. I don't admire that kind of writing. I don't admire Vonnegut. Well, that's a lie. I do admire Vonnegut as a man, and I admire his moral stance in the world. I think he's a brave man and a good man. I admire many of his talents, some of the things he can do. But I just reviewed *Breakfast of Champions,* and I find some of those things sophomoric and maudlin and too easy and too simplistic. No, if we *are* in a watershed time of fiction where what's going to develop is this long string of didactic, propagandistic, tract-thesis sort of writing, it seems to me that that's a decline. That's a decline of the spirit, of the country, of the people, and even of the nation.

Dealing with that sort of thing is not like dealing with that woman in Faulkner's *Light in August,* for instance. In Vonnegut's fiction or any sort of fiction like that, that didactic stuff, you remain on the level of ideas rather than on the level of blood and bone and the rest of it. I don't think it's nearly as painful, nearly as excruciating to read Vonnegut as it is to read Flannery O'Connor. Never are we going to have as many people reading Flannery O'Connor as we do people reading, say, Fletcher Knebel's *Seven Days in May* and all that stuff. Or that guy Hailey. Hailey's fiction is not didactic fiction, but it works in the same way, because for human terms and human considerations he substitutes a mindless catalog of detail.

That guy Fletcher Knebel was a newspaper man in Washington for thirty years, and he knows what color bathroom tissue is in the President's bathroom; so he puts that in the book. And people'd much rather read that than they would Flannery O'Connor's grandmother in "A Good Man Is Hard to Find," sitting there in the ditch with her shoulder broken and this madman leading the family off one by one to shoot them in the woods. It's much better to stay with the colors of bathroom tissue and how a president of General Motors gets up in the morning, what his day is like, how many appointments he has, and how many vice-presidents he has.

J.D.B.: But isn't it true that one craving the novel has satisfied historically is to make that trip into a place you couldn't go unless you had the novel? It's a behind-the-scenes exposé of an airport or a hotel or a karate school or an auto-wrecking company. Frequently you have exotic settings in your books, and the reader gets to go there and find out what the people are like.

H.C.: Mind you, I don't think there's a thing wrong with exotic settings and detail, or even catalogs of realistic detail. But you mustn't allow the exotic setting and the catalog of realistic detail to become a final, ultimate substitute for the heart underneath, the blood and bone of some human beings. It's only when those details substitute for the human thing underneath that it becomes of little or no merit. I think the Haileys of this world, among other things, can't write. Reading books like that'll make you have wooden ears. That's my own opinion anyway.

J.D.B.: One trait that makes me very interested in your work is that you really do seem to portray a kind of surrealistic world in many ways, but there's always a clear relationship between that world and what we really know.

H.C.: I feel that's true too. Maybe this is a conscious thing. I think about it when I'm working. Again and again and again things seem if not surreal then so extraordinary—the things people believe, the things that people do—that they might as well be surreal. Maybe this is a conscious thing because I like to start with something that is obviously a world that nobody can quarrel with. Here is the porch and there is the chair and here is the man and we're all happy, right? Then in a very slow kind of left-handed way, left-handed in the sense that you don't call attention to it, it just slides off the edge of the real world into a thing that can't possibly be true. Except it *is* true; at least, I think it is.

It's a little like Cheever. Somebody said that in Cheever's stories the character turns the corner and walks into madness or something like that. In a story like "The Swimmer," for instance, a guy goes off the beach and he swims home. He swims across people's swimming pools and down the canal, and as he's swimming across these suburban swimming pools getting home, the landscape gradually changes and when he finally gets home, hell, the house is boarded up, his family gone. Everything's changed and the story slides off into this screwy, unreal madness. I'm sure what some people would say, and I'm one of them, is that the reality underlying it, the psychological, emotional reality is a valid perception of reality. The guy left that morning, and he comes back and it's years later and his family's gone and everything's boarded up. Well, on the level that most people use the word "reality," that ain't real; that can't be real; that's screwy. But the suburban madness that put all those swimming pools in backyards to start with—that reality is valid.

In other words, it seems to me that many writers, and I think I'm one of them, feel that they have to distort the real world in order to be able to render accurately and truly the psychological reality or emotional reality of people in this age, in these circumstances. Because, among other things, the readers are so bombarded with stimulation that unless you have some sort of distortion they can't read. The world we live in being what it is, we're so accustomed to freakishness and freaky behavior that "ordinary" freakishness we don't see as freakishness at all, not at all.

I saw a circus act on television not long ago where they wheeled out this bed into the center ring, and this damned horse came out and got in bed and laid down. He put his head on the pillow and then lifted his head up and took the sheet with his teeth; and the poor horse's eyes were rolling and his tongue was lolling out and his flanks were heaving. He was incredibly awful, unnatural, dreadful, and of course the audience was laughing and clapping and shouting because it was a marvelous thing that the horse had been trained to do this thing. Well, I don't bleed for animals very much. I thought it was a shitty thing to train a horse to do, but we are all busily being trained to do the human equivalent to what that horse was doing lying down in the bed.

J.D.B.: They must have beat the poor thing to death to get him to do that.

H.C.: Well, they didn't touch him out there, but I don't know how they went about training him to do it. No, he came right out there and did it, but he didn't like it, that was the thing. It's a terribly unnatural thing to do. Among other things, horses almost never, unless they're dreadfully ill, lie down broadside because it hurts their stomachs. They don't put their heads down flat because they aren't built to do that. They don't sleep that way. They don't do anything that way.

AL BURT

Harry Crews: Working the Kinks Out

Harry Crews has decided maybe he will get off the freaks for a while. Maybe it is time to try something else. He is getting a reputation as a kinky guy. For seven novels now, a fascinating menagerie of freaks has crept out of his typewriter. Inside their heads, they have some normal ideas, but they are trapped by their outsides.

There are freaks of beautiful bodies, and freaks of incredibly misshapen bodies, but either way the burdens are too heavy. There are midgets and fat men and cripples mixed in with go-go dancers and sideshow entertainers and evangelists and physical culturists. They intertwine through a bizarre kind of counterpoint that produces unusual appetites and enterprising means of satisfying them.

In his new book, for example, Crews's hero is a deaf mute whose legs are so useless he ties them under the seat of his trousers. The young man lives in a gymnasium with an elderly weightlifter and two wasted boxers, and makes a living with a sensational hand-balancing act. Marvin may be the world's greatest hand-balancer. He can pirouette slowly on one finger, holding it for applause. But he is too grotesque to make the big-time. Ed Sullivan could not use him because his head is too big and square and his body is too ugly with his legs all tied up like that.

Crews calls this parable *The Gypsy's Curse* and it is a gem. Underneath the sex and hairy language, there is the anguish and pain of the freak who can live only by exploiting his freakishness. The Curse, for

From the *Miami Herald*, June 30, 1974, G1+.

Marvin, is finding the perfect sexual partner in Hester, a blonde beach beauty looking for someone who will love her enough to kill her for being faithless. Even in perfection, Marvin loses. Again, a theme of unbearable cost in perfection and unbearable burden in imperfection. It is all very kinky.

"Not long ago," said Crews, "*Playboy* magazine sent word they wanted me to do something for them. The guy said they had a very kinky idea they thought I would like. Cocaine. They wanted me to write something about cocaine. I said, 'Aw, no, man. Do you know where I live? Not that. Maybe something else'."

Crews paused for a moment, making his point. "Yeah. Oh, yeah. No question about it. I got a reputation as the guy who writes the kinky stuff. Somebody pretty soon's gonna call me up and when they do I'm gon' say, 'Yeah, but I want you to come down here and talk to me about it first' and then I'm gon' beat the shit out of him. Somebody's gon' ask me if I don't want to go somewhere and cover a carnival of freaks, you know, and watch a guy eat a live chicken, or something." He laughed.

Crews, thirty-nine, looks a little like a primitive who has tried civilization and was unimpressed. He lounges about his lakeside cypress cabin, about twenty-five miles east of Gainesville, in faded jeans and wrinkled shirt and tennis shoes without socks. His hair is long. He has the expressive face of an actor and his hands leap about in emphatic gestures. He is a remarkable man who seems to speak several English languages, in addition to the one he writes so beautifully. He shifts roles, going from the Georgia farm boy to the boisterous ex-Marine to the philosophical recluse, to the college professor.

Crews teaches a course in writing two nights a week at the University of Florida in Gainesville, and helps conduct a writer's conference once a year. But he lives and works here in the cabin, which has a fireplace, a couple of beds, a kitchen and a table in the back where sits the old Underwood standard typewriter on which he has written all seven novels, plus numerous short stories and essays. He has no telephone, either here or in his university office, and he will not permit mail delivery at home because he finds it distracting. His ex-wife and their son live in Gainesville.

"One doesn't mind the fact of the matter," said Crews, getting back to the business of freaks. "It's just the harping on it."

"I have to insist when somebody starts talking to me about freaks . . . That's not my word. We're all freaks, but just in different ways, most of us. To dwell on this business of the freaks and to dwell on what they call the Gothic novel offends me, yeah. I hadn't even heard of one until everybody told me I was writing 'em.

"Another thing, they talk about me being a southern novelist. It's true I write in the South and it's true that's where my sense of place is and sense of people is and sense of language is. But hell, every writer has to have that. You know, some guys are in the Midwest, some guys . . . Norman Mailer's a New York Jew, you know, and he knows about that. John Updike knows about Pennsylvania and he's got that little town there . . .

"But even if those things are true, it seems to me sort of beside the point to harp on them. It doesn't demonstrate anything, it doesn't prove anything, it doesn't open anything up, illuminate anything. You know, I'm just not particularly fond of that.

"But I tell you, I have the feeling in me, and maybe it's just a feeling. I've had wrong feelings before, but I have the feeling that there is going to be some sort of departure in my work, that I'm going to do something else. I mean, I'm going to still write novels. Man, I started out to be a novelist. That's what I want to be. That's what I care about.

"I also like to write short stories, but unfortunately what you gonna do with them? Yeah, you can publish them in literary magazines, which is where all mine have been published, and they've been anthologized. You can publish them. But man, it gets back to audience and the rest of it. Short stories are hard to write. Hard to write as anything else. So what've you got? If you're lucky, you've got 1,900 or 2,000 readers. Shit, man.

"What I'm trying to say is, I think either the subject matter is going to change—and I don't know what I mean by subject matter because you know I got novels about boxers and sponge fishermen divers—I guess it's not subject. I guess it's more the form of the thing. Maybe that's what's going to change. I don't know. But I just have this feeling in me. Maybe I'll do two or three books of nonfiction."

The National Endowment for the Arts, a federal project based in Washington, recently awarded Crews $5,000 to use professionally as he pleases. Two years ago, the American Academy of Arts and Letters gave him a grant of $3,000. "I like those grants, man," he said, smiling. "Yeah."

Crews has decided to use the money for an exploration of his own life as a boy in Bacon County, Georgia. "It will be a biography of place. The focus will be me, autobiographical. It will be about those people up there and that time." It also would be his first book-length nonfiction. Whether it will be a conventional narrative, he does not know. "Something in my head resists that. But it can be nice, if it's done right."

The idea began last summer, when Crews spent seven weeks walking the Appalachian Trail from Georgia to Maryland, carrying along a photographer and a tape-recorder, collecting information and anecdotes. "I talked to people all along. You'd be dumbfounded, you'd be just dumbfounded at the stories that I got off that trail. Things that people told me and I heard and I saw. Really kinky, great things, right?" Part of that time, the description might have fit Crews himself. His hair grew down over his shoulders and he wore one golden earring.

Crews tried to splice together his experiences on the trail with memories of his boyhood in Bacon County. But later, he decided that wouldn't work. Now, he plans to separate the two. The trail hike will be one story, and Bacon County another. He likes this better. The last couple of years, he has had this feeling that he needs to know more about himself and his beginnings. Going back to Bacon County will satisfy that urge.

"I think so. I think so," he said. He speaks rapidly, often in broken sentences, but the communication remains clear. "Yeah. For a long time I didn't know that. I grew to manhood without . . . Some of the language, you know. Some of the things we said. Things like, 'He's so stingy he wouldn't give you the steam off his shit'. A beautiful line, the steam off his shit. But the kids that always had bathrooms and things, they didn't . . . That must be a mystery to them when they heard it. Be out in the woods, or out on the ground, or even the outhouse. Hell, when it's freezing, it steams. You know, the ground's frozen. Very colorful, immediate, graphic, concrete language and those people, you know . . ."

The University of Florida has given Crews an indefinite leave of absence and he will go up to an uncle's farm in Bacon County and get reacquainted. "I want to talk to guys that knew my daddy," Crews said. "My daddy died when I was eighteen months old. I never knew him. I grew up on faded photographs and, really, kind of legends. He was really a good man, but a strange man, a mean man, a lot of kinds of man. He died on the farm in the winter time, of a heart attack."

Although the language and the themes of his novels are not exactly what the rural folk in Georgia might find pleasant reading, Crews thinks the state has treated him well. In Bacon County, or over near his mother's present farm closer to Tifton, Georgia, he has celebrity status. One reason for that may be, he thinks, that more have heard he is a writer than have read his writing.

"My mother only went to the second grade, and they just insisted she be on the board of the little library. Ma's never read a book, except the ones I've written. Only ones she's ever read. Takes her about six months to get through one of my books, but she's one of the best readers I ever had. People find that strange. I mean, I've got a Baptist mother that's lived in the country all her life, one of those good women, and I don't mean that pejoratively. I mean that straight out, good woman. She never blinks at anything that I've written. She knows what's in the world. Doesn't bother her. She knows a word's a word, that it's not the deed or the fact, you know. No. Ma at one time is primitive enough and sophisticated enough to know that it's all magic anyway, and that's the way she feels about it.

"She's dumbfounded, for instance, that anybody would pay you money to write something that wasn't true. You know. That really amazes her. When I wrote *The Gospel Singer*, when I finished it, I called her up and said I sold it, I got this much advance, and so on. Later on, when I saw her, she said, 'Son, you didn't pass that off as the truth, did you? You didn't tell 'em that?' I told her, 'No, Ma, that's not the gig'."

Everything started for Crews in Bacon County, his love for the physical side of life, storytelling, his awareness of the perfection and imperfections of people, an annoying conscience, an insatiable curiosity, absorption with the unusual, a boiling kind of drive inside him to try new things, a battle with self-doubt, a compulsion to illuminate the whole thing.

"I got started in all this long, long before I ever had any notion . . . I was writing stories when I was just a little kid. I wrote 'em for my family and told 'em. I started telling 'em, before I started writing 'em, for my friends. Mostly, with the exception of my brother, my playmates were black. You know, we were out on the farm. We used to get together and . . . I can tell you exactly how it started.

"The way it happened, it started with Sears, Roebuck catalog. We used to spend a lot of time looking at the thing and, among other things, here were all these perfect people. Everybody we knew was damaged, had sores on their legs and their fingers cut off, but here were all these beautiful, perfect people in this book and they were so well dressed and they were obviously human. I would make up stories to account for the things they were doing. You know, 'See this man in the red coat, well this girl here's his daughter and she's gonna marry him on this page back here and he don't like him because he don't make his money just by standing there in that red coat. He's the deputy sheriff on the side . . .' So, anyway, I got into that."

Crews joined the Marine Corps at seventeen, served three years, and enrolled at the University of Florida. Predictably, he became restless and left for eighteen months, but the burden of writing ambitions brought him back in 1958. Andrew Lytle was a writer-in-residence at the University of Florida, and Crews became first his student and then his disciple. "The only reason I've never dedicated a book to him is that I've never written anything I thought he'd want his name on. He's a demanding man," Crews said. The Lytle encounter was important to him.

One year of teaching junior high school English in Jacksonville, after graduation, sent Crews scrambling back to Gainesville for a master's degree. With that in hand, in 1962, he shifted to Broward Junior College in Fort Lauderdale, again to teach English. The year *The Gospel Singer* was published (1968) he returned to the University of Florida, where he has remained. Since then, a new Crews novel has been published each year. The others: *Naked in Garden Hills* (which he thinks was his best), *This Thing Don't Lead to Heaven, Car, The Hawk Is Dying, Karate Is a Thing of the Spirit* and, this year, *The Gypsy's Curse*.

"I wrote another book called *The Enthusiast* which I really liked a lot, at least I liked it a lot while I was writing it. I suppose it came out of my life in a way. It was about a guy that just everything he got into, he made a passion of. I got into karate and I did *Karate Is a Thing of the Spirit.* I got into hawks. I trapped and trained hawks and wrote *The Hawk Is Dying.* The books are somehow always after the fact. But anyway I wrote this book and it felt good the whole time I was writing it. But I never sent the damned thing off. Put it in a drawer. It just didn't work, finally. You know, you try to lie to yourself at first. It'll come back another time. The work is never wasted. Ten years from now, all that'll come back," he said.

Sometimes, something just works. The first time he drove to the farm near Tifton he got lost. He was working on *The Gospel Singer* then. He wandered into a town called Enigma, Georgia. "I said God, that's where it happened. It's gotta be it. But I changed a lot of things around like the highway, and the swamp. You know, I didn't want to piss off the people in the town. I got nothing against them. But I did manage to do it."

Naked in Garden Hills found its way into a phosphate excavation because Crews was driving from Vero Beach to Tampa, and wandered through Mulberry, the phosphate capital. *This Thing Don't Lead to Heaven* came after a visit to a nursing home, during which he feigned sickness in order to leave quickly.

Despite the pace at which he drives himself, and his expanding interests (he has written and sold screenplays of two of his books and sold a third to the movies with the script to be done by someone else), teaching has never seemed a burden to Crews. He not only likes it, but in a way depends upon it to bring order to his life.

"No. It's not a burden. I'll tell you why. I guess the biggest reason is this. You get stuck when you're writing. Everybody knows that. You get stuck and you just don't know what to do, and it looks like the thing's gonna die on you. Maybe you've got three or four months in it. So you sit down . . . I work every day. I don't give a shit whether I know what's coming next or not. I work. At least I sit at the typewriter. I tell myself, 'You go sit there three hours. You don't have to write anything. Just sit there'. So pretty soon you write something, just try something; and you find your way out. But sometimes it's bad, and you know it's bad. When that happens, at least me, I get really down on myself. I begin to doubt everything. I think, 'Hell, you weren't a writer to start with. Now you've got this charade. You really ought to . . .' I just say terrible things to myself. Then, voila, I go to school.

"I like to teach, see. That's the weird thing about it. I really do. I enjoy it. The students, they're honest, they'll run you up a tree. They won't take much phony stuff. I go in there and teach a sensational class. Just get in there and just wing and talk and get 'em excited and get all . . . When I come out of the class, I think, well, buddy, you might can't write, but goddam, you sure can teach.

"I've got a sort of theory in my head about that. I think every man ought to have more than one thing he does well. He doesn't have to get his bread by it, but if he's just really a good, competent, fine, amateur butterfly preserver or coin-collector or Sunday painter or bicycle rider or anything, so that he can go out there and get his head clean . . .

"You see, I don't think of writing as a job. I think of it as a, almost like an avocation. I would be writing novels if nobody was publishing them. I'd write novels if I had to send them out to sea in a bottle. I just know I would. So I really don't think of it as a job. At school, that's a job and it kind of gives direction to my life and, you know . . . I'm pretty bad to drink. As a matter of fact I will stay drunk on you for a while, from time to time. I would rather, all things being equal, I would rather not disappear into a bottle. It seems to me that's a cheap way to go. Having a job, having to go to the university, having students I'm responsible for, keeps me straighter than I otherwise would be. The hardest thing for me is to control my personal life so I can do the amount of work I want to do. I need to work. I have guilt feelings if I don't work, sourceless anxiety."

When writing first-draft material, Crews forces himself to sit at the typewriter three hours a day. Three hours at that stage exhausts him. Later, rewriting or revising, he might stay with it eighteen hours. When he started writing *Naked in Garden Hills,* he had an idea and one line, "Wherever he was, it looked like he had been there forever." That started as the first line in the book, describing the fat man, but at the end could be found 200 or so pages back.

"When you've got that first page in the typewriter, of course, you been thinking about something for a long time, but you don't know what it means. There's a little bit of an idea in there. I start with a place and somebody and then I just try to know the story.

"Robert Frost said all his poems ended in surprise and discovery—discovery for himself. You know, when he started out with a poem he really didn't have much at all. He talked about that little poem, 'Stopping by Woods'. He said, 'When I started that poem all I had was the first line, and so I then proceeded to try to write a second line in which I was consistent with the commitments made in the first. Then I wrote a third . . .'

"Well, that's the way I work with fiction. What apprentices don't understand is the important thing is not the fucking story. It's not any of that. The important thing is the writer whose perceptions all of this is being filtered through. The writer's vision of the world. It doesn't matter what he writes about. My writing will have a certain taste and a certain smell and a certain sound. Nobody's going to confuse Faulkner and Hemingway, no matter the story. I go on feeling when writing fiction. I don't give a rat's ass where the novel's going."

Crews said he has learned more from reading Graham Greene, the British author, than anyone else. *The Power and the Glory* is his favorite. "It's not so much the subject matter as the consummate skill. He's as accomplished a writer as I know, and both a popular and a critical success." He noted that Greene suffered the blackest kind of melancholy and depression. Both Greene and Crews have been accused of sacrilege in their books, a charge that bothers Crews.

"I wouldn't do that," he said. "I take all my books to be about the nature of faith. How does a man come to believe what he believes? How do you get to belief and how do you hold on to it? God, wife, job, whatever. I feel a sense of responsibility.

"Greene always insisted upon the right to portray the unbeliever as powerfully as the believer, the crippled and the halt as powerfully as he portrays the perfect. What most people want, out there in the suburbs, is a papier-mâché villain. A guy really powerful and really bad at the same time scares them. The devil in Milton's *Paradise Lost* came out heroic, saying it was better to rule in hell . . ."

Romantic, sentimentalized writing angers Crews. "Chekhov said learning to write is learning to murder your darlings. We've all got this kind of mush thing in us. We can't write about that. We've got to write about it the way it works."

The way it works, for Crews, is parable and metaphor. His darlings came out of the Sears, Roebuck catalog and he murdered them long ago. He trotted them out and brutalized them with truths that made people squirm. Now he will go back to Bacon County, Georgia, where it all began, and turn that withering vision upon himself and his people.

Meanwhile, another novel percolates. "I'm going to call it *The Feast of Snakes,*" he said. "It's about these snake roundups. I went to one up in south Georgia not long ago. What's got me wanting to write the thing is the fact that here are these people catching these goddam rattlesnakes and they're eating them and they've got a beauty contest... People hanging on the wire and looking at the snakes. Lester Maddox was there and led us in a little hymn while he played his mouth harp and all this shit.

"Now, I want to find out what that means. Your ordinary guy on the street will say it don't mean anything, folks get together and they just eat the snakes. No, no, no, you can't shit me. I watched those ladies. They want to eat some of that rattlesnake and they just been hanging on the pen looking at 'em where they're all writhing in there. And they get over there and the husband says, 'Aw, come on Dolores, just put it in your mouth, honey. It's just like fried chicken'. I don't know what all that is, but I want to know. That's the kind of thing..."

STEVE ONEY

Harry Crews Is a Stomp-Down Hard-Core Moralist

It was all of two o'clock on a sultry Thursday afternoon and Harry Crews was poured into a corner booth at an ersatz nautical bar in Gainesville, Florida, called the Winnjammer. Bits of sailing rigging were scattered about. The place was as dark as the hold of an East European freighter. Light from a flickering wall lamp played upon Crews's face, and there was a shock in seeing him, discernibly electric, as if he were stripped of psychic insulation: stripped like a badly wounded animal that has retreated to its lair.

"The craziness is in me," he was growling. "I'm self-destructive. Masochistic." He was slouched into the booth, and one of his legs, crippled from childhood polio, hung limply to the floor. Crews's large, brutal torso, fitted into a decaying mauve sweatshirt, coiled lazily. His viper-like skull with eyes set an inch back into the brow was turning on a thick snake's neck, a neck resplendent in a silver and turquoise necklace.

"My private life is a shambles." The voice was almost indiscernible, lost in a glass of Scotch and milk he was draining. "I get into trouble. I can't cope. I louse things up, wreck cars, lose money. But a fictional world . . . I can make it do whatever I can't do with my own life."

Here at the Winnjammer, Crews was fighting to gain control of himself. He had just endured a long, soporific drive back to Gainesville

From *Atlanta Journal and Constitution Magazine*, May 15, 1977, 7+.

from Ashburn, Georgia, where his mother was ill with appendicitis. He was trying to pull his mind together before going home to finish writing a magazine article about jockeys for *Sport*. Facing him at 7 P.M. was the initial meeting of a quarterly fiction-writing class he teaches at the University of Florida. And in the back of his mind, hanging like a cerebral millstone, was the thought of the work he still needed to do on his first nonfiction book, *A Biography of a Place*.

Scheduled for release in the fall, *A Biography of a Place* is to be a dissection of past and present in Bacon County, Georgia, Crews's birthplace. It will be his ninth book, and it follows a string of novels that began appearing yearly in 1968, when *The Gospel Singer* was published. Whether the new book will come from what could be called Crews's world—in the same way that Yoknapatawpha County is called William Faulkner's world—is difficult to divine. For one thing, it is difficult to understand Crews's fictional world. He doesn't understand it completely. A line which Flannery O'Connor wrote about her own work hints at the substance of Crews's writing, though: "It is in the extremities of evil circumstance that the possibilities of grace are more nearly perceived."

"Oh man, man, I feel like I'm gonna die. My mama just worries, worries, worries. I had to go up there to do what I had to do because a son has got to do what he feels he's got to do." A second Scotch and milk was in Crews's hands. "I may die though. Damn drive."

Crews backed up from the thought of his demise and lit a Marlboro. "I ain't gonna die, but damn if I don't feel like it. Bring me another of the same, and less milk," he called to the barmaid.

* * *

Harry Crews's eight novels abound with the extremities of evil circumstance, the products of evil circumstance. There is Joe Lon Mackey, protagonist of Crews's most recent novel, *A Feast of Snakes*, a novel set in Mystic, Georgia, at the time of the town's annual rattlesnake roundup. Joe Lon is a college-caliber football player who is left with nowhere to play because of poor high school grades. Joe Lon rechannels the brutality his high school football coach taught him to cultivate by blowing away a number of acquaintances with well-aimed shotgun blasts.

Then, there is the Gospel Singer in the novel of the same name, a golden sheep born from the fold of a depraved white trash family in Enigma, Georgia. The Gospel Singer has a honeyed voice that has allowed him to escape the insularity of Enigma. He returns to sing at one last tent revival and ends up being hung from a tree. The people of Enigma perceive that the Gospel Singer is a charlatan and set him free by a noose.

And appearing in almost all of Crews's books are midgets, people without legs, the deaf, and the dumb. And there are crowds in all of his novels—milling, destroying, running awry with that violent sense of freedom one finds in a large group where one is guaranteed anonymity.

★ ★ ★

Writers like Harry Crews always run the risk or create the risk of being mythicized, of being enshrouded in a mystique replete with its own parables. Already, certain caretakers of literature have consigned Crews to a place that one writer said was underneath a dark root of the southern literary tradition. But what that really means is difficult to discern. Because Crews writes about people who on the face of it are freaks and evil interlopers—Jean Stafford once called his bailiwick "a Hieronymus Bosch landscape in Dixie"—it is probable that critics can't get around the abnormal, gut-wrenching fireworks that are always going off in a Crews novel. "Obsessive," "violent," "grotesque," "gratuitous," "bizarre," "macabre," "harrowing," "wild." Critics are fond of labeling Crews's fiction with these words. "I don't even read that crap anymore," Crews will bellow. "It's too hard to write, and if you read enough reviews, you'll flip and lose your confidence. It does happen."

It's a fact that Crews is an easy target for literary potshooters. He's received his share of plaudits, but a rumor that has reached minor mythic proportions holds that Harry Crews is nuts; that he writes about nuts; that his work is gratuitous, rife with uncalled-for violence and perversity; that he sits at his 1920s Underwood typewriter in his stultifying stucco home in Gainesville and busies himself in creating even more gratuitous scenarios to be test-marketed for the freak-reading public.

Even his friends promote the rumor. *Playboy*, for which Crews writes frequently, once labeled him its "resident weirdo." *Esquire*, for which Crews writes a monthly column called "Grits," packages the column with a logo that looks like the peeling skin of the comic-book character Hulk. And if, stumbling through a bookstore, one happens to find a paperback edition of one of his eight novels, those potato chips of writing known as excerptable blurbs which appear on their jackets will reaffirm the story: "obsessive," "violent," "grotesque," "bizarre," "macabre," "harrowing," "wild"—all the words except the one which Harry Crews detests, "gratuitous."

Aside from the bizarre fictional population which Crews gives critics to ponder, there are the hard facts of his own life, the facts that have led some to accuse him of being drunk on machismo. Already this year, he has been forced into an out-of-court settlement with a man who, he says, "leaned on me too hard, just wouldn't let me out of there without going back to the parking lot and then, what could I do? When it's gotten that far, there's nothing to do but go on with it." Anyway, Crews ended up breaking the man's hip in the brawl behind a Miami bar. And there have been other incidents. He was thrown in jail in St. Augustine after a ruckus at an establishment known as the Slip Disk Disco. While in Tulsa, Oklahoma, working on an *Esquire* story about the sexual life of evangelist Billy Ray Hargis, Crews took up for a Tex-Mex whom he felt was being wronged by an immigration agent in a pool hall and was subsequently jailed. Because of his lifestyle, Crews feels critics attack him without considering the merit of his work.

* * *

Jed Smock was gyrating like a drunken top on a worn spot of grass in a quadrangle outside Crews's office in the University of Florida Fine Arts building, an aging gothic edifice. Smock, an evangelist who interprets the impending doom of the Old Testament with considerable embellishment from his own febrile imagination ("Do you think those people on the two 747s that collided in the Canary Islands knew they were going to die? Did they know Jesus? Will you know Jesus if you are called tonight, if time runs out tonight?"), considers the student body of the university to be his personal flock. It was Friday morning, and Crews was ensconced behind his office desk, already well into a third large Styrofoam cup of Krispy Kreme coffee. The previous night had been taxing. It began with a two-hour lecture to his fiction class and ended with a drop-in friend sleeping in his living room, curled up with a stun gun for protection from an amorphous, never clearly defined danger. Crews was pulling at his scalp, slurping coffee, and smoking, stoking himself and his nerves. Outside, Smock was telling a group of Krishna Consciousness people that they and their saffron robes would burn eternally.

"I don't know, God, I don't know," Crews was musing. "One of the things that writers live with is the terror—fear—that they're not going to be able to write a book. And if you write one, you're scared that you're not going to be able to write another one or that if you do write it, it's going to be terrible. And writers who are truly writers, that's about all they got to live for. It's what keeps them together. It gives them something to hold onto. This playwright who wrote *Picnic*. Los Angeles guy. I've forgotten his name. Anyway, he killed himself because he couldn't get any work anymore."

Crews drained the cup of coffee and grunted. "I think precisely what people mistake in me as being macho . . . that thing in me that wants to get as far on the edge as I can of anything that I can, the thing I like to call getting naked . . . is my need to keep myself going as a writer. You can't find out about a thing . . . well, you can find out about a thing vicariously and you can find about a thing from a book, but you can't find about it as well as you can when you're naked and vulnerable to the experiences of the world.

"And that's the only reason that I can live more or less in a university community and still not write academic novels. I go out into the world and do whatever I do. Now people can just say what they want to say. I don't think anybody who's ever met me or known me for any length of time, intimately, would say that I go out and do these things, this machismo stuff. I'm just out there, and if you're out there long enough, things happen to you. And then you write about them.

"But there is a cost. There is. My gig is to get naked, but guys make me out as a brawler and a drunk, and sure, I howl sometimes, just like anybody, I howl.

"But what I wonder about are things like when I went into this bar last week and a guy I don't know from Adam asks me about the time I was out at the Blue Pine and got in a fight with a cue stick with some guys . . . I say to this character, 'That never happened, man. How do you think I get my work done, huh?' That's the thing they don't realize. People think I'm always lying in some gutter someplace, sleeping something or other off . . . and there are times I am . . . but not that often. I try to take reasonably good care of my talent; I figure I'm just hitting my stride. A good writer ought to be able to get twenty-two, twenty-four, twenty-five books in a career. And after all, no matter what anyone says, we're all just trying to get through this thing, trying to have something to do until we die."

★ ★ ★

It was getting near 10 A.M., and Crews was in need of alcoholic sustenance. The Gainesville bars opened at 11, so he limped out from his office to make the drive to his ex-wife's house for a couple of vodka and tonics. Pulling himself into his silver van, Crews jammed Randy Newman's *Good Old Boys* tape into an eight-track player and pulled out onto the blistering macadam of the highway. Driving loosened him, as if it worked the coffee out of his system.

"Yeah, it's very difficult for me to talk about it. It's very difficult for me to intellectualize on all the work I've done, although it's easy enough to do about the work someone else has done." Crews was humming along with the tape, which was into a song about Huey Long, "Kingfish."

"For instance, people have written that there is a midget in my first three novels, and when I gave a copy of my third one [*This Thing Don't Lead to Heaven*] to my ex-wife, Sally, she said, 'You don't, do you, intend to make a career out of midgets?' And that was the first time it ever occurred to me that there were midgets in my first three books. There was Jefferson Davis Munroe in *This Thing Don't Lead to Heaven* and Foot in *The Gospel Singer* and Jester in *Naked in Garden Hills*.

"This thing I'm writing for *Sport* about jockeys. I was down in the jockey room at this racetrack working on it, looking at all them little people, and they don't walk, they tick, like a watch. They're fine. And I say in the piece that they are perfect of their kind. They are the absolute essence of what is needed to do what they do, which is ride thoroughbreds."

★ ★ ★

Crews wheeled the van off one of Gainesville's main drags and onto a quiet,shady street. "There are these guys," and he spat the words, "who say I write gratuitously about freaks. Some guy at the Atlanta papers wrote a review of *The Gospel Singer*, and I wonder about that guy, who he is, if he's ever written anything himself. He wrote just an awful review of the book . . . saying such things as this guy is an awful writer; you'll never hear from him again; he'll never write another book.

"Anyway, there's a guy who has his head on wrong. Some writers never get over that kind of criticism. I'm not saying this to be self-serving, but to be a writer and to sustain yourself for a long period of time, you need raw courage. You have to say to the world . . . okay . . . say what you want about me, do whatever you want to do to me. And I'm still gonna write and I'm gonna write the way I want to write and I'm not gonna write books to satisfy you.

"And if they're gonna say I gratuitously write about freaks and violence, let them go ahead and say it. I have a helluva lot of compassion and sympathy for those people who, as I said about Foot in *The Gospel Singer*, are special under God."

The van had pulled to a halt in a driveway leading to a ranch house. "See, I can walk around and I'm not going to get any static. People will look at me and no one is struck by how ruined I am. I can think dreadful things, have dreadful notions in my mind, and no one is going to know. But a guy who is three feet tall is going to have to deal with being three feet tall every day. And every time he turns a corner, he looks at a guy and he sees his own predicament in that guy's eyes.

"To write about one thing you have to talk about another thing, and that's the whole nature of fiction and poetry. You can say more about what the world out here calls normal by dealing with what the world calls abnormal. This is what I do.

"The reading public bothers me, though. They don't want to read about the blood and bones and guts of an issue. They want to read about something they're not going to have to think about, and if it does hurt them, as say *Love Story* does, it won't last very long. What has happened in this country is a failure of the imagination."

Crews eased himself down out of the van and began fumbling around with his key chain for a house key. He pushed the black beret he was wearing back on his head and shuffled over to a brick enclosure in front of his wife's house, where he keeps his dog, Brutus, a massive black mastiff. "I write out of this kind of outrage," he was saying. "And to write about the violence and the stuff I write about, you've got to be angry . . . People wouldn't understand it if I said I was a moralist. They'd think I was some academic dude holed up with a bunch of facts and books and didn't live in the real world. But to write out of my kind of outrage, you've got to be a stomp-down hard-core moralist."

Crews was teasing the dog now, growling at him, and the vision of Crews and the dog conjured up a scene from *The Gospel Singer* where a character named Didymus contemplates throwing himself to a massive dog.

And Didymus said, "Go into strange lands where people have never heard of you and tell them things they do not want to hear and cannot understand. If you are lucky, they will kill you and eat you . . . or throw you to vicious dogs. That is the way to God, righteousness, and the moral life."

**DAVID K. JEFFREY
AND DONALD R. NOBLE**

Harry Crews: Part of an Interview

Harry Crews tells his freshman classes at the University of Florida that he is "a writer who teaches, not a teacher who writes." Crews is a writer who, in fact, writes almost constantly, even more than the ten books he has published in the last eleven years would indicate. In an interview in early December 1978, in Gainesville, Crews discussed his life (the first six years of which he treats in the recent book A Childhood: The Biography of a Place), *and his eight novels (of which he considers* Naked in Garden Hills *his "favorite" and the more recent* The Gypsy's Curse *"a goddamn triumph"; his latest novel,* A Feast of Snakes, *has, however, gotten the best critical reception). The excerpt which follows is a small part of the five-hour interview; in this excerpt, Crews discusses his works in progress and* The Enthusiast, *a book for which Harry feels a zeal not shared by his publishers.*

D.J. & D.N.: You seem to use a lot of your personal experiences in your novels. But you seldom make use of your experiences at the university or your experience as a writer.

H.C.: *The Enthusiast* is about writing.[1]

D.J. & D.N.: *The Enthusiast?*

H.C.: It's a strange book. Creatures out of all my other books come and kidnap me and take me to Disney World. It's a very, very very

From *Black Warrior Review* 5.2 (1979): 89–92.

curious book. And I think a goddamn fine book. And no son of a bitch'll publish the goddamn fucking thing. Those rotten bastards.

D.J. & D.N.: When did you write it?

H.C.: I guess it's about the eighth book. I've written four books since I've been at this university that ain't been published.

D.J. & D.N.: You say *The Enthusiast* is about writing?

H.C.: It's about how it happens, at least to one guy. How one guy perceives it, understands it, comes to it, discovers it—the reality of it. Now, that's a strange phrase there, maybe, "the reality of it," but, and this is going to sound like a lie, there are times when I'm writing and things are going well that what is real and what is not real becomes unclear, the distinction is not very clear to me. You can get lost.

D.J. & D.N.: Your characters come alive for you?

H.C.: Yes, and most of the stuff never really gets into the book. You know a helluva lot more than you can put in the book, or that you need to put in the book.

D.J. & D.N.: *The Enthusiast* sounds very autobiographical. Could we hear part of it?

H.C.: [*Reads from manuscript.*] Harry loved his son very much, whom he neglected when he was caught in a book, which seemed to be more or less all the time. But Byron, being the beautiful boy he was, knew that his daddy was about half crazy, and never expected more than Harry Crews could give. They had a pretty healthy respect for one another, everything considered.

"Oh, he's been playing hard today," Sally said, "and he went to bed early." There was a wary, almost shy pause. "How's the novel coming?"

"Well, when I get through saying this, I'll have exactly one hundred ninety-eight words into Chapter Four of Part Two."

She knew that was all he could tell her, how many words or how many chapters. How the novel was, whether it would die in the middle or had never started to breathe in the first place was something he never knew until he was through. And even after he was through, as Duffy said, there were some people who had been unkind enough to point out that in their opinion Harry Crews didn't even know then.

"You're going out to the lake now?"

"Yeah, I thought I'd go right on out and work some tonight."

"Will you have a drink first with Johnny and Ward?"

"Not tonight."

"You know I love Johnny Feiber and Ward Scott, but you really shouldn't have any vodka and stuff with them and then drive thirty miles to the lake."

She knew Harry's predisposition to have some vodka and stuff, lying to himself, saying that he could write after he'd had a little vodka and stuff to relax, which he had never in his life been able to do.

"No. When I hang up, I'm going straight to the lake."

"Work well," she said. "Catch you later."

And she and Harry hung up.

It was always a pleasant drive from Gainesville to Melrose. The flat country, the road without traffic at this hour, and straight except for a few gentle curves that were bordered on both sides by dark standing pines that left their needle scents in the damp air.

But arriving at the cabin was not pleasant at all. He did not want to be out there by himself. Except that he wanted to be out there by himself. There was no way to win.

He had left a light on in the house to come home to. He always did. He doubted he would get out and go in if there were no light. He flipped a cigarette and started toward the lake. He took a deep breath, as though diving in the water, and got out of the car.

He stood in the doorway, regarding the room. On the sideboard by the fireplace were the quinine water and the vodka. To the left of it in front of the window looking out on the lake was his desk. Among the unanswered letters and notes and bills and complaints from various people, he sat down to a typewriter, its shift bar and frame bent from being dropped when he was drunk, the same typewriter he had written ten novels on, four of them never published, three of them not even submitted for publication because they died.

His gaze swung from the vodka to the typewriter. He really wanted to get drunk. He deserved to get drunk. Hadn't he worked hard today? Hadn't he done everything the university had asked of him? Hadn't he listened to students who had nothing to say? Hadn't he tried to give things to students who seemed unable to accept them? And in any case, did anyone care? If he didn't deserve a little vodka, then who the hell did?

The answer, of course, was "yes," that he did deserve the vodka, that everybody deserved it, and that it spoke well of anyone to need a little vodka to get through this world, and that he distrusted anyone who did not need it. Not needing a little vodka from time to time means that you're either stupid as hell or you're simply not paying attention.

Still, he could have got drunk in town anywhere. He did not need to come out here to this empty, dreadful, lonely cabin to drink vodka and tonic. He had trapped himself here alone with his typewriter so it would take less courage to use it. There is something encouraging and rewarding in knowing that you are capable of being the basest, most craven of cowards. Harry Crews had known this about himself for a long time.

Trying to pretend that he was not going to do it, being as casual as hell, he went over and sat down. That was the great, grand secret of writing, the secret that certain students lusted after, the secret that some people wrote him letters about, the secret that he was sometimes paid money to lecture on, the great, grand secret of writing, which he never told audiences anywhere, because, if he did, they would have been disappointed and would have demanded their money back. The great, grand secret of writing is Put Your Ass on the Chair. Repeat. Put Your Ass on the Chair.

The next step is much easier. He sighed and put his fingers on the keys and disappeared.

D.J. & D.N.: That is a strange kind of Harry Crews book. What are you working on now?

H.C.: I'm writing a novel now called *Crab*. And I'm also writing a play, the first play that I've ever attempted. I know nothing much about plays except insofar as I've read them. Tennessee Williams said that, if you want to be a playwright, attach yourself to a company in whatever capacity. You know, if you can be a scene designer, or whatever; draw the curtains, but just be there. That's the best thing you can do for yourself. Well, I've never done that, but I am writing a play, and I won't go into that.

Crab, though, I will say is, as you know, the astrological sign of Cancer, and the book is about a woman who has a radical mastectomy, two of 'em. They cut the whole front of her off. There's only three people in the story . . . father, mother, and this boy. He lives close by, and he's the kind of boy that, for whatever reason, people have the unfortunate habit of telling the most dreadful things about their lives.

I have actually myself been across the table from a guy and the guy'd start telling me something about his wife or whatever, and I hold up my hands and I say, "No, no, man, wait. Don't tell me that. Don't tell me that. It's not so much that I don't want to know it, because I would like to know everything, but I don't think I can bear that. I got enough on my back already." Same thing in the book. The boy does not want people to tell him their horror stories, but for whatever reason—his face, the way he walks, however he talks, whatever—they do, just awful things.

Man has a private life and a public life, and you really go down when you confuse the two. Or most people do. I'm not sure writers do. If André Gide had not been concerned with his private life, there would have been no André Gide, right? So there you are.

Note

1. *The Enthusiast* was the working title for a novel that would be published in 1987 as *All We Need of Hell*. An early version of the first four and a half chapters of that novel was published in 1981 as *The Enthusiast* in a limited edition by Palaemon Press; it was reprinted in a collection titled *Florida Frenzy* (University Press of Florida, 1983). The excerpt that Crews read to Jeffrey and Noble does not appear in either of these two books, but was later incorporated in another limited edition, *Where Does One Go When There's No Place Left to Go?*, published by Blood and Guts Press in 1998.

DAVID K. JEFFREY
AND DONALD R. NOBLE

Harry Crews: An Interview

D.J. & D.N.: When do you write? when you have a story? or every day?

H.C.: I write every day of my life.

D.J. & D.N.: How many hours a day?

H.C.: I can work about three hours, sometimes four, on first-written stuff; you know, the page is blank, and you're trying to kind of find out which way you're going.

D.J. & D.N.: Do you write at home or at your office?

H.C.: My office.

D.J. & D.N.: Do you look forward to it? Is it fun for you to write?

H.C.: No. There are times when things are really going well and you know where you are and you know what you're doing; you have a sense that you know what it means. Those times are pretty good....

See, you don't want to go there. You say, "I don't know what to write! I don't know the next paragraph!" The Hemingway thing—always stop when you can write another five hundred words—well, that's real nice advice, if you can follow it. But sometimes, you know,

From *A Grit's Triumph: Essays on the Works of Harry Crews,* ed. David K. Jeffrey (Port Washington, N.Y.: Associated Faculty Press, 1983), 140–51. Originally published in a shorter form in *Southern Quarterly* 19.2 (1981): 65–79.

you can't follow it. So you say to yourself, "I can't write today because I don't know anything." Then you say back to yourself: "I'll tell you what you do; you go there and you put it in the chair. You get to the chair and you just stay there three hours. And you can't write letters, and you can't clean your fingernails, and you can't pick your teeth or anything else. You just sit there. You don't have a window to look out. You look at the wall. And then in three hours, get up, and you're cool. You've done your best." Well, three hours is a long time. After about twenty minutes you'll say, "Hell, do *something*, even if it's wrong."

I'll tell you something else. When I start writing, I say to God, "God, give me five hundred words. I don't want to be greedy, although I am at times a very greedy person; but I'm not greedy today. Give me five hundred words and I'll be satisfied. I don't want to know the whole rest of the book. All I want to know is the next five hundred words. Thank you. Amen." And then, do it. Five hundred words, after all, isn't much. If you double-space and you've got good margins so you can make notes to yourself, you're only writing two hundred and fifty words a page. That's two pages. And, as the young Jules Verne said to the somewhat older Alexandre Dumas, "How do you write so much? How do you turn so much out?" Dumas said: "A page a day gives a book a year. Two pages a day gives two books a year." Now, that's going to sound very mechanical, very arbitrary, but that's the way I do it. That's the way I think. Many times those two pages go somewhere else, usually the trash basket or the furnace. Andrew Lytle used to say, "Fire is a great refiner." And it is.

D.J. & D.N.: Do you know when you start them how your novels are going to end?

H.C.: Never.

D.J. & D.N.: The ending is decided as you move along in the writing?

H.C.: I move toward where the story seems to be going. You don't make up a story; you discover a story. Robert Penn Warren says a writer does not need to know his story; he only needs to trust his knowledge of craft and technique to discover the story. And the bottom line is what Flannery O'Connor said: you never do really discover it. She said that no matter what the subject, the writer is interested in the mystery of that subject, which he cannot hope to solve but only to deepen. Ain't that *fine?* That's *fine!* That's fine. And you can't do it much better than that.

Many times you start a novel or a short story or whatever from the wrong point of view. You don't know that then, but as you move, it becomes clearer and clearer. *A Feast of Snakes* was about five times as long as it is now. I wrote it all the way to the end, and I saw that I had done it wrong. I'd put it together wrong. So then I just had to go back and do it again.

D.J. & D.N.: Do you do a lot of revising? Do you rewrite, or do you tinker with what you've written?

H.C.: I think of changing a word or transposing words, deleting a line—I think of that as polishing, not rewriting. I think of rewriting as touching a book structurally, when you say: "This thing's in the wrong place. I don't know where it goes; maybe it doesn't go anywhere; but it doesn't belong here." So you move it. You change the structure. That's rewriting. I do rewrite a great deal.

D.J. & D.N.: How do you feel when you sit down to start something new?

H.C.: The fear that I think many writers live with (maybe even *all* of them; certainly, I do), the fear that I live with is that I won't ever be able to do it again. I mean *anything*—a novel, a story, a thing like *A Childhood.* This is not false modesty. When I sit down to write, I sit down with an absolute terror that it's not going to work. I also think that in every book you write, in the middle of the thing it looks like it's not going to work. Because most of the time, as I said, you don't know where you're going. Mr. Lytle, who took me in like a lost dog and was as much a father to me as any man, except for my Uncle Alton, ever was, told me: "Son, the middle of a place, the middle of a thing is no place to judge it from. Suck it up and go on." Well, I'm sure Mr. Lytle never said, "Suck it up." He's a very formal man and a gentleman. I told him, "We both say we're southerners, but you're a southerner, I'm not a southerner." Like Jimmy Carter and me. We're both from the South, though; well, we ain't from the South. He's . . .

ain't a tenant farmer's son; I am. I'm not bad mouthin' him or tenant farmers, I'm just stating a truth.

D.J. & D.N.: Mr. Lytle, of course, encouraged you while you were a student at the University of Florida, and you've also quoted Robert Penn Warren and Flannery O'Connor admiringly. Are there other writers you think you've learned from?

H.C.: I think I've learned more from Graham Greene than I've learned from any other writer. To the best of my knowledge, I've read everything that he's ever written. I like *The Power and the Glory* an *awful* lot. But, you know, there are no perfect books. Faulkner said, if I remember correctly, that he read *Madame Bovary* every year; it's a fine book, but it's not a perfect book. For starters, the beginning is very, very wrong. But I love it. I love that book, and I read it quite a bit, too. André Gide I read and think I've learned much from. I could go on. As everybody knows, people who write, more often than not, are voracious readers. If I get caught in a house where there are no books, I go nuts.

D.J. & D.N.: Do you read Faulkner much?

H.C.: I've read him all, but I never read him when I'm writing. There are a lot of writers I don't read when I'm writing. I think Thomas Wolfe was the best writer this country ever had because he took the greatest risks and made the greatest failures, but I wouldn't touch Wolfe when I was writing.

D.J. & D.N.: Any others you admire?

H.C.: James Agee: he was born a prince of the language and so he remains. Truman Capote: I don't care what kind of stupidass remarks he makes, he can write; he really can. When he's on, he's really on. Updike would be twice the writer he is if he weren't such a hot dog. God knows, he's a word man. Eudora Welty: great writer. Erskine Caldwell, by the way, is a helluva lot better than he's ever been given credit for. Mr. Caldwell is much, much better than his peers. But if you ask me, "Who's your favorite writer?" there's no answer to that. That's like saying, "What do you like best for breakfast?" Some mornings you want a beer; some mornings you want strawberries; some mornings you want, God help us, Frosty Crispy Flakes with a lot of sugar; and some mornings you want your old lady.

D.J. & D.N.: Did you ever feel you'd outgrown a writer you'd once admired?

H.C.: My first hero in letters was Somerset Maugham. I outgrew that. When I was a freshman, I thought Ayn Rand was a hell of a writer, and unfortunately I read all of her books. By the time I was a sophomore I knew she was no good. She's a tract writer. The theme, that the English teachers love so much, comes first and the characters come later. It's something that people have said about me. They're wrong, of course. That's what's wrong with Sartre's fiction; every character has to come in bearing the burden of his peculiar, or particular, brand of existentialism. It constitutes a flaw in the work he does. To some extent James Baldwin is the same way. I think James Baldwin is one of the best essayists, if not *the* best essayist, in the country. "The Fire Next Time" is a beautiful essay, wonderful essay. I don't like his novels or his play. I think the preface to the play is marvelous.

I would much rather these people write essays. That's an honorable and wonderful and difficult profession. It always seemed to me that, in the novels that Ayn Rand or Sartre write, the subject comes before the people; the subject doesn't come out of the people and their predicament in the world.

D.J. & D.N.: You don't think of your novels as novels of ideas?

H.C.: Not in that sense. People have said I write thesis novels or tract novels. That hurts. I'm not ashamed of admitting that that hurts me. Real honest-to-God pain. Because I don't believe it's fair and I don't believe it's true, and I believe it comes out of a superficial reading.

D.J. & D.N.: How so?

H.C.: Well, all books deal with subjects. Every novel will make an economic statement because the people in them have to get their bread somehow. And every novel will make a theological statement, and on and on. It all depends on the characters. Faulkner said, generally, that the characters should be so solid they cast a shadow. I think that the people in my books—I've missed a couple of times; who hasn't?—I think that most of the people in them are people, not just names clunking around imitating people. They have substance, I think. I am not, despite what I think of as the tight narrative line of my books driving towards what I at least believe is an inevitable ending—despite that, I'm not a very conscious writer. I don't say, "I've got this character here and this one here, and I'm going to do this with that and that with this."

Any character of mine is difficult for me to talk about, in the same way that anybody—any friend, any enemy, anybody I know—would be difficult for me to talk about in any real depth, because they're complex. You know a lot more about them than you can put in a book or than you need to put in a book. I think that I talk more cogently and more succinctly and more sensibly about other writers' work than about my own, and we all know why: you're closer to it, and it is very often a mystery, a mystery that you can't solve, but a mystery that you've been involved in. To ask me to unravel that mystery and elucidate upon its parts or how it got put together is something I don't do very well.

D.J. & D.N.: You talk about other writers' work a good deal here at the university.

H.C.: I lecture to freshmen in a course called Introduction to Fiction. And then I work with graduate students who think they want to be writers. I try to do for them what a good editor would do for them, if they had a good editor. They write and I read, that's the name of the game. We do have a class and we read accomplished writers and we talk about them. We discuss the stories that the students write; every student that writes a story has a conference with me in my office.

D.J. & D.N.: What do you think about that? Do you think that works?

H.C.: I think if the student's a writer, it works; if he's not a writer, it doesn't work. If you ask me, "Why is a man or woman a writer, what's in there that makes him that?" I have no answer. Unfortunately, most of the people that teach that stuff don't write themselves, and a lot of bad information is given to people who take such courses, because the people giving the information don't know what they're talking about, because they haven't done it. They studied with someone who didn't write.

I read their stories, and I read them very carefully, and then I talk to them: "This transition is too fast," or "You have a mechanical break here." Now, some of the best stories that we know of have mechanical breaks in them: "The Dead," Joyce's story, I think has five. There are no Thou Shalt Nots in fiction. A writer can do any damn thing he can get away with. As Flannery O'Connor said, unfortunately, he can't get away with very much. Or I'll say to the student: "Look, this language you've got here. This is rhetoric. This language doesn't do anything. It doesn't carry itself. You're in love with the sound of your own voice" (which, God knows, all of us who write, and some of us who don't, are) "but it won't do." There is a soft spot in all of us who write that's got to be killed, squashed, exorcised, before we can write truly, as Hemingway would say, God love his soul.

D.J. & D.N.: Writing the way you do, you must sometimes get stuck or blocked. What do you do if and when that happens?

H.C.: Well, I run a lot. I don't run fast when I run, but I run a long way. It takes a long time. When I run, I think about my stories, and I think about what's going wrong. I think about how things are developing. I think about things I don't know. I think about a lot of things, but it all has to do with writing. I have got unstuck running more than I ever have other ways, because it's almost self-hypnosis.

I pretend (and I pretend as soon as I hit the street), I pretend that there is a little man in my forehead who is running this machine, which is my body. I've been hurt a lot, so it hurts when I run. The machine—the legs, the neck, the back, the ribs—sends messages up to the little man behind my forehead. It's like a ship, and a guy down in the engine room is calling up to the captain: "Ah, engine two, in trouble. Engine two, firing badly. Smoke coming out." The captain says, "Never mind. I've checked that out all right. Maintain speed." Hangs up. After a while, no matter what comes up to the little man, he sends it back. He sends it back to the foot: "Foot is all right." Foot hurts, feels as though it may be fractured again. "We've checked it out fully. Foot is maintaining well." Phone hangs up. So then, after, say, about three miles, your body goes away. I get the feeling of becoming total mind, free mind. You get a focus, a concentration that you can get nowhere else.

D.J. & D.N.: Despite your earlier disclaimer, we would like to ask you about your novels. Many of them seem to deal with the nature of man's evil.

H.C.: It is more fascinating, perhaps easier, to write about that which is diabolical and evil. We somehow feel, I think, that we understand goodness and love better than we understand badness and evil. Who would be evil? Why would you be evil? Why would you starve the Georgians in Russia? Why would you shovel people into furnaces? You can't think about that. And yet, my God, my God . . . It is the thing in us that keeps us fascinated with ourselves. It fascinates us with ourselves much more, the animal in us, the flesh-tearing, brutal animal in us, fascinates us much more than the kissing, licking sweetheart who sends valentines, who cares enough to send the very best.

D.J. & D.N.: You like to end your novels in the midst of holiday crowds. Do these mob scenes reflect this sense of mankind?

H.C.: It has been my observation, perhaps faulty, that we live for that. We make our bread, we earn our living, we do whatever we do in some form of isolation, and it's highly controlled. We all have these facades, these images of ourselves. But if you go to, say, Fort Lauderdale Beach [for the university's spring break], that which is in us that we deny, either consciously or unconsciously, seems to emerge; and that seems to me more what we really are than what we would have people believe we are. I'm afraid I don't have a very high opinion of the disguised human being, "disguised" meaning his identity, his family, where he came from, what he believes in. When all of that disguise is gone, he then becomes a thing that none of us can be proud of or pleased with (and I think it's in all of us).

You can call it a form of mass hysteria, if you want to, but, you know, good men, and I mean large numbers of good men, have done absolutely atrocious things for no other reason than that they were caught up in the frenzy of the lack of identity. And when you get caught up in that frenzy, then you revert to the cutting edge of the front teeth and the grinders in the back.

D.J. & D.N.: Another of your preoccupations, as you suggested a minute ago, is with the family. *A Childhood* is about your own family, and each of your novels deals with the families that the characters form after the break-up of their real families. Would you comment on that?

H.C.: It's a thing that's very much on my mind all the time, the disintegration of the family. I see it everywhere I go. I think about the marvel of growing up in the same house. I think that's a very beautiful thing, to be able to do that. And I think it's a very beautiful thing to have your mama and daddy and your brothers and sisters there. You know, you write out of the manners of your people and the customs of your people, and that is all you've got.

But we're all so mobile; we're all so . . . voiceless is a real good word, used in that context, because accents have almost disappeared. You can take a disc jockey from Gainesville and take him to Los Angeles and nobody would ever know the difference. They've all got that banana-smooth sameness. When we lose our voices, there's no communicating. When we lose that, then we begin to lose the family. You know, damned little was passed on to any of us—voice, place, manners, customs. When that begins to break down, it diminishes the human family. That's what I think.

D.J. & D.N.: Your novels comment, too, on the American preoccupation with the consumer economy, our propensity to devour, to gorge it all in. Do you think of yourself as a social critic, a social satirist?

H.C.: Well, I've certainly never thought of myself as anything like, say, Sinclair Lewis, but I think that any writer that writes about anybody living in any culture is going to be to some extent a commentator on that culture and on that system. Maybe because of how I was raised and where I was raised, I just don't care much about clothes and about food. If a man's got a place where he won't freeze to death when he puts his head down to go to sleep and if he's got enough to eat, well then he's pretty much all right. When I lived out on the lake in Melrose, there was not a bed in the house. I slept on the floor. I wrote *The Gypsy's Curse* sitting on two concrete blocks at a desk made out of a door.

You know, if everything has to be plastic and polyester color-coordinated, that kind of world, it makes me nervous. I don't like it and I don't want anything to do with it. Such circumstances would diminish whatever intellect or perception of feeling I have about my fellow man. To pile up all that stuff is an effort to resist the fact that someday you're going to lie down and die. I just know that's the way that works. I don't think that *not* piling it up is going to keep you from doing it, but it just seems to me that you can spend your time in a better way.

D.J. & D.N.: Earlier, you mentioned your prayer to God. *A Childhood* has a remarkable scene dealing with your religious conversion, and your novels often take as their protagonists or contain minor characters who are men of God or religious fanatics. Would you talk about your view of religion?

H.C.: I have no book that does not in some way concern itself with man's relationship to God. That's my own judgment. Somebody else can say something else. But I am a believer. I am not a spark of electricity. I am not an accident. I was made. Natural law is a phenomenon that never ceases to amaze me. I have in *Karate Is a Thing of the Spirit* that if you take a rock and contemplate it long enough and concentrate on it, touch it with your tongue, and look at it, that the whole mystery of the world is in it. Strangely enough, they all, if you turn 'em loose, they all fall down. They don't go up or sideways, anything else. Peanuts put their flowers on the top of the ground and their fruit underneath the earth. I don't believe, although I've tried to understand it, I don't believe that we really know why sap rises in trees; but I expect somebody could give me a long documented thing on that . . . I've read them, and I still don't believe they know.

But I go to no church. I am not of any denomination. I think of worship, if you want to use that word, or I think of thinking about God as contemplating the inadequacies of my own heart. But churches, organized religion—I have tried, I've been to just about every church you can think of. Catholic churches: the great T. S. Eliot said, if God is to be worshiped, He ought to be worshiped with all possible pomp and circumstance. The icons, the water, and the gettin' down and gettin' up, and the wafer and the wine. But a little later it all goes sour. So I can't be a Catholic. I can't be a

Baptist and I can't be a Unitarian. The Unitarians, God love their hearts and souls and may they all be right, they talk about things like the cavities in your teeth. If you've never been to a Unitarian fellowship, you ought to go; guys in there talking about Watergate; which is all right.

I went for a while over here to the temple—not Orthodox, not Reform, Conservative Judaism—I think it's called Conservative Temple. I think there's three of them. That guy gave a talk on, a lecture on Abraham Lincoln. You think I'm lying? My right hand to God. He gave a lecture on Abraham Lincoln. At one point I'm standing there and I don't know anything about it and I've got my yarmulke on and I'm kinda watching everybody else and some of it's in English and some of it's in Hebrew. Anyway, all of a sudden, I'm standing there, first time I went—later on, I know what it means, but I'm with nobody—and all of a sudden they all turn around, this way . . .

D.J. & D.N.: They're all looking at you, right?

H.C.: Yeah. Well, I'm a slower learner, but—used charitably to be called a late developer—but I got myself around too, and it turns out we're looking toward the Wailing Wall.

So anyway, I can't go to church. I can't go to church.

D.J. & D.N.: Organized religion is clearly not something that holds any . . .

H.C.: No, because there's too many . . . things in there; just as Oliver Wendell Holmes said, "You'll have to pardon me if I cannot believe your fairy tales." I think that's the way he said it. In any event, he was not an atheist; he was an agnostic, but he was clearly a moral and a good man. I am not an atheist or an agnostic, I sometimes act and say things that would lead people to believe it, things that clearly would indicate such a theological position. Not true. On the other hand, it is a thing with which I'm fascinated, and, to be pompous, a thing with which I flagellate myself more than a little.

And if I was in one of those monasteries where the monks slept in their coffins, I'd be right in there sleeping. But I don't have to sleep in my coffin. Some of us know the ground we're going into, and some of us have already smelled our rotting flesh, and some of us have already had the worms in our eyes, and the rest of it, so, after you've had that, well, you don't need to go to church; you've already been, and got everything they've got to give you. All you've got to do is wait and see how it turns out. And I for one find the fact that every mother's son and daughter of us is gonna die, I find that one of the most beautiful and terrifying and surely informative things that will ever happen to us, 'cause we gonna get to find out. We gonna get to find out.

I've always thought a writer has an obligation to show the skull. This is not original with me. I think Flannery O'Connor may have said it—that if you don't show the skull behind the smile, then you haven't shown it all. That's related, it seems to me, to what Hemingway said—that all stories end in death and that him that would keep you from that is no true storyteller. When I'm writing, I want the novel to be terrifying and beautiful and joyful and full of anguish and laughter at the same time, so that you're thinking, "My God, my God, what are we in here?" Now, why do I want to do that? I don't know. It's just part of who I am. I can't explain it to you. It's just the way it comes out.

D.J. & D.N.: Are you surprised when people find your books funny?

H.C.: No. They're funny books. I never set out to be funny. I've never thought of myself as a funny person. Not many people *laugh* when I'm around. I walk into the bank and all the guards put their hands on their guns. It's just that that terror and anxiety that we all live with is as necessary and real and important as the joy and the beauty that we live with. And there wouldn't be any joy and beauty and ecstasy and all the rest of it, if there weren't at the end of the road the worms for your eyes. There wouldn't be.

D.J. & D.N.: We read your novels. We've been reading them for a long time. Do they sell?

H.C.: They don't sell very well.

D.J. & D.N.: Well, I'm curious about that.

H.C.: I am, too.

D.J. & D.N.: Do you have any theories, any notions about why not? and how do you feel about that?

H.C.: I feel bad. I feel bad about that. Because anybody that tells me he doesn't lust for an audience, I think he's crazy.

You may or may not know that this has been said, and you may or may not agree with this, but the audience for fiction in America is suburban and middle class. Suburban housewives, around thirty-five or six or seven. That's who buys the books. Now, are they gonna buy a book with a guy walking on his hands, hitting a lady in the head with a hatchet [*The Gypsy's Curse*]? They gonna buy a book with a guy in it that's got the biggest foot in the world, and he himself is a midget [*The Gospel Singer*]? Practically everybody that's written anything about me maintains that I put that stuff in those books—midget with the biggest foot in the world; guy who walks on his hands, can't talk, can't hear, and the story's told from his point of view, which is a goddamn triumph—they say I put that stuff in there to sell books. Well, if they knew anything about selling books, they'd know that wouldn't sell books. I don't *put* anything in my books anyway. Middle-aged women don't buy those books, and middle-aged men don't buy them. That criticism hurts me.

D.J. & D.N.: Have you ever sold any of your novels to the movies?

H.C.: All my books are or have been under option for movies. One of them's sold outright, *The Gospel Singer.* People ask me things like: "Won't you feel bad if they make your book into a movie? You know, the producer does something, the director does something, the actor does something, everybody's screwin' with it. . . ." I say: "No. They haven't done anything to my book. My book's in the library. Nobody's touched my book. That's what *they* did."

D.J. & D.N.: Do you read reviews of your work?

H.C.: I sometimes read the first lines of reviews. Then I quit.

D.J. & D.N.: You mean if the first line isn't good, you hate the review?

H.C.: Well, I'm not quite that tender, I don't think. But maybe I am. I can get hurt really quickly and really deeply emotionally, and it hurts for a long time. Nobody needs that. You don't need that very much.

Geoffrey Wolff reviewed one of my books, a two-page review, but, you know, he's gotta start out by saying, "Harry Crews has written eight novels, four of which I have read, one of which I have liked, but if you have come here for me to knock Crews, you've come to the wrong place." And then from then on, all roses, which I didn't read. I'm not gonna listen to somebody tell me he's read four of my books and liked one out of eight of them, and now he's gonna give me a good review. I just don't need that. It's probably true. Maybe they're all bad. Hell, I don't know. Let somebody else decide. I just write 'em. I don't review 'em. I don't ever recall reviewing a book of mine. Well, not in public.

D.J. & D.N.: Well, I've reviewed them, too, and I don't think they're bad; but you're not exactly getting rich from them, are you?

H.C.: If I wanted to make money writing, or if I wanted my son to make money writing, I sure as hell wouldn't tell him to become a novelist. Not that you can't make money being a novelist, but it's rare that you can make money being a novelist and make it honestly. You gotta be a fraud, a cheat, a hypocrite. You gotta study the market, what's *in* this year, and go do one of those. I never do that. I write what I write. I write what comes to me.

D.J. & D.N.: Are you bitter about reviewers? Do you really care about that?

H.C.: I've stopped reading them.

D.J. & D.N.: You've gotten a lot of good reviews.

H.C.: Yeah, well, that's nice to know, but it doesn't help very much.

D.J. & D.N.: Reviews don't sell books.

H.C.: Nope.

D.J. & D.N.: What does?

H.C.: I don't know. I got a kind of theory about it. "Theory," that's sweet. I got a feeling about it. It's that I go down and buy a book and read it, and then I meet you at the post office. I say: "Hey. Richard Price's *Ladies' Man* that just came out. Get it. It may upset you a lot, but it's a helluva book. You oughta get it, and they've got two left down there. If I was you, I wouldn't mail that letter. I'd go get it right now." And then you go get both of them and you send one to Iowa. And then somebody in Iowa says, "Hey. This is not bad." Like that.

D.J. & D.N.: And then he goes to the post office . . .

H.C.: Yeah. I think that must be the way it happens. If it doesn't happen that way, then maybe some of us just weren't meant to be . . . See, the ultimate criticism, and it's a killer, it *is* a killer, the ultimate criticism that a writer gets is that what he is, is not worth being. I mean, after all the work is in. Maybe by that time you're dead; hopefully, you're dead.

D.J. & D.N.: I asked Truman Capote that question about reviews, and he said that reviews were of no use unless they were so orchestrated that they came out within about one week. He said if you could get the *New York Times* and *Newsweek* and *Time* and *Harper's* and the *New York Review of Books* all to come out with the same thing in about ten days or two weeks, this would create a kind of effect.

H.C.: Well, if nothing else, people'd be talking about it.

D.J. & D.N.: Yeah, it'd be all over New York. But if the reviews come out slowly, one at a time all over the place, then no one review does anything for you. You get raves but they don't have any effect.

H.C.: So much of it's luck. Eudora Welty said you don't just need talent and hard work and the rest of it. To write a good book or a good story you also need luck. And I think most writers would agree with that.

D.J. & D.N.: I've also heard that something like forty percent of all hardcover novels are sold within the city of New York. That can't help you.

H.C.: The way I get it is "within an eight-hundred-mile radius of New York City." But it could be "within New York City." That's true. Whatever reputation I have does pretty much exist, strangely enough, within the urban North. There is none down here, much.

When *Esquire* asked me to write a column for them every month, I didn't much want to do it because I knew it was going to get in my way. And I didn't start just to be a columnist. But, I told 'em I'd do it for a year. I wrote as well as I could. I wrote things that I thought were real and of some consequence. But I also thought it might get my name around and might help my books to sell. I want my books to sell. I ain't ashamed of saying that.

D.J. & D.N.: You took the job in order to promote your name, right? Nobody else is doing it, so you've got to do it. Right?

H.C.: That's right. You got it right. And that does not speak well, I don't think, for a man to admit that.

You know, all we've got is time. I'm halfway to eighty-six, and that's getting on. I'm on the downhill side. How damn long do I expect to live? I always wanted twenty titles. I always wanted twenty titles because I thought if you did—hell, this sounds so mechanical and arbitrary to say, "I wanted twenty titles," as though that meant anything—but, if you wrote as well as you could and as honestly as you could and with as much concentration, focus, diligence, whatever, as you could, well, then, out of twenty you might get a good one. You know, you might get a good one.

D.J. & D.N.: Douglas Day wrote that *A Feast of Snakes* reveals for the first time your "radical despair." There seems to be some of that here, in your conversation, in your personal life.

H.C.: My personal life is, and has been, as long as I can remember, a shambles. I don't live, I don't do it very well. But the one thing in the world that I can have some control over and shape and feel good about is whatever I can write.

If you look at any writers, if you really look at them, what you see is a trail of mucus and blood and guts and everything else. I think that every writer of any consequence or a writer that tries to be of consequence and write something of merit, that it costs him an awful, awful lot. If you're married, what you give to the typewriter, you can't give to the girl. That may be all right for a year or two. It may be all right for eighteen years. But sooner or later, it's going to catch up with things. While fathers are out teaching their sons to fly-fish, you're trying to teach yourself how to do something with your craft. If you're a person of feeling, if you feel things keenly and deeply—and I don't think you can be a writer unless you feel things not just for the moment but they live in you—that costs you. I don't think you can be a writer of consequence and merit unless you have grave doubts about yourself, about what you've done and who you are and whom you've hurt. And that costs you. And so, it all costs you. What is left is what all of us are going to get, a chance to know what it's like to die.

AL BURT

The Troubles with Harry

Violence follows Harry Crews around like an oversized lapdog, eager to spring upon him with bone-crunching love. "I don't know why I attract it," Crews said, shaking his head, making the gold earring on his left lobe jiggle and gleam. "But I do."

He kept rubbing his right eye, still blurry from a recent concussion. The doctor has told him it will be all right. The razor cuts across his body are healing nicely, too. The knees are still a mess, though. "I can go upstairs, but going down, I have trouble with that," he said.

He mused. "Maybe it's the way I talk. Abrupt, ragged sometimes, like that, you know. But I don't mean it that way. Maybe it's how I walk. Sort of out-front. I don't know what it is, but something I do gnaws at people.

"My reputation is not good. That's part of it. The things I get into are highly suspect. Send me to Alaska and what do I write about? Whores getting tattooed on their ass while they're blowing cocaine up their noses. What is that? But it's what was up there."

He got the concussion and razor cuts and fresh damage to battered knees while researching a story on dogfighting. "Making the connection was like a dope buy," he said. "I followed instructions. Flew to Miami, flew to the west coast, drove to Boca Raton, on and on. No names. Louisiana rules. The dog don't have to take his killing. All he has to do is 'cur' out."

From the *Miami Herald*, December 31, 1978.

Pit bulls fought in an old barn. "It was madness, man," Crews said, lighting up at the memory. "The whisky's out, the money's out. Lot of guys holding heat, lot of guys holding knives, lot of bullshit coming down. Two or three fights and the crowd's in a frenzy. Just madness."

Crews went near the pit, leaning to see better. "I just asked this guy, who was really a big guy, I would never have thought to fuck with him, I said, 'Hey man, you got a good shot of the pit. You can see. Just move over a little bit because you're in my way'." Crews put pleading into his voice, to show how reasonable he had been.

He shook his head, bewildered. "Maybe it was the tone of my voice, but that was all it took, man. Before I knew it, I was on the ground and he was on the ground with me. He had three guys with him and they started coming. I had one guy and he told 'em, 'If you're gonna get in this you gotta come by me'. Which they did, just like that. Really big guys. Nobody tried to separate us 'cause it was all just madness."

One guy worked him over with a contrivance that let the edge of a straight razor fit around his hand like brass knuckles. The four left him bloody and broken.

Crews had no hard feelings. "They were pretty decent guys," he said. "They didn't want to kill anybody." He recalled it with satisfaction, like a man cataloging his pain following a day of manual labor on his dream house. "After the fight, my guy gave his dog a shot of Demerol and cortisone," Crews said. He smiled. "Hell, he gave me a shot of Demerol, too."

Legends already have begun to build around Harry Crews, novelist and University of Florida English professor. At forty-three, his long hair and heavy mustache graying slightly, his tall athlete's body beginning to puff, he has had ten books—eight of them novels—published, and lifted himself to the upper levels of American letters. He portrays evil so powerfully and naturally and empathetically, extending in his own way the tradition of Graham Greene and Flannery O'Connor and the young Erskine Caldwell, that he disturbs people who cling to fashion and convention for sanctuary. He makes a roller-coaster ride of the bizarre twists and violent lurches that people take when struggling to free themselves of cursed lives.

Yet more than that distinguishes him. His own life had such unusual dimension that it threatened to compete with his work for attention.

In that respect, he was the Ernest Hemingway of his day, buoyed by myth-making, distracted by it, becoming one of his own best characters, though Hemingway alongside the earthy Crews might have seemed a pompous straight-arrow.

Not long ago, with a pocketful of money from one of his journalistic exercises for *Playboy* or *Esquire,* Crews and a buddy went to St. Augustine to play. "Expressly to spend that money," was the way Crews put it. For the occasion, he shaved his head, setting off a full beard nicely and complementing the single earring.

A discotheque became headquarters. After three days of drinking and dancing and romancing, the inevitable occurred. He returned from a momentary diversion to find a sailor with his girl. "He knew damned well I was with the girl," Crews said, explaining the provocation. "I'd been dancing with her, buying her drinks and everything. But he was talking to her and he had his back to me."

First thing the sailor knew, a warm stream of water came coursing down his pants leg. Honor demanded, and got, a fight. "Cops came out of the woodwork, six carloads of 'em," Crews said. "They got me and the girl in the back seat of a car. She was beating at them and yelling, 'You can't do this to us'. And I'm trying to calm her down and telling her, 'Yes they can, darlin', yes they can'." Crews's attorney, checking the shaved head and earring, advised him not to contest the misdemeanor in court. He left his bond, if not his heart, in St. Augustine.

Things like that just happened to him, out of nowhere. Once he was in Encino, California, with actor Vic Morrow. They had been talking about making a movie from one of his books. They had a few drinks, naturally, and Morrow decided to drive Crews to his Pasadena hotel. They got lost. About 5 a.m., somewhere in Pasadena, Crews announced he felt like walking. Morrow reluctantly agreed.

Crews explained that something Morrow had said, "just turned my head around. I wanted to walk awhile and think." It was a story about a woman who had a flower bloom in her mouth when she had an orgasm. "I was taken with that image," Crews said.

Preoccupied with that, he turned a corner and discovered he had gone into a dead-end alley and two guys had walked in behind him. "I caught it," he said. "I got hurt bad." Another misfortune.

Through other misfortunes, as well as automobile and motorcycle wrecks and a tour of duty with the Marines, Crews has had his neck broken, ribs on both sides broken, sternum broken, both knees and both feet broken, his entire body bruised and sliced. Still, he remained a man passionate about all things, unslowed. "I have an incredible recovery rate," he explained.

Not long ago, Crews walked into a Gainesville bar, and saw a guy and a girl sitting there. The girl spoke. "She looked vaguely familiar to me and so I said, 'Hey, how are you? You're lookin' good'. Then I walked over to the bar and ordered a draft. I had that glass almost up to my mouth when I caught this shot on the side of the head."

The punch wiped out a row of teeth and cost Crews a $700 dental bill. He was mystified. "Never saw the guy before. It was between him and her. He had his balls up because he thought I'd been fooling with his girl or something. I swear to God, three weeks later I was in Atlanta and the same thing happened.

"Man, listen, it's like a snowball. I go in a bar somewhere and some jackass walks up to me and tells me a long story about something I did somewhere, some outrageous thing, and I wasn't there and I've never been there. I used to try to correct all that. I used to say, wait a minute, man, you got that wrong. But now I just shrug."

One misfortune he did not plan to risk was old age. One of his books, *This Thing Don't Lead to Heaven,* dealt with the horrors of an old folks' home. "I forgot who it was but somebody said when you die you ought to be just a little puff of dust, that somebody could put in their hand and go Poof! and blow away, all used up, nothing left. I don't plan to get old; I plan to wear out.

"I am forty-three years old, but I don't have any friends forty-three years old," Crews said. "People forty-three years old usually are worried about their annuities, life insurance policies and the mortgage on the house and all that shit does not interest me.

"It's damned near against the law to be vulnerable anymore, but that's my whole gig. I want to be vulnerable. I want to be naked. I want to be right out there and just let it all hang out."

Never doubt that Crews does exactly that. In his latest book, *A Childhood,* his story of growing up in Bacon County, Georgia, he lets so much hang out that he engages the sensitive reader with a familial concern. Crews grew up among a loving, tragedy-prone family in an atmosphere that accepted the maimed and deformed as commonplace. He narrowly escaped crippling polio, and death by being boiled alive in a vat prepared for scalding a hog. It was a physical, back-against-the-wall world.

The book even told how his father, while still a bachelor, got "the clap" and feared sterility, of Crews's loss of his father as an infant and the succession of a drunken stepfather, and of the local code of conduct in which a man settled his own grievances and considered it a dangerous revelation of weakness to call in the law.

A Childhood was a beautifully written book, a southern classic really, and it explained a lot about Crews. He dedicated it to his only child, Byron (whose mother he married and divorced twice and still spoke of lovingly), and said it was written so that Byron would know who he was by knowing who his father was, a circumstance denied to Harry. Harry searched out that father by talking with Bacon County families and old-timers. At one point he wrote disquietingly, "For half of my life, I have been in the university, but never of it. Never of anywhere, really. Except the place I left."

Curiously, he felt alienated from the two places to which he was most attached, the University of Florida and Bacon County. Within his family, his mother was an exception. "I asked her if she wanted to read the book before I published it and she said no. She said if it's the truth, write it. She has never objected to any of it."

His other kinfolk were decent to him but he felt alienated. "They act like I'm a goddamn leper," he said. "My brother thinks I write stomp-down, hardcore pornography. I'm welcome in my uncles' and aunts' houses, and my nephews', or at least they make me think so. But it's different. If I go to their house and it's cold or there's something there they think's not quite right they apologize to me in a way they would not apologize to their other blood kin. It doesn't make you feel good. It makes you feel bad.

"I don't know what it is, exactly. I talk differently, dress differently, eat different food . . . And there's the notion of a man making a living without sweating, without calluses on his hands, without the use of his physical self. Something seems slightly askew about that, too."

Crews believed the university and his kin saw him in exactly opposite ways, producing the same result. At the university, he appeared the primitive. "See, I just don't do anything the way they do it much. I don't go to all those standup tea parties. Me and a couple of black cats are the only ones that's got an earring in our ear. I don't own a pair of trousers that aren't Levis. I wear whatever comes to hand, and back when I was drinking bad I'd go three or four days without shaving and I'd go to class just looking bad.

"I'm quick to speak my mind, too, at faculty meetings and other places. They are used to people who are much more careful than I am. If they want to tell you you're not doing your job right they don't say, 'Hey, you're not doing your job right'. They come at it this way and then this way and over the hill and everything and finally they get down to it.

"Whenever we get a new department chairman, and we've had four or five since I've been here, I always go in and tell him, I say as long as I don't hear from you I will assume I'm doing my job well. If for some reason something begins to eat on you, don't let it nag you for three weeks before you tell me. Just say, 'Crews, you've got to change'. And if I can't change, I'll walk.

"The university has been good to me," he added quickly. "I'm not sure what they think of me, but they treat me fine. When I was up for full professor, I remember what one sponsor said in a letter. Something like, 'Harry Crews was not to the manner born, but the university not only can stand him, it ought to stand him. He might not do things just the way we would have him do them, but it'll be all right'." He thought that sounded fine.

Crews's eight novels have dealt with the theme of the ugly being beautiful, and vice versa. Curses were blessings, and blessings were curses. Most of his characters live on the edge of violence, and often fall in. His reputation soared on grotesque comedy, beginning with *The Gospel Singer* (1968), which depicted a golden-boy singer whose extraordinary gift led him into scenes of seduction, rape and righteous murder. The other books followed, one a year: *Naked in Garden Hills* (a fat man gets fatter on Metracal, and go-go dances in a phosphate pit); *This Thing Don't Lead to Heaven*; *Karate Is a Thing of the Spirit* (again, the study of a troubled mind, for which he became a karate expert); *Car* (a man eats a car, bite by bite); *The Hawk Is Dying* (a man tries to save his sanity through the discipline of training a hawk);

The Gypsy's Curse (a crippled deaf mute finds the perfect mate, a blonde looking for someone who loves her enough to kill her for being faithless, and obliges her with a hatchet); *A Feast of Snakes* (a football hero goes mad at a snake festival, commits multiple shotgun murders and leaps into a pit of rattlesnakes). His book *Blood and Grits* was a collection of essays.

Two scenes from the last novel, *A Feast of Snakes,* typify the Crews commitment to scenes of shock and violence. In the first, a woman repeatedly runs away from her husband and each time he finds her and drags her back. She gives up. The daughter finds her one day, slumped in a rocking chair, a plastic bag over her head and a one-sentence note pinned to her dress: "Bring me back now, you son of a bitch." The daughter goes mad.

The other scene involves a young girl pushed to the brink of insanity during a rattlesnake festival by a deputy sheriff who keeps forcing his passion upon her. Sitting in his squad car, she goes over the edge. She sees a snake in his lap and with a swift slap of a straight razor she severs its head. The deputy, transformed into a fountain of blood, bleeds to death.

Despite an uninterrupted string of successful novels, Crews lives with the fear that one day the magic would be gone, that he would not be able to write another book. He calls it the "dark twirlies . . . that awful, cosmic anxiety." In a strange city, overcome by twirlies, he sometimes goes to the library and looks himself up in the card catalog for reassurance.

"Writing gets harder, not easier, as you go on," he said. "You can write fifteen books and then if you blow the sixteenth and you try the seventeenth and it dies, too, then you know. Then it's the hell with the fifteen. They don't even count any more. I'm always scared I ain't gonna be able to do it again." He might be a professor but he still loved to roll the language of south Georgia off his tongue.

Crews had just come through a critical period in his life. The crisis came when he stepped on a stage to speak to 700 university freshmen. "I was standing there, and I thought to myself, 'If I don't get out of here in about four minutes I'm going to start crying'. So I just said, 'I'm sorry', and went to my chairman. I was straight with him. I said, 'Whatever's gotta come down has gotta come down'. He was great. We worked out some time and, hell, I've taught a better quarter this year than I've taught in ten years." The doctor called it nervous exhaustion, but Crews said he was on the edge.

"I had stayed drunk for about three years. You know, I'd just get up in the morning and drink half a quart of vodka while I shaved and took a shower and then I'd just ride it. I can ride on whisky because I can control how high I am. You start to go down, and you just take a little bit, don't let it get away from you. I could drink a quart of vodka and go to a dinner party and be perfectly civil and talk and everything. Of course, if I drank bad enough, I'd get so I'd be out of control. But I've beat that shit. I've been off everything, except a little beer, for eight months now. Beginning to feel good again."

The legends of Harry Crews go on. They build and build. There was the story, for example, of the time he and a buddy were out bicycling before sunrise on a country road. A young man in a car ran them into the ditch. Harry got the license number, traced it, and bicycled over to the fellow's house. An older man came to the door. "Whoever was in that car, I want him out here on the grass," Crews demanded. The man said it was his son, asked Crews not to curse and it was stalemate. The boy would not come out.

"What we ought to do," Harry called to the younger man, "What we oughta do is get down right here in the door but because your daddy's here and because your mama's inside and I don't want them to get all upset, we'll just forget it." He started to turn away, and thought better of it. "Let me say one more thing," Crews added. "If you get to thinking about this, and change your mind, here's my name and where I live. And if you ever do this again, like we say in Bacon County, I'll see whose ass is the blackest."

Crews has a good heart, in his way, whatever the legend. He is generous with time and gentle of manner with those he perceives to be handicapped or innocent. He had a chance, several times, to turn that withering writer's vision of his on fellow south Georgian Jimmy Carter. Magazines wanted him to do a hatchet job. Crews went over to Plains, but he never would write about the Carters or about their hometown. "I just didn't want to," he said. He did not explain further, but to me, at least, it seemed he thought that Carter had earned grace by being able to spring, unscarred, from his harsh home country and to bring it high honor. He wants no part of sullying that kind of miracle.

"I'm from Bacon County, Georgia," Crews said, defining himself. "Everything about me starts there. I spring from those people. Wherever I go and whatever I do, I'm one of them." Writing *A Childhood*, dredging up all those truths about himself, the kind many people would lie about, meant risk and pain. The writing was difficult and the research did violence to his already precarious peace of mind. Ordinarily, he would not mind a little violence, of course. But he prefers the conventional kind.

TOM GRAVES

Harry Crews

I came to the world of Harry Crews through a different path than most readers. I had read his profile of actor Robert Blake in Esquire *magazine and had been profoundly disturbed by it. This was the mid-seventies, and I was a journalism student at the University of Memphis, trying to mold myself and my writing in the style of the celebrity New Journalists of the day, such as Tom Wolfe and Hunter S. Thompson. Nothing I read had prepared me for the Blake profile. Crews used his subject more as an excuse to talk about himself than anything, cutting away from Robert Blake's life to long autobiographical asides. The back and forth of the piece was almost dizzying, until I got the point that Harry saw Blake as a sort of doppelganger of himself. It was then that the logic of the piece fell into place.*

After that, I cut a wide swath through Crews's novels and magazine work. A budding writer myself, I proposed an interview with Crews to the editors of the Paris Review, who agreed to consider the finished piece. A date was set with Harry to meet at his university office in Gainesville, but at the last minute he seemingly disappeared and I was forced to cancel my flight. Another date was set in January 1979, and I decided to chance the flight when he told me his van was in the shop—he was stuck in Gainesville until it was repaired.

I caught up to Harry at his office at the University of Florida, and he seemed in particularly good spirits and ready to talk. The interview, I thought, went splendidly. I had no idea how close he was to a personal abyss,

Portions of the following interview appeared in *Southern Exposure* 7.2 (1979): 252–53; *Chouteau Review* 4.2 (1980/81): 62–78; and *Memphis Flyer*, October 22–28, 1992, 12–13.

one that would keep him from writing another novel for nearly ten years. *A Childhood* and *Blood and Grits* had just been released to great acclaim, and Harry Crews seemed well on his way to becoming a literary icon.

The Paris Review *declined the interview because, I was told, George Plimpton did not appreciate Crews's "rough" sort of fiction. Thankfully, other publications saw the value in it.*

T.G.: In your writing there has been an inordinate interest in blood and violence. You've talked about things such as cockfighting that most people would consider to be a revolting, unpleasant part of the American underbelly, something that ought to be hidden from sight and not discussed. How did you develop your interests in these kinds of subjects?

H.C.: I've always loved blood sports. Cockfighting, bullfighting, dogfighting, and the rest of it. In fact, I have a piece coming out in *Esquire* about dogfighting. But this article is no defense of it. Rather it is an effort to see whether or not we tell the truth rather than being hypocritical, hippy-dippy bullshitting jack-offs about it. Whether or not we tell the truth, so that we might be able to say something about the culture we live in, the society and country we come from, which God knows has gotta be among the more bloody countries that we know in history.

I point out that when Indian Red Lopez fought David Kotey for the featherweight championship of the world, it took thirty-seven stitches to close up Kotey's face. It took seven I think to close Indian Red Lopez's face. What's football if it's not a blood sport? You know, guys getting broken legs. Leroy Jordan played a whole goddamn season with a broken bone—a nonweightbearing bone—in the bottom half of his leg.

T.G.: Certainly during the first half of this century, baseball was considered America's favorite pastime. It now seems that football has taken over as America's favorite sport, and I'm wondering if it's because it's a more violent sport.

H.C.: I'm not really sure it has, it just seems that way. If you read and look at the figures that baseball teams and ballparks draw and television audiences and so on, you'll see that it's comparable to football. I'd be the last one to say it's because we got bloodier or because we got more violent or because we see in it a microcosm of our macrocosm of the world that we live in.

It's true, however, that when a player gets hurt on the field, the camera always pans away from him. The camera goes somewhere else, or the announcer guy says something like, "Well, we see a player is down on the thirty yard line. He doesn't seem to be moving. He's not getting up. We'll be back after this message." After you come back the player's already gone, they've toted him off the field. It's the same with baseball when two dugouts empty. When they come out with baseball bats in their hands, they always cut away from it. I don't think people like that though. They wanta see the fight. They wanta see the race driver at Sebring or wherever fry in his own car. "His back end is getting loose, he's up on the wall. He's spinning, my God, he's on fire! We'll be back after this word from our announcer." Or some bullshit thing like that. Well, yeah, uh-huh. Everybody's saying, "Aw, why couldn't you pan in on him close? See him a-squirming."

T.G.: In nearly every one of your novels there is a scene of a crowd that goes on a rampage. Do you have a fascination with crowd psychology, what we as a people do when we're in a crowd together?

H.C.: That's true. Maybe I am fascinated or appalled or dumbfounded with them. We are a crowd society. Whatever crowds do are likely to get more news coverage, whether they be riots, whether they be sit-ins, whether they be pickets at a big company. Whether they be a whole bunch of Iranian students with paper masks over their faces trying to get rid of the Shah, which, thank God, they've already done now. The sonofabitch will never get back in there again. I don't know that that holy man's going to do much better, but at least he's not going to do as bad as the Shah did. *I don't think.* This is just my own personal opinion; one might even say bias or prejudice. Whatever.

The point is that in a crowd men and women, because of a certain anonymity, because they are less likely to be identified and held responsible for their own actions, what they are, what's back there lurking, always comes out. And what comes out, coach, I'm sorry to say it—I ain't a doomsayer, I ain't pessimistic, it doesn't matter to me. Well, it does matter to me because I'm in the world with them, and I don't want to get killed or mutilated—but what comes out inevitably is just the worst kind of that thing that we all hide. We're meat eaters, that's the thing. There are vegetarians—spiritual vegetarians, emotional vegetarians, political vegetarians, and those who are vegetarians in fact—who deny that the front teeth are cutters. A human being has got in his mouth a 550 pounds per square inch bite. You don't need that kind of bite to eat asparagus. You need that kind of bite to eat meat. These are cutters and these are grinders. They pretend we are something else.

It gives me no pleasure particularly to talk about that we are not what we would seem in the world. But that we are in fact meat eaters, killers, suckers of blood, and riders of one another. But in all that, there is beauty, there is humor, there is joy, there is ecstasy. I think all my books are obviously funny, there are places in them that are funny, with the possible exception of the last one, *A Childhood*. It's not that I *meant* to put humor in there, it's just in there.

Graham Greene said that he reserved the right to depict unbelievers of the Roman Catholic faith with the same kind of power he depicted believers. Of course, that got him into a lot of trouble. By and large, people want to confirm what is weakest in them. That is, their propensity for charity, sympathy, contributions to the afflicted, smiles, happy home life. They want all that confirmed, when in point of fact that is what's weakest in them. Because it is the least substantial in them. Who's ever got close to a marriage that didn't find a rotten core, a nest of snakes at the middle of it? Okay, there's joy in it, happiness in it, and there's pleasure in raising kids that go and do something. That's cool. I'm all for that. The fact that it's a sham, the fact that it's bullshit, need not necessarily upset us too much.

They want that confirmed. As soon as you start writing about the other things, that are just as much a part of us as any of the other, when you start writing about blood and violence and the predisposition to put your foot on another man's neck and let him carry you, then everybody objects.

It takes my dear old mother as long to read a book as it does me to write one. She went through the second grade. She reads everything I write. She's never blinked at any of it. And she talks about it well. She says to me, my dear old mother, "Son, why don't you write a book that's happy and nice and full of smiles?" And I told her, "Mama, when one comes to me, I will."

T.G.: Don't you think your mother knows that what you write about is a part of her as well?

H.C.: Naw, I don't really think so. When I used to work for *Playboy* so much, she used to always get the magazines and look in them. She didn't even know such a thing as *Playboy* existed in the world 'til I started writing in it, and God only knows what went through her poor ol' dear mind when she opened the book and saw all them naked ladies in there. I bet she thought, "They touchin' theyselves, they touchin' theyselves, Godamighty they touchin' theyselves."

T.G.: In the beginning of your book *The Gypsy's Curse*, you quote Diane Arbus. The quote, "My favorite thing is to go where I've never been," seems doubly appropriate because it appears to echo your own life, and Arbus in her photographs portrayed a dying world much like the one you depict in the book. Would you agree that your outlook is similar to hers?

H.C.: I don't know. I am a great admirer of Diane Arbus, dead now, as you know, of suicide. I'm a great admirer of hers for one thing you'll notice: all of Diane Arbus's people that she photographed are looking dead into the camera. Next time you look in her book, notice that. Not looking off. Lookin' dead into the camera. Every last one of them. I know her brother, Howard Nemerov, a very fine poet.

I read her preface, which was really a kind of talk she had given to a class, and they put it posthumously as an introduction to her book of photographs, where she talked about, "My favorite thing is to go where I've never been." The real point is this: Not that I feel she and I . . . that she's one of us, although I do feel that way. But rather that business, "My favorite thing is to go where I've never been," has to do with the fact that many writers, painters, playwrights, so on—artists of whatever kind—have said that when they become American expatriates and live in Europe, you see America so much better from Paris than you do from Alma, Georgia. You see America so much better from Munich than you do from Chicago, and it's because there is the distancing of the subject. Get back so that you can see it.

Working in carnivals, living as I did with them . . . I traveled twenty-seven hundred miles with a gambler for a piece that I wrote for *Playboy*, called "Carny," being with, I don't know, what society considers outcasts or not very nice folk. Being with them, minorities of whatever sort, Chicanos, Jews, blacks, south Georgia tenant farmers, and also gamblers, pimps, prostitutes, street hustlers for smack, scag, coke, that whole sort of thing, you get a view of the world from where they are that you would never get sitting in this office in this boondoggle of a building on a multimillion-dollar university.

T.G.: There is a freak of some sort in every one of your novels except *A Feast of Snakes*. Why is this book the exception?

H.C.: If you are determined to find freaks, think of them in that way, obviously the sheriff with a peg leg shot off in the Vietnam war, is a freak. He rapes the black girl, she subsequently having all manner of hallucinations and distorted perceptions about snakes in her world. Her mother's hair is snakes. She sees snakes and all the rest of it. She then emasculates him with a razor out of her shoe. I suppose that if you are determined to think of it in terms of freaks, that's as freaky as anything I've done.

The thing people won't admit is that when somebody says the word "freak" you think of somebody with eight toes or three legs or something like that. But there are spiritual freaks, emotional freaks, political freaks, educational freaks, people who are distorted and asymmetrical. People whose equipment, whatever it may be, arms, legs, whatever, don't work the way they oughta work. I suppose that if I were of the mind to think that way about freaks, I would say that *A Feast of Snakes* is part and parcel of everything I've ever done. People dumping poor Joe Lon over the fence into the snake pit, and him surfacing like a swimmer with snakes hanging from his cheeks. I mean, if that ain't freak city, what is it? I'm saying this for *your* benefit. For the reader's benefit. I don't think about it that way.

T.G.: How do you answer the critics who charge that your work is filled with gratuitous violence and characters that are grotesque?

H.C.: I answer the charge by saying that they can't read fiction, that they don't know anything about fiction, that they don't know what fiction is. There is *nothing* gratuitous in my work. There are no descriptions of landscapes that are gratuitous, there are no descriptions of people that are gratuitous. There is nothing in my work that is not necessary and inevitable to the action, the place, and the circumstances that I'm writing about.

Faulkner once said to someone—not that I'm comparing myself to Faulkner, God forbid—but this person asked him, "Mr. Faulkner, what do you think of people who read your books and say they don't understand it?" And his response was, "Read it again." Yeah.

So, the dumbasses out there that are watching television until they are rotting in their souls, watching Walter Cronkite and *Happy Days,* who cannot read my fiction, and say that it's gratuitous, I say they have no eyes, no ears, no heart, no mouth, no sympathy, no charity for the human predicament. And they think that the human predicament and situation is living over in suburbia with a high wall around yourself and worrying about your annuities and your tax-sheltered income. That's my answer.

T.G.: What do you think of the type of violence Sam Peckinpah depicts in his films?

H.C.: All Sam Peckinpah ever did in his movies was show that getting hit on the chin doesn't sound like [*makes a small popping noise*]. When one grown man hits another grown man in the face, it splatters like an overripe tomato. And it's not fun getting killed. It's bloody and gory and altogether unpleasant. That's all Sam Peckinpah ever did.

T.G.: What about the fact that Peckinpah's violence and death are often done in slow motion, which is usually associated in the language of film with romance and eroticism? It makes one wonder if the American public is now equating death with eroticism.

H.C.: Naw, the American public isn't doing anything but worrying about its tax-sheltered incomes, as far as I'm concerned. They only know slow motion from *The Bionic Man,* where the guy is supposed to be able to run—I don't know—nine hundred miles an hour, and supposed to jump fifty feet in the air. The way the director and the producer and the writer have got around that is when he's going nine hundred miles an hour to put it in slow motion. And hippy-dippy America out there thinks, "Man, he's going *nine hundred miles an hour.* Wow!" Now why Sam Peckinpah did his thing in slow motion . . .

T.G.: Going back to *A Feast of Snakes*, have you been to the rattlesnake roundup that they have every year in Sweetwater, Texas?

H.C.: No, did not. I've been to Sweetwater, Texas, but not for the rodeo. I think it was in the Blake piece in *Esquire* where I said I was in jail in Grapevine, Texas, a couple of years ago. But I get in jails. All the time.

T.G.: From raising a lot of hell?

H.C.: Just that. Getting drunk. Whatever. It's nothing. It's nothing to get excited about. I'm not proud of it. I really am not. But, I'm not ashamed of it either.

T.G.: How did you become interested in rattlesnake rodeos like the one you depict in *A Feast of Snakes*?

H.C.: Charné, this girl who I lived with for five years, and I went to—just fucking off. I work very hard when I work and when I don't work, I don't work very hard. And she and I went to a place. I'm trying to remember the name of it. It's just down from Mystic, Georgia. There really is a Mystic, Georgia, and it was just down from there. A little town in south Georgia, just about seventy-five miles from where my people live. And we went up there to one. I went as a participant. You know, to catch snakes. And of course they had a big place there where you could eat it. You didn't have to buy it. They gave it away to the hunters, the rattlesnake meat cooked.

It's good stuff. I cook my own, though. They don't exactly have my recipe. My recipe that's in the book [*A Feast of Snakes*] I got off a guy in Mississippi. It's good firm meat if you don't overcook it. It's a little like fish; if you overcook it, the tissue breaks down. It's mush. Most people need a thermometer to cook fish or snake or meat, for that matter. But I can pretty much do it with my fingers. I can just reach in the oven and press it and know when it's about right.

T.G.: So you don't fry it?

H.C.: I fry it to begin with, then I finish up in the oven. It makes it crispier. I deep-fry it, but then I take it out of there when it's about three-quarters done, put it on a dry, flat pan and bake it, and then it gets all crispy and nice.

T.G.: Did Auntie, the old black woman you talk about in *A Childhood*, inspire your fascination with snakes?

H.C.: I don't know if she did or not. I suspect that Auntie inspired more than I'll ever know. 'Cause I was young. I'm convinced that those years up to the time you're six or seven years old, that's where you really get bent. That's where you get towards wherever you're going.

T.G.: Many of the characters in your work appear to be allegorical. For example, the Fat Man in *Naked in Garden Hills* seems to represent a person who is imprisoned within his own soul. Of course, he is literally imprisoned by his own flesh.

H.C.: The same with the Gospel Singer. The Gospel Singer was given his voice. He didn't work for it, it was a gift. His problem was, and it's as old as literature is, he did not want to be God's man in the world. He did everything he could do, possibly think of, to get rid of it. He didn't mind singing and making money, and making people happy. But he didn't want everybody's soul on his hands. Or on his conscience. Again, that's a thing that goes back about as far as we know in literature. Denying what you are, the chosen of the gods . . . that sounds like a marvelous thing to be, chosen of the gods or God. But it is not. It is a terrible responsibility. They end up hanging him on a tree limb when he tells the truth.

The simple fact is that I think of everything I do as being—I don't know quite how to say this—as violent and as despicable as many people find it, I think of it as all work, man's relationship to God, man's relationship to his own true nature, as opposed to what he bullshits people into thinking his own true nature is. Most of my work, almost all of it if you look at it, the novels anyway—well, there's nothing to write about except good and bad. That's all the reader's interested in. Who's at fault and who's not. It's all a moral question. Dylan Thomas was asked why he wrote his poetry, and he said he wrote it in praise of God, "and I would have been a fool to have done otherwise." I can't really say I've written in praise of God, but certainly the thing that preoccupies me the most is affairs of the heart, which always translates into who's right and who's wrong.

As we all know, there are no black hats and white hats in the world.

We're all wrong and we're all right. We're all mixed. But try to get people to admit it. I mean, some of our greatest saints, at least in the Roman Catholic view of things, the greatest saints were some of our greatest sinners, cheaters, fuckers of ladies, dicers, you name it. St. Paul, who was on the road to Damascus when he saw the burning bush, was a real son of a bitch. Before he got the word. Just a son of a bitch. And you don't suppose all that went out with him as soon as he saw the burning bush?

It's like courage. All courage is, is fear controlled. Everybody's scared when the heat starts coming down. You're terrified. Whether it's in a fight, whether it's some jack-off in the Marine Corps says you got to slide across a rope over boiling rapids or in a river or whatever it is. Sure, you'd be a fool not to be scared. It's the control of the fear. And when you look inside yourself and see that you are . . . well, I give you a quote. Johann Wolfgang von Goethe said, "There is no crime of which I cannot conceive myself guilty." It seems to me that he was simply a great poet admitting his involvement with mankind. But all these people that say [*in exaggerated southern accent*], "He's jest writin' about all them nasty thangs. You ought to do what Shakespeare did." The hell. What is Shakespeare all about? It's about regicide, betrayal, lopping off heads, you name it.

T.G.: You and I both were raised as Southern Baptists and rejected it when we came of age. Why do you think Southern Baptists have the reputation of being among the meanest, most prejudiced, most narrow-minded . . . ?

H.C.: I'm not sure I can subscribe to that or do. The fact [is] that they are mean in the sense of being small, their angle of vision—what they admit into their society, into their lives, into their emotions, into their charity, into their sympathy is very small.

Up where I come from, for instance—not to get into political or social matters—but the plight of the blacks has not changed one bit. They still go to the back door, they still live on whatever they can find. Black real estate, the shanties, is very valuable, because there is only a few places those folks can live. So if you've got a little shanty, and you want to charge seventy dollars a month for it, and the damn thing has no running water, no electricity, and the outhouse is in the back and got cracks two inches wide in it—you can get the seventy dollars a month, 'cause they got no damn alternative. It's not as though they can go in town and rent an apartment for seventy dollars. Right around where I come from they still got everything nicely compartmentalized. And they still run in all those old things about, "some of my best friends are . . ." or "I've always been good to them." Or whatever. I'm glad that they've got the burden of that on their hearts and not me. Because I don't know how the hell I'd deal with it.

T.G.: The people I've known who were the most racist, the most hawkish during the Vietnam War, the most conservative in the rankest sort of way, the ones most eager to trample on the Bill of Rights for their own personal agendas are nearly always Southern Baptists.

H.C.: I suspect it has to do with the God they worship. Southern Baptists, generally if you talk to them, really think they are worshipping the God of the New Testament. They aren't at all. Matter of fact, I talked to an old guy in Georgia last time I was home and he said, "I don't know what it is everybody wantin' somethin' new, new all the time. Talk about the New Test-a-ment. What's wrong with the Old Test-a-ment?" Now here was a guy never read the damn Bible—*damn* Bible . . . musn't say that . . . Jeez, forgive me—never read the Bible, he just carried it around in his hand. Southern Baptists worship the God of wrath, the God that gives to schemers, the God that benefits the strong and lets them walk on the weak. The New Testament God obviously is a God of forgiveness, and a God of love, and a God of the rest of it.

It's very curious if you really get to talking to cradle Catholics or cradle Baptists or cradle Lutherans or cradle Methodists or cradle Unitarians, or whatever, just how little they really know of their religion. They go in there, they're like a mule grinding cane. He grinds cane all day and you put him in a lot and he still walks in a circle.

There's much about myself and what I believe and what I do that I don't know. That I can't answer for. That I can't talk rationally about. I don't apologize for that. It just happens to be the way things are.

T.G.: There seems to be an awful lot of bitterness in your writing. Several critics have called this bitterness your method of revenge towards our society. For example, Paul Zimmerman in his review of *A*

Feast of Snakes in *Newsweek* says, "There is a strong smell of revenge in his writing. Behind his comic grotesquerie keens the angry cry of a man enraged that life can be so cruel, and people so victimized by the lumpen conditions of their lives."

H.C.: [*interrupts*] The last half of it I would agree with. The revenge part I would not agree with. The bitterness I would not agree with. If you say bitterness toward the people in my book, I have a feeling that you can't write about people that you are bitter toward, that you hate. I'm not bitter toward the people in my fiction. But, yes I am bitter, and I am angry that the human situation is what it is. That we out of hand destroy whole cultures, as the Indians were destroyed. As we have tried to destroy the Chicanos. That we destroyed the blacks. That we are busily still destroying them. For all our protestations to the contrary, that we are anti-Semitic. All the Jew jokes. The Chief of Staff of the Armed Forces saying the Jews control this and that not too long ago. If somebody sounds different than we sound—that is, the voice, accent—we are right on his back. "Southerners are obviously ignorant and dumb because of the way they talk." People from Brooklyn.

I think that the collective consciousness of America would make us all sound like disc jockeys if they could. All alike. You take a disc jockey out of Gainesville and put him in San Francisco, and he won't have any trouble. He's got those pear-shaped notes and those mellow tones. He wouldn't have any problem. It is that lust for standardization which will be the death of us all eventually. They would have us all sound like a disc jockey if they could.

T.G.: Why is the lead character in every one of your novels an alienated male?

H.C.: I don't know, I don't know. You see, these are questions that writers can't answer. Many times they develop convenient lies about these questions that they can tell at cocktail parties. "I did this because of this, this, and the rest of it." I think my characters are men because I have grave reservations about my ability to create a woman that could sustain a novel. That's first. That's the male part of it. The alienation part of it, I have never thought of it, I've never thought about it just in those terms. But I have, of necessity, been alien to the place I have found myself since I was very, very young. I left the farm when I was seventeen, and I have never been back there to live.

I wrote recently that I have been in the University of Florida for more or less twenty years, but I've been *in* it, never *of* it. I have no friends in the university, as we would count friends where I came from. Not one. I don't see 'em, I don't go to the places they go, I don't go to their parties. I talk to 'em in a professional capacity if we have common problems in the university. But friends, no.

I don't suppose you could imagine a more alienated human being than a south Georgia sharecropper who must move every year from one leeched-out patch of soil to another. Never owning anything. With his back continually to the wall. Other people get medical care. He gets none. Other people get oranges and grapefruit or lemon to keep from getting trench mouth or scurvy, but he has none. Other people have children who have shoes. But his have none. I mean, if he's not alienated, who the hell is? Maybe if I write about alienated male characters, maybe this alienation comes just from my own life.

T.G.: Are Marvin Molar in *The Gypsy's Curse* and Joe Lon Mackey in *A Feast of Snakes* really the same character? Extensions of the same psyche?

H.C.: They have both been trained throughout their lives to do something they thought would save them. And then they had the rug jerked out from under them. How the hell was Joe Lon supposed to know he was supposed to read? Nobody ever told him. He was supposed to run over other boys, which he did with great efficiency. And then it came up all of sudden that he wasn't able to go to college, and he had been trained for violence. Trained to run over people. Then it was all ended. What the hell was he supposed to do? That's enough to drive anybody to a breakdown or violence or murder or anything else.

T.G.: Are these characters maybe extensions of your own anger?

H.C.: I don't want to push this anger thing too far. I'm not *that* angry. The reason so much of what is said about me by so many people again gets back to the thing I told you when we first started. Most people can't write fiction. They don't know what fiction is about. They know nothing of craft. They're not readers. And they do not have the emotional capacity to put themselves into other people's shoes. Suck themselves out of their own skin and get into somebody else's skin for awhile. If they did they would be readers of fiction, supporters of plays, and readers of poetry. They are not.

I don't pay much attention to those people who say I'm alienated, bitter, or put gratuitous violence or this or that or the other. I mean, I spent thirty years learning what I do and I take gross exception to your basic female book page editor or male book page editor who is worried about everything except books. My life is reading and writing and some few things to divert me when I'm not doing that.

T.G.: Your prose style has a power and punch to it I've seen in very little other work, but obviously you've had your literary influences. Who were they?

H.C.: I don't pattern my style after anybody consciously, but obviously we stand on other people's shoulders. I probably learned more from Graham Greene, the English novelist . . . *The End of the Affair, Brighton Rock, The Power and the Glory,* and so on. His autobiography, called *A Sort of Life,* I wrote a long thing on for the *Los Angeles Times.* I learned a lot from him. My first [hero] in letters was Somerset Maugham. But then after I got to be about twenty-two, I began to understand why he was called, by certain writers, "that old whore of literature." So I got off him. Faulkner has influenced us all, on whatever continent. Flannery O'Connor. Currently the young writers that I admire: Cormac McCarthy, Richard Price, Thomas McGuane—not necessarily *Ninety-Two in the Shade,* but other things he has done. There's a whole bunch. Don't matter. When you ask somebody what books they learned on, or what writers they admire, it's like asking somebody which of their own novels they like the most.

T.G.: Who would you say are some contemporary writers that are overrated? Let's start with Norman Mailer. He gave you a nice little plug on *A Feast of Snakes.*

H.C.: Overrated? Oh, I don't know, man. Norman Mailer is a genius by anybody's accounting, but he spreads himself thin. He takes on assignments that he really shouldn't take on. Norman Mailer's willing to talk, if he's got the time, to anybody about anything. Much of it I should think—although God knows I would hope he forgives me if he sees this—because of all those wives and all those children. He has to turn about a million dollars a year before he makes a nickel himself. You know, whatever he's got, eleven or twelve kids, and three or four wives.

T.G.: What do you think about the feuds he's had with other writers?

H.C.: Like Gore Vidal? You take a book of Vidal's like his collection of short stories, *A Thirsty Evil*, is just a marvelous book. His first novel was *Williwaw*, which he wrote when he was about twenty-one and still in the service. I don't admire the things that he is best known for. I don't admire *Myron*, although I read it, I don't admire *Myra Brecken-ridge*, which I also read. The guy just about can do anything. He's a great researcher. He has a good mind. He's a journeyman of the language.

When James Agee died, his obituary was in the *Sewanee Review*. He went to prep school right outside of Sewanee at the Episcopalian high school called St. Andrews. When he died his obituary read, "He was born a prince of the language, and so he remained."

Well, I believe the same thing is true of Truman Capote. Capote's reputation rests primarily, well, almost exclusively among people who know, with his short stories. And with his short novels. Things like *Breakfast at Tiffany's*. Short things. Ever since *In Cold Blood*, beginning with *In Cold Blood*, starting with *In Cold Blood*, everything thereafter we can dismiss, I think.

T.G.: Such as those excerpts of *Answered Prayers* that have appeared in *Esquire?*

H.C.: Yeah, right. But Capote is a marvelous intellect. Has a marvelous, a most wonderful sense of perception. But he's about done for.

T.G.: It seems like he's more into that New York disco Studio 54 bullshit these days than writing.

H.C.: He's always been sort of a jet-setter. But he just about went apeshit on a radio program in New York not long ago. He started talking about suicide, and they cut him off the air. This was about eighteen months ago.

T.G.: Is this when he was having his heavy bouts with drinking?

H.C.: He's always had a drinking problem. He's had a drinking problem for twenty fucking years. I felt very sorry for him. I know it's kind of clichéd to say it, and the rest of it, but my heart went out to him because I know what it is to be locked into that kind of world. Yeah, he's a class A alcoholic. I guess he's not beating it, and don't want to beat it. You know, the whole uppers and downers kind of thing. You take five milligrams Dex to get up in the morning. You take a Valium or a Quaalude, or a bootleg Quaalude, which you can get fairly easily, which will put you to sleep. Which will give you a case of, as Terry Southern calls them, "the whips and jingles" the next morning. You know, you sleep well that night and when you wake up your fucking hands are shaking, your eyes are jumping, your spine is pogo-sticking. You get into that world where you just keep doing pills and alcohol and you get into a *bad thing*, man. That's a one-way street. Won't get you anywhere.

T.G.: Can people write stoned like that?

H.C.: You can't write that way. You can't write messed up.

T.G.: Are there any books you think of as failures in some way?

H.C.: Yeah, there are books that have already been labeled as failures in many cases. *Across the River and into the Trees,* by Hemingway, I think is a failure, also in Hemingway's case *To Have and Have Not,* which was actually three separate pieces of stuff put together—that was a failure. Faulkner's *A Fable* is a failure.

T.G.: What do you think of the Beat movement? Did Kerouac or any of those writers have any impact on your work?

H.C.: That Beat thing was just a little ripple in a very large pond. If Jack Kerouac had only been able to keep it together, hold it together. You know he died a rank conservative about a hundred and fifty miles from where we sit, in the Tampa–St. Petersburg area, living off his mother, with a John Kennedy half dollar taped in his navel?

T.G.: A what?

H.C.: A John Kennedy half dollar. He wore it all the time.

T.G.: That's a new one on me. Why did he do that?

H.C.: He admired the guy, and he was a little nuts. He was dying and he knew it. There are some writers who, apparently, never make a false move, but they are very, very far and few between. That's why a writer wants twenty or thirty titles.

T.G.: So he can be assured of having a couple of good books under his belt?

H.C.: You see, you write twenty or thirty in hopes that you will have *one*. My life is justified if I can write one good book.

T.G.: Are there any of your own books that you don't like now, looking back on them?

H.C.: My books? No, no. I like *all* my own books. I really do. I think *Naked in Garden Hills* is probably as good as I'll ever do. I know everybody takes exception to that. I like the *Snake* book. Well, what the hell, I like the *Karate* book, the *Gypsy* book. I mean what can I say?

T.G.: Out of curiosity, what has been your biggest seller?

H.C.: Far and away *The Gospel Singer* made more money than anything else.

T.G.: I know it was the first novel you published. Was it the first novel you wrote?

H.C.: It was the fifth novel I wrote. The other four were not published and will never be published simply because they were not good enough. They were finger exercises or something. *The Gospel Singer*, the *Karate* book, the *Snake* book, the book I just did, *A Childhood*, those have been the most successful, if you measure success in terms of money. And I like money just as much as anyone else. It buys you time. It buys you freedom. It buys you food. It helps the people you care about and have responsibilities to. So I ain't knocking money.

I don't guess any writer I know, I can't think of one that I know personally who measures the success of his work in terms of the money it makes. Any guy who tells you he don't like money up to a point . . . I don't mean that you have to sell your ass to get it, sell yourself to get it. But money keeps your child warm. It gives him some orange juice for breakfast, a couple of eggs, some very expensive bacon. It gives him three dollars to eat lunch on. And that night when he comes in he has a nice meat loaf, a baked chicken, or a steak or something. So, yeah, you try to raise a boy that's going to grow up with his bones right and strong and durable. You want to feed him right. You want him to sleep right. So, money's important in that way.

But in terms of the satisfaction you get from doing something or the way you feel about it, money ain't shit. Money does not count. It just simply does not. If money meant anything, then you would never become a writer anyway. You would make more money, certainly initially anyway, certainly in the first four or five or six or maybe even ten years, you could make more money if you could get some money together and get yourself a filling station. Hire a couple of guys. Pump a little gas. Lube a few cars, change some oil. You'd make more money that way.

There are obviously exceptions. Some people who have their sensibilities tuned in to the lowest common denominator the way we were taught in school. Maybe you weren't. You're younger than I am. In the multiplication of fractions you gotta find the lowest common denominator. They got their sensibilities tuned into the lowest common denominator. They write a book that an awful lot of people buy. But one has to remember that art is not democratic, it is aristocratic.

T.G.: That is exactly what the critic John Simon has said about art and language.

H.C.: Well, if we went out there and looked at a motor in a car of a certain sort, maybe somebody would look in there and say, "Gee, it's all shiny and looks impressive." But somebody else looks in there and they see what the parts do and they see what they are. They see the essential nature of the machine and the parts. And to suppose that the people who can only say, "Gee, it's shiny, it looks nice," that their opinion is equal to people who know why the damn machine does what it does, is madness.

T.G.: In *Car* you hit on our American obsession with cars, particularly here in the South. Do you think there is a kind of Cadillac American dream we all buy into?

H.C.: I think there is a kind of Cadillac dream, a kind of Cadillac conception of America. It does not exclusively belong to southerners. Stock car racing and the rest of it came out of the South because of running moonshine and because a powerful, shiny car was one thing that poor people could get ahold of. I do not mean to slur black people or mean this to be pejorative, but a black that lives in a shack because he can't go anywhere else, can't know anything else, he can get himself a great big car. Those of us in the South who were tenant farmers are the same sort of folk. I didn't learn to drive a car until I was twenty-one years old. My brother didn't learn to drive a car until he was twenty-five. We knew all about mules, but nothing about cars.

Talk about anger and the rest of it, the thing I got a case for is cars. Every man in this country has his car to eat. And we will, by God, eat it. Because Detroit is spewing them out one every so many minutes. They have taken over Detroit. Why would you have at various intersections, four gas stations on each of the four corners available? Do we need that many gas stations? The answer is no. No we don't. The pollutants in the air—you can check me on this in the statistical abstracts in the library, but I think one out of every six people in America works for the automobile industry or in a related job. The whole business of fat people who are out of shape and can't do anything, can't be, in prison terminology, "a stand-up guy," they step on that accelerator, squeal those wheels. It's not the car so much, this powerful squealing of the wheels, it's *them*. They feel that. It's all out of that enormous thing that the novel comes.

T.G.: What does the South represent to you?

H.C.: The South represents to me a place, first and foremost. People who have, in Flannery O'Connor's words, "manners." Which doesn't have to do with saying thank you, or wiping your mouth, or not sneezing on your sleeve. Manners—simply to her in the sense that she used it posthumously in a book called *Mystery and Manners*—means just the way we view the world, the way we view ourselves. The way we proceed in our day-to-day activities with other people. You have to know about the manners of your people before you can write about them. The South is about the last people, the last area of the country, who have that sort of communal manners. We are among the last people who have a certain way of talking, accents.

T.G.: Why is it that a southerner from Florida can feel a kinship with—

H.C.: [*interrupts*] 'Cause I don't come from Florida, I come from Georgia. Florida's not the South. Florida's got nothing to do with the South. There's a little panhandle up there that has to do with Alabama, that should have been given to Alabama. But Florida's not the South, not the South at all. It's almost like being in exile.

T.G.: But aren't there parts of Florida . . . ?

H.C.: Up around the panhandle. This is the watermelon-growing capital of the world right through here, but no, by and large Florida's not the South.

T.G.: Okay, your point is taken. Let's say for the sake of discussion that a person from Georgia can go to Arkansas and feel a kinship simply because he's a fellow southerner. I'm trying to get at why this is so.

H.C.: Because we are the only people in these United States that have been defeated. Had an occupying army and had tribute exacted of us. That's all. One doesn't want to be a professional southerner. One doesn't want to hash over that stuff too much. But the fact remains that the rest of the country doesn't know what it means to have the equivalent of tanks roaring through the countryside. To having tribute exacted of it.

T.G.: What do you think of the genteel South we see depicted in so many novels and plays? The kind of writing I call "granny fiction," where we have a lot of reminiscing about sitting on the front porch swing smelling the azaleas in bloom and all that stuff. Things like some of Eudora Welty's later novels.

H.C.: I happen to like Miss Welty and her work. I've met her. I met her in New York at the American Academy of Arts and Letters. And they gave me an award which came with three thousand dollars, which

I promptly blew. But I like her work, I like her stories. I don't think there's a finer story in the language than a story like "Powerhouse." How does a little old lady in a white hat who belongs to the garden club in Jackson, Mississippi, write about a black jazz band on tour? This is in "Powerhouse." How the hell does she come up with a line like, "And it was hello and good-bye and they were all down on the first note like a waterfall"? What marvelous symmetry of sentence and language and sound and image. Now her novels are quite another matter.

T.G.: Like *The Optimist's Daughter?*

H.C.: I just have to beg off here and say . . . Well, I don't like Henry James either. I always thought that was a flaw in me somehow. I've learned a lot from his prefaces, but I can't read him.

I've got a good friend named Dan Wakefield, who's one of the contributing editors at the *Atlantic Monthly,* who wrote *Going All the Way* and *Starting Over,* and Dan told me, "I'll teach you to read Henry James if you'll teach me to read Faulkner." See, he can't read the other guy. I cannot read Miss Welty's novels. I cannot. I can start and I can struggle, but I can't finish it. But that's all right. Katherine Anne Porter, that thing on Sacco and Vanzetti that she published two years ago was a goddamned embarrassment. It was garbled and badly organized. *Ship of Fools* was a big novel that was a best-seller that nobody read. But her place in American literature is safe on the basis of *Flowering Judas* and *Leaning Tower* and other collections of short stories.

T.G.: We now have the New South to deal with and in Eudora Welty's South we had the slow, genteel, well-mannered place you just talked about. But the South you depict is explosive, fast, often violent, and unpredictable. Tempers flare. Is there such a thing anymore as this slow, polite South?

H.C.: I think there probably is to some extent. I mean, I was taught to say "sir" to anybody who was older than I was, and I even say it to people who are younger than I am because I grew up saying that. I grew up not calling a man by his first name until I knew him. You just didn't do that. There is a certain restraint, a certain reticence for people who are not of our kind and of our place. There is that isolated, insular quality of the South that nobody can deny. Course, if you talk about the slow pace of the South in terms of elbows and knees and rolling eyes and shuffling along and "feets don't fail me now" kind of bullshit, then no, there is not a slow South. But anyplace where the sun shines hotter, people are going to slow down. That's just a fact.

T.G.: I'm curious—did your depiction of women such as Hard Candy in *A Feast of Snakes* or blacks such as Lummy in *A Feast of Snakes* stir up any cries from feminists or black groups?

H.C.: Nope. Nope. I don't have anything like that, don't get anything like that.

T.G.: Do you think it's because the people who read your books are perceptive enough . . . ?

H.C.: I don't know what it is. There was a time, when I figured if I got a letter from a reader—it usually comes by way of the publisher; they send it to the publisher 'cause they don't know where you live—I assumed it was a bad letter, and generally it was. But that's all changed. The specific examples you reference—Lummy and Hard Candy—no. No fem libbers, no black groups, no black people have said things. That doesn't necessarily mean they weren't thinking it.

T.G.: There are parts, particularly in *A Feast of Snakes,* where it seems to me things could pretty easily be misconstrued.

H.C.: Anything that I have written could be misconstrued.

T.G.: One thing I think you've done a splendid job of getting into is the jock mystique that is so prevalent in our culture, particularly in football. Joe Lon Mackey seems to represent a certain type of dangerous jock mentality I've seen a lot of in our society. How did you go about tackling this subject?

H.C.: Well, a writer doesn't choose a subject. A subject chooses a writer. Physical attributes, whether of strength or swiftness or stamina or whatever, is something that is measurable and seeable. We can see it, witness it, measure it. What do you do forty yards in? You can't fake that. We can put a watch on you, and if you do that in four or five or maybe in six, we can sign you up. If you don't, say if you're a seven, shit, you're nowhere. Just one second makes the difference. Most of the people with whom I am friends are athletes. I dedicated *A Feast of Snakes* to an All-American football player, Spider Jourdan. I like sweat, I like to put your ass on the line. There's so much fudging. So many lies. "To hell with it. Let's put a watch on him. Let's put a tape measure on him." You can't fudge with that.

I just admire that because a good friend of mine not long ago said, "Harry, I wish I could find just one thing in the world, just one, that I didn't have to cheat at." This is a guy that's got a Ph.D. This is a guy that's in the *Guinness Book of World Records*. A guy that's just a super stud jock. This is a guy that's married. What he's saying to me is, "I just wish there was just one *fucking* thing that I didn't have to cheat at." I understand what he was talking about. One thing that you could keep pure, one thing that you could keep untainted, and one thing that is pure and untainted is a watch on forty yards. There ain't no way you can fuck that.

T.G.: I'm surprised you haven't written a book about boxing. Of course that's a subject that's been covered by a lot of other writers, and you've covered subjects almost nobody else has. I can't think of too many other karate novels for instance. You did a number on that one. But boxing . . . I know Norman Mailer's written a lot about it, mostly nonfiction. Has it been a subject you've thought about?

H.C.: Yeah, I almost went to Zaire to cover that fight myself for *Playboy*. Mailer'd already got the job. They would've sent me if they hadn't already signed him. I don't know, man. The next two or three years are so lined out. See, I don't have any time for the next two or three years. By the time I get through with the novel I'm writing, by the time I get through the play I'm writing . . .

T.G.: Have you ever made the talk show rounds to promote your books? The reason I ask is that I've never seen you on television.

H.C.: I don't like to talk about those things. I've been on national talk shows. They've all been an unmitigated horror. If you ain't seen me already, you'll never see me, 'cause I'll never do it again. You end up talking to people who have never read your book. Whose staff prepared some questions, and they can hardly read the questions, much less understand the answers you give. West German television, which has the biggest audience—bigger than the BBC—in Europe, came here and stayed with me two weeks and made a documentary. We went back to the Okefenokee Swamp and visited houses I had lived in, in Bacon County. We went to the place I work out over at my house, which is down by a creek in some woods. You see, my work has been translated into German and into French. *Car* did pretty well over in France. For the film we also went and saw my mom and my farm and the rest of it. I've done my share of those talk shows, although I wish I hadn't done any of them. The German thing was all right. I didn't mind that.

T.G.: In your novels you use a method of enhancing your story that is something like editing techniques in movies. Like when a guy is falling off a cliff and the film cuts to another scene to enhance the emotional impact. How did you develop this technique?

H.C.: It's one of the things I worked out on my own, by watching movies. One of the things was working with editors, and one of the things was talking to my betters. People who knew more about it. It was all a hit-and-miss sort of thing. The thing that you see, the thing that the public sees, is the finished product. They don't see all the fuck-ups you made. All the blind alleys you ran up.

T.G.: Do you think your novels could catch on big with the American public some day the way Kurt Vonnegut's have?

H.C.: Of course. I'll probably be dead. Maybe my heirs will be dead. I know how vain and full of myself this sounds, but I have every confidence that my books will endure.

T.G.: Critics have said that you have one of the blackest senses of humor to be found in American literature. Do you think they are right?

H.C.: They are probably right. Forty acres and a mule will give you not only a black sense of humor, but a black view of the world. Forty acres and a mule is a bad way to go. It's been a long time since I've been there, but I remember it *all* in an incredibly graphic sort of way.

T.G.: Do you find yourself sometimes enraged at the America of today? From reading *A Childhood* and your comments on the injustice of being poor in this country, I think you are.

H.C.: Dismissing *A Childhood,* the answer is yes. Anything that man has put his hand to is flawed. There is no perfect novel, no perfect short story, no perfect plays, no perfect poems, no perfect painting, no perfect photographs. Necessarily flawed. Appreciating and being able to identify the flaws of this country is every bit as important, it seems to me, as being able to appreciate and identify the strengths.

T.G.: In *A Childhood* you say that the world that was depicted by Sears and Roebuck in the catalogs they mailed to your family was a lie. You said that there has to be scars underneath the facade of those perfect-looking models. Do you feel this is true of life in general?

H.C.: Of course. *Of course.* It was then, and it is now and always has been and always will be. Insofar as we present our best face to one another. How many marriages have you known that the man and the woman would come into parties, they were smiling to one another? They were holding hands, they were arriving in the same car. They, as they say, "maintained appearances." And then one day you hear from a friend, "Did you know that Pete and Sally's gettin' a divorce?" And you think, "No, man! Wait a minute. I didn't know that. No, you gotta be wrong. Pete and Sally came to my house and they were all huggy-bear, kissy-mouth kind of bullshit thing." [*Lowers voice.*] But no. Underneath the worms were crawling. They're eating eyeballs.

The face we present to one another is an ideal face. I'm not immune to that. None of us are. We don't want other people to know that we have failed. Failed in marriage, failed in jobs, failed in money, failed with the wherewithal to look to the future, so that we take care of our children. So that we send them to college. You made X number of dollars and ten years later you're broke, and you can't send your kid to school, and you can't take care of your wife or whatever it is. We all know that. It is our weak, misguided effort to be godlike. Everybody wants to be godlike. The family wants to be godlike. The government wants to be godlike . . . Nixon, Lyndon Johnson, "Naw, we ain't bombing Cambodia." [*Lowers voice.*] "Huh-unh. We ain't doin' thay-yat." And of course, hell, we'uz bombing them motherfuckers out of existence. "So I appear to you as a man, but I really am a god." Nobody would be courageous enough or foolish enough to say that, but that's what all of us think. "I look like a man, but I am a god. I can see through to the other side. Come to me."

Of course there are the big hucksters and shysters, shucking and jiving. Great fortunes have been built on it. "You can't see on the other side of it, but I can. So you send me, each of you, three thousand dollars and I'll take you down into Guyana there and give you all cyanide. And you will like to drink it because I'm me and you are you. And I'm different than you are." Well, no. Not really. Fucker thought he was dying of cancer. He wasn't dying of cancer. Had people run out the shacks with chicken livers and chicken gizzards, and he told people they were cancers he had taken out of other people. And on and on and on.

All very sad. All very tragic. And all very ugly enough to make a man almost murderously angry. But that's the nature of the world. I don't know about you, but the only world I know is the one I see.

KAY BONETTI

An Interview with Harry Crews

K.B.: Mr. Crews, you said that *A Childhood* was the hardest book you've ever had to write. Could you elaborate on that a little bit?

H.C.: Well, yes. I wanted very much to write the book, but I wasn't sure I could. It is first of all about people, many of whom are still alive, or their children are, and since I wanted to be true to that time and that place and that experience, I put them in the book as they were. You and I know that most people don't want to be set down as they are. They want to look better than they are. It's a perfectly human thing, but you can't do that when you're writing.

Over and above that, and probably more difficult in the writing of the book, is the fact that my childhood was a kind of nightmare. I know that everybody's tired of hearing about unhappy childhoods, but I was raised on a tenant farm, and the man I thought was my daddy was not my daddy. He was my uncle. Everything was turned six ways of Sunday. I fell into boiling water. I had infantile paralysis. I had to call all those incidents back to memory. I knew it wasn't going to be pleasant when I started, but it was a book I very much wanted to write, so I did it.

K.B.: Why do you call it "the biography of a place"?

H.C.: It has to do with the fact that we moved so much, with being tenant farmers. I've never sat down and tried to count out how many different places I lived between the time I was aware of myself—say four years old—until I left to go into the Marine Corps at seventeen. We moved practically every year, sometimes twice a year. So I had to write about the people, about that place—Bacon County, Georgia—about the fact of the lives of tenant farmers of which we were a part. You made a crop and you moved on. After harvest, sometime in late summer after the tobacco was in, we'd get the mule and wagon and load up a few sticks of furniture, a few ladder-back chairs and a bed or two and whatever, a washpot and two or three washtubs and the rest of it, and we'd move five or six miles down the road. I mean, it *is* the biography of that place, those people, and that time. Yes.

K.B.: It's also a place of the mind, isn't it?

H.C.: Well, yes, because I am told that as you are shaped in the first six, seven, ten years of your life, so you will grow. And the curious thing about human beings is they carry their past with them. We can record things in writing and remember, and I think in a very real sense you never leave your childhood. It's as though you had a sack on your back. It's always very much on your shoulders.

K.B.: How conscious were you, when you were writing, of the structure of the book? It is very beautifully structured, in the sense of Thoreau's *Walden.*

H.C.: If you're writing a thing honestly, there are plans you can make, there are outlines you can make, there are notes that you can make to yourself about your intentions. All of those things invariably change. They are reshaped and rethought. Writing is a very, very messy business. I left Georgia when I was seventeen years old to go into the Marine Corps, and I thought I was going to do the seventeen years. It turned out to be about up to my seventh birthday. So the thing was shaped as I went along. You're never quite sure which way the thing is going to go when you're working on it, and you are concerned to make a thing that has integrity, that has unity, and to some extent you are controlled, and the writing is controlled, by that narrative line that you finally discover.

It is very much a process of discovery. The best way I can tell you how that works is a thing Frost said about "Stopping by Woods." He said, "When I started out to write that poem all I had was the first line. So I wrote it down. And then I tried to write a second line in which I was consistent with the commitments I had made in the first line. And then a third line in which I was consistent with the commitments I had made in the first and second line." Well, with poetry that's very easy to see. Frost is concerned about the length of line, all his poetry scans, he was concerned about rhyme schemes and so on. So you make that commitment and you do it. You write a line with ten syllables, you write another one with ten syllables. And then you just go on till it finishes, trying to remain consistent with what you had done before. He said, "The poems I have written that pleased me most have ended in surprise and discovery." And the key word there is "discovery." In the best work, the writer is literally trying to discover something in his life—about himself, his view of the world, his understanding of what it means to be a human being and caught in this that we're all caught in. He's trying to find out exactly what he thinks, what his values are, what his priorities are.

All of my friends who are science fiction writers and detective story writers, please forgive me, but I think that if you're writing science fiction or detective stories, you can plan it all out ahead of time, make a little outline and run your characters through it, and the plot is a surprise and has all these twists, but I don't much admire that writing. I think that the stuff that is closest to blood and bone you cannot plan really, ahead of time. You've got to write a sentence down and see if it works. And if it doesn't work, you've got to scratch it out, and try another one. And you've got to do the same thing with a paragraph, and a page, and a chapter.

K.B.: You have said that *A Childhood* is your struggle to find out exactly who you are.

H.C.: The real genesis of books is a mystery. And it's every bit as much mystery to the people who write them as it is to the people who read 'em. If I may, my first novel, *The Gospel Singer*—now I'll do this quickly—the way that happened. I was much younger then, than I am now, and I happened to be up at my mother's farm to visit. I'd written four novels and never published one. I'd written a roomful of short stories and never published one. But I was working, and it was just something I did and wanted to do. Okay, Sunday morning, I'm still in the bed, and she's up and she's going to church. A very famous gospel singer was raised right around where her farm was, and he was in town, in the countryside. He comes back once a year to sing for the folks.

My mom comes into the room where I am and she says, "Get up, son. Come out here, I want you to meet this fellow." And so I got out of the bed and I'm—you know, it's early, for *me* it's early—and I got up and I walked out on the porch of this farmhouse. And here is this man standing in about five hundred dollars' worth of silk suit. And he has this very red, sensuous, erotic, obscene kind of mouth—or so I thought it was. He had on his fingers about nine rings, all catching the sunlight and flashing it back to me. And I looked at him and I thought of Christ, of Christ that he sings of, the man who rode the donkey over the palm leaves, and I thought, well, yeah, all right.

But he had with him some other gospel singers who were Native American Indians. They had their regular fringe buckskins, and they had long feathered headdresses. Standing there in a farmyard, mind you, and they're going to sing in about an hour down the road in this church. He'd brought them with him. They were real American Indians, they really were. But I happened to know that their tribe didn't have headdresses. They might have had a feather in their hair, but they didn't wear the long headdresses. That was the Plains Indians, and others, but not their tribe. But they had it.

And so, I looked out there in the yard. And when I looked, I thought, "freak." That's the word that came. "Freak." "FREAK!" But then I looked back to my mama, who will travel three hundred miles to hear what she calls all-night sings. And I looked at mama and I thought, "Well, now if they're freaks, they couldn't exist without your mama and people like her. So if you're gonna call them freaks, you gotta call your mama a freak." And I love my mama. I happen to think she's a magnificent, courageous, great woman. So there I was. I thought, "Well, your mother is the other side of this coin." I wrote *The Gospel Singer* out of that concern with trying to see both sides of the thing.

Most fiction writers, the best fiction writers, don't know what you ought to do with your life. They don't know what's right and what's wrong. They're just out there thrashing around. They have to have a rather enormous capacity for forgiveness. Your sexual preferences are not my sexual preferences, your economic preferences are not my economic preferences. You have blind spots in your character. You may be a drunk, you may be a needle freak, you may be promiscuous. Well, a fiction writer generally can get past that stuff, at least in his art he can; he has to. You are a human being, you get hungry like I get hungry, you grieve, you're depressed, you're hurt, and my heart is with you. I don't approve of everything you do, but I'm with you. I understand. I hurt too. Unless you've got that, I think the chances of being any good at writing fiction are remote.

K.B.: You say in *A Childhood* that when you had infantile paralysis that you felt like a freak. People came and stared at you. Your novels are full of folks that the world would call, for one reason or another, cripples or freaks, either psychologically or physically. Do you think that early experience is what attracted you to that sort of observation about the world?

H.C.: I don't really know. I just know that I grew up feeling that way about myself. I was the only one in the county that had that particular ailment, so far as I knew. And people did come by to see me, and I do know what it's like to have people stare at you. They can say whatever they want to say. They can say they've come to cheer you up. They can say they've come to bring flowers. They can say whatever. But you can see in their eyes that they are obscenely interested in those marvelously crooked legs that you have. They're looking. And when you're a little boy, you don't know how to deal with that. Maybe if you were grown, you'd have a greater fund of resources to call on. So I do know what it's like. And then there is something about what the world calls freaks, folks that have special consideration under the Lord. That's the way I like to think about it. They *are* special.

K.B.: The point is, you dramatize this point of view.

H.C.: If it works at all in the fiction, it works as a kind of metaphor. You and I can be as freakish as we want to in all ways except physically, and nobody'll know about it. You and I can be as kinky as we want psychologically, emotionally, all these ways that are disguisable. But if you're two and a half feet tall, and go to New York for the first time, the first person you see is going to look at you as what you are:

"My God, you're two and a half feet tall." The world gives you back a mirror that you have to deal with.

I have just an enormous sympathy for and empathy with people who have to deal with that crushing reality every minute, every hour, every day, every week, every month of their lives. It never gets finished. What makes your life and mine possible is that the problems we have, we feel will someday be over. You're in debt, you get out of debt. You've got pneumonia, you get over it. But you don't get over being two and a half feet tall.

I cannot convince anybody, of course, that I don't sit down to write a novel thinking, "Well, I have to have some freaks." I've had people say, "Hey I thought you were normal, that you were just a regular, normal, civilized person, and then I read that terrible stuff you wrote," little knowing that it is about the nature of belief and faith. Look at Flannery O'Connor's *Wise Blood.* There's Hazel Motes in there, forming the church of Jesus Christ without Christ, binding his body with wire, blinding his eyes with lye, walking around with shoes full of rock, when she herself [O'Connor] is the most orthodox, believing Roman Catholic that ever came down the pike.

What would possess her to write such a thing? Because it was by writing about that that she could *illuminate* something. It's a way to tell somebody one thing by telling them something else. A way to illuminate things. Flannery O'Connor went to Lourdes, for God's sake. As a matter of fact, she's got an essay that begins, "I am no vague believer." I mean she believed it all. And yet you look at her books, and well, how could a good Christian girl do that? Because she was an artist. Because she was trying to make *real*—make flesh and blood—those great abstract nouns: "hope" and "despair" and "anxiety" and all the rest.

The serious writer who wants to do something that has some validity has to deal with everything. What if you had something wrong below the waist, and you went to your doctor, and he said, "Yes, what can I do for you?" and you start unbuckling your belt, and he says, "Oh my God, is it below the belt? I can't look at that." Well, no, of course he's got to look at that, and look unblinkingly. And what you have to do in a book—there are three questions: What did the writer try to do? How well did he do it? Was it worth doing? Now if the answer to the last question is yes, then whatever the writer found it necessary to do is valid.

K.B.: You said something in *A Childhood* about telling good stories. First of all, you said, "Nothing is allowed to die in a society of story-telling people. All, the good and the bad, is carted up and brought along from one generation to the next. And everything that is brought along is colored and shaped by those who bring it. If so, is what they bring with them true? I'm convinced that it is. Whatever violence may be done to the letter of their collective experience, the spirit of that experience remains intact and true. It is their notion of themselves, their understanding of who they are, and it was just for this reason that I started this book because I've never been certain of who I am."

H.C.: I think that one of the problems, if you want to call it a problem, that makes fiction writers is they aren't real sure who they are. They have to slip in and out of identities, other people's skins. People think of writing as a very marvelous, very glamorous type of occupation, and it's like other jobs. There's some good things about it and some bad things. I have a nineteen-year-old boy and the last thing I'd want him to be is a fiction writer. It's too painful. All my friends who are newspaper reporters mustn't take exception to this, but newspaper writing isn't writing. You can do that and lead a happy, normal sort of life.

Being a fiction writer is a good way to go crazy, it's a good way to be a nervous wreck, it's a good way to become a drunk. You continually pick at yourself, the little sores that you have. They scab over and you pick them open again. Other people not only let them scab over, they let them scar over. They leave it alone. Writers don't do that. They can't keep their fingers out of the sore. They've got to keep it bleeding. And it's off that blood that they make their stuff.

K.B.: You also said, "it was always the women who scared me. The stories that women told and that men told were full of violence, sickness, and death, but it was the women whose stories were unrelieved by humor, and filled with apocalyptic vision. No matter how awful the stories were that the men told, they were always funny. The men's stories were stories of character, rather than of circumstance, and they always knew the people the stories were about. But women would repeat stories about folks they did not know, and they'd never seen, and consequently without character counting for anything, the stories were as stark and cold as legend or myth." Care to comment?

H.C.: I'm not sure I can say it any better than I said it there. It was just my experience in the Georgia I came from, the tenant farms I came from. We didn't have electricity—no radio, no television. Consequently, uncles and aunts and brothers, sisters, cousins, we'd all be around the fire every night. And when women started to talk, I always heard it with a sinking of the heart. Women scared me. They always seemed to talk about such dreadful things, and it was always a step removed.

The men would say, you know, "Remember when we went down to the creek with Ernie?"

And, "Yeah, whatever happened to Ernie?"

"He's over in Blackshear. He's dipping turpentine."

And you know this is Ernie. They know Ernie, and they start talking about him. Ernie becomes very human and very real.

Women, on the other hand, would say something like, "Did you hear about that woman who came into the shop over there in Waycross?"

And then one of them would say, "Yeah, I heard of that."

And then they would spin this thing which had its point of departure from the woman coming into the place at Waycross, and then it would just get horrific.

Women, maybe because they are closer to the process of birth, are therefore closer to the process of death. Women's vision of the world is so much harder, closer to the way things really are, than men's. Man set against a woman is a pretty weak stick. Despite all the macho stuff and fighting and brawling and falling down the street, women are the strong people. Men are not quite so strong, so their stories are full of humor. A woman will tell you truth. A woman will look you in the eye and tell you how it is. I can remember something Margaret Mead said. She said that women are committed to motherhood in every cell and fiber of their being. Men have to *learn* to be fathers. And obviously some of us learn it poorly.

K.B.: You said that men and women are different. You also said that they can't be equal. I think the feminist response to that would be equality doesn't have anything to do with difference or sameness, but in fact biologically, we are both male and female. William Carlos Williams said that the female principle of the world "is my only appeal in the extremity to which I have come." Do you buy that? Do you see the female side of yourself being the writer Harry Crews?

H.C.: I understand your statement that we are both male and female. We have both of that in us. But no, I don't think of myself as the female side of me doing what I am doing. It is true that I love the direct statement, the direct way of looking at a thing. I can live real well in my life with a "no." I can't live with a "maybe." I want you to tell me just the bottom-line worst thing. I want no sham, no gimmick. The truth hurts, but I'd rather be hurt by knowing it than not knowing it.

Men are able apparently to deal with small pains, like a headache or an aching ankle without complaining about it, better than women, or are more disposed to do it than women are. But women deal with profound hurts better than men do. I mean, when the stuff is really on the line, it's the women who stand up to it. Most men spend the first half-century of their lives—if they're privileged to live that long—they spend the first half-century of their lives finding wherein real manhood lies; better said, humanhood. Where humanhood lies. It's all right to be stand-up and uncomplaining and stoic, and those other things. There's nothing wrong with them, unless they begin to distort and warp, *as they do.*

K.B.: When do you write?

H.C.: In the morning. I try to write when I'm rested, and do everything else when I'm tired. For instance, when I was married, I tried to be a husband when I was tired. I got up in the morning and exhausted myself at writing, and [then] I took care of being a husband, I took care of whatever job I had to have to feed my family while I was trying to teach myself to be a writer. If I get up every morning and write for three hours, just three hours a morning, if I do that, no matter what happens to me, I feel good about myself.

K.B.: When do you revise?

H.C.: Once I get a draft of something, once I get the page filled up, I can work eighteen hours at a stretch. When I said work three hours a morning, three hours on a first composition is about as long as I *can* work. After three hours, I feel like somebody's been beating me over the head with a baseball bat. It's as far as I can go. I revise in about the same way, but don't stop after three hours. I mean, after all, it's there in front of you. You can noodle it around, try this, try that, take it out, put it back in, extend it, delete it. Sometimes I work all day and into the night with something like that.

K.B.: You mentioned in *A Childhood* that you and your friend Willalee and his sister would take out the Sears and Roebuck catalog and make up stories about all those fancy, perfect-looking people. Did that just carry on in adulthood?

H.C.: I think so. I think so. It's a natural extension of that exercise. We were way out there in the country, eighteen miles to the nearest farm, and the only book that we had access to besides the Bible was the Sears and Roebuck catalog. We'd look in there at all those people—those models, and mannequins, whatever—and make up stories about them. This is that guy's daughter, and that's his wife, and then you turn back to the lady in the lingerie, and this is his aunt, and the aunt did this. We'd make up histories for these people. And if a fiction writer does anything, that's what he is busily doing, spinning out of more or less whole cloth histories of lives: why somebody did this, in this place in this time, and what the person most cares about in the world, what he wants, what he's willing to give up to get it.

K.B.: When did you come into consciousness about this thing you were doing, this spinning tales and writing stuff down, that this was writing, and that there were other people in the world who did this?

H.C.: Not for the longest time. I was about sixteen before I first came to any real notion of writers as living, breathing human beings. I had read some novels by a man named Frank Slaughter, who lives over there in Jacksonville. I was in Georgia, about a hundred and ten miles from Jacksonville. I hitchhiked there. And I looked up Frank Slaughter's name in the phone book. And it was *in* the phone book, curiously enough. And I dialed the number and I spoke to his wife, a kindly, generous lady. I told her who I was and that I wanted to speak to Mr. Slaughter, or see him, that's what I wanted to do. I wanted to see him.

And she said, "Well, I'm sure Frank'll talk to you, but you'll have to call back. He's at the barbershop. He's gettin' a haircut."

And I said, "Well, thank you, ma'am," and I hung up.

And I never did go to see him. I went back in the street and put my thumb in the street. Because the notion that a writer had to get a haircut! I mean, writers don't get haircuts. They don't have to deal with everything the rest of us do, do they? Really? I just couldn't put together my own love of literature—the mystery, the overwhelming, profound grandness of literature—with going to the barbershop and getting your hair cut. I thought, if the man's getting his hair cut, he can't be the man I want to talk to. It just threw everything I thought about writing out the window, and I went back home.

K.B.: Well, when did you decide this was a thing you were to do?

H.C.: I never considered anything else. It's the only thing I ever cared about. It's the thing I've worked hardest at, most consistently at.

K.B.: Even when you were a kid?

H.C.: The need to fantasize has always been with me. I have a publisher, Harper and Row, at the moment. But I'm a free-lance writer. Nobody has guaranteed to publish anything I write. I write it, and I send it up, and if they want it, they publish it. If they don't, they say, "I'm sorry, go away." I really believe that if I never published another book, I would continue to write them as long as God sees fit to leave me here. It's just a need to do it. I don't even think that I'm more maladjusted than anybody else. I think I get along all right in the world. I get up in the morning and take care of things. But it's just something I need to do, and that I find rewarding to do. I don't like to write, I don't know any writer who does. In the moment, it's a painful, frustrating process. But after it's done, when you look at the thing, and it's finished, and you think, "Before me, this was not. Because of me, this is." It's as close as a man can get to knowing what it feels like to have a baby. Up to, including, postpartum depression.

A guy who was writing a book just recently wrote to me and he said, "I'm writing to all writers I can find and asking them, when you finish a book, how do you celebrate? Do you have an expensive meal, or let yourself have some of your favorite wine, or how do you treat yourself?" And my response, genuinely, was that when I finish a novel or a story, when I finish a thing, I go into just the deepest, bloodiest, bluest kind of funk. And the only way I can get out of it is start to work again on something else. When I finish it, I'm glad it's done. But the farthest thing from my mind is celebration. The thing uppermost in my mind is staying alive.

K.B.: And this is the Harry Crews who doesn't think it's the female part of him that writes books.

H.C.: All right, well, maybe you've got me there.

K.B.: Why'd you go to school? Did you go in the Marines so that you could go to school when you got out?

H.C.: No, I went in the Marine Corps because at seventeen I didn't know how to do anything, and there were too many mouths to feed already. There was no work in the county, and it was a way to stay alive. So I went down to the post office in Waycross, and there was a Marine recruiter there and he was glad to have me. He shook my hand and signed me up. I wrote the whole time I was in the Marine Corps, stories and things.

K.B.: How'd you do that?

H.C.: Well, you just get on your footlocker at night and get yourself a tablet and start writing. I mean, I wasn't publishing anything, you understand, but I was writing like a house afire. But I knew how dumb I was, how unlearned, and how much work I still had to do. It was during the Korean War, and I had the G.I. bill, so—I didn't go to the university because I thought somebody'd teach me how to write. I knew that wasn't true. I went there because it was a place to be for four years, and I would get money from the government. It was a way to eat, have a roof over my head. I wasn't married, I didn't have any responsibilities, and so I really went to school in order to write. As spotty an education as I had, I thought going to college was about the easiest thing I ever did. I mean, you go to class, you write the hippy-dippy stuff they have you write, and you know, you make the grades and—do it. And the rest of the time you got to yourself.

K.B.: What about teaching? Is it something that you enjoy, or is it just something you do to get by so you can write?

H.C.: I got into teaching by accident, and I like it. I think it's a marvelous way to spend your life. Association with young people has a tendency to keep you going, particularly the way college students are these days. College students these days will run you up a tree. They are questioning, in some instances, almost belligerent. But they'll keep you honest. And I need a certain order in my life. Truthfully, I had planned to quit teaching when I was forty, which was almost seven years ago. I thought, "By then you'll be old enough that you can just write, and you won't need this stabilizing influence in your life." But a couple of days a week, I have to be somewhere. That means on that day I have to get up and take a shower and shave and put on my clothes and look decent, or decent enough to pass, and go do my job. It's a way of maintaining.

K.B.: You're unusual in that you publish in a market that's pretty scanty, anymore, hard to crack into: *Esquire*, *Playboy*. Did you get into that easily? Did you seek it out?

H.C.: No, I did not seek it out. I wrote four or five novels, and the people at *Playboy* had read the books, in some instances reviewed them in the magazine. One day, they called me from Chicago and asked me how I'd like to go to Alaska, to cover the boomtown at the southern terminus of the pipeline and to cover the building of the pipeline. Well, I'd never been before, and it seemed a long way to go from Florida, but I said, "Sure. I'll go." And that's the way it started. I went, and I did the job, and they liked what I did.

K.B.: Has it ever struck you that one reason, perhaps, that you're misread is that a magazine like *Playboy* is publishing you for the wrong reasons?

H.C.: Maybe. Maybe. This will sound presumptuous and immodest, but I have great faith in my work. If it's misread now, all right, so be it. I mean, it is what it is. I believe the work'll hold up. And whether it's published in *Playboy* or *Harper's*—the journal doesn't make your writing good or bad, the *writing* makes your writing good or bad. I don't worry about that stuff. I refuse to let myself think about it. It's like a book being made into a movie. People say, "Aren't you concerned about what they'll do to your book?" And my reaction has always been, "They can't do anything to my book. My book's in the library. They can't touch it."

K.B.: Do you always finish the books you begin, or do you ever abandon things?

H.C.: I am not much given to abandoning things, because I have learned that in the middle of most things that you write, they look impossible. You think, "Oh, my God, this is no good, it's not gonna work, I can't finish it." But those things that you felt most hopeless about many times turned out to be your best work. So I would prefer to go on through with it and gut it out to the end and do the best thing I can by it. Then if it's a failure, ditch it. Now I've done *that* song. In the last eight years, I've written three novels that I never even sent off. I mean, up to and including getting them typed up. Because ultimately I saw that even if I *could* get them published, I didn't want my name on them.

K.B.: What did you do with them?

H.C.: I've got them. If I had any courage, I'd burn them. The first novel I published was the fifth one I wrote, and the first four never were published simply because they weren't good enough. I still have those things in the file. God, that oughta be burned. My God, they're embarrassing. But I was young, I was just trying to find my way. The second one's better than the first one; the third one's better than the first two, and, you know, you can see it coming. It's getting a little better and a little better, but they're still pretty bad.

K.B.: Who are some of the writers you read?

H.C.: Graham Greene, who is still turning out about a book a year. I think he now has thirty-five titles, thirty-five books. I've read everything he's written, all the essays, all the critical pieces, all the novels, the plays. I've read all of Somerset Maugham, I've read all of Faulkner, I've read all of Flannery O'Connor, I've read all of Eudora Welty. I think that John Updike is a much better novelist than anybody gives him credit for being. Most of the people in the business like to look down their nose from time to time at John Updike; I think he's very fine. I was just reading a collected book of stories of his called *Problems*. I've got it by my bed at home. I think he's very fine.

K.B.: He's one that Norman Mailer mentions every once in a while in his weak moments.

H.C.: Mailer is what I love in a writer. He's willing to take a risk, to take enormous risks. And when you take enormous risks, you're going to fall sometimes. But I read Mailer, I have read him. And Erskine Caldwell is a much, much finer story writer and fiction writer than almost anybody gives him credit for being.

K.B.: Why do you read?

H.C.: I guess I do it for the same reason I write: I like to do it. It must give me something back or I wouldn't be doing it. I've always thought if I were so unfortunate as to get locked up forever, I think I could do time pretty easy if they'd let me have some books. Just get up there in that cell and read all the time. Things have come down in my life that are pretty terrible, and if I can get myself a book, man, I can get past it. I can get past anything if I've got something to read. I've been reading all my life. As a matter of fact, people who do not read, I feel this great sympathy for them. I want to go up and hug them and say, "Don't you, darlin', realize what you're missing? Why aren't you reading?"

K.B.: When did you start reading, then? In the school system?

H.C.: Yeah, in the school system and whatever I could find. And the more stuff I could find, the more I read.

K.B.: Did your mother encourage you?

H.C.: No, not really. Nobody in my family ever finished high school, much less went to college. As a matter of fact, the first book my ma ever read, by her own admission, is the first book I wrote. And it takes her about as long to read a book as it does me to write one. She reads very slow. She's a good reader, though. She's not stupid; she's a bright, quick person. She's just never been to school. Got a good mind, a good, analytic mind, really. And a great heart, which is always a bonus if you can have that in fiction.

Early on when I was writing and starving, couldn't sell anything, and didn't have a job, didn't *want* a job, I remember my ma tried to get me to take a job in a filling station. She wanted me to start pumping gas. She said, "Son, you could pay into your social security. You're not doing anything."

And when I sold my first novel, I called her and said, "Ma, I sold a book."

She said, "You mean one of them made-up books, like you make up?"

And she said, "You mean you made it up, and they taken it and give you money for it?" And my mother to this very day does not understand why somebody would give you good money for something that was made up.

As John Updike said when he accepted the National Book Award, "Fiction is a tissue of lies that's truer than anything that ever happened." Yeah, the nuts and bolts in there may not be the truth, but the truth of the heart, again, those great abstract nouns, "hope" and "despair" and "love" and "ambition," and all the rest of it. Those are the only things that are worth considering anyway, aren't they?

RODNEY ELROD

The Freedom to Act:
An Interview with Harry Crews

R.E.: What do you think is the most important quality a writer can have?

H.C.: Well, it will sound simplistic, but the desire to tell stories. When I say desire, I mean that it is a necessary quality of your life. That you are compelled to do it and can do nothing else. If that is in place, then all the other necessary shit—craft, subject, and the rest of it—will come to you. First the compulsion.

R.E.: As a writer and teacher, can you characterize the writing of the generation that followed you? Are there any trends?

H.C.: The unfortunate trend is to write science fiction when they have no qualifications for it. The really good science fiction writers—Bradbury, Asimov, and others—knew a great deal about science and could make it at least interesting and credible; but most people writing now have nothing but a floundering notion of science and science fiction that they got, unfortunately, from the movies. Their writing is characterized not by a literary heritage but by an electronic heritage, and you can see it in their writing. Reading the work that many of them begin doing before I can convince them it's bullshit, reading that stuff will give you wooden ears.

R.E.: Do you think storytelling is disappearing because of that electronic influence?

H.C.: No. I don't think it is disappearing, but it has changed radically. Much of what is published today is terrible, terrible stuff. I just read a Barthelme story in the *New Yorker*. It was just a terrible story. The crap he gets away with. All of the so-called postmodernist stuff, not all of it but most of it, is just dreadful. Look at the five or six novels of the black writer Ishmael Reed, which is that postmodernist stuff, and most of it is on the level of a sitcom intelligence, like television. On the other hand, the strong storytelling sense is still there. It's not disappearing. This is just a bad time we're going through.

R.E.: What importance do you place on the title of a novel?

H.C.: I fool around with titles a lot. That doesn't make me unique. Hemingway wrote out pages and pages of titles. By and large I like short titles, though *Naked in Garden Hills* is long and *Karate Is a Thing of the Spirit* is long. Mainly, though, I like short titles: *Car, The Gypsy's Curse, A Childhood, The Gospel Singer*. I think *Naked in Garden Hills* works well with the theme of the novel. I think the reader, once the novel is read, ought to be able to see where the title came from and where it fits.

R.E.: Your titles all seem to have a certain rhythm to them.

H.C.: Rhythm is the name of the game for me. I like language, and I like the sound of it in my ears and on my tongue. When I'm writing, if a sentence doesn't want to have that kind of rhythm, doesn't want to feel like it's moving, undulating, I just change the damn sentence till I get it where it does.

R.E.: Traditionally, young writers have started with the short story and graduated to the novel, as you yourself did. Do you think this will continue?

H.C.: Yes. The short story, although there are precious few places to publish them now, is sort of a training ground for young writers. It's more intense, more compact. There is much less room for mistakes.

R.E.: Are there any obvious dangers that you would warn a young writer against?

H.C.: Only this. Getting stuck under the influence of somebody else's writing. Everybody was in the beginning tremendously influenced by somebody else's writing. There is nothing wrong with that. After all, a master carpenter didn't get to be a master carpenter by just walking out of the woods. But at some point, you have to make that break and do your own work.

Mr. Andrew Lytle, the great southern critic and writer, always said that if an apprentice were any good, he would end up by attacking his master. Now I've never attacked Mr. Lytle in any sense, but I've known for a long time that he wasn't nearly the fiction writer that I once thought he was. His great book, his best book, *The Velvet Horn*, is incredibly flawed by the dialect, which is so fucking strong you have to work to figure out what the hell he is talking about.

R.E.: He's probably talking about what Hemingway did to Sherwood Anderson with *Torrents of Spring* and what he did to Gertrude Stein and what Faulkner did to Anderson.

H.C.: Exactly. But what is the point in that? I ain't knocking Hemingway or anything and don't want to appear holier-than-thou, but those people seem to feel it necessary to say, "Nobody ever helped me or influenced me, I was a genius when I was born," or some shit like that, which is a stone fucking lie and they know it. It's a species of insecurity to feel it necessary to attack someone. That's what prompted Hemingway to say he was going to knock Turgenev off, or, in the initial version of "Snows of Kilimanjaro," to put Fitzgerald right in there, saying, "Poor old Fitzgerald." Why the fuck do that? Fitzgerald never did anything to him. Never had an unkind word for him.

R.E.: Do you think it's true that all writers are congenital liars, as Faulkner said?

H.C.: Oh, yes. I think the business of being a fabulist—that is, to be involved with fabrication and making things up and living in the world of the imagination—all that spills over into lying even when you don't have to lie, just because you want to tell something that is memorable and compelling. In your own mind, this isn't what happened to me at Daytona Beach, but this is the way it should have happened. You tell it, and it's a great story. It's not true to the facts of the matter, but very true to the spirit of what happened—truer in spirit than the facts are. When you give someone the spirit of the thing, that's better than the facts.

R.E.: Are your books made up?

H.C.: Damn straight. If I didn't have invention and the balls to invent, to let an outrageous thing happen and then make it work in the fiction, I wouldn't be the writer I am. By "outrageous," I don't mean outrageous in the normal sense of the word; you have to let characters be people and give them the freedom to act like people.

R.E.: So you don't do research for any of your novels?

H.C.: Not a bit. It's hard enough making the damn things up without doing research, too. Though for the *Childhood* book I did go back to Georgia. I took my boy with me, and we rode around Bacon County in my van, talking to farmers. I spent hours and hours with a tape recorder listening to my mom talk about my daddy and how things were back then, but after that the book had to come out of how I felt about it all.

The *Karate* book is based on research that I didn't know was research. I was in karate with no notion of writing about it, but at some point I hurt my knees and quit. I had all this body of knowledge that I later used to inform the novel.

R.E.: Why do you think writers like Pynchon, Salinger, and Faulkner go into hiding for so long?

H.C.: This may sound a little hippy-dippy, but all writers of any significance are tremendously sensitive. That is to say, sensitive to criticism, to social pressures, and I think that the people you mentioned do that, though none of them would admit it, because they recognize their own intense vulnerability, which they can't deal with out there, so they hide.

R.E.: Have you had a purpose in mind while writing your fiction? Have you tried to do anything with it?

H.C.: I can't go very far in explaining this—not that I would want to—but it seems to me that all my books have dealt with the nature and quality of belief. Belief is normally associated with matters religious, but there are other beliefs. Belt believes in the salvation of karate. Easy Mack, in *Car*, believes in the American automobile. The people of Enigma, Georgia, believe in the Gospel Singer. The nature and quality of belief, that is the thing that has been with me since I was a little boy. I suspect that's because of my experiences in the Baptist church and the great fear that was instilled in me about the nature of God and his wrath/love, which as it was given to me were the same things.

R.E.: The impact of contemporary literature on our culture remains small. Do you ever wish you had given your energy and talent to something that might have had a more immediate effect?

H.C.: No. I don't think novels cause anything much to happen that can be calculated or measured or most generally seen. The changes that a novel, a good novel, makes are in the individual who reads it, in his psyche, in his notion of despair, honor, anxiety, or whatever. You can't write a novel demonstrating what this society has done to the black man or the Indian and have it change anything. The people who believe that are jacking themselves off. I don't write for that reason.

R.E.: Why do you write?

H.C.: Because I'm good at it and it gives me enormous satisfaction, not in writing, but after it's done; and finally, for whatever reason, from an early age, it seemed to be the thing that gave me some sense of release. It always seemed like the thing to do, so I did it.

R.E.: Are there more Harry Crews novels to come?

H.C.: I sure hope so. As you know, I'm involved with movie work right now, and I guess I won't fool with novels again until I finish that business; but once I get done with the contracts already formed or being formed, I intend to leave that stuff alone for the rest of my life. It does not give me the satisfaction that writing novels does.

R.E.: How seriously do you take movies?

H.C.: I take them seriously in that it's a legitimate form, but I don't take all movies seriously. Movies can be fantastic experiences, but if one out of twenty or one out of forty is worth a shit, then you're lucky. Writing screenplays after writing novels doesn't really seem like writing to me at all. And besides, I find the tendency for more and more science fiction movies appalling.

R.E.: You said you were going to get away from movie work. What about journalism? Do you anticipate staying with that?

H.C.: I don't think so. In a little while, the necessity to make a lot of money, which I don't care about one way or the other, will pass. I don't write novels for the money and, matter of fact, I'm beginning to feel a little foolish at my age going around asking people questions. I always felt a little foolish, but now the fun has worn off. I hate it. I'm gone back to novels. I want twenty titles.

R.E.: You are a man of few possessions. Why do you think that at this point in your life you don't have a home and . . .

H.C.: I don't have anything. Say it right. I think that's because I move a great deal. I like to keep on the move. I like to have things in my life such that if I need to move across town or across country I can be ready in fifteen minutes. I had possessions once. I mean, I had them up around my fucking neck. I thought and felt that I was not in control, that they owned me. After all, if you have a house and a car and nine jillion pieces of furniture, you're not mobile. You're not anything. You're stuck. Some people will say it's a great way to be stuck, and maybe it is for them, but the notion of having a bunch of shit that I have to stay around and take care of doesn't wear well with me.

R.E.: Most writers whom I know try to stay out of the university and teach only as a last resort, but you like teaching. Why?

H.C.: I teach because I like it. It gives me some sense of myself when my writing's not going well. I can go and teach and that's pleasant. The only problem I've ever had with the university is the professors and the people who run it. I try as best I can to stay out of their way. But you're close to great libraries, close to great ideas; you have time to read, time to write. And when you hit a slack period in your work, you don't have to stay drunk all the time or chase women all the time. You can go to the university and truck around up there and do your job. I've got a good job and try to do the best I can. Those students pay good money to sit in my class.

R.E.: Do you regret that most writing now is coming out of the university?

H.C.: I don't think it makes any fucking difference where a writer is. Whether he is in prison or the university. Some of the best writing we have was done while a guy was starving in a room. Do I think that's good? No. But I don't think it's bad either. A writer is going to do the work that is in him to do, and the notion that the rarified, pristine atmosphere of the university is somehow going to destroy him is wrong.

R.E.: To what extent can you teach someone how to write?

H.C.: Only to the extent that you can be a reader for them and try to get them to see what it is that they have done, and see wherein what they have done is not effective. If it's effective, you say you like it and it's a great thing, but you can't dwell on that too much. Mr. Lytle has done that with me. All my editors have done it. They don't talk about the good shit. They may give you a passing line. "Okay, son. It's a good thing." But that's all.

That's what happened to me when I took the *Childhood* book to New York. For three days I talked not only to my editor but to the publisher, the guy who ran the house. He admired my work and liked me and everything else, but he said the book wasn't right. And it wasn't. They were right, and I was wrong. I brought it home under my arm and fixed it, but it took three days of talking to convince me that what I had done was not effective.

That's all you can do when you teach writing. You can only show them how what they've done is not effective.

R.E.: Do you think times are as good for young novelists now as they were when you came up?

H.C.: The publishing industry will tell you otherwise, but I think the times are better for young novelists than they have ever been. Markets are everywhere, and even in the economic mess we are in now, the publishing houses in New York are rabid for good novels. The work has got to be good, but if it's good, there is no problem getting published.

R.E.: I recently read Erskine Caldwell's autobiography. It seems that on many of his books, he wrote one draft in longhand, then typed up a clean, revised copy, and that was it. Have any of your books come that easily?

H.C.: Well, when you stop and think that *Car* took, from the moment I started working on it till the time I sent it off, about six weeks, you realize that doesn't leave much time for revision. It was sort of given. And the same thing is true of *Naked in Garden Hills,* my second book. Almost nothing was changed from the first draft. Those were the two easiest books for me to write.

R.E.: What about your first novel, *The Gospel Singer?*

H.C.: No, fuck no. That went through different beginnings and endings and everything else. I lived and struggled with that book forever. I was fortunate to have another writer who was reading for me and talking to me about what I was doing. He kept me from sending off a bunch of shit I shouldn't have; and when I sold the book, I had an editor who was willing to spend as much time as necessary to help me get it right.

R.E.: What has been the most difficult book for you to write?

H.C.: Without question the *Childhood* book. I was writing about people who had lived and many of whom are still alive, including my mother. I wanted to tell the truth on one level, talking about the spirit of the thing, but I also wanted to be factual. Many of the facts were terribly unlovely—worse than that, ugly—and I didn't want to unnecessarily pain any of those people. That book hurt me the worst. It burnt me bad. I have never been quite right since I wrote that book. I thought it would take me four or five years to get over it. I never was so glad to turn loose of anything in my whole life.

R.E.: You've said to me in conversation that you felt every young writer should have at least one writer whom he knows extremely well, from top to bottom.

H.C.: Yes, I do. I think you should read all the stories, all the novels, letters, biographies, and articles. You get a sense of the whole creative life. You see how someone else managed what you yourself are trying to do. And if you're honest in your work and let the shit come out the way it ought to come out—though you might not know the direction in which you are going—after five or six years of work, you'll see what your subject is. You'll see a certain direction. It'll have a certain smell and a certain taste and a certain subject matter.

R.E.: I have a friend who is thirty-three and has been writing hard for ten years and still doesn't have a place or subject that he feels is his own. This is puzzling to him.

H.C.: It probably ought to be. That, it seems to me, is a man who hasn't had the courage to examine his own life: who he is, where he came from, and what it all means to him. One of the things that prevents people from becoming writers is the inability to look at their lives and look at what they believe. They can't look at themselves honestly and say, "Okay, that's how it is." Society makes it damn near necessary to disguise yourself. To appear "normal." To appear like everybody else. For good or bad, I've never given a shit. Whatever people think of me is fine. I made peace with that a long time ago and realized that I'm not gon' be like most people, not gon' be what most people called decent. I'm not like most people, and I don't act like most people. I can live with that just fine and always have, but most people can't.

R.E.: What are your reading habits?

H.C.: I don't follow any particular writers. I read a lot of writers I've never heard of. Books that are sent to me and stuff I pick up off the shelf cold.

I think as writers grow older, they read less and less. They read like a house afire for fifteen or twenty years, then it begins to slack off. There was a time when, if I started reading a novel, it could be the worst thing in the world and I'd read it on through. Now I'll give a novel thirty or forty pages, and if the damn thing isn't working, I say to hell with it. I drop it.

R.E.: Do you associate with other writers much?

H.C.: Not much. I go to certain places—conferences, universities, and the like—for no other reason than there are writers there whom I know and admire, and I like to spend a few days with them. But to my mind, hanging out with five or six other writers all the time can be a shitty experience. The reason being that writers have such enormous egos that they are hard to deal with on a day-to-day basis. For that reason I've never understood how good, publishing writers are married to each other. I don't see how they make it, and by and large they don't.

R.E.: Do you think it is possible for a writer to live a normal life, complete with wife and family and still write meaningful fiction?

H.C.: Yes, I think it's possible. I have to think it is possible because people such as Cheever have done it. Updike did it until he finally got divorced, but only after a long marriage and when his kids were up and grown.

I think it's possible, but highly unlikely. Of course, it's highly unlikely that anybody's going to stay married, but I think the nervous energy and preoccupation with what you are doing is such in writing that you have very little time to give to anyone else. Inevitably, women become—I'm speaking here of women, though if it were a woman writer I suppose it would be true of a man—women become jealous of the typewriter. All the hours and distracted moments that you give to the typewriter can't be given to her. A writer needs time, and when he needs it, it doesn't matter if the kids are sick or you're supposed to have dinner with her mother. Fuck it! You ain't going! That doesn't set well with wives.

R.E.: You said in *A Childhood* that you knew from an early age that you wanted to be a writer above all else. Now that you are forty-seven and recognized as one of America's best writers, has it all been worth it? Has it been what you thought it would be?

H.C.: It's never what you thought it would be because before you've published a novel, you think it is going to change your life and change it significantly. That it's going to lead to some sort of salvation. That it's going to make you happy. It doesn't do that. Looking back over the shambles of my personal life, I can't say it's all been worth it. I have paid a lot. Everything I've owned or loved. I looked around one day, and I had made it; but I hadn't brought anything or anybody with me. That's a question I can't answer. I don't suppose any man could.

R.E.: How would you respond to statements by your peers in Gainesville that you once had a great mind and a great talent but have destroyed them both with alcohol?

H.C.: Number one, I don't have any peers in Gainesville. I think you're talking about those guys at the university by and large, but those guys are professors, not writers. But my answer to them would be that they are wrong. Wimps always think that things are destroyed. Wimps see a little blood and bone, and they think the game is over. They don't know you can go out and get taped up real good and shoot up with a little dope and get back in and hit somebody. No, they're wrong. I'm a long ways from finished.

R.E.: Do you think that in your work you have emphasized the blood and bone and pain and chaos at the expense of beauty, peace, and serenity?

H.C.: Not at the expense of it because I think that blood, bone, mutilation, and being in extremis is wherein beauty, peace, and serenity lie, or that it is out of such things that beauty, peace, and serenity come. I've never learned a damn thing from peaceful or good things. I never have. But a writer or somebody who creates things stays in such things at his own risk and expense, because a creative life is not quiet and peaceful and serene. It is often chaotic and ugly.

R.E.: A man who will sit on a bar stool and drink three triple vodkas in fifteen minutes seems to be making a statement of some kind.

H.C.: Damn straight. And that statement is that I'm looking for oblivion. For different reasons at different times. Nothing bothers me when I'm drunk. When I'm drinking, I'm drinking to get away from it. To stop the wheels from turning.

R.E.: So you're not a social drinker.

H.C.: No. Never have been. Maybe when I was very, very young, but that wasn't drinking.

R.E.: At this point, do you think alcohol has been an asset or liability for you as a writer and as a person?

H.C.: It's been an asset right up to and including now, but the time has come, simply because the body has worn out, for me to put it down. Somebody asked James Dickey the same question, and he said, "Whiskey has been a great and dear friend. I just wish the body would have held up so I could go longer with it." But it has beaten me. Whipped me. So, I'm goin' back off of it for a while. Try to. And I will. But no, whiskey is a great thing. I'm glad it's in the world. Anybody who is totally against whiskey, I've got to wonder about. People abuse whiskey, but then people abuse apple pie and blow up to five hundred pounds.

R.E.: Do you think you're lucky to be alive?

H.C.: Lucky as hell. Tremendously lucky inasmuch as I've broken my legs, my feet, my sternum, ribs on both sides, fingers, broken my neck, had concussions, fallen in boiling water, done dope, and have been out in company where people were often maimed, mutilated, or even killed. Yes, I'm lucky to be alive.

But some people feel compelled to put themselves in harm's way. They climb mountains, hang from rocks, jump out of airplanes; and I think that being out there makes them see the world clearer, more graphically, more vividly than they would have seen it if they had stayed in safe places. Danger makes you alive. Almost getting killed is a marvelous experience. It makes everything all new again. The phrase I use when I come back from being hurt real bad is that I come back "purified and holy." Purged. And then you're safe. You don't need to do anything like that right away. That's what the edge is all about.

R.E.: Have you ever lived in any other way?

H.C.: Never. Not even when I was married, which is why I'm not married now and haven't been for a decade.

R.E.: I find it curious that a man such as yourself has only been married once. Why is that?

H.C.: Because I came to peace with myself a long time ago about that and realized that a happy marriage and home and children and grandchildren and all the rest, that all that was not meant for me. I had more than a few good years with Sally, the mother of my two boys, one now dead, and I've loved other women since her. But I didn't marry them and won't marry them in the future. You can have an ex-wife, but you can't have an ex-family. The one or two times that I've been tempted to get married again, I've asked myself the question: "With whom does my ultimate loyalty lie?" The answer has always been: "With Sally and Byron."

And besides that, listen, I'm all for the institution of marriage. I think it is great for those people who can do it, but the whole notion of tranquillity and domesticity just bores the living shit out of me. And when I get bored, I have to go out and make something happen. And wives don't take kindly to that. They send you out for a loaf of bread, and you come back three days later all beat and broken up and full of vomit. They naturally don't like that.

R.E.: What kind of women do you like?

H.C.: I like a woman who is open to the experiences of life in all its forms. One who is not easily shocked by something, or better yet, not shocked at all. One who knows that to be human is to be full of the most outrageous urges, actions, thoughts, and desires. Physically, I like lean little women, though most of the time I'm not choosy at all.

R.E.: Have you always gotten along well with women?

H.C.: I get along well with women for short periods of time. As a rule I get along very well with women if we're not sleeping together. If we're sexually involved, that's a different story. I require an enormous amount of space, and I try to give the women in my life just as much space. Most of them can't stand being that alone that much. I'm the easiest man in the world to get rid of. All someone has to say, as long as they don't say it belligerently, is that they don't want me around, and I'll leave. Walk. Fuck, I'll go! I don't like to argue or fight with women. I'd rather put my feet in the street, and have, more times than I can remember.

R.E.: Tennessee Williams said, after watching Rip Torn perform on stage, that he didn't see how any man could be so sensitive and not be queer. What are your thoughts on homosexuality?

H.C.: It doesn't bother me whatsoever. I get along great with fags. Unless they hit on me, that is. Then I have to tell them in the most out-front way, "Look man, I don't bat from that side of the plate. I don't go that way, but it's cool with me if you do." And if they honor that, we're fine. It's too bad that the world gives them such incredible heat. I think it drives them to greater extremes of behavior. Anything that drives people underground makes for extremes of behavior.

R.E.: What was the scariest moment of your life?

H.C.: Let me see. I guess it would be the time I sat across the room looking at a guy in the corner holding a 12-gauge shotgun on me. It was a double barrel with exposed hammers, and they were cocked. The guy was just a little freaky, being in the middle of a major speed run. Fact is, he was very freaky. If I hadn't had a woman there with me who knew about such things—that is to say, knew about frustrated, fucked-up people—I might not have made it. I knew I couldn't get across the room before he let those hammers down. As it was, she talked the gun out of his hands, but not before I sweated off about twenty pounds.

R.E.: What do you think would make you happy?

H.C.: Like a happy marriage? I don't think that is in the cards for me. Besides, I think everybody puts entirely too much emphasis on happiness. They think too much about the concept of happiness, as though there were going to be a time when *everything* would be right and stay right. It's like people trying to get their house the way they want it. Or their yard, their marriage. It's impossible. And besides, it seems to me that conflict and turmoil are much more productive than is the notion of happiness. Tennessee Williams said that the mind and heart of man were constructed and meant to exist better in the white-hot cauldron of conflict. That is an imprecise quote, but he's right. That's when we do best.

There have been times when I've been laid up in a great hotel under the air conditioner with a great lady and money in my pockets and had everything working right, yet I was in such a slough of despond, so on the ragged edge of going nuts, that I didn't know what to do. So what's the problem? The problem is that there ain't nothing to resist in a situation like that. Nothing to fight against. I've got to have something with teeth in it. Something that will bite back.

R.E.: In what ways do you feel yourself aging?

H.C.: Only in one way. I feel as young as I ever did except that I don't come back as fast. I don't heal as fast. I've said that the most appropriate thing anybody could put on my tombstone is, "He got well a lot." I've spent an enormous amount of time healing up. If I get hurt bad, I'm just like a damn dog. I back up somewhere where it's cool and dark and just cool out and heal up.

R.E.: Any ideas on how you would like to die?

H.C.: Only that I'd like to go out quickly; and I would hope that if I knew I wouldn't be able to go out quickly, I would have the wherewithal to take it on out myself. I think suicide is a perfectly honorable alternative to dying naturally. I think people have the perfect right to kill themselves. It makes everybody around them unhappy, but to hell with them. It's not their life. But I think that if they're gon' do it, they ought not fuck it up. They should do it in such a way that the chance of survival is nil. I'd like to go naturally though.

R.E.: Do you think you will?

H.C.: There's a good chance. Listen. If I'm not dead from drugs at this point in my life, I never will be. The shit I've beaten in my life, man, you wouldn't believe. That's why alcohol doesn't bother me nearly as much as it does everyone else. It gives me moments of pause sometimes, but it doesn't worry me. I'm gonna be just fine. And besides that, if I dropped dead right now, if I don't get out the fucking door, I got no complaints. I've lived my life the way I wanted.

If other people are happy living over there in the northwest section of town, behind their walls, with their gardens and grass and four cars that they don't need, that's fine with me. I don't go around knocking them. Even those dusty old professors that marshal all those facts, spending their whole lives in the stacks, that's a perfectly honorable way to make a living and spend your life. Now that doesn't mean that I have to go spend a lot of time talking to them. I try to be polite and straight, and if I find something I can't deal with, I just say something pleasant like, "Well, I've got to go see a man about a dog," and I walk.

All you have to do is put your feet in the street and let others live their lives and you live yours, because people will live your life for you if you'll let them. Your mother will; your daddy will; your wife will; your children will. I know some children right now who are busy living their parents' lives because the kids won't get out and work. They won't do anything but bitch and whine and piss and moan and lay up in the house smoking dope and let their daddy take care of them. And the fuckers are twenty-two, twenty-three years old. My boy is nineteen, and he knows goddamn well that he's got to do it himself. That doesn't mean that if my boy is in trouble that I can't help him. But I can't help him by giving him everything in the world. That's no way to raise a kid.

I never had to wonder, man. When I got to seventeen, nobody had to tell me to leave. I was expected to leave. I knew it. And I wanted to go. Going in the Marine Corps was the only way I knew to get out, to leave the state, leave everybody whom I knew, and see if I could do it alone. I'd been so damn isolated and knew it, simply because I'd gone to some trouble to get books. I knew the bigger world was out there, and I wanted to see it.

R.E.: Are you optimistic about the future of America?

H.C.: I'm not given to optimism, but I don't let it worry me.

R.E.: What about your own future? Are you optimistic about that?

H.C.: Sure. Optimistic in this sense. I'm gonna keep writing, and to the extent that I do keep writing, everything else can do what it wants. I can be hungry, homeless, wet, in debt, fucked up; but if I'm writing, that's enough. It really does give me that kind of payback.

R.E.: A writer from New York closed a recent article about you by saying that he had the distinct impression that you wouldn't be around much longer, that the final chapter in the tumultuous life of Harry Crews is now being written. What would you say to that?

H.C.: That just goes back to those wimps who say that I'm burned out, that I had a mind and talent and destroyed it with alcohol or whatever the hell it is that they are saying. That's just because most people can't deal with chaos. They can't deal with blood and bone and pain. They think that once you're hurt, you're hurt forever. And, of course, you are if you're a wimp. Immodest as it is of me to say so, I ain't a wimp. Never have been. I get down sometimes, but I always get up again. To answer your question, I'll piss on his grave.

A. B. CROWDER

Harry Crews

A.B.C: Do you worry that the so-called Southern Renaissance is in decline? Or do you feel that it will stay on for a while?

H.C.: The South has certainly had more than its share: Eudora Welty, Faulkner, Walker Percy, Flannery O'Connor, and on and on and on. I very rarely hear Truman Capote mentioned as a southern writer, and yet much of his work, even when it's not set in the South, has about it the flavor of the South, the flavor of southern writing—that is to say, a strong sense of place, a strong sense of things being tied together by virtue of blood or convention or manners or whatever, and other things.

And as to whether or not it's in decline? I don't think so. Here's why: nobody's going to confuse me, my voice, my inflection, my accent, with somebody from the Midwest or with somebody from Brooklyn. We in the South not only sound like *somebody*, but we look like *somebody*, and we act like *somebody*, and we know pretty much who the hell we are, while the rest of the country is having a very serious identity crisis. One of the reasons we are distinctive, of course, is because we were a defeated nation. The Yankees beat us and exacted tribute. I'm not a professional southerner, I'm not dragging all that stuff out to reminisce, but it does happen to be true. Our history keeps us going.

From *Writing in the Southern Tradition: Interviews with Five Contemporary Authors,* by A. B. Crowder (Amsterdam: Rodopi, 1990).

A.B.C.: What about the southern storytelling tradition?

H.C.: We listened to our grandfathers talking about their fathers. We heard stories and knew things that we otherwise would not know and would not hear. This American society (and I don't know if it's necessarily a bad thing; it's just a thing that seems to be inevitable) is a society of standardization. So [if] writing is in danger in the South, it's because there is the danger of its children learning their voices from television and from radio rather than from their granddaddy's knee or their daddy's knee. And we are in danger of becoming standardized; half of folks you'd be around are wearing something out of New York. So it melts down. There is reason to believe that standardization will kill the very thing that caused the flowering of southern writing. I hope it ain't true, but it doesn't look very good.

After having said that, my gut reaction is that a lot of writing is still happening. There probably won't be another Faulkner, but we don't know where there's another really good one coming from. I'm sure he's out there somewhere.

A.B.C.: If we had another great writer like Faulkner, do you think he'd have trouble getting published?

H.C.: No, I don't think so. The publishing industry *is* in financial trouble, and very often a publishing house is owned by some electronics company that is not interested in literature. The country is starved for good writing and good stories, good storytelling. If you show up at a New York editor's with a really first-rate story, well done, they'll just make you think you're the king of the world. They'll wine you and dine you and kowtow to you. Nobody's going to make me believe that a good writer will have difficulty getting published. If people can't get published, they often want to pretend that the reason they can't publish is that the publishers "just don't like this kind of writing, or they just don't like me, but I'm too independent, and I'm unique, I write experimental writing myself," and so on. No, the answer is, you're just bad.

Now, there are horror stories that all of us could name about certain books being turned down. The author of *A Separate Peace*, I happen to know, was refused by everybody in this country—everybody. Finally the manuscript had gone to England, and an editor at Scribner's happened to be in England, looking for a good manuscript. Scribner's had already turned down *A Separate Peace.* So this editor over there saw the thing and wired back the script. We'd better buy this book, he said. Now, hell, the book had already been in the house. Why didn't they buy it the first time? Well, just because that's the way it works.

You see, when you get through writing a novel or story, if you have the grit and the guttiness to do that, by God, you ought to have the grit and the guttiness to put it under your arm and go out there and kick down a few doors and see some people. You can say, "I got to see an editor; I got to see him . . ."

"Gee, I'm sorry, they're all in conference."

Say, "Hell, that's all right, I'll just sit down here and wait." And then the next morning, come wait again. As long as you're civil, they're not going to call the police or anything. You've got a manuscript; you want somebody to see it. Do it. Get out there and shake the bushes.

I suppose you know that Kosinski story, *Steps,* which won the National Book Award. He actually won the damn thing for *Painted Bird;* they didn't give it to him for *Painted Bird,* so the next one comes out—they give it to him for that. And *Steps* is not nearly as good as everybody made it out to be, and I like Kosinski. Here's the horror story: some boy recently typed the thing up, typed up *Steps* in manuscript, this winner of the National Book Award—typed it up in manuscript form and put his own name on it and sent it to various agents, various editors, who read it. It is just incredible, but nobody recognized it as *Steps.* You figure, what the hell have these guys been doing all the time; I thought they *read;* I thought reading was their business. They didn't recognize it, and not one accepted it. They turned it down as too perverse and unclear and turgid.

So there are all these horror stories. And I imagine you'd have trouble getting published something like *The Sound and the Fury.* Can you imagine that damn thing coming into the office in manuscript? Can you imagine some editors dealing with the first part of it? A writer has just got to keep on keeping on.

A.B.C.: To what extent have you met with rejection?

H.C.: I have, for whatever it's worth (but it might be of some encouragement to aspiring writers), been rejected by every publishing house in this country and every slick magazine (I mean by "slick magazine," you know, *Atlantic, New Yorker,* and whatever—*Esquire*). I've been rejected by most of the quarterlies—the *Virginia Quarterly, Prairie Schooner,* the *Missouri Quarterly, Sewanee Review* . . . on and on and on. This was back when I was starting.

But hell, I just felt like, from the very beginning when I was young, I just felt like, look, if I keep writing and the damn stuff is good, sooner or later somebody is going to bite. I mean it's like fishing, man: keep your hook in the water. You ain't going to get no fish if there ain't no hooks in the water. Keep putting them in there. Wait.

A.B.C.: Is your audience really important to you?

H.C.: Many of us would sell our books for ten cents apiece just so more people would buy them, if we could arrange to get them printed and do that.

A.B.C.: I enjoyed your piece in *Esquire* on where you live and why. Can you add anything about your origins and your present connection to them?

H.C.: You know I live in Florida, north Florida, but I'm *from* Georgia—I'm from south Georgia. I was raised on the edge of the Okefenokee Swamp mostly. We went to the swamp because the fish were there, frogs were there, crawdads were there, the bear was there, and that was before it was a national refuge, and we hunted and fished in the swamp because it put meat on the table.

I now live in north Florida. I live where I live partly because I love small towns. I live in a very small town. It's getting almost too big for me; I probably better move back out of the way. I am presently living in a house that has a glass wall in the room I write in (my typewriter faces so I can't look out the window). Outside the glass wall there's a creek called Hogtown Creek. And the house is on three acres of land with marvelous kinds of trees and bushes and brambles and whatever.

One thing I don't want is a lawn. Three things I refuse to do in the world—wash a car, mow a lawn, what's the other? There's another one somewhere.

But I can look out the window; this is why I love where I live: I look out the window at Hogtown Creek and in my imagination follow it upstream to where it joins the Suwannee River; and then I can follow the Suwannee River upstream to where the headwaters rise in the vastness of the Okefenokee Swamp, the swamp I was raised in. And I was raised around guys telling stories about that swamp. Where I am now, I am just a hundred miles from where I was born and raised to manhood. I'm not too far away from it to [not] be able to hear the accents, the rhythms of the storytellers that still live in my own mouth and, more importantly, in my own ear. Everything that I write has its source, I think, in my childhood. Again, it reminds you of what Flannery O'Connor said; I think she said that anybody that survives his childhood has enough to write out of for the rest of his life—something like that.

A.B.C.: Andrew Lytle thinks you went wrong somewhere. Would you comment on Lytle's criticism?

H.C.: Well, Mr. Lytle—Well, I'll tell you, now, Mr. Lytle was sort of like a father to me at one time, and he sort of disowned me. And that's all right; I can live with that. You see, he was a great teacher and a demanding taskmaster, but he was about as curious a fellow as you'd want to meet, too. He has these ironclad principles and theories of things, which he will not deviate from. And that's fine; there's nothing wrong with that. He doesn't have to like me, and he doesn't have to like my work. As a matter of fact, when I was studying with him, he said, "Son, every apprentice that's any good eventually turns on his master." But I've never said anything bad about him.

Lytle is a grand old man, and every time I see him, and every time I'm around him, I dutifully sit at his feet and listen to him lecture me about the errors of my ways, and I have no interest in arguing with him. He's been too good to me, and he gave me too much. He spent on me the only thing any of us owns—time. He gave me his time when he was writing very hard, trying to finish a novel he'd been on for nine years. Every hour he gave me he couldn't give to his novel.

So I'm not going to ever—he can say what he wants to—I'm not ever going to say anything about him bad.

A.B.C.: Lytle thinks the true hero in southern writing is the community. What do you think?

H.C.: I know how Mr. Lytle means that word "community." I'd like to go with Mr. Lytle, but here's one of the things you must understand: my South, the South I'm from, is entirely different from Mr. Lytle's. He doesn't know anything about the South I'm from. He knows it in an intellectual way. You see, Mr. Lytle's daddy sent him to France to study. Mr. Lytle's family gave the land that Murfreesboro, Tennessee, is built on. I mean, his daddy was a planter and never touched a plow in his life, not once, and was very proud of it.

Reynolds Price is, among other things, a really fine scholar. I'm not a scholar. I've read a lot, but my education has enormous holes in it because I didn't have any of that great discipline that study for a Ph.D. gives you. I'm not wimping and crying. I guess if I'd wanted it bad enough, I'd have gone and got it. So I'm not prepared to debate or argue with people of the caliber of mind of Mr. Lytle and Reynolds Price, or people who come out of that kind of life.

Still, they don't understand my South. Even Erskine Caldwell did not understand my South and the experience of living there. Oh, he wrote about sharecroppers, and he wrote about tenant farmers and all that sort of thing. But his daddy was a Presbyterian minister or something, and he had a secure life. He went to college—very nice and easy. Our views of the world were so different. It doesn't mean we can't communicate; it just means that I can't talk their language because I don't know it. On the other hand, I'm immodest enough to say that they can't talk my language because they don't know it. They just think they do. They think they know my language; I *know* I don't know theirs. But they don't know they don't know mine, but they don't.

As a matter of fact, I know Reynolds Price; I've talked to him and everything. I know him, but I really don't know him. It's always been a very formal kind of . . . but Price has always been that way with me, around me. I don't know if he's that way around everybody or not. There was a certain reserve there, and it's not my nature to be reserved. But if I'm off somewhere and that's the game we're playing, I'll play by those rules, you know, or try to. I fouled out a few times, but I try to play by the rules.

A.B.C.: Are you the typical writer with an academic affiliation?

H.C.: While I *am* a professor in the graduate school of the University of Florida, we mustn't fly under false colors here. I am not your normal, everyday professor. One of my major triumphs in the world is that I now direct a degree that I was turned down to study for at the very school that turned me down. After the University of Florida graduate school turned me down, I went off and wrote some things, and wrote some more things, and wrote some more things, and then they invited me there. So I'm not a Ph.D. It's a very nice thing to be a Ph.D. A poet you may have heard of, Donald Justice, who not long ago won the Pulitzer Prize, his office is next to mine. Donald Justice is not only a very, very fine poet, he's also a Ph.D. So, you see, the two are not mutually exclusive. But I just want you to know it's not one of the things that I have.

A.B.C.: How did you come to write the various personal essays in *Blood and Grits*, "Cape Coral," for example?

H.C.: The way that piece came about is that *Esquire* asked certain writers around the country to address themselves to some specific subjects. For instance, a very fine writer, Walker Percy, who lives in Louisiana, wrote about whiskey—yeah, bourbon. They asked me to write about cars because I have a book called *Car*. And they know that I think the car is an abomination before the Lord. That's how that piece happened to be written.

A.B.C.: What about the Bronson piece?

H.C.: *Playboy* called me up and asked me if I wanted to spend a week in a boxcar with Charles Bronson in Idaho. And I said, "Sure." He was making a movie called *Breakheart Pass*. We stayed in the Lewis and Clark Hotel, in Lewiston. We stayed there and every morning the cast and the cameraman, the grips and the gaffs, everybody would climb into all these buses and go up and get on this train. It went up in the mountains, and we stayed on the train all day long and into the night.

It had a special boxcar for Bronson—very fine with big dressing rooms with beds on each end, a kitchen—heavy gravy, real nice.

But you see, I wasn't there very long before I discovered I was in deep trouble 'cause I was there to do a piece on Charles Bronson, and Charles Bronson doesn't talk. So I got a little frantic. I only had a week, and I'd been there three days, and I had half a page of notes—nothing on tape. Very personable guy, but he doesn't talk much. So that piece is an exercise in getting the job done. So you notice in that piece I write all around Bronson. I mean, it's the only thing I *can* do. I can't say it was a bad experience; it was very frightful; it was freaky but nice.

A.B.C.: Before we leave *Blood and Grits,* tell us how you came to write "Climbing the Tower."

H.C.: The "Climbing the Tower" thing was just at a time in my life that I have every two or three weeks—sometimes every two or three months—when, because of overwork and stress and abuse of alcohol and that sort of thing, I get way out on the raggedy edge of what I would think approaches borderline insanity. And that's the way I came into that town [Austin, Texas]. And when one of the professors who had invited me to come there said, "Here's where they started dropping" and all that, I wasn't even aware that I was on the campus where this boy had climbed up on a tower and started shooting people. And when they started talking about it, it was just, you know, too much for me. But then I had this great sympathy for him, and it's out of sympathy that I wrote the piece, out of a justification of the deed.

You mustn't, you wouldn't, I hope, think that I was saying I approve of those actions—certainly not. But I quote the thing from I think Germany's greatest poet, Johann Wolfgang von Goethe, who said, "There is no crime of which I cannot conceive myself guilty." You just think about that. I mean, would you sell your mother for a Baby Ruth candy bar? It's been done. If you've got a starving child, and he needs a Baby Ruth candy bar, well, you don't *know* what you'd do. That's why it won't do to be too self-righteous. It won't do to be too sure of your own wherewithal to withstand the evil and temptation of the world. That only leads to some kind of pristine silliness.

So you don't know those things. That's why, when you write, everybody who writes ought to bring a measure of humility to his work. You don't *know* how *everybody* ought to live. You don't know how *everybody* ought to think and believe. And what *everybody* ought to read. You might know what you would like for you and yours to read, and live, and be, and think, and the rest of it. You might even think you know what you wish for the community you live in.

A.B.C.: How do you feel about the sort of criticism that forever seeks to identify the source of fiction in the writer's life?

H.C.: I despair of the sort of criticism that continually does that sort of thing, the kind that says a guy wrote a play about fags because his mother was a very dominant figure and he didn't have a father and because he was a latent fag himself. I mean, a fag is a fag is a fag is a fag. And a heterosexual, a hetero, hetero, hetero, hetero . . . Who gives a rat's ass?

A.B.C.: It seems that "Climbing the Tower" began as a powerful emotion. Do most of your stories begin with a strong feeling that you have to write about?

H.C.: I think, by and large, what you suggest is true. I think you have the very, very strong reactions; certainly, if it's going to be good fiction, or a good piece, it ought to get an emotional reaction of some kind. You see, if you have a very strong intellectual reaction to the thing, and you write fiction about it, it's liable to turn out badly. It's liable to turn out as kind of thesis fiction, meaning fiction that's there to prove a point. Good fiction is not there to prove anything. Good fiction is there to make you breathe with another human being, bleed with him, to suck you out of your skin for a little while and put you in somebody else's skin, to let you participate in another man and a woman's doing the best they can with what they got to do with. So if it's too intellectual, then it might turn out to be less than it ought to be.

I have a book called *Car.* And my reaction to cars is emotional, but it's more intellectual than emotional. Did you know that with the vehicles that we have right now—and I'm not talking about flatbed trucks, or something like that—I'm talking about cars, we could load every man, woman, and child in America in a car and have room left over . . . . It's madness. It's madness for a hundred-and-ten-pound woman to get into a four-thousand-pound piece of machinery and drive two blocks to get a thirteen-ounce loaf of bread. Now there's something in those figures that simply does not synch, you know.

I often think, what would life have been like if they couldn't have made that sucker work, you know, the car, if it just didn't work. If they couldn't have got it off the ground, didn't get it off the drawing board, I guess we'd have cooked up something else. I don't know.

The point of this rather long harangue is that *Car* would have been a much better book if I had been able to get a little more distance on the subject. The book did very well, did better in France than it did in this country—but though I don't think it's a bad book, it could have been a much better book than it is.

Likewise, you can't write any character in fiction that you have contempt for. You take a story by D. H. Lawrence called "Rocking-horse Winner." It's about a boy and whatnot. The woman in that story is something of a monster. But D. H. Lawrence gives her what Flannery O'Connor calls "a moment of grace." It would have been all too easy to make her just a monster; she's not just a monster: she's doing the best she can. She really is. And Lawrence knows that. Hate is counterproductive in almost everything, I think.

A.B.C.: Getting back to *Car,* how can you defend a story about such an outrageous event as a man's eating a car?

H.C.: It's just sort of a bad joke. A guy does eat a car; they cut it up—bumpers, fenders—into half-ounce cubes of metal, and he swallows a certain number every day, and consequently passes a certain number every night. This is a kind of promotional stunt. After he passes them, they take the little cubes and they mold them into miniature Mavericks, which is the kind of car he's eating, and they sell these as mementos, which you can hang on your key chain. And this goes on and on and on. And of course, things like glass and oil out of the crankcase they simply encapsulate so he can swallow them.

You say, "What? You wrote a book that said what? I mean, get back! No! Wrong!"

But it's better than it sounds. It would almost have to be, wouldn't it? You don't have to invent very much in the world we live in because madness and absurdity are everywhere about us. It truly is. But of course, we have become so accustomed to it that we do not see it. The thing is, eating a car sounds far-fetched to the rest of us, but it's not far-fetched at all. A Swede ate a Fiat in Argentina. He got through half of it in five years. I saw it in a little blurb thing that big [*gestures with his thumb and forefinger*], and I thought, "Suffering God. Yeah, so say we all. Now, looky here."

In the book the guy eating the car is a metaphor; it doesn't work very well perhaps, but the obvious metaphor is that all of us have our car to eat, and we're going to eat it. It's become a substitute for everything. You get in the car, you know, and you're in the kind of shape I've let myself get in, and you get in there: oh, boy! You got that gas pedal down, and "Wheeah!" You think it somehow seems like you could "do it" knowing full well that your knees have gone bad, you're nine thousand pounds overweight, drunk half the time. You think, "Wheeah!" You're in a car, your little jowls just shaking. The sexual imagery, both in the design of the cars and in the advertisement of them, is too obvious to merit discussion.

Easy Mack, the character in the book, says, "About a quarter of the children in America are conceived in the back seats of cars." They were these mobile motel rooms for generations. Then it got to the place where you didn't have to have a mobile motel room. You just took Suzie home to your parents, said, "Well, Mom, we're going up to my room."

A.B.C.: Have you done any writing for films and television?

H.C.: I just finished writing a screenplay for Michael Cimino, the boy who made *Deer Hunter* and, unfortunately, *Heaven's Gate,* which lost forty-four million dollars. Of course, he lost forty-four million dollars of other people's money; he got rich on it. So he hired me, and I did a screenplay for him. And I have just finished the first draft (I have three months more of the contract) of a film called *Clown,* based on the life of Emmett Kelly, the great Barnum and Bailey, Ringling Brothers clown. Weary Willie was his persona, sad mouth and all of that.

But I think that after I do this screenplay, I'll never write another one. The money is seductive, if you want to know the truth, to say it straight out. I've only been married one time in my life, but I carry an alimony and have carried it for better than a decade. It would kill an ordinary man, and I've got a boy in college, and so, you know, I need some bread. Still, I find working in films very unsatisfactory. It doesn't give me anything back.

For one thing, you don't need to be a writer to be a film writer, in the sense that I think of being a writer. In a novel, the whole business of passing time, just that aspect, is an enormously complex, difficult thing to master. In a film, you just write, "Cut to, colon." Hell, if you've got a scene in Jacksonville, and you want one in Conway, Arkansas, you just "Cut to." In the next scene, the exterior or interior tells you where you are. That's all on the script.

And then underneath that you describe what the camera sees. You can say the camera pans the room, you can walk in through the door, you can have a tracking shot: camera behind him, he walks in, does this (got to have a railway laid down for that, by the way, to put the camera on, unless it's a handheld one, which is very rare, but sometimes very effective, too). But then, in describing what the camera sees, you can write Sears and Roebuck prose. That's what I think of it, the kind of prose that you get that describes how you use a lawn mower. You don't even have to write in complete sentences.

Now you got to be good with dialogue. And you also have to somehow be good with constructing the narrative line of the film, just the line of the action—after all, you've got to have the story.

Now one story I wrote for Michael Cimino was an original screenplay, based on nothing. At my second meeting with him in New York, we made the deal, shook hands, and he went to my agent, and that was cool. And I thought the guy had some sort of synopsis, or maybe what is called a treatment. Sometimes a treatment is very brief, and sometimes it's many pages long. I thought he had something; he didn't have anything. He took out a piece of paper cut out of the *Los Angeles Times*, and it was about Giddings, Texas, and a bunch of ore. As a matter of fact, the town had as much ore as is found on the north slope of Alaska. They always knew the ore was down there, but the technology and the price war didn't make the work good.

He said, "Go to Giddings."

I said, "Well, good. What am I supposed to do there?"

He said, "Put the story there." So that was the instructions I had, as much as I had. And so I went to Giddings three different times, lived there for a while, and wrote a story called *Boomtown*. Now that was an original screenplay.

In most instances you are given a book; maybe it's your own book. I wrote the screenplay for my first book, *The Gospel Singer,* and I could tell you why it hasn't been made yet. It's kind of a long story. The director just got in trouble. We already had the location, we'd already done the casting, we had the money to make it, and, anyway, the prime mover of the project got into some very serious trouble with something called the Mann Act, and it cost him everything he had to get out of it. I thought he'd do time, but he didn't. But now Tom Jones owns the play. See, I sold it outright. So there's a little more money in it for me if they make it, but they own the screenplay I wrote.

A.B.C.: How did you learn to write screenplays?

H.C.: There is a director named Frank Perry, whose first movie was called *David and Lisa,* a classic in its time. He also did *Diary of a Mad Housewife* and a lot of other films. After I wrote *Naked in Garden Hills,* the second book, the phone rang one night. I picked it up, and a voice said, "This is Frank Perry."

I thought it was one of my friends. I said, "Look, I've had a long day. I don't need this. I'm not in the mood for a joke."

He said, "No, no, this *is* Frank Perry." Finally, he convinced me that he was. "I want to buy an option on your novel."

And I said, "Fine. Call the agent. I'll give you his number. He's right here in New York."

And he said, "And I'd like you to write the screenplay."

You know what the first rule is: Get the job. Get the job and get paid; get some money up front. Then worry about how you're going to do it. So when he said, "I want you to write the screenplay," I said, "Sure."

He said, "Have you ever written a screenplay?"
I said, "No."
And he said, "Have you ever seen a screenplay?"
I said, "No."

But he's cool, see. He knows something about writers and writing and what a good writer looks like.

And he said, "It doesn't matter. I'll send you a screenplay for you to look at, just so you get a look at one first. Then you do it any way you want to do it."

Well, I already knew you cannot translate a novel directly the way it's written from the novel to the screen. It always has to be taken apart.

Anyway, I got the screenplay in the mail, and I wrote the thing in three weeks—very young man, I didn't have to sleep, didn't have to eat, didn't have to do anything, just write. I did it in New York, stayed at the Plaza Hotel; right across the street was Perry's office on the tenth floor. He got a typewriter sent to my room in the hotel, and for three weeks I would go across the street, and he would show me something: "No, you see, you can't do this. See, son, it's a *picture*." And he'd explain why you couldn't do it that way. Just like going to school. I knew this was one of the greatest opportunities. I was going to school with a master. I'd go back across the street and write all day, and then that evening he would send a messenger over, not from his office but from his house. He'd get my stuff, read it that night, and the next morning I'd show up in his office. And we'd have another little lesson. That's where I learned whatever I may know about writing screenplays.

The same people I'm working for now on the Emmett Kelly film want me to write sort of simultaneously a biography of Billy Martin, who's a terribly interesting guy, and a screenplay of his life. I think probably the book and the screenplay would do well; I think it would make everybody money. But I tell you something—now you think this is a lie, but this is stone truth—if I just wanted to make money, there's a lot of things that I would have done and I could have done. There's nothing wrong with money, but I feel terrible when I use whatever talent I may have as a writer for no other purpose than to make money. You see, I could go to Madison Avenue and write jingles for Coca-Cola and get more.

I would rather write novels. Writing novels is a way of understanding the world, a way of understanding yourself, a way of coming to some passion and empathy with your fellow beings, and I know that sounds awfully like some kind of sermon, but it's only the truth. When I write fiction, I feel good about myself. I write fiction and I'm a better human being. I'm more at peace with myself, more at one with myself. When I write screenplays and certain other things, nah, nah. I'm full of stress, full of anger half the time. So I don't want to do it. I can get through with *Clown*, and then I'm going to try to finish a novel I've been working on for a long time. And I'll finish it. I figure I've got about another year on that novel.

A.B.C.: Are you pleased with all of the serious work that you have done?

H.C.: No, there are things, for instance, in *The Gospel Singer*, certain passages—I find them rather embarrassing, simply because they're overwritten. The passages are called variously "purple prose" or "rhetoric." When somebody says, "Well, that's just rhetoric," he simply means that the language is not carrying its own weight.

Now *Naked in Garden Hills* I take to be the best thing I've done. It is an enormously complex book, the way time is dealt with, the way point of view is dealt with—very, very complex. It is powerful. What you're doing has got to be so deeply hidden that even when somebody cares enough to look for it, they have to look terribly hard, and then they're not even sure they found it.

People continually come to me and say, "Hey, I really like your book, *Naked in the Garden.*" Well, who was naked in the garden? Well, Adam and Eve, I reckon. *Naked in Garden Hills* is supposed to sound occult or something (it is meant to evoke that kind of response in readers without their ever really knowing it). It is meant to appeal on the subliminal, almost unconscious, archetypal level.

The theory, as I understand, of archetypes, is this: presumably, and I think it's probably true, there are certain things that have happened again and again and again and again in the history of human development. A colt, when it's born, can get up and outrun a dog, you know. It's got those long legs. But a baby? Naw, even a five-year-old boy. Put him anywhere; he'd die in a minute. There are certain ways of taking care of children, certain rites of passage. They happen so often that when you write about them, when you bring them into the experience of the reader, it triggers something back there that is deeper, more profound than his conscious intellect.

A.B.C.: Have you written anything that you are not pleased with?

H.C.: I wrote a book dedicated to my first son. I had a boy drown when he was four years old. I didn't know what to do. "I'll write another book, that's what I'll do," I said. I didn't realize until just not long ago that it's quite a bad book. It really is. I was shocked the other day when some guy that I thought was a good reader and fairly perceptive told me he thought it was my best book. It's not. But, you know, baseball players have bad days; writers sometimes have bad years. That's just one of those things you live with. That's why I always thought, if I were lucky and worked very hard, wrote twenty books, I'd have some chance of one of them maybe being of true merit and pretty damn good. Not great. Your chances of writing a great . . . how many great novels can you name in the first fifty years of this century? Probably fifteen or twenty. So your odds against writing a great book are just overwhelming. So you mustn't think about that too much. What you do is just do your work according to your own best lights.

A.B.C.: Do you sit down and write every day?

H.C.: I do. I try to write every day except when I'm visiting classes at some college or when I have to go away on business, because there's something about just staying in touch with it. I try to do it in the morning when I'm rested. And I try to be gentle on myself. Many times, you know, it's hard to get going the next day; the clock rings, and you wake up. This little voice in your head says, "Well, Harry, you're not even sure what comes next. You don't know exactly how this thing goes. You'd better think about this for another day." And there's another little voice, in a somewhat firmer but gentle tone, that says, "No, no, Harry; go sit down for four hours and if it comes . . ."

You see, it's so easy to lie to yourself, to fool yourself into thinking that you can have it both ways, that you can go sit somewhere in a bar all night and half the morning *talking* about life and that somehow talking with somebody else who wants to talk about life will somehow result in [a novel]. Learning may come of it. Insight may come of it. A great many things may come of it. But not a damn word's getting written. I mean, you got to get there and do the work. That's what I do.

A.B.C.: Are there times when you sit down, and you just sit and stare?

H.C.: Oh, yes. I just have some rather strict rules for myself. I can't clip my nails there, I can't clean my nails there, I can't write letters there, I can't read books there, I can't read the newspaper, and I can't do anything there. The desk faces a wall, so I can't go looking out the window there. I'm not married. I live with my boy, who's nineteen. He's never been up before about ten o'clock in the morning in his life, I think. But I have a hard and fast rule. There must be no radios. So, yes, you're sitting there, and you *are* stuck. You don't know what's going to happen. And you sit there, man. Four hours? Sitting there in a chair? Looking at the wall? So what happens after a while, you just snatch up a piece of paper and put it in the typewriter and say, "God, I'll do something, if it's wrong." You know, anything is more entertaining than this. Boring. You go to work.

Lawrence Durrell talks about writing in terms of chopping wood. He says, "I just go in there and I chop out a cord. And if it, you know, is not right, won't burn, and long lengths won't fit in the fireplace, I just throw it away." I mean that's the metaphor he has, one of his stopgap metaphors. But you just do it.

A.B.C.: What sort of instrument do you write with?

H.C.: I normally compose on the typewriter, but not always. Sometimes I use a pen. But when I do get stuck, I have a bunch of those Flair pens, different colors—a red one, a green one, a yellow one, a blue one—different colors of pens there, and I have a yellow legal pad, and I write one paragraph with the red pen, and every paragraph I begin, I change pens. I do one with a red one, then I do one with a green one, and then I do one with a blue one. There's something about changing the colors that makes you say, "Hey, you're making progress, you know, because you're moving this thing right along," because you can see it. It's a ritual that you just sort of go through to get yourself going. Somebody, Hemingway maybe, sharpened twenty pencils every time before he started writing. That's just one of the things he did to crank himself up. At the twentieth pen[cil] he was ready to work. My ritual works for me. And I often write long pages, sometimes a series of pages, in these different colors.

A.B.C.: The thought of you rolling out those rainbows of good stories is a good one to stop on. Thank you.

HANK NUWER

The Writer Who Plays with Pain: Harry Crews

This interview was conducted on a Saturday morning at Crews's Gainesville, Florida, home. It was apparent that Crews had forgotten the interview. He was naked and slumped low on the easy chair he'd coupled with that night. A female graduate student stirred on a couch on the right. Outside, the day was stinky hot. Inside, the air-conditioning was blasting. Empty Schlitz cans and other clutter in the main room contrasted with the order in the room to the left, where a typewriter and neat stacks of manuscripts lay atop a spotlessly clean table.

Crews ordered the student into the kitchen to see what the fridge held. She came back with a lone frozen container of orange juice that had no chance of melting in that cooler of a room. Crews struggled with the lid, cursed, and reached down past the chair's cushion to come up with a knife long and sharp enough to gut a mule.

A few minutes later, he bellowed in pain when he stood up to go to the bathroom. Explaining that his short ribs in back were broken, he dropped the blanket covering him to expose massive bruises the color of rotted fruit. He said there were two stories to choose from as to how he'd been injured: either he had fallen in the tub while washing his short, badly butchered hair,

---

From *Rendezvous with Contemporary Writers*, by Hank Nuwer (Pocatello: Idaho State University Press, 1988). Previously published in the *South Carolina Review* 18 (Fall 1985): 63–73. Parts of this conversation were published in *Dynamic Years* magazine (September–October 1984); that article also included some remarks made by Crews at a University of Tennessee–Chattanooga symposium.

or he had incurred the wrath of some thug in a girlie joint. Later, he offered a third scenario: possibly he'd been in a pool-hall fight. When he came back to his chair, the interview commenced.

H.N.: What gives you the drive to create?

H.C.: There's probably only one good thing about being a tenant farmer's son: You've seen it all. You've been hungry; you've gone to bed cold. You didn't have a fire; you couldn't go to school. You've *been* there. When it gets too bad for everybody else, it's getting just right for you.

H.N.: What renews you as a writer?

H.C.: As a writer you're as close as a man can come to knowing what it means to have a baby. You don't like it while it's going on, but man, when that baby comes out and you see that bloody, ugly, wrinkled, little guy, then you know the thing came out right. Before me this was not. Because of me this is.
[*At this point, Crews introduced his boy, Byron Jason Crews. The love and friendship the two obviously have for each other was touching to see. Byron told his dad his plans for the day and departed.*]

H.N.: What do you say to your peers at the University of Florida who object to your hard-living lifestyle?

H.C.: To start with, I ain't got no peers in Gainesville, but I guess you're talking about them professors. They ain't been around no blocks. They ain't seen blood, and all their bones are intact. When they see a little blood, they think the game's over. They don't realize you can go to the sidelines where the coach'll say, "Can you go?"

And you say, "Yeah, Coach, I can go."

If you can't play with pain, you can't play. You don't know what game you're playing, you don't know what the score is, you don't know what quarter it is, half the time you don't know what position you're playing. And whatever blood there is you just tape up a little bit, and if you've got them kind of doctors, he'll shoot you up a little bit. It'll fuck up your mind and fuck up a lot of things, but shit, I played a year with my goddamned left arm chained to my fucking chest. Couldn't use it. I played defensive tackle. This is in high school.

H.N.: While teaching at the university do you ever get any material from that group for your fiction?

H.C.: No. I have no interest in writing the academic novel, the novel set in the university. Now, there is a great book that *is* an academic novel called *Stoner,* by John Williams. It's the kind of book you've got to give about one hundred and fifty pages before it starts to take over. But man, by the end of it, it's just like *Madame Bovary.* It just kills you, breaks your heart. You'll never forget Stoner. Stoner is the last name of the main character in the book.

But no, I stay away from my "peers." I don't know what they think of me; I think they're decent people. But I don't know their names, and I don't know their faces, and I don't know anything about them. I stay away from them. I don't go to parties, and I don't go where you hold the thin stem, and everybody walks around and makes nice.

H.N.: Any worries about the effects of hard living and drinking?

H.C.: The thing about the body is that if you just get out of its way, it can handle it. We ain't talking about cirrhosis. You get cirrhosis of the liver and you're in bad shit. But if you get out of your liver's way, your whole goddamn liver can be white except for a little red spot about that big. And if you ain't got cirrhosis, that son-of-a-bitch will come back.

H.N.: What memories do you have of serving in the Marines?

H.C.: I went into the Marine Corps when I was seventeen years old. I had a nineteen-inch neck, nineteen-inch arms, and nineteen-inch calves. I was 219 pounds and nothing but ligament and bones. I was ready to go. Physically, it wasn't that hard on Parris Island, but they mess with your mind. They slap you around a little bit and bloody you up some. I don't know if they still do that anymore, but in those days they did it to you.

H.N.: Have any of your Marine Corps experiences helped you as a writer?

H.C.: What it put into me is what a writer *has* to have: discipline. When I went into the Marine Corps, I was a sorry S.O.B. There wasn't nothing too low for me to do, including stealing old ladies' purses. But fourteen months later when they let me off the island, I "sirred" everything that moved, and I spoke kindly to little old ladies with purses. People think they have to continue in the same mode forever, but they don't.

H.N.: They probably took one look at your size and figured they'd put you in line.

H.C.: Yeah, they did. But the Marine Corps saved me. If I hadn't gone in the Marine Corps, I wouldn't be a professor in the university; I'd be in the state prison because I was a bad actor and a bad boy. Just rage. Just sourceless fucking rage. I'd like for you to see this five-thousand-word essay on violence [I did for] *Playboy*. I don't come off looking real good at all. Matter of fact, I come off looking pretty fucking pitiful. But it's just the truth. The piece is called "The Violence That Comes to Us."

There are a few sociopaths, psychopaths—whatever you want to call them—out there, who go around looking for trouble. Christ, you can be walking down the damn street, turn the corner, and walk square into the face of madness—you might get cut. This scar on my arm here, which ain't a bad scar, right here—a boy cut me. He cut me because I live in this little town, and there's a lot of all this shit on the street about my name. I'd be in bars, and some guy'd come up and tell me a story about something I'd done. He'd be chuckling, and telling me about how it was, and, truth of the matter was, I never even went near the place. Somebody told him or he told somebody else, and he got it fifth hand, and he thought it was true. When I was younger, I used to try to correct those damn stories. But any more I just shrug. It's all so boring.

H.N.: How did he cut you on the underside, instead of the outside?

H.C.: He just reached under there. I was sitting on a park bench, and he just reached under and cut me. I didn't even know he cut me. I was wearing a short-sleeved white shirt, and it felt about a quarter as bad as a bee sting. It didn't hurt. Goddamn guy was leaning right in my face. I looked down, and the damn whole left side of my shirt was just full of blood. Course I ain't much of a squaller, but it bled a lot.

And he said, "I cut you," and then he ran.

I say in the piece he didn't need to run. Anybody who chases madness deserves what he gets. Deserves what he catches.

H.N.: I was going to ask if *this* is a true story—Did you pee on the head of a guy in St. Augustine one day?

H.C.: Yep, off the bar. It cost me some money, too. They put us in jail; we bailed ourselves out. At the time my head was shaved, I had a big fucking earring in this ear, and I weighed about one hundred and sixty pounds. And just looking for shit—just looking for it. I don't know why. It certainly is not complimentary—it's degrading—but I was. If you wanted to go, I wanted to go with you. Goddamn it, we'll go out to the parking lot and *see* who's got it. I don't give a shit if you weigh three hundred pounds—just get out there and get it on. Yes, I did. I stood on a bar and pissed on a guy's head. I had two friends who were in the bar. It cost us a little money, but we got out of it all right. We survived.

H.N.: You once said you'd like to shoot for twenty book titles in your lifetime. Your newest book, *Florida Frenzy*, puts you more than halfway over the hump. I guess that's eleven, if I'm not mistaken. Do you think you have the push in you for another novel?

H.C.: No, I ain't got eleven; I got fourteen now.

H.N.: You've got fourteen?

H.C.: Yeah, but that's all right. It don't mean nothing. I ain't just got the push left in me for another novel, son. I'm going to get twenty or twenty-five. I think it was Miss Eudora Welty who said—no, maybe it was Katherine Anne Porter—I can't remember which one said it—but to write a good book or a good short story, one of the things you need is luck. Take hold at the right place, get out at the right place. And I figure if I could get twenty that one of them would have a chance of being a book that would be around for a while.

H.N.: Some of your essays in *Florida Frenzy* come from the *Esquire* "Grits" column you used to write. I wish you were still doing that column. I liked it.

H.C.: *Esquire* called me up and asked me to write a column.

And I said, "I never wrote a column."

They said, "We didn't ask you if you ever wrote a column; we asked you if you *wanted* to write one."

I told them I'd sign on for a year; I did it fourteen months. I did it fourteen months, and they didn't fire me; I quit. The last piece I wrote was called "Climbing the Tower."

But the thing was, when they asked me to write the column, I said: "What is it about? Is it about politics, or sports, or whatever?"

And they said, "No. Just whatever you want to write about."

Which, at the time, I thought was a great deal. But it turned out not to be a great deal, because you gotta come up with something; then you got to get some kind of slant on the son-of-a-bitch so you can write about it. It was hard. It was only a twenty-five-hundred to three-thousand-word column. That's not much for one month. But I was writing [other things] at the same time. As a matter of fact, it's from writing those columns that the *Childhood* book came.

H.N.: Did it take you a long time to learn the form of writing a magazine nonfiction piece? It's a shorter haul than writing fiction.

H.C.: If you look at the pieces I've done for magazines, they all have the elements of fiction. There's a place, there's a tale, there's dialogue, there are characters. It just all happens to be true.

H.N.: My favorite story of yours so far as essays go is "The Knuckles of St. Bronson." I enjoyed that one very much.

H.C.: Boy, that was a hard piece to write 'cause he wouldn't talk. Shit, he probably doesn't say three hundred words in the whole article.

H.N.: He didn't give you a lot of action, either.

H.C.: No, I was desperate. I'd gone all the way to Lewiston, Idaho, and I'd been out there a week. I knew after about two days, "Man, you ain't getting the story." If you look at the piece, I write all around him. I write about this publicist, women in bars, and so on and so forth.

I titled his piece "The Knuckles of St. Bronson." That's how I put it in the collected book of journalism—that's what I called it. But damn if *Playboy* didn't change it to "Charlie Bronson Ain't No Pussycat." And not only that, but they put [in an illustration of] a pit bull with Bronson's face on it. If it'd been me, I'd be in jail somewhere up there in Illinois somewhere, 'cause I'd be going up there and kicking somebody's ass. Put my face on a goddamn bulldog, no way! I wrote Bronson. I said, "Look, I'm sorry. I have no control over that."

H.N.: To paraphrase something in *Karate Is a Thing of the Spirit* that you said about William Faulkner's work, your novels all contain one damn freak after another. Which of these freaks, in your estimation, casts a long shadow?

H.C.: I don't know that any freak casts a long shadow, though what the world calls freaks, I don't think of [as freaks] at all. See, we're talking about physical freaks here. You and I are freaks—or we could be. I get so fucking tired, so *sick* of people talking about me writing about freaks. Well, they just gotta move over and give me room 'cause I ain't going away.

And my old mother, seventy-two years old, when I wrote the *Childhood* book, I said: "Ma, you're in the book. I got you saying the things that you said. You've probably forgotten; you're seventy-two now, and all mellowed out. Do you want to read this before I send it to New York?"

And she said, "No, son. If it's the truth, tell it." She said, "The truth never hurt anybody."

Which is not true, bless her darlin' heart. God love her. It ain't the truth. You ought not to write shit that hurts people—not living [anyway]. If they're made up, if it's fiction, it's all right. Sometimes you protect people. See, you protect them. There are guys you go with to do interviews and stuff, and right off the bat you know you're going to protect them. I mean if they're, you know, if they get drunk, or fall down, or whatever they do. You walk out and say, "Hey, this guy's bent, twisted, and hurt. But underneath all the bent, twisted, and hurt, he's a decent human being. And I ain't going to fuck him over."

I've had guys come in to interview me that just killed me. Well, maybe they made me look like what I am. There have been guys who've come here and shit on me, and other guys have come here, and that didn't happen. But you can't have it both ways. You're going to write about a guy, warts and all. Just how stuff was, and how it looked, and how it smelled, and how it tasted, and how it felt, and the rest of it.

Are you going to write some kind of bullshit confection that won't do you or anybody else any good? Frankly, I don't give a shit what anybody writes about me. I've been a little bit hurt a couple times by what guys have said, but if that's what they want to say, that's what they want to say.

H.N.: There's a saying that hard work is for fools and mules. How do your friends and relatives living in Bacon County feel about the way you make your living by writing?

H.C.: Absolutely mystified. Absolutely mystified. My mother cannot believe that somebody would give you good, hard, honest money for telling a story that never happened—that's false, that's a lie. And she doesn't to this day. It's a mystery to her. And it is to the rest of my people, too, including my brother. What it's amounted to is alienation from my cousins and my aunts and uncles who raised me. Uncle Alton, may he rest easy where he is, Uncle Alton raised me like a daddy—I lived with him—but I was writing and selling things before he died. He didn't understand, either.

And so what it comes down to is an alienation from blood. I do not have one single blood connection, as we say in the South, that I can talk to. They just look at me like I'm a bank robber because, after all, you're making up stuff that are lies and selling it to people; they're paying you money, so you must be a thief. They've got some kind of thing in their heads. It doesn't make it easy, but I've come to grips with it. It makes me unhappy somehow, but I don't want to think about it. I *try* not to think about it.

H.N.: Do you think that the tragic South that you, Robert Penn Warren, and James Dickey write about is gone?

H.C.: I don't know. I *do* know we're being assimilated into the culture of the rest of the country. Kids are not hearing stories from their granddaddy's knee the way I did. My granddaddy had a white beard down to his navel; he was a rough old man. He kept a Mason fruit jar of moonshine up on the mantel shelf. Every now and then he'd go over there and take a little sip and come back and sit down. But I heard dialectical English from his mouth. When the English sent folks to Georgia in the early 1700s, they sent thieves and whores and pimps and burglars—whatever—to keep the Spanish from coming up out of Florida. My granddaddy spoke the same dialect as those folks. They didn't say "chimney," they said "chimley." And that's how I grew up saying it.

Yeah, it may disappear; it *will* disappear. We're all going to become—God love our hearts—radio disc jockeys with interchangeable parts. If you don't have phrases like "He'd rather climb a tree and tell a lie than stand on flat ground and tell the truth!"—then who the hell *are* you?

H.N.: "You don't have a pot to piss in or a window to throw it through."

H.C.: That's right, that's right. You gotta have something. You've got to *be* something and be from some*where*. And if you got that, you can tell the world to kiss your ass—that you're going to be what you're going to be, and I ain't going to be what you want me to be. I'm going to be what I'm going to be; I'm going to be what's in me to be.

The reason my brother and I fell out with each other—I haven't seen my brother in nine years; I don't care if I ever see him again—was we were up there at the farm walking out back toward the lot. He was saying, "Goddamn, Harry! I know everybody's got to make a living, and you gotta do what you can do, but I just don't know why you let our mother read that stuff." Now, he was talking about the shit in *Playboy*.

[I said,] "Now, why don't you just turn around and go back in the house and tell our mother what she can't do, 'cause I don't do that. I wouldn't presume to do that. I'm *not* going to do it."

We're grown men, I'm in my fucking forties; he's in his fifties; he's older than I am. He fucked me over as a child, beat me with a belt when Ma wasn't home. Everybody's got to get whipped sometime, but if I never see him again as long as I live, it'd be all right.

Contrary to popular belief, I'm not a violent person. But if you wrong me, I'll kill your fucking ass, and I'll spend the rest of my life in jail. I'll kill your fucking ass, and you can count on it; depend on it. You don't want to kill your own blood; you don't want to kill your brother. I just don't want to see him any more. Question?

H.N.: Did you bury a four-year-old boy?

H.C.: I buried a four-year-old boy, and I've got this one that you saw go out the door. Yeah, I found him, yeah. It was a Saturday morning in

Fort Lauderdale, Florida. I, for whatever reason—probably drinking or something—was still in bed. This bunch of little children came running and beating and banging and screaming at the door. I got up, and they said, "Your son's at the bottom of the pool, and we can't get him out."

The people next door had a pool; they had a fence around it, and ordinarily it would be locked. For some reason it wasn't locked. And I'm out of bed—I don't give a shit whether I'm dressed or not. I got on a pair of drawers. I went there, and the little bastard had taken off his fucking shoes and put them by the pool. I guess he thought he was going wading. And he got in there, and he couldn't swim. I got him off the bottom, and I held his fucking nose and gave him mouth-to-mouth resuscitation, but it wouldn't work. I knew there was something wrong; at first I thought it was his tongue. I thought he'd swallowed his tongue. But I got his tongue out and it still wouldn't work. I could tell the air wasn't going to his lungs. What had happened was he had eaten cereal that morning. When he started to drown, he threw up the cereal and sucked it back in. He was dead as a duck when we got to the hospital. Yeah.

H.N.: What was his name?

H.C.: Patrick. Yeah. What the hell were we talking about before that?

H.N.: I dunno.

H.C.: We were talking about whippings.

H.N.: Have you read a lot of Flannery O'Connor?

H.C.: I wouldn't want to put any money on it, but to the best of my knowledge, I've read everything she's written—*Mystery and Manners*, letters. I can't count her as an influence on my work, although you don't know the people who influence you.

H.N.: How's Jim Landis to work with as an editor?

H.C.: Landis is the best editor I ever had. I'll give you an example. When he got that book *This Thing Don't Lead to Heaven*, he sent me the check for the advance and he said, "I'll get back to you." He got back to me. He wrote me a thirty-two-page single-spaced, not double-spaced, letter. And man, he had *read* the goddamn thing. I mean, he had just eaten it. That's the way he is. And that's why he is the head of Morrow [Quill division]. He ain't no senior editor no more. "Senior editor" sounds big time, but it's just a fucking title. Kinda like the fucking title I got. I'm a full professor in the goddamn graduate school, and I feel about as much like a professor as a rat feels like a hippopotamus.

H.N.: I guess when you're teaching writing classes, point of view is very important. I was wondering if your viewpoint as a person is shifting as you go into your middle years?

H.C.: [*Shaking his head.*]

H.N.: Does that mean no?

H.C.: No! No! No! There are about a million ways to define point of view. If you read E. M. Forster's *Aspects of the Novel,* a series of lectures that he delivered at Oxford University, you'll see when he comes to point of view he says it is the most difficult aspect of fiction. Did you see the little book I got called *Florida Frenzy?*

H.N.: Yes.

H.C.: Did you read the front of the thing?

H.N.: Uh-huh.

H.C.: All right. I said somewhere in that tiny introduction that sometimes you'll write for a year on a book, only to discover, after a year's work, that you have chosen just that point of view in which the story you're trying to tell cannot be told. Then there's nothing to do but start again.

I want to get away from this kind of—what do I want to say?—"confessional" fiction. Usually apprentice writers, young writers that come to you, what they give to you is thinly disguised autobiography. I'd like to get away from that.

Also, if you want to know the goddamn truth, I'm sick and tired of writing books. Goddamn! I've had a couple of books that you couldn't have had any better reviews. And they died. I really want to write a book that's just going to knock everybody's dick in the dirt.

That's what I want to do. You know, when it's read by one hundred thousand, one hundred fifty thousand people. Christ, if you're going to spend a goddamn year writing a book that two thousand people read, I mean, what kind of business is that? You know what I mean. If you had a chain saw and you had some timber, you wouldn't cut down nine thousand trees just to sell five of them, would you? You'd just think, hell, I'm in the wrong business. If the shoe business were handled like the publishing business, we'd *all* be barefoot.

There's a deal that's kind of cooking. Lord, it would take so much heat off, just so much heat. I could get out of town, get about ten acres, put my own fucking vegetables into the ground, get my chickens, be on the lake, put a damn house out there, and all that kind of thing if I write—there's a deal in the works—the so-called Billy Martin story. It's his biography. At the same time this biography comes out, the screenplay's gotta come out, called "The Story of Billy Martin" or "The Billy Martin Story." If you sign a deal like that, man, you just write your name on the contract and you get a ton of money. More money than you ever thought existed in the world. I don't want to do it—I want to write another novel—but if it comes down, I don't see how I can help but do it.

Besides, it can be a great story. Billy Martin is a little guy, a tiny guy. He played second base for the old Yankees. Billy'd tell you about two words before he hit you. He don't give a shit about how big you are, how small you are, or anything else. He'll just fuck with you. No, it won't be a bad book; I'm just hungry to write another novel. I don't want to waste my time—not waste my time, but spend my time—doing that [Martin project]. But maybe I'll have to. I've been carrying alimony enough for twelve years to kill two other men. I mean, to feed a damn horse for twelve years that you ain't riding—that's hard. I'm just sick of it. Question!

H.N.: Do you feel bitter because you think you've paid your dues by writing good books already?

H.C.: Listen, son—ah, this is going to sound wimpish, but let it sound however it sounds; ain't nothing but the goddamn truth—when you come off a tenant farm, and you had the life I've had, and you're a full professor in the graduate school at the flagship university of the state of Florida, and you've written fourteen books, then yeah, yeah, yeah, I've paid fucking dues. As a matter of fact, I think somebody ought to pay me.

I'll tell you one other thing. A lot of people are predicting my death. No, I ain't going to die. I *ain't* going to die. I ain't going to go down. I'm not going to do any of those things. You see all these blinds drawn and doors closed? It's dark in here, like a cave. I'm like a goddamned hurt animal. Like a dog. Just get back in a dark place, lick your wounds, heal up, cool out. And when I come out, I'll come out biting. I'll do whatever I do. I'll either do the Billy Martin thing, or I'll do another screenplay, or I'll do a lot of things I don't want to do. I'll be back. It'll be all right. I'll be back.

MARY T. SCHMICH

Still in the Game: On the Straight and Narrow with Writer Harry Crews

Crews is losing it, they've said. Dissipating his talent. Wrecking his body. Down for the count, vodka bottle in tow.

He hasn't been a shy drunk. He didn't try to keep his self-destruction secret. He is such an irrepressible spinner of yarns and so compulsively autobiographical that the drunken nights, the brawls, and the broken bones became the stuff of stories, of Harry Crews lore, as told by Harry Crews to the world.

He wrote about the alcohol, celebrated it even, and the likes of *Playboy* and *Esquire* paid him to do it. He elevated drinking to sport, blood sport, like raising pit bulls or poaching gators or fighting cocks or any of the other blood sports he has written of so reverently, so irreverently, so cleverly and clearly.

Readers of his Charles Bronson profile know how during the interview he slipped into the bathroom of Bronson's movie-set trailer for a much-needed nip from his vodka flask. Readers of "Going Down in Valdeez" know that on an assignment in Alaska he passed out, and some pranksters tattooed a hinge on the inside of his right elbow. It is that craving for excess, in alcohol and experience and self-revelation, that's threatened to bring him down.

"Experience . . . experience . . . experience what?" Professor Harry Crews is alone this Monday in his little fourth-floor office in the University of Florida English Department at Gainesville. He is talking

From the *Atlanta Journal and Constitution,* January 27, 1985, M7+.

to himself as he writes, chin pressed to chest, eyes closed, that dense helmet of a forehead pinched in thought. Hunched over his typewriter, he looks pained, as if he's sitting on a cactus.

"Have a seat, coach. Nice to meet you. Be with you in a minute." He bestows the title "coach" apparently indiscriminately, on women, waiters, friends, students, the scholar who is chairman of the English department.

His eyes squeezed shut, he types a few quick lines on the manual Royal typewriter, a temporary replacement for his 1920s Underwood, which is out for repairs; he had hurled it across the office in a fit of pique. The last time he did that and sent it to be fixed, it came back with a coat of paint that covered the patina and the scars that had lived with him through several novels. He was furious.

He whips page 87 of his novel in progress from the typewriter and lays it on the manuscript stack, next to a corncob pipe and a retirement plan brochure. This novel is his first sustained attempt at fiction in five years.

He finally looks up and smiles. It is a smile that makes sense of that hackneyed phrase, "his face lit up with a smile." His teeth flash, his blue eyes blink like a Morse code lantern. Instant creases radiate up from his eyes and down along his high cheekbones in curves that match the line of his salt-and-pepper mustache. The Harry Crews lore doesn't necessarily prepare you for Harry Crews's warmth.

He suggests lunch, warns apologetically that his choice of restaurant is restricted by his "semiprecious diet," and begins, without prompting, to talk about alcohol.

"Alcohol whipped me. Alcohol and I had many, many marvelous times together. We laughed, we talked, we danced at the party together; then one day I woke up and the band had gone home and I was lying in the broken glass with a shirt full of puke and I said, 'Hey, man, the ball game's up'."

He swivels forty-five degrees in his desk chair and pulls some photos of himself from a low file-cabinet drawer. He thumbs through several—"There's a righteous picture, there's the kid in shape"—looking for one in particular. "There. There's the alcohol." In the photo he is squinting and disheveled. "There I am, half in the bag, enjoying myself. God, disgusting . . . disgusting." He closes the photo file and shoves it back in the drawer.

"I sort of looked askance at people who didn't drink. I thought anybody who could get through this stone-cold sober wasn't paying attention or was just dumb." He has been lipping an unlit Merit filter cigarette for a couple of minutes. "Try getting through a quart of vodka, half a case of beer, and maybe a little wine every day of your life and see what it does to your nerves." His hands tremble slightly as he lights the cigarette. He draws on it so hard that his cheeks sink into twin hollows.

He unfolds himself stiffly from the chair. Bad knees, he explains. Riding motorcycles. His blue jeans droop in baggy folds around his hips. "Everybody's predicting death for me," he says, pacing his six-foot, 199-pound bulk, radiating energy so strong you can almost feel the heat. "They thought I was out of the ball game. Everybody sees a little blood and they think the game's over. Well, there's those that want to stay in the game and those that don't."

Crews has put his mind to staying in the game with the ferocity he brings to almost everything he does. The regulars at the Gainesville Gym know he's still in it, at least in whatever game it is that pits sweat against iron.

"Harry's a wild man," says Clovis Watson, the bodybuilding champion who runs the gym. He half smiles. "You'll see."

The gym air is stirred by overhead fans. The bodybuilders grunt with strain. Metal clanks. Boy George sings, "Do You Really Want to Hurt Me?"

A self-described "world-class sweater," Crews, forty-nine, moves from machine to machine, stopping only briefly between strenuous repetitions. His brow drips sweat. His hair—which he once kept shoulder length, has been at times shaved right to the scalp and now is in a military crewcut—is matted to his head with sweat. Sweat has soaked a large V onto the chest of his gray sweatshirt.

Thanks to the semiprecious diet, which is heavy on fish and vegetables and light on alcohol, and to his three-hour workouts almost every morning, he dropped forty pounds in five months.

Between machines, Crews tells stories to the other gym clients. He and Clovis talk. "We talk about being great at whatever we're doing," says Clovis. "Me at bodybuilding. Him at writing."

Crews admires perfection, but even more the tenacity it takes to reach perfection. He admires bodybuilders, short-order cooks, roofers in midsummer, anybody who can take the heat, go the distance, fight the good fight, shoulder the burden, whatever the burden is, and who can do it without therapy. He admires survivors.

Crews is a model of the mythical "man's man," a hybrid of Ernest Hemingway and Charles Bronson with a *Dukes of Hazzard* streak. He doesn't have his hair cut in a barbershop because he can't find one without the chrome-and-plastic salon nonsense. He fishes. He roasts goats. The south Georgia sandpaper in his voice often knocks the "g" off "ing" and the "h" off "th," turning "with" into "wit" and "writing" into "writin'." He rides motorcycles and bicycles. He despises cars; if he owned one, he says, it would be an old six-cylinder Chevy pickup.

Asked how he envisions himself twenty years from now, he simply recites his broken bones: "I've broken my neck and broken my nose nine times and had my left cheek crushed and one leg broken and the other one at the knee entirely torn out, had fingers on both hands broken, ribs on both sides broken, had my sternum for God's sake cracked. I'll quit there."

A violent man, you might think, just the kind of man who would write, as he did in a recent *Playboy:* "I don't know a hell of a lot about manhood, wherein it lies or what it's made of. I'll leave that question to better minds than mine—the fem libbers, for instance. They could tell you in a New York minute. But whatever it is, a good part of it seems to be bound up with violence of one kind or another, on football fields, high school and college wrestling mats, karate dojos and—God help us all—the Armed Forces that defend this land of ours."

Just the kind of man, you might think correctly, whose writing would be punctuated with fights and bawdy sex scenes. Just the kind of man who stops at the passing of a tight-skirted woman on the sidewalk and utters a slow, unprintable, three-word exclamation of amazed admiration.

But don't call him macho. He knows people do, and he doesn't think it's true. In fact, he calls himself a feminist.

"Aw, I get my licks in every now and then just to be ornery," he says. He sounds somewhere between peeved and hurt when he talks about the frequent criticism of his character. He'll argue that the sex in his books isn't gratuitous, like sex in Harold Robbins's novels. (It's also much wittier.) He notes that the women in his novels (like those in his life) are often as strong as any man he's ever met or invented.

Of that woman on the street, he says convincingly, "I would say, she meant for me to look."

As for the violence, well, violence exists. Sure, he and his friends (and his enemies) have flattened each other in bars a few times. The point is not to win or lose or maim, but to feel. "Nose-to-nose combat is better than a psychiatrist, is never as humiliating and is not nearly so expensive," he wrote in *Playboy*. Violence doesn't make us bad, "it only makes us human."

Understanding Crews demands understanding where he came from and the distance between that place and his life today. In miles, it isn't all that far. Take I-75 from Gainesville across the Florida–Georgia line, cut east through Waycross, Georgia, and within three hours you're in Bacon County.

It is not the geographical distance but the cultural distance between the south Georgia tobacco fields and the academic halls of Gainesville, between the five-year-old boy with the infantile paralysis and the big man obsessed with the idea of stamina, between the tenant farmer's son and the man of letters he became.

"My daddy died when I was twenty months old and mama married my daddy's brother," he has written. "Until I was almost seven years old, I never knew he was not my real daddy. I know how strange that sounds, but I don't remember ever knowing. He was daddy, and I called him daddy and loved him as daddy in spite of the fact that he was drunk going in and coming out, and incredible in his violence, with the scars of a perfect set of somebody's teeth in his cheek under his left eye. Every night I lay in bed trembling, thinking, this time he's gonna kill mama. Her screaming and begging ripped and shook through the house as he beat her and beat her, usually stopping only when he got too tired to go on."

He can't recall a day in his childhood that he wasn't beaten. His mother finally left his stepfather in the middle of one violent night. She hustled the five-year-old Harry and his older brother, Hoyet, onto a bus to Jacksonville, haven of employment for Bacon County refugees. She took a job rolling cigars in the King Edward cigar factory. Harry took to stealing hubcaps.

Five months later, they moved back to a small Bacon County farm. The house was so run-down that Harry used to lull himself to sleep by counting the stars through the roof shingles. His Uncle Alton, his mother's brother, became his surrogate father and the most important man in his life. He didn't see his stepfather, the man he'd grown up calling "Daddy," until he was grown and a student at the University of Florida.

He described that meeting in his acclaimed 1978 autobiography, *A Childhood: The Biography of a Place*. "I found him in the Springfield section of Jacksonville not far from where I lost him. He was sitting in the back of a tiny store, huddled beside a stove in a huge overcoat. He was very nervous. He did not want to talk. I left minutes after I got there. We never touched each other, not even to shake hands."

Harry doesn't go home much now, but when his elderly mother, Myrtice Turner, who lives in Ashburn, Georgia, about seventy miles south of Macon, went into the hospital for cancer surgery, he sat by her bed for two days. That visit was the first time he had talked to his brother, a devout Christian who shuns alcohol, since the two had had a falling-out ten years ago. "I think Harry is leaving off drinking, and I am so grateful to God," his mother says. "He is so precious. I told him the other night when he called that his brother was so proud of him, and I said, 'I am, too. You just seemed so different this time'. He didn't say a word. I don't know whether he was proud of that or not."

Crews has been writing for almost as long as he can remember. "One looks at this in hindsight and has reason to suspect that one of the paybacks for doing this was a failed marriage," he says. "It's Friday night, the wife's been in the house taking care of the kids the whole week, and everybody else is going to a movie, or there's a party somewhere, and 'No, I'm not going. Go if you want to. I've got to work'. I just was locked in in such an obsessed way, much more obsessed than I am now."

He is wary of marriage now. "I have lived with various women off and on, three or four or five years. There haven't been that many. Two of them for five years. But then I'd go off for a year and be—dreadful phrase—hitting targets of opportunity, feeling bad about yourself so you don't give a rat's ass what you do. Somebody who was as obsessed as I was with writing doesn't have an awful lot of room in his life for another person."

After his marriage ended, he moved to Lake Swan, outside Gainesville. For five years he lived without a telephone, television, radio, newspaper, mail. There was no furniture, and the fireplace provided the only heat. He slept on a quilt on the floor. To write, he sat on a concrete block and perched his typewriter on a concrete-block stack. He calls it the most seductive period of his life.

Maggie Powell met him during that time, on a 1977 visit with her boyfriend, one of Crews's students. "The first time I ever saw Harry," she says, "he was completely naked. He was on the floor in front of a glass door. I knew I was in for an interesting experience from then on." They have lived together off and on for five years. The off time occurs whenever she's decided he's gotten, in his words, "too rank" and kicked him out.

Maggie could be a character in one of Crews's novels. She is smart, tall, lithe, steely when she puts her mind to it, and, Crews says almost reverentially, possessed of an "oceanic sympathetic sense." When she met Crews, he had already begun to drink heavily and was taking drugs.

She has since become a competitive bodybuilder and is working on a graduate degree in exercise physiology. Her prodding helped persuade Crews to trade his daily vodka for daily workouts. She was fed up with turning him out and taking him back and turning him out again. Confronted with the suggestion that he's an awfully big man to throw out, she grimaces good-naturedly. "Yeah, but even harder to carry in."

In the sultry stillness of a warm afternoon, we drive to his small cabin on Cross Creek, the closest thing to a home Crews owns, though he's rarely here. He's tried to pare his material possessions to the simplest: he doesn't own a house or a car or a suit or a pair of leather shoes. His Nikes, his motorcycle, and occasional visits to the cabin satisfy his acquisitive urge.

This afternoon on the screened porch, sweating and downing sixteen-ounce Diet Pepsis, he talks about books, God, death, and screenplays. He's a nonstop talker, as much actor as raconteur, the consummate product of his south Georgia storytelling society. He is in constant motion, his forehead rising and falling, his hands somersaulting over each other in illustrations. He throws his arms wide, the tattooed hinge on the inside right elbow opening and closing, opening and closing. He hugs his chair as if to crush it.

He has sold most of his books to producers or screenwriters. He has written screenplays for his own works and other people's as well.

Director Michael Cimino hired him to write a screenplay. Robert Duvall called shortly after winning last year's Best Actor Oscar to talk about Crews's writing a screenplay for him. Donald Sutherland called recently to discuss film possibilities for Crews's novels *Karate Is a Thing of the Spirit* and *The Hawk Is Dying*.

The list of possibilities seems endless and the list of disappointments almost as long. So far, though Crews has made substantial money from the projects, nothing has made it to the screen. He doesn't say it, but others do: the drinking has gotten in the way.

He talks long into the afternoon, the rise and fall of crickets the only sound besides his Grit voice.

On his novels: "All my novels deal with the same subject: the nature of belief. Most of them, one way or the other, are about believing in—I don't want to say God or something stupid like 'The Great One'. I don't know what to say. If you look around you at the natural world, rocks don't fall sideways, do they? They fall down. And what happens in the waters, and the miracle of our bodies, and the sap rising in the trees in the springtime, and peanuts putting the flower on top of the ground and the fruit underneath the ground. It just all blows me away. So that's part of it. But it has to do with believing in anything. It has to do with believing in writing."

On his grown son, Byron, the person he loves most on earth: "He met me at the airport not long ago. I'm tired, getting off the plane, just really dragging, I said, 'Son, I'd kiss you, but I don't think I could reach you'. He gave me a great line. He said, 'Hell, I'll bend down for an old man'. And right there, in front of God and everybody, he kissed me."

On his own death: "I don't like funerals, don't like memorials, and don't like memorial services, and don't like eulogies, don't like any of that, and so in my will, when I die, however I die, I am to be taken posthaste to the nearest crematorium and burned up without anybody seeing me. Byron is charged in my will, and this other boy, an ex-rodeo-rider, with taking my ashes to the Little Satilla River—where in my boyhood I spent many, many happy days—and feeding the fishes with my ashes. Anybody who feels moved to do things like markers and memorials or weeds or anything like that, should take whatever money they think they may have spent and give it to whatever children anywhere they think need it."

That night, Harry and Maggie eat a dinner of oysters at Lafitte's, a small restaurant in downtown Gainesville.

Crews orders Perrier, then changes the order to a carafe of white wine. He can drain a glass in a swallow. With the clean wrist-flick of an expert, he downs several that way. Another carafe, please. Maggie's eyes narrow in disapproval. They argue about whether he is getting drunk or not. The argument waxes and wanes, digresses into an ornery discussion of war and pit bulls, and eventually passes. The next morning she will say that's the first time he has drunk that way in a long time, though he doesn't really consider drinking white wine drinking.

Not everyone is convinced that Crews can beat this thing, but he is, and Maggie is. She has seen him beat drugs, and she's convinced the alcohol has to be easier.

Earlier that day, in the late afternoon light, he had leaned back in his chair, stroking the tips of his mustache, searching for a way to describe the novel he is writing. "It's about a guy," he said, "who thinks he's really got a handle on the world. He is suffering badly from the sin of pride—hubris, the Greeks would call it. He thinks he knows a great many things he does not know. He detests weakness of any sort, physical or anything else. And thinks he can hack it.

"Circumstances just collaborate to show him he's been wrong about what he thinks about himself and other people, his family included, his son specifically. He's been wrong, wrong all this time. He did not know. He was too proud—of his intellect, of his physical prowess—too proud of his ability to make his body do whatever was demanded of it.

"And it all contrives to bring him down, to bring him to a place where he is humbled, because there is no other way to do it. He comes to the place where he has to face that he is wrong, and he's been wrong for a very long time, and that his being wrong has caused an enormous amount of grief to other people, to his family, to the people he works with. To just a lot of people. And that's what it's about."

In many ways, though he doesn't say it, that is also what Harry Crews is about. And at the count of nine, Crews is on his feet.

MARY VOBORIL

Harry Goes Cruising for a Bruising

Harry Crews aches all over.

He's bruised, he's limping, his left cheekbone is cracked and he's "hurtin' to the ends of the God-damned earth." His apartment is dim as dusk, but he squints and squints, as if he were standing outside in bright white daylight. He drinks long, flooding gulps of Budweiser from a sixteen-ounce can. It is 10:15 in the morning.

"Whenever I finish a new book. I always go a little bonkers. I finish a book, and I drink," says Crews, speaking in the slow, countrified rhythms of Bacon County, Georgia. He holds the beer protectively, as if someone might snatch it away. He's wearing tan slacks, a sleeveless gray zip-up shirt, black Reeboks. His limp becomes a lurch as he moves toward a velour couch that's the deep purplish hue of good port wine.

"Uhhhhhhhh," says Crews, collapsing on the couch. Heidi, his golden retriever, trots over and plops down at his feet. She thumps her tail against the scarred terrazzo floor. Crews glances down and smiles. "Daddy loves you," he says. He looks up. "Hey, do you know about mules? How mules are made? I wrote this thing about mules. Let me read it to you...."

So begins a visit with Harry Crews, purveyor of Grit Lit, a serio-comic brand of regional writing that also goes by the name Southern Gothic and Redneck Macho. Crews is a novelist, essayist, book critic, profiler of such men as Charles Bronson and Robert Blake, playwright-

From the *Miami Herald*, June 28, 1987, G1+.

in-the-making and, since 1962, a college professor. He wrote about himself in *A Childhood: The Biography of a Place*, and his screenplays include *Clown*, based on the life of Emmett Kelly, and another based on his novel *Car*.

The manuscript for his thirteenth book, *The Knockout Artist*, is at the typist. "And hell, I had a book that came out in January, the *Hell* book," says Crews. *All We Need of Hell* is the tale of a fitness-crazed, Zen-obsessed yuppie lawyer who plays tapes of Hitler speeches as he sits on Florida beaches in a Winnebago with a built-in gym. The first printing of 7,500 sold out in twenty-three days. "An excellent, edgy novel," said the *New York Times*. "Bizarrely hilarious. There is vividness to his characters. There is ease to his prose."

The *New Yorker* praised it too ("highly entertaining"), but a *USA Today* critic derided it as "a repellent little book. . . . Shame on you, Harry Crews. And shame on Harper & Row for publishing you." The author is not charitable toward such critics. "I'm going to have to tear that guy's head off and puke down his lungs," he told *People* magazine.

Crews composed *Knockout* on a beat-up, dust-colored manual typewriter, working in the north Louisiana woods in a remodeled worm barn. He and Heidi lived there ten months. The barn had no running water, an outdoor toilet, a wood stove for heating and cooking. "In other words, what every writer needs if he can stand it," says Crews. Six words decorated one wall: "Only the dead have no fear."

He and Heidi returned to Florida in May, and for the last three days they've lived in the dingy two-room $195-a-month apartment, "a God-damned cell." He wants to move. He hates the plastic, hates the Formica, but the University of Florida campus is only two blocks away, and Crews doesn't drive these days.

"You know why I'm living here? Oh, darlin', I totaled my truck. And totaled a Cadillac. Drunk," he says. It happened the morning of May 20 as Crews drove to a Gainesville gym. So did the accident cause the bruises, the cracked cheekbone, the limp? "Nah." Then what did? "Drinkin'," Crews says. "Drinkin'. Drinkin'. Drinkin'."

Anything worth doing, he says, is worth overdoing. When he drinks, he overdrinks. He teeters, he falls, his legs buckling and twisting at odd hurtful angles. He's also had concussions, razor cuts, both knees broken, both feet broken, ribs broken on both sides, a broken sternum, a broken neck, a nose broken nine times. "I have an incredible recovery rate," he says. He also says, "I get up and I write, every day at four in the morning, no matter how bad I hurt."

His recent troubles are "minor tragedies, boring," not picaresque enough to qualify for a story he plans to write someday, a story called "Jails I Have Known." He gets hurt at cock-fights, pit-bull fights—he's addicted to blood sports, including football—and once at a disco at St. Augustine Beach, where he was arrested. Police officers, he says, "almost always leave you living. I mean, after all. If they don't, they've got all those forms to fill out."

It's time for lunch. Crews wants to go to the Yearling, not far from Marjorie Kinnan Rawlings's home at Cross Creek. But this is Monday, and it's closed. His second choice is Lafitte's, a wood-paneled seafood restaurant run by a former student.

Crews sits in a booth, his back to the wall. He eats three forkfuls of shrimp salad and drinks six glasses of white wine. He drinks as if they were cups of warm coffee on a cold day, long throaty swallows, no pauses, half a glass at a time.

"Say, did you read the piece I wrote about my mama? For Mother's Day?" This was in the May issue of *Southern* magazine, to which Crews is a contributing editor. It's an affectionate, deftly worded tribute to his mother Myrtice, whose schooling ended at the second grade. She taught him lessons in self-respect, such as, "It's no disgrace to get dirty; the only disgrace is in staying dirty." She still adds an admonishment to her goodbyes: "Now, son," she tells Crews, "be good and do right."

Harry Eugene Crews was born on the fringes of the Okefenokee Swamp in the "hookworm and rickets belt" of rural Georgia to a life that would be marked by calamity as much as by creativity. His father, Ray, helped carve the Tamiami Trail out of the South Florida swamps, returning home in 1925, when "farmers were saying there wasn't enough cash money in the county to close up a dead man's eyes." He died before Crews was two. Never having known his father, Crews writes, "I knew I would be looking for him the rest of my life."

In a Georgia farmhouse, Crews fished for chickens by dropping a string and corn-baited hook through cracks in the floorboards. He loved possum, but his mother wouldn't cook it: "she said she knew it would taste like a wet dog smells." The Sears catalog beguiled him.

"All the people in its pages were perfect. Nearly everybody I knew had something missing, a finger cut off, a toe split, an ear half chewed away, an eye clouded with blindness from a glancing fence staple. But the people in the catalog had no such hurts." He survived polio, then almost was boiled alive. In a game of crack-the-whip at a hog butchering, he was flung into a trough of scalding water. A bystander immediately hauled him out, but Crews's skin and even his fingernails began sloughing off, falling into bloody puddles at his feet.

At seventeen, he joined the Marines. At the University of Florida, he was denied admission to the same graduate English program in which he now teaches. He and his former wife had two sons. One drowned in a neighbor's pool at age four, when Crews was teaching in Fort Lauderdale. Crews recovered the body. His surviving son, Byron, now twenty-four, plays guitar professionally.

Crews orders more wine. He's described himself as "nervous, energetic, a shifter in seats, a chomper at bits, revved pretty tight all the time." A tough guy. Mean. Yet there is about Crews a substratum of likability, a subtle, inconstant current of warmth and nice-guyness. Physically, he's out of shape. "The thing about drinking, it bloats you up like a horse," he says. His stomach is big as half a basketball. It pokes out over a pewter-colored belt buckle that's stamped with a hawk. He makes a muscle with his right arm, the arm with a tattoo of a blue hinge on the inside of the elbow. The hinge was burned on in Alaska, where he'd gone on assignment for *Playboy*. He passed out, drunk. When he woke up, there was the hinge.

Crews keeps the arm tautly muscled. "Feel that," he says. The bicep feels hard and stony, like a new baseball. Crews sees it differently. He looks at the arm and talks to it. "A gun," he says. "Fifty-two-year-old guys don't normally hold that kind of heat. That's a gun." He unmuscles his arm and spreads his fingers, palms up. They're ridged with thick calluses, a legacy of weight training.

More wine arrives. "The plan," says Crews, "the plan is to stay alive." He wants his body to wear out, not grow old. "Burn it all up," he says. "American society is so disgusting. You get a house. You build a big, big fence. You buy a lot of insurance. You save your money for your Golden Years. Has anything ever in the history of the world been more of a misnomer than 'Your Golden Years'? Christ, your teeth are gone, your eyesight's gone, you can't have sex, your mind—

everything's gone. Screw 'em, man. Not this one," he says, jerking his thumb toward his raised chin.

He's studied karate, hiked the Appalachian Trail, scaled mountains, used drugs that made an orange light big as a pumpkin explode behind his eyes, then pulse for four days. He rides motorcycles coast-to-coast and wrecks them, including "the foggy Christmas morning of 1958, just before daylight, when I laid a motorcycle down and went under one side of a semi—an eighteen-wheeler carrying U.S. mail—and came out the other." He teaches because "every man ought to have more than one thing he does well.... When my writing is going badly, it is absolutely necessary for me to have something else I can do that makes me feel good about myself.

"I teach a sensational class. When I walk out of the room or the lecture hall, a little voice is going off in the back of my head saying, 'Son, you may cain't write, but you sure as hell can teach'." He has written, "It's not unusual for a twenty-year-old boy to tell you that you don't know a damn thing about a subject you've been studying thirty years." Even so, he critiques the boy's writing so that his spirit, his desire to excel, is not killed. Of fifteen students a year, he says, perhaps four could succeed as writers.

Crews shoves aside the shrimp salad plate. He gulps another half-glass of wine. He's answering unasked questions. "Talent. Ahhhh, everyone talks about talent. Talent helps. Listen, get all the talent you can. But writing is guts and it's courage. You cannot have a failure of courage. Everybody in the world is telling you you're no good, and you can't do it, and it's not going to work. You've got to keep talking to yourself, say, 'Come on, son. Come on . . . .'"

He is helped out of the restaurant. He has written, "When I feel a case of the black twirlies, or free-floating anxiety, or just the need to cool out from the typewriter, I go to Cross Creek." He's on his way there now. He buys more beer at a convenience store. He reaches the passenger door of a rented Buick Regal and stands swaying in the heat. He is asked: Are you all right? He closes one eye, squints with the other, as if sighting through a rifle scope. His face is savage, his voice harsh: "Don't be kind to me." His mood has shifted.

"Let the rest of the world say what they want," says Crews, working his way into the car. "Let 'em say, 'Weeeeeelll, Crews is drunk'. I'm not well thought of, champ. I'm not well thought of by my, uh, 'peers' at the university, and we put 'peers' in quotes, because I sure as hell don't consider them peers.

"Like I told you a while ago—or as we say in the English Department, *as* I told you a while ago—man, teachers are not my favorite people.... Do I stink, by the way? If I stink, say, 'You stink'."

When *A Feast of Snakes* was published in 1976, Jonathan Yardley, a Pulitzer Prize–winning critic who now works for the *Washington Post*, called it "absolutely stunning." Crews, he said, had reached the first rank of American novelists. He had crossed an invisible but important line. He no longer was a writer of promise. He was a writer of achievement.

Cross Creek is a kind of shrine to writers of promise. Crews will not leave the car. "Not when I'm like this," he says. "I'm not always like this. I wish you could see me when I'm not like this." A broadcasting crew saw him like this. "Two goddamn weeks they were with me. Know what they said? They said, 'It's a disgrace to have a man like Harry Crews on a university campus. The students have to watch him self-destruct'. Well, this was five years ago, and I haven't self-destructed yet. I'm too mean to die."

That may be, but he's not too mean to cry as he talks about Flannery O'Connor, to whom he's been favorably compared. He cries again as he says, "I stay scared about half the time of my life. I run scared. I look strong but I run scared." What makes him scared? "I have nobody. A man needs a woman he can love, even if he can't get along with her." He married and divorced the same woman twice.

Crews cites Dylan Thomas, Arthur Miller, Goethe ("There is no crime of which I cannot conceive myself guilty"). He's been drunk with Tennessee Williams. He's rescued a wounded hawk. He has rescued a wounded graduate student, who phoned at 3 A.M., saying he'd hit a deer on his motorcycle. "I'm hurt bad," he told Crews. "I told him, 'Hang on, hang on. I ain't lost a graduate student yet, and I ain't gonna lose you'."

Crews has written that he shares a dream with Robert Blake: Wherever he is, he doesn't belong. He's written that nothing human surprises him, that the evidence does not support Norman Rockwell. And also, "It's two kinds of people in this world. Us that wants a drink and them that don't want us to have one." Right now he wants a drink.

The rented Buick pulls up to another convenience store near Cross Creek. Crews hands over ten dollars, asks for a six-pack. He drinks the beer the same way he drank the wine at lunch. It's twenty-two miles to his home in Gainesville.

His characters tend to be hard-drinking, hard-talking, hard-living, back-against-the-wall misfits who have a taste for ex-cheerleaders, men who find no peace, their souls seething and beset by sourceless rages. The prose can be memorable and elegant, the sentences beautifully balanced, the commentary on human nature shrewd and true and funny. People don't just die, they "bite the big bagel." Another tells her son his father "was not wrapped real tight. His loaf was missing several slices." One man says, "Damned if I don't feel like somebody just told me I didn't have cancer."

In Crews's books, a man reaches over and pats the rear fender of his pickup "the way men in an earlier time patted the withers of their best horse." Drag race audiences stare at the track "with the same intensity as a surgeon staring into an open chest cavity." A man who suffered buckshot wounds now has a back "full of little purple holes, like somebody set it afire and put out the fire with an ice pick."

The *Hell* protagonist "didn't mind being thought crazy. But he did mind being thought a fool." As for craziness, "old folks can't go crazy, not in the South they can't. In the South they're just 'that way'." A pro football player is asked if he ever thinks about death; he answers, "Everyone thinks about death." And what does he think about when he thinks about death? "I think . . . I think death will annoy me."

In the car, Crews shifts suddenly. He wants to know, "Did you hear what the governor said about me?" This is former governor and now senator Bob Graham, who delivered the UF commencement address last May. He advised the graduating seniors to do five things: Keep their running sweats and Reeboks in the front of their closets, visit museums, go to concerts, travel. And also, "Read Professor Harry Crews's new novel."

On the two-lane road back to Gainesville, Professor Harry Crews falls silent. He squeezes his eyes shut. He looks as if he aches all over. His head falls back. He contorts his mouth in a soundless howl. His head falls forward. He covers his face with his left hand. His right hand looks as if it's fused to the beer can.

In the narrow parking lot of his one-story, concrete-block apartment building, Crews is helped from the car. He's in a sour, damn-the-world mood. He mutters something about handguns. Heidi, the golden retriever, stands inside the door, inside the dimness. Her tail wags and wags. Crews's mood loses its edge. He collapses into a recliner chair. He says, "If you ever, ever get in trouble and need help, call me. Collect." And also, "Will you get me another beer before you go?"

The refrigerator light is burned out. The wire shelves are empty, except for a cellophane bag of hard candy and five sixteen-ounce cans of Budweiser. He reaches for the fresh can and holds it protectively, as if he fears someone might wrest it away. He takes a long, flooding swallow. He cannot stand without falling. It is 3:15 in the afternoon.

Harry Crews is not always like this. It's just that he's finished a new book. And whenever that happens, he always goes a little bonkers. He finishes a book, and he drinks.

WILLIAM WALSH

Harry Crews

Harry Crews has a reputation of being a hard-driving, hard-drinking, bar-fighting writer. The horror stories of his harsh life run rampant in literary circles; half of them are true and the other half might as well be. To sit down and talk with him is a powerful experience; he stares you in the eye, cusses, gulps his coffee, puts out his cigarette butts on the table edge, sits broad-shouldered, and asks why anyone would drive all night from Atlanta to Gainesville to talk with him. He is straightforward and to the point, and I couldn't help but believe he could be any one of his characters from the meanest to the nicest. This interview was conducted on January 10, 1988, at his office at the University of Florida.

W.W.: After serving in the Marines, you attended the University of Florida, where you met Andrew Lytle.

H.C.: Right. I didn't meet him for a good long time. I always knew he was on campus, but I didn't go to any kind of writing classes. I think it's generally true the more serious a young man or woman is about writing, the more steadfastly they refuse to go to anything called a writing class. Primarily because they have the wrong notion of what goes on in the class. No, they probably know what goes on in there and they stay away for good reason.

But if you can go to a writing class in which the writer, the person holding the class, understands that writing cannot be taught, but can

From *Speak So I Shall Know Thee: Interviews with Southern Writers,* by William Walsh (Jefferson, N.C.: McFarland and Company, 1990).

only be coached, and if the teacher is really undertaking to do for you what a good editor would do for you, if you had a good editor, then it's worth going to. Anybody who really is out to "teach" writing—you want to stay away from that son-of-a-bitch.

Anyways, I lived with some veteran friends in a place called Twelve Oaks Bath and Tennis Club. They were apprentice writers and they knew about Lytle, and finally they got me to sit in on a class. After one class I knew that's where I ought to be. That was the first glimmer, the first notion I had of how truly ignorant I was of what I was trying to do and how much I had to learn if I was ever to write. I was with him for a couple of years—a good long time. The game was—I wrote and he read, and sometimes he talked to me about what I wrote, sometimes he didn't, which was precisely right. Much of what I wrote wasn't worth talking about.

W.W.: In mentioning editing and workshopping a writer's work, do you agree that in a workshop the students are editing work they are incapable of editing? How do you feel about the workshop?

H.C.: No. No. It's up to the person running that thing to try to give the class direction, to cut off long monologues that aren't going anywhere and have no point. But it's all part of the process, having everybody talk about everybody's work.

It always seems like wasted motion to the person whose work is being considered. They want to know what the writer thinks and not what their peers think. Not only are you trying to coach what the people write in the workshop, but you are trying to develop in them editorial skills only because they're going to have to edit their own work. If they don't edit it, no one will.

We don't have any editors at publishing houses much anymore. I don't know what they pay editors for at houses anymore—like Random House, Knopf, Morrow, or Viking. They don't have editors in the sense that Maxwell Perkins was an editor—people who really did edit work. Editors think that if they quarrel about a fact or two, or an image, that they are editing manuscripts—that's not editing at all.

While apprentice writers may object to other apprentice writers talking about their work, that's all part of the process, part of the pain of it, but just as long as it is understood in the workshop that the writer is under no obligation to do anything anyone tells him. If you hear something you can use—use it. If you don't hear anything you can use, then just disregard the whole goddamn evening and go do what you want to do.

W.W.: How much editing do your editors do, say on your latest novel, *All We Need of Hell?*

H.C.: I can't speak for what may have happened to other writers' manuscripts, but my editor goes through the manuscript and quarrels with language. They say this is too fast, this is too slow, I don't believe this—all that stuff—most of which can be disregarded. I believe that if a good reader has trouble with something you've written, the least you owe to yourself is to take a good hard look at it.

As far as I'm concerned, editors are a goddamn nuisance and an obstacle to get over. I've had two editors that were good—Jim Landis and Chuck Corn. Landis edited my first five books. He's a good reader, a very conscious worker, and he was fine. Charles Corn, a boy from Macon, Georgia, helped me a lot with *A Childhood*. He was a good editor, but I only worked with him on one book. So with six books I've had good editors, and maybe I'll run into another good editor.

W.W.: When you first began writing, you dissected Graham Greene's *The End of the Affair*, where you broke it down to numbers—the number of characters, scenes, rooms, etc. Why Graham Greene and not Faulkner or Hemingway?

H.C.: Because I had read everything Greene had written up to that time, and still have read him right along over the years. I honor the man's name. I do. I hold him in high esteem.

Why not Faulkner? At the time I was doing this, I probably wasn't a good enough reader, and I had not read as much Faulkner as I should have read. Reading Faulkner isn't going to make you a better writer, because he was such a one-of-a-kind writer that much of what he does is very useless to the rest of us. Faulkner, when Faulkner is bad, is as bad as it gets. There are similes and metaphors and language in Faulkner that are absolutely terrible. There's a story called "Wash," where Faulkner is writing about a shack and it's built down by a stream, and the shack is tumbling down. He says the shack looks like some ancient primeval beast that has dragged itself there to the stream to slake its thirst and die. Terrible, dreadful. And all that doom is terrible.

Don't misunderstand me, because I concur with a great many other people that Faulkner is a genius, but whether or not he is a great place for a young writer to go to emulate . . . I have problems with that. You sure as hell can't take any of his things as a design that you're going to use as a model. That won't do. Of course, you have to understand I'm talking about very young writers. I'm not talking about guys as old as I am. With luck there comes a time when you're not trying to model yourself after anybody. You're trying to discover whatever is in you, which you were doing from the beginning, to release as dramatically and compellingly as you possibly can. But in the beginning, you are trying to find your voice, your subject, whatever you do well, what you don't do well—all those things—then you're subject to do anything. There's nothing wrong with modeling your story on someone else's.

The bottom line on this for me is—you do whatever you have to do to get where you need to go. You dig that? You do whatever you have to do to get where you need to go. And no two writers do it the same way. If whatever it is you feel is necessary for you to do, and if other people make fun of that, well, my feeling is—to hell with them. If you find that it's a good thing to do, go do it. Because the world is full of bad advice.

As a matter of fact, the world doesn't want you to do anything. The world wants you to work the lawn or walk the dog or paint the house—anything but write, just so you bleed whatever energy you have away from writing, and if you're not careful that's exactly what you're going to end up doing. There are writers who manage to be good husbands, good fathers who paint the house, water the lawn, and do their writing, too. If that's the case, wonderful. There's nothing wrong with that. I've never been able to do that.

You have to hoard that energy and keep it for the work and not spill it willy-nilly here and there. Obviously, you have obligations to husbands and wives and children and to a job to keep bread on the table. I know that and I accept that, but we have too many examples before us of writers who simply wasted their energy and talent by using it up in other things. There are a number of people who would point to me as an example of one of those writers who has used up his talent and energy doing things he should not have been doing instead of writing.

W.W.: Much of your writing generates out of those experiences you've had while not writing.

H.C.: Exactly. If I had not done the things I had done, I would not have written the books I've written.

W.W.: In reference to your work, Allen Shepard wrote in the *Dictionary of Literary Biography*, "It is not something one wants to [read] too much of at a single sitting. The intensity of his vision is unsettling." How do you feel about that description of your work?

H.C.: I resigned myself a long time ago to not have very many readers, because I have enough sense to know that not many people are going to want to read or are capable of reading what I write. There simply aren't many readers of fiction anyway.

Unfortunately, fiction, if it is equated with anything, it is the movies and television—that is to say, as entertainment. There's nothing wrong with being entertaining. Fiction ought to be entertaining in the sense that it takes you out of your own skin for a while and puts you in someone else's skin. But over and above that, good fiction, unlike most of the other forms of entertainment that fiction competes with, ultimately, ought to turn you back upon yourself and force you to make judgments about your own life and the rightness and wrongness of your life. This should happen to your particular reader. He should see your particular vision of the world. It should force him to make judgments, and most people don't want to do that.

W.W.: Your books are funny. Some of the passages had me rolling on the floor, but that's not what drew me to your books initially. Essentially, it was the craft of storytelling, especially in the understatement of your descriptions. In *Car* specifically, there is a scene where a family of four is killed, and instead of going into the bloody gore like you could have, which a lesser writer might have, you described the little boy, who, instead of going through the windshield or being cut up—you said there was a spot in the glass where someone's head had stopped. Reading that scene was a startling experience. That understatement is seen throughout your books, and it's very powerful.

H.C.: Very often the horror and the terror of the thing becomes magnified by simply drawing back and understating.

W.W.: Let's discuss the grotesqueness of your work.

H.C.: People have brought it up and reviewers talk about it—they use words like "Gothic" and "grotesque," and if that's what I am, then that's what I am. That's all right. I take no offense at it. You've got to understand that I think of myself as a storyteller. I tell stories. That's what I do.

All of my stories have a certain flavor, smell, taste, texture—whatever you want to say—as do most writers' stories. If a reader finds what I write distasteful, then I'd be a fool to argue with him. I'd say don't read it. And many people do find what I write distasteful. It's more than that—they're absolutely outraged. The first review I saw of *All We Need of Hell*, I was in a little cabin in Louisiana and a boy brought me a *USA Today* and the review was just terrible. Initially, I wondered why the guy went on as long as he did. If you think something is absolutely dreadful, without any merit, why the hell go on at great length about it? Just say it's terrible and stop. That fellow simply doesn't need to read any more of my fiction. I hope he doesn't upset himself that way. Life's too short for him to read something that's going to put him off so badly.

W.W.: The grotesqueness is brought about by the character's actions, but, also, to a large extent by the character's physical features—like the boy, Marvin, with no legs in *The Gypsy's Curse*. There isn't any of that physical grotesqueness in *All We Need of Hell*.

H.C.: Right, and there isn't any in my new book coming out in the spring, called *The Knockout Artist*. Except there is in a way. The kid can knock himself out. That's his claim to fame—he can knock himself out . . . I've been asked time out of mind why the boy in *The Gypsy's Curse* walks on his hands, can't talk and he can't hear, and so on. I have no ready answer to that. I've been asked that nine million times, and I guess the quickest and best answer to that is that I can write better about the "normal" world by writing about the "abnormal" world.

It seems to me that this is in no way unique to me. All we have to do is look at *Gulliver's Travels*. Why write about little tiny people? Why write it the way he did? Obviously, it's saying something about you and me or it wouldn't have stood up for this long a time. But from the number of times I've been asked about it, you'd think it was unique to me.

W.W.: The reason I brought it up was because you have been heavily criticized for it. I mean, who wants to read about normalcy? Many of your characters border a fine line between normal and abnormal.

H.C.: Fiction always deals with extremes. Fiction is always about someone whose ass is on the line. He has to jump left or jump right, he can't stay where he is. And the reason for it is very simple—it is in a crisis, conflicts, in what I think of as "blood moments," that you find out who the hell you are, what you really are, what you really believe, what you're really capable of—that's where you find it out. You don't find it out otherwise. Most of us are never caught in those circumstances so we won't know. Are you a coward or are you able to control your fear and behave with what the world calls courage? Most people won't know, because they've never been tested.

In fiction, if the fiction turns you back upon yourself, then despite the fact that you've never been caught in those circumstances, you have to deal with those issues. That gets to the heart of why I write as I do, and why all other writers write the way they do. If you look at a really good novel, like Norman Mailer's *An American Dream,* most of us aren't going to kill our wife and leave her by the bed, dead, and then go down the hall and screw the maid, and then come back and throw our dead wife out the window. I suspect none of us are going to do that. But, Mailer forces us to consider it in his novels. If we read the novel, we are forced to psychologically and emotionally (spiritually, if you will) deal with those circumstances.

W.W.: In *A Childhood* you state, "There wasn't enough money to close up a dead man's eyes." You grew up on biscuits made of flour, lard, and water. You would eat dirt to get the minerals you needed. Was this the hardest part about your childhood?

H.C.: We didn't have to eat the dirt, but we did. That's not too unusual for kids to do. They don't know why they're doing it but their body knows why.

The lack of money wasn't the hardest part, but it didn't make my childhood particularly pleasant. Not to have food, clothes, and to not have a place with any permanence was hard. There were all sorts of problems: my father dying, a mother who was uneducated having to raise two small children, getting involved with a second husband whom I loved very much, but unfortunately was locked into an alcoholic mist, and my brother and I were thrown back upon our mother's resources that were nonexistent, except for courage and determination.

I think the worst part of my childhood was the absence of a father. But, as the logicians say, I'm reasoning contrary to fact. I don't know what it would have been like if my daddy had lived. I never knew him. I don't know him now. I know him insofar as I wrote about him in that book, and whatever I know about him is what people have told me. And since memory is always suspect, I don't know if what I know about my father is true or not, or if my notion of him is true or not. It's just the one I'm stuck with.

W.W.: On page 14 of *A Childhood* you wrote, "And more marvelous still, to be able to return to that place of your childhood and see it through the eyes of a man, with everything set against that long-ago, little boy's memory of how things used to be."

H.C.: Place is very important to me. What I was writing about there was about my part of the county, the land I was raised on, the house I was raised in, and to come back and see it as a grown man. As a kid we moved a lot, so we never were in one place for too long. I never had a lot of things. I still don't have many things. I don't want a lot of things. I never buy myself anything. I did not buy these shoes I have on. I didn't buy these trousers. This vest was sent to me from New Orleans, as was the shirt, by Maggie Powell. She bought them and sent them to me. I don't think having things is a great plus.

I don't know if I'm making any connection necessarily with my childhood. Am I this way as an adult because I was that way as a child? That's too simplistic, to reason that way. It may very well be a natural extension of my childhood, but I don't know. I don't own many things. I don't have many things. Whether they be books, clothes, or furniture, I think of them as an encumbrance. I could pack up everything I own and put it in the back of my truck along with my dog and I could leave town today.

W.W.: *A Childhood* was beautifully portrayed, from making up stories from the Sears catalog to the neighbor raiding your smokehouse. Out of that do you have a favorite childhood memory?

H.C.: Yes, it's sitting around the house telling stories. But it's got to be cold outside and it's got to be dark and you're tired and you have the foot tub in front of the fireplace and everybody's washed their feet—that's about the only thing we washed. We told stories.

Tobacco-selling time was always a favorite time of the year because strange things came into the house. Tobacco was a money crop and you got new overalls, new shoes, and weenies, which you never saw—store-bought goods—sliced bread and all that good stuff. So that was a great time. Hog-killing time was a great thing.

W.W.: What was the worst part of your childhood?

H.C.: Probably the episode when my legs drew up so that my heels were against my buttocks. I couldn't walk for a year. Whether it was infantile paralysis or polio I don't know. Some doctors said it wasn't, but that it was an hysterical symptom, and that there was nothing wrong with me. Maybe I just retreated to the bed because I couldn't deal with what was outside the bed.

W.W.: Could you discuss *The Knockout Artist,* your new book coming out this spring?

H.C.: No, it's complicated and too complex. I like the book a lot and the publisher likes the book a lot. I don't have the foggiest notion what reviewers, the public, or anybody else will think of it, and I don't care. It's done now, and whatever reception it has, that's the reception it will have. I'm on a play, now.

I will say that it's about a twenty-year-old boy, a fighter, and he's had thirteen fights. His manager abandons him in New Orleans after a fight where he was knocked out. That boy comes from where I come from—Bacon County, Georgia—right off a farm as I came off a farm. He has to make do as best he can in what for him is a foreign land. I went to New Orleans to write the novel. I'd been there many times before, but I'd never written a novel set in that city. Since he comes from a farm the way I did, why not let the boy have my sensibilities and feelings—I mean, I know how a person from Bacon County, Georgia, would react to New Orleans. Said more specifically, I know how I would react to New Orleans.

So that boy very much has my own knowledge, sensibilities, and prejudices. I probably identify with the boy in that book more than any other character I've written.

W.W.: You would say that this is you under the circumstances that you could have put yourself in?

H.C.: Yeah. Pretty much the way he reacts is the way I would react when I was his age, given who he is, had I been who he is. And at the same time I am, I'm not.

W.W.: The thing I found with your books is that you have never trampled the same ground twice, you never backtrack. You must have a wide range of interests and knowledge as you cover so many different things, from manning a hawk, to putting headliners in cars, to karate.

H.C.: I've trapped and trained hawks like the guy in *The Hawk Is Dying* at a place called Payne's Prairie. I caught two hawks out there; I manned them and flew them. I didn't do that to write a novel. After I manned them, I just happened to write the novel. I studied karate with a guy named Dirk Mosig, here in town, and I never would have written *Karate Is a Thing of the Spirit* if I hadn't studied karate. I never would have written *The Knockout Artist* if I hadn't spent a good bit of my young manhood around a fight gymnasium with boxers, managers, or if my brother hadn't been a fighter.

In *The Gypsy's Curse*, the guy's name is Al Molarski. Well, I knew a guy named Al Berkowitz, who owned a gym. He owned the Firemen's Gym in Jacksonville—I just moved the gym to Clearwater when I wrote the novel. There was in that gym a guy who walked on his hands and was a deaf-mute, and he had been raised by Al Berkowitz. But I never knew the guy. I saw him. I saw him running up the stairs on his hands to the gym. I saw him hand balancing, but I never knew a deaf-mute in my life. I didn't know him; I just saw him. This was thirty-five years before I wrote about it.

My fiction is a visceral response to the world I live in. I guess to some extent it is an intellectual response, too, but it's a gut response to the world I live in, much in the way that some people, because of certain body chemistries, can walk through the woods and break out in a rash because they are allergic to certain plants. Artists are people who walk through the world, and because of a certain psychic chemistry, they break out into novels, poetry, paintings, and music.

ROB MICHAELS

Harry Crews: Pen-Packin' Old Boy

Mr. Harry Crews is one of the grittiest, funniest, and most compassionate writers ever to emerge from the American South, and considering the competition, that's no mean feat. His roots extend deep into the mean and sweat-stained soil of the southern-Georgia dirt farm where he grew up in the wake of the Great Depression, a brutal season stunningly chronicled in A Childhood: The Biography of a Place. *A man with hogback wanderlust, Crews has left a trail of some of the most side-splitting, tear-jerking, gut-wrenching pulp you'll ever read—mad and vital tales of Chevy-eating, snake-sucking, and bible/beaver-thumping heels/heroes staring down their fates and leaving their own crazy stains on an alien and unforgiving world.*

Motorbooty spoke via telephone with this deadeye potentate of weather-beaten wisdom and transcendental profanity.

R.M.: So, you've published a new book?

H.C.: Yeah. It's called *Body* and I could have gone to any number of places to get it published, but I ended up at Poseidon Press because they got me laid.

R.M.: Are your dealings with the publishing industry often a source of trouble?

H.C.: I'm not sure there are any generalities that one could make about the publishing world that'll hold up, except that most of the

From *Motorbooty* 5 (Winter 1990): 18–22.

people involved are assholes. I've been treated pretty well, though. When you have a publisher, many times the only person you know there is the editor, and it's not so much that there's an adversarial situation between writers and editors, but the truth of the matter is this: a writer spends a year, year and a half or whatever it is writing a book and then some editor sits on the toilet for a weekend reading it and tells you what's wrong with it. You learn quickly that they might be right and they might be wrong. I *do* think a good editor is a good thing to have, but a good editor is nothing more than a good reader, someone simply saying I do believe this, I don't believe that; this is too fast, this transition doesn't work, etc. Editors, like agents, are a necessary evil. I never read a contract—I leave that up to my agent. I just make sure they promise me a lot of pussy whenever I come into town and sign on the dotted line.

R.M.: Have you written much nonfiction lately?

H.C.: Yes. A little while ago I found out that Sean Penn and Madonna are bibliophiles, both of 'em—not only do they buy and collect books, but they read 'em too. After they read *The Knockout Artist*, they asked me to go to the Spinks–Tyson fight with them, and I did, and later I wrote a piece on Madonna for a magazine. So yeah, I do some of it, but I started out to be a novelist, and that's where my heart is, so I do less and less nonfiction.

I'm currently writing a screenplay for Sean Penn. He wants to stop acting and direct, which should make everyone happy. We got along real well off the bat. He treated me like blood kin, and I'd trust him with life. I don't mind writing screenplays, but it's Sears, Roebuck catalog prose. It doesn't matter how it's written, just so you know what the camera's looking at. It turns me off—it reminds me of writing instructions on how to run a lawn mower.

R.M.: A lot of your books involve sports: football, boxing, karate . . .

H.C.: Well, my new book is informed by the world of female bodybuilding. I trained a girl that won a bunch of titles—she could have won the world if she'd have wanted to get heavier than 124 pounds, but she wouldn't. The girls that win the world now do it at weights like 155, and they look good so long as they're in briefs and under posing lights and at a distance from ya, but put one of 'em in a dress, and they don't look so . . . well, it depends on the man. I admire them greatly, but I've never been to bed with a 155-pound world-beating female bodybuilder (or a male bodybuilder for that matter), and I don't know what it would be like, but it seems like huggin' one of 'em would be like huggin' a guy. But I don't know, fuck it, I don't want to pass judgement on shit like that.

You're right, I follow a number of sports, boxing more closely than anything else. And strangely enough, I love track and field. I'd just as soon go to a goddamn track meet as just about anything that I can think of going to. Shit, I can remember when the seven-foot high jump was an insuperable barrier. I can remember when the four-minute mile was an insuperable barrier. Let me tell you something about that shit. Everybody knows that Roger Bannister was the first guy to run a sub-four-minute mile, but almost nobody knows how long his record stood. His goddamn record stood seventeen fuckin' days, bud. All them years everybody said no one was going to run a sub-four-minute mile, but once one man showed that it was possible, a whole slew of guys came in and ran a sub-four-minute mile.

I can tell you in just a heartbeat what my fascination with sports is. It's this: I think all of us are looking for that which does not admit of bullshit. You can't get it in a marriage, you can't get it in a—to use a word I hate—relationship, you can't get it from the church or the government. The government for godsakes, don't get me started on that. Every government in the world is just a tissue of lies, and anybody who doesn't know that just hasn't thought about it very much. But if you tell me you've got 4.4 speed in the forty, hell, we'll just put a watch on you and see if you've got it or not. If you tell me you can bench press 450, hell, we'll load up the bar and put you under it. Either you can do it or you can't do it—you can't bullshit. Ultimately, sports are just about as close to what one could call the truth as it is possible to get in this world.

R.M.: Do you think writing cuts through bullshit in a similar way as sports?

H.C.: Well, I think that, but I also think there's a connection in another way. If you wanna find out what you're made of, then you undertake to write a novel. In the popular mind, I think writers are thought as kind of panty-waisted, limp-wristed, semiprecious people. But it takes a brand of courage and a tolerance, a very high tolerance, for failure, frustration, and self-doubt, for running up into something that looks like it's totally impossible, and instead of turning around and abandoning it, you sit to it and say, no, goddamn it, there's an answer in here somewhere, and I'm going to find it or fuckin' die.

It requires a tolerance for self-doubt and anxiety that most people have no notion of. Most anyone can deal with that sort of thing for a day or two, maybe even a week or two, but try dealing with it for a year or two. You get up every morning and it's still there, right where you left it. I've never started a book in my life that I knew the ending of. I've never made an outline in my life. Discovery is what it's all about. If you already knew all the stuff you're writing about, there'd be no reason to write about it. Writing is a form of thinking and a form of finding out at some kind of gut, blood level what you think about a thing.

Playboy recently bought a chapter from my new novel, and it was written in a way that almost nothing that I write is ever written. I wrote the whole chapter in one sitting. I wrote much longer than I usually do, but I was so in love with what I was doing and it was working even though I didn't think I could make it work because it's a fuckin' love story, kind of a sub-story to the rest of the novel.

There's this world-beating male bodybuilder, and among other things he's got the greatest back in the world—nobody's ever had a back like that. He falls in love with this young girl who would be pretty if she was about a hundred and fifty pounds lighter. She's got good bone structure and all that but she's just a very fat girl. It's the first time they ever get down and get close. With her being as fat as she is, she hasn't had that many guys hit on her in her life, and all that shit's alien to her. It's nice. It's real sweet and it's pretty. I don't write that many sweet and pretty tender things. I don't have anything against them, I've got something for them, but they rarely come to me.

The odds are so overwhelming, statistically, against the thing that happens between men and women that it's a wonder anyone ever gets married. But by God, when it works, fuckin' money or where you live and all that other shit don't mean shit, man—you've got some*body*.

They ain't your blood, but in one way they're more than your blood. Despite the fact that I haven't been married in eighteen years, I still hold that shit in great awe.

R.M.: Your books also feature a lot of sideshow-attraction-type characters. Aside from the nonfiction piece "Carny," there's obviously the very big-footed Foot in *The Gospel Singer*, Herman in *Car*, and even Eugene in *The Knockout Artist*.

H.C.: Very often you see the "normal" world better, more clearly, and in a light which you would not otherwise see it if you are seeing it through the perception of "abnormal" human beings. I often see people that are special in the consideration of God, they're all twisted and warped and in wheelchairs with motors, and they've got two appendages on their one hand that they can sort of push buttons with. A great many things always occur to me. One, these people need to be hugged just as much as you or I do. They need to make that connection with another flesh.

Also, I want to look at 'em in such a way as to say, "Hell, man, it ain't nothing, you got fucked up, it was the hand that was dealt you and you're dealing with it, fuck it. I'm with you." On the other hand it's difficult for me to look at them because the sympathy—or whatever you want to call what you feel about somebody getting hit with something like that—is bound to show on your fuckin' face.

I remember living with a woman who was a sculptor, and a damn good one, and she had a show of all these big things that she'd made. A fuckin' blind boy came in and wanted me to tell him about what was there. Everybody else—hippy-dippy types standing around with long-stemmed glasses and shit—was treating him like it seems people always treat blind people. And then suddenly it occurred to me, I said, "Wait a minute, fuck, man, give me your hand." And I started leading him around, putting his hands on the sculptures and telling him about what he was feeling. You could just see it all over him, he was grateful that somebody wasn't treating him like a goddamn leper.

R.M.: Do you think there's any similarity between the performance aspect of a sideshow act and the act of writing—sort of exposing flaws, things that may cause shame?

H.C.: Well, I never thought about it just that way, but since you mention it, there probably is.

R.M.: To what extent are your characters based on people you know?

H.C.: It's definitely "based on." I've always thought the imagination makes nothing out of whole cloth. I'm not prepared to make that a categorical statement—maybe it does—but if you're writing about a building, you're probably thinking about a building somewhere, even if it's unconsciously. Then it all gets modified and transformed into something else.

I know writers are very fond of saying that they're not in their own books: "Don't look for me in my book, I'm not in here anywhere." Well, they probably are not in there in full form. But their prejudices, their sentiments, their biases, their angle of vision on the world—to say that's not in the book is bullshit and they know it. It's impossible for it to be otherwise. What they're trying to say is "Don't confuse me on some kind of one-to-one basis with somebody inside the book." This is particularly true if they're writing a first-person novel. Readers are often inclined to confuse the voice, that "I," with the person that's writing it, but that's a distinction that writers insist upon, and I think rightly so. I know I sure as hell do.

My whole life isn't writing. I might be shootin' pool, or out in the woods, or hunting or fishing. Certainly fishing. But writing is central in my life. I may only work on it two or three hours a day, but I do it seven days a week. If I get those hours, it's kind of like an anchor to me in the world, and if you don't like "anchor" then it's kind of like a stabilizing influence on me. Particularly if I think I've written something that's not bad, that's half-ass good. Then it doesn't much matter what happens to me the rest of the day, it can't fuck with me.

The truth of the matter is that we've all got strong suits and weak suits and there's no such thing as a perfect piece of writing. There's going to be flaws in everything, but some people are so goddamn strong in the things they do well that the flaws can be overlooked. Faulkner comes to mind. Shit, Faulkner could write some of the worst motherfuckin' metaphors that have ever been imagined in the history of letters, and when he just gets purple, when his prose gets out of hand, he's capable of turning a passage into rank, sophomoric bullshit. But he's so goddamn strong in so many other ways that it just doesn't matter. Obviously, Faulkner has been an influence on the whole world, and I don't dare go near one of his books when I'm writing something. His voice is so goddamn overwhelming that I just don't.

R.M.: You've got to be at least sixty now. What do you have to say about that?

H.C.: Well, there ain't a hell of a lot to be said for getting old. But I'm not as hard on myself. I've always run on a tight wire. I've got a nervous temperament and if I want to do something, I want to do it at least one hundred percent full bore, like if I can't have too much of something, I don't want anything at all. But in recent years, that's gone away, or been modified. I rather like myself more than I did earlier. I've got a little more patience with myself and with my failings and flaws and the things that I can't do. And a little more patience with other people. There's no goddamn reason to totally go nuts because some poor sonofabitch is doing the best he can and his best just ain't worth a shit. There's no reason to beat on the motherfucker or get upset about it, but I used to do a lot of that. I backed off that pretty good and I'm glad about it.

R.M.: Those other people are probably pretty glad about it too.

H.C.: Oh yeah.

R.M.: Do you think that your change in temperament has shown in your writing, or maybe it's because of your writing?

H.C.: I don't know if it's shown in my writing, and it's not that I've made peace with my writing, with what I'm capable of doing. It's not as though I've said to myself, "Well, you're a pretty mediocre motherfucker," which I don't believe. Modesty's not my strong suit. I'm not a modest man. It's not that. It's just that for many years I would literally tear my guts out doing the very, very best that I could and then, on top of that, beat on myself because it wasn't better. Well fuck that, man. If you've already opened everything that you could get open, if you've given every fuckin' thing you've got, well then, if you're going to do anything, you ought to say to yourself, "Well, old son, it ain't

Shakespeare and it ain't Dostoyevsky, but what the fuck, it ain't too bad for an old boy out of south Georgia." Have a little forgiveness for yourself. I've always been hard on other people, but harder on myself than I was on them. Nothing was ever good enough, and nothing ever is good enough. I've never finished any fuckin' book, including the one that I just finished, where I didn't say, "Well, son, you blew it again." That's what led Graham Greene to say that the artist is doomed to live in an atmosphere of perpetual failure.

Conception is pristine and pure and has all manner of hope in it, but between conception and execution, something gets lost. I'm sorry, bud, but don't let anybody shit you, there's a big gap there. There's always going to be a big gap there, and you can drink yourself to death over it or you can shoot yourself in the head over it or you can be an asshole to your family about it. There's a lot of ways you can handle it, and everybody, every man and woman, comes to their peace with that however they do. I got no advice here, everybody works it out for him or her self.

DINTY W. MOORE

An Interview with Harry Crews

Harry Crews is known for doing nothing halfway, be it drinking, writing, or lifting weights. During the interview, he was gracious, talkative, and obsessed with two things: finding a gym, and finding the end to his novel in progress, Scar Lover, *which has just been published this month by Poseidon Press. He has been sober for two years. The interview was conducted at last year's Associated Writing Programs Annual Conference.*

D.M.: You've been teaching some twenty-five years now, most of them at the University of Florida . . .

H.C.: Right. I teach two writing seminars for graduate students, with about eleven or twelve students in a class. I've got twenty-three years marked up on my fuselage, and I could retire if I wanted, but I like working with young writers. I don't like working with all of them, but I like working with most of them.

D.M.: You studied writing yourself?

H.C.: I studied at the University of Florida after I left the Marines, and just by the grace of whatever, I met Andrew Lytle. He took me in like a lost dog and read my stuff for me. I raked his leaves, cleaned off his roof, or I would drive him around every week, and that went on for a while. Then I took a couple of classes with him, and that's where I got it.

D.M.: *A Childhood,* your autobiography, talks quite a bit about the storytelling tradition among people in southern Georgia. Your people. But telling a story orally is much different than writing a novel, isn't it?

H.C.: It is, it is. Much different.

D.M.: But this oral tradition shaped you?

H.C.: Yes, if I couldn't have been a southerner, as a writer . . . I don't know. It's the only thing I've ever wanted to do and the hardest thing I've worked at. Man, if you want to make money, you ought to open a gas station, because it will be a long damn time before you ever make money at this. And anybody who wants to be famous is crazy, because I've known a lot of famous people.

I knew Erskine Caldwell when he was alive and he was very kind to me, and I always went a lot of places with him, and the first time I was with him, I was a fairly young man, about thirty I guess, and they simply would not leave him alone. I mean, we would be in a restaurant, and they would ask him about stories he had written so long ago. He had written so fuckin' many, that he couldn't remember them, and I could see then what an enormous pain in the ass it was.

Mr. Caldwell told me one time a thing I've always remembered. He said, "You know, I wish that when I was a young man I had read more, but I wanted to write so bad that I didn't read so much as I should have." Today, when I get in the company of people, other writers or academics, who are talking about writing fiction, half the time I don't know what the hell they're talking about. I mean, I'm a storyteller. That's the way I've always thought about myself—I'm a storyteller, that's all. It's all I've ever wanted to be, and all I've ever tried to be.

D.M.: You wrote four novels before you published your first one, right?

H.C.: Yeah. I did and I still have them and oughta burn them before somebody gets hold of them and does whatever they might do. The reason they weren't published, of course, wasn't because of some conspiracy against me, but because they weren't any damn good. The first one really wasn't good, the next one was a little better, and the third one was a little better than that, and the fourth one was almost there. But I have no intention of going back and trying to fix them.

D.M.: What kept you going all that time? All those years where you weren't published?

H.C.: I don't know. I can't say. I really don't know.

D.M.: No idea?

H.C.: Well, when you ask anybody why they do what they do with their life, they have answers they give you, but they're convenient answers, and I've always thought those answers were pretty far from the truth. Nobody really knows. How you and I happen to be sitting in this hotel room in Miami is a collaboration of circumstances we could never figure out if we had ten thousand years to devote to it. But no, it never crossed my mind to quit.

D.M.: When do you write?

H.C.: I get up about three in the morning and by four I'm writing, and I write until the gym opens at nine. When I was young I wrote a lot at night. I had to. I had a wife and two sons. But nowadays, whatever doesn't get written by nine o'clock doesn't get written.

D.M.: After a dozen novels, does it get easier?

H.C.: It gets harder.

D.M.: Why?

H.C.: It gets harder because an amateur, if he's got something to do, a transition, or moving some people from Miami to Jacksonville, he probably knows only one or two ways to do it. But a professional—and I don't particularly like that word when it applies to writing, writing is an avocation—a professional knows that there are an infinite number of ways to do it, and that somewhere in there is a best way to do it. So it doesn't get easier.

D.M.: You keep writing though?

H.C.: Well, I certainly don't compare myself in any way to Faulkner, but Faulkner had a thing he said. He said, "Nothing, nothing, nothing, brings peace like work." I can be full of anxiety and nerves, and literally coming apart, now that I can't drink, which used to be the way to get out of it, to fix it—I can be that way, and I can sit down with a piece of paper and a pencil and, man, in ten minutes I'm calm as a cucumber. You do your work, and maybe what you do that day is good work you can keep and maybe you have to throw it away, but that's just part of the turf, and after this long time you understand that. If you took writing away from me, I don't know, it would be difficult to live in the world without writing. I know that sounds precious, and probably very few people would believe that, but it happens to be true.

D.M.: In *Blood and Grits* there is an essay entitled "Carny," in which you say, "Some people have only one or two heroes; I have hundreds. Sometimes I meet six or seven heroes in a single day." Reading your novels, this seems very true. You make silly, comic, even deeply flawed characters seem heroic.

H.C.: Well, I got a young girl in my class now that a medal ought to be struck for every day of her life. She's blonde, she's pretty, she's in a fuckin' wheelchair, and I don't know how she gets done what she gets done because her hands don't work very well. And crippled people, and fat people, and whatever kind of people, need to be hugged and touched and loved and cared for as much as Olympic athletes. I'm not wise enough to know if it's a blessing or a curse when a person born that way has a brilliant brain. There's that guy who writes those books about the theories of numbers . . .

D.M.: Hawking?

H.C.: Right. And he's in a fuckin' wheelchair, and no one can understand a word he says except his mama, and where does he live, man? Now try to get into where he lives.

D.M.: But why does Harry Crews see these people and see heroes?

H.C.: I guess I know what it means to be a freak, and I know what it means to have people look at you as a freak. If you read *A Childhood*, you remember I had this thing with my leg. It was diagnosed as infantile paralysis or polio or something, but hell, it was country doctors that did the diagnosing. A while ago, I gave these lectures to some psychiatrists at the teaching hospital at the University of Florida. The lectures were on creativity, as though I know anything about it. Well, the consensus of these psychiatrists was that I didn't have polio at all—my leg had drawn up that way, my heels were up against my ass for a year, and it was an hysterical symptom.

You know, people go blind and they have no organic reason to be blind, they just can't see. Well, there's shotguns going off in the middle of the house when you're four years old, and you don't understand anything that's happening around you, and the shit gets bad enough, you just retreat. With my leg drawn up that way, I got to stay in bed, and I got the food brought to me.

D.M.: In your essay "Climbing the Tower," you mention Graham Greene's quote: "The artist is doomed to live in an atmosphere of failure." Is this sense of failure part of what keeps you writing?

H.C.: If you're lucky and work really hard, you might have thirty titles in a decent working life. That means you only get to roll in the paper thirty times, and roll out the last sheet thirty times. This French poet, I forget his name, he said a poem is never really finished, it's just abandoned. The same thing happens with a novel. You get to this point where you say, "Well, I've either got to send this thing on to New York or spend the rest of my life working on it." You try to get it as good as you can, but you never know when that is. You never know what's going to come to you. And you never know where it comes from.

D.M.: You evidently don't plot your novels out ahead of time?

H.C.: I've never written an outline in my life. I've never worked from an outline. Publishers have this thing about three chapters and an outline—well, hell, my answer has always been the same. I could write a great outline of the thing after I'm finished with it, but I can't write that shit now, because I don't know.

D.M.: There was more than a ten-year gap between *A Feast of Snakes*, your eighth novel, and your ninth, *All We Need of Hell*. You were still writing during that period, but why not fiction?

H.C.: Ten years?

D.M.: You wrote *A Childhood* during that time, and the magazine pieces.

H.C.: Yeah, right. Well let me tell you how I happened to write *A Childhood*. I thought if I wrote all that stuff down, in as great a detail as I possibly could, talking to as many people as I could and reliving it, it would be cathartic. I thought that it would in some sense relieve something. And it may have, but it didn't do what I thought it would do. It didn't work out that way.

D.M.: How did writing *A Childhood* compare to writing fiction?

H.C.: Writing that damn book damn nearly killed me. It was a very, very, very, very hard book to write.

D.M.: Why?

H.C.: For some reasons that are obvious if you've read it, like having to relive that shit. There were a lot of places in that book where I simply could not write, type, use a pencil, or anything. I didn't know what to do, but I was going to write it one way or another. So what I did was I got a tape recorder and would go into a room and make it as dark as I could, a lot of times at night, when it was really black, and lie down, and just talk into the microphone, and then give it to a stenographer. And of course, it would be all fucked up and stuff, but at least you'd have some words, and actions, and dialogue, and stuff there. You wouldn't be looking at a naked page. I don't know, if I hadn't hit on that, maybe I wouldn't have got the book written. That took a lot out of me.

D.M.: You also wrote some screenplays during that period?

H.C.: I don't consider that writing. The problem with all these film schools is they teach these kids all this shit about camera angles, and dissolves, and whatever, and they forget to tell them if you haven't got a story, you haven't got anything.

D.M.: You're finishing a new novel now, right?

H.C.: Right. It's called *Scar Lover*. Jim Dickey's got a line out of a poem, "Guilt is magic." I'd like to put that on the flyleaf.

D.M.: Why?

H.C.: The book's about a young boy who accidentally totally maims his little brother with a claw hammer, and because his parents were south Georgia farmers with no money, they haul their brood sow to the market to sell because they need the money for the boy's medical care, and they happen to run into a Sunoco truck, and are burnt alive. And the problem is, everyone blames this boy, and he blames himself. He's just carrying a load of guilt that is killing him.

It's not as funny as my other books; even a book like *Feast of Snakes* has got a few laughs. I'm not a funny person, I've never said a thing that made anybody crack a smile, but for some reason it gets into my books. But this book is the darkest by far. The darkest, blackest book I've written.

D.M.: Is this based on a story from your childhood, something you heard about?

H.C.: Hell, no. I don't know where it comes from.

D.M.: Total fiction?

H.C.: Of course, except where I come from, everybody I knew had an eye missing, or a finger missing, or something. So I suspect the book just came out of that generally. I come from the hookworm and rickets capital of the world. There's very few healthy people there. Nobody's got any money to see a doctor.

D.M.: This new book is almost done?

H.C.: Yes. But who the hell knows? Just because I already spent twenty-seven thousand dollars of the publisher's money doesn't mean it's going to be published.

D.M.: But you're close?

H.C.: If I can just find the fuckin' ending. That's all. It's driving me totally ape-shit, but that's something nobody but another writer would ever understand.

JOANN BIONDI

Still Macho after All These Years

Deep inside the ivy-covered campus of the University of Florida, room 1011 is a stark, white cinder-block cell with harsh fluorescent lighting and rickety plastic chairs. A hint of chalk dust hangs in the air. It's 7 p.m., and fifteen students sit in a semicircle listening to their English professor, who lapses into a soliloquy on the craft of creative writing.

"Some writers just throw up on the page and expect the readers to pick out the good little globs that stick," says Professor Harry Crews. "You can't do that. Writing fiction is not an exercise in emotional indulgence."

As usual, Crews looks like a madman who eats roofing nails for breakfast. His light-brown hair is cropped boot-camp short. He wears sweat pants and sneakers. His blue-gray eyes dart around the room as he speaks. His thick lips occasionally shift into a grin that is insane-asylum frightening.

His latest novel, *Body*, is set in Miami Beach and is a tragic tale of female bodybuilders who compete for the Ms. Cosmos title. The book's heroine is the strong and sinuous Shereel Dupont, formerly Dorothy Turnipseed of Waycross, Georgia. Shereel's sister is the bovine Earline, who becomes the infatuation of Billy Bateman, a compulsive bodybuilder who eats only boiled fish and protein powder. For Billy, Earline is the most erotic encounter on earth because her undulating

From *Sunshine: The Magazine of South Florida*, June 9, 1991.

layers of soft flesh smell to him of the fried chicken, greasy burgers, and fudge brownies he has denied himself.

★ ★ ★

Crews's own life has frequently wobbled on the brink of the bizarre, and his reputation as a crude, cocky tough guy is not unwarranted. Most of his favorite topics come from his own life: poaching alligators, getting drunk, camping in the Okefenokee Swamp, and fighting—cockfights, dog fights, human fights—the bloodier, the better.

His days as a wild man, now mostly a thing of the past, seem to seduce rather than scare away wannabe writers who sign up for his courses. "My classes close quicker than any classes on campus, so I think they like me pretty good," says Crews, who has been teaching in Gainesville since 1968. He is surprisingly gentle and nurturing toward his students.

"No job is a good job for a writer who wants to stay home and write, but I've got such a good deal teaching here that I feel like it's theft," Crews says. "And it's good for me because it keeps me from getting too full of myself. These young people are real honest. Eventually their honesty gets bled out of them, and they become brain-dead like the rest of society. But while I have them here, they're *alive*."

Crews is not crazy, though he enjoys letting people think he is. He confesses that some of the photos on his book jackets look like "Here comes crazy Johnny and his chain saw." His conversation is spiked with four-letter words, but he insists that he never swears in front of his mother. He drives a mud-splattered pickup truck and often fiddles with a pocketknife when he talks.

At fifty-five, he looks much older. His body appears to be at war with itself, and he moves as if he is always in pain. Years of karate, motorcycles, and reckless living are responsible for his messed-up knees. He stumbles when he walks and his hands shake. After a rough childhood and countless barroom brawls, he boasts of having broken his knees, feet, sternum, ribs, and neck. His nose, which squats on his face below a massive forehead, has been busted nine times.

A protruding middle-age paunch, probably the result of the quart of vodka he poured into it daily for twenty years, seems a permanent appendage despite morning workouts at a gym.

The most startling news about Crews these days is that he has quit drinking and doing drugs. It's been more than a year since he sobered up, and it has definitely made a difference in his life. "I drank goddamned hard for over twenty years," he says. "I'd start drinking and I'd stay drunk till I ran out of money, passed out, or was put in jail. I sure as hell never expected to live this long, 'cause if I had, I would've taken better care of myself."

Drugs, in the illegal form available from the students on campus, and Valium prescribed by doctors were also once a part of Crews's life. During his stoned escapades, the author was known throughout central Florida for smashing up his cars. Once he managed to wreck a car directly in front of the Gainesville police station.

Bartenders in town all have their favorite Harry Crews drinking stories. One heard often has Crews and playwright Tennessee Wil-liams getting drunk together shortly before they were to make a presentation at the university. "For a long time it was just one great big brotherhood of intoxication," says Tom, bartender at Lillian's Music Store, Crews's favorite Gainesville good ol' boy watering hole. "Harry would get so drunk he would have to crawl to the men's room. But his literary groupies were always around to pick him up."

Crews has tried to quit drinking before, even checking into detox centers several times. But he has never stayed sober this long. He attends Alcoholics Anonymous meetings and is on antabuse, a drug prescribed for alcoholics that causes them to get violently ill if they imbibe even a minute amount of alcohol.

"Sure, I miss it. Oh, God how I miss it," Crews says. "I wish I could kick back with a martini almost every day at about four in the afternoon. But I can't. I'm an alcoholic. It's all behind me now. Gone. And the world has certainly changed since I quit drinking."

He does make clear, however, that one thing has not changed. "A lot of alcoholic men become impotent when they quit drinking," he says. "They feel like they're on a stage and they just can't do it. Well, I just want you to know that that hasn't happened to me, darlin'."

When asked to explain the reason for his sudden reformation, Crews says, "My liver was just saying to me it was time to quit. I heard that old clock ticking and realized that I still wanted to do a lot more writing before I die, so I had better quit. And besides, it was getting in the way of my work."

Nothing gets in the way of Crews's work. Writing is his life.

"Others will tell you different, but I write because I can't help it," he says. "Writing fiction gives me back something I get nowhere else in the world. Faulkner said that nothing brings peace to a man like work, and that work he meant was writing.

"And besides, there ain't nothing else I'm any good at."

After more than twenty-five years of writing, Crews admits that it's as difficult as the day he started. He says he found his own "writer's voice" by "fasting, praying and working damn hard for years. There's not enough money in the world to make a man go through what he has to go through to write a novel. It's hell. I'm a mess when I'm working on a book. I'm absent-minded, I get lost and confused, and I need to be put on a leash and taken around."

Crews knew he was going to be a writer ever since he was a kid growing up in backwoods Georgia. In his 1978 book, *A Childhood: The Biography of a Place*, Crews told the painfully honest story of his past. Bacon County was a place where babies were named Leroy and Bertha and families went hungry because of a bad crop. It was a place where men drank moonshine, ate possum, and chewed tobacco, and where women grew old before their time. Crews wrote about how, when his daddy died, his family had the body embalmed and buried the blood in the yard behind their house. Their hound dog Sam howled over the burial mound for days.

"Harry's childhood was terrible," says Maggie Powell, his girlfriend of thirteen years. "His family was so poor they never celebrated Christmas. There was only one time he got a Christmas present, and it was a Baby Ruth candy bar. He has spent his entire life trying to put a buffer on that painful past."

Powell, a thirty-eight-year-old former bodybuilding champion, has experienced the many moods of Harry Crews. They have lived together and broken up several times. "Harry is an extremist," Powell says. "There were weeks when he could not, would not, get out of bed. There were empty vodka bottles everywhere. And when he did go out he was awful to a lot of people. But he's also a wonderful, kind, loving person. He's always looking after Gainesville's street people. He gives them money whenever he sees them. He's been violent with a lot of other people, but he's never been violent to me. Except, of course, when he would beat me to a pulp verbally.

"You see," she continues, "Harry knows his talent is a gift, and since he doesn't know where it comes from, he's afraid he'll wake up one morning and it will be gone."

Crews lives in a large, rustic house off a main road in Gainesville. Its two-story windows look out onto a deep, heavily wooded lot. A sundeck juts out from the rear of the house. A framed black-and-white photo of Crews as a young boy sits on the bookshelf in the living room. The house is clean and comfortable and decorated with plenty of plants. His constant companion is Heidi, an old golden retriever.

When not writing or teaching, Crews practices yoga, bakes pies, and calls his mother, Myrtice, in Georgia every day. He quit smoking before he quit drinking, and he no longer eats meat, preferring steamed vegetables. If he goes into a bar now, he orders a Perrier.

His life seems almost tame, though he was involved in a fistfight a few months back. But that, he says, wasn't his fault. Some guy came up to him and wanted to find out if the writer was as tough as his reputation. "I may do a lot of shucking jive with people I know, but hell, I don't pick fights with strangers," Crews says. "They pick them with me. It happens all the time."

If no longer a drunk and a brawler, Harry Crews does know what explains his existence, and will until the day he dies. "I am a writer," he likes to say, "or I am nothing."

DAVID ARONSON

Writing Is an Act of Discovery: Harry Crews

David Aronson spoke with Harry Crews at his home in northwest Gainesville, shortly before his retirement from the University of Florida. Crews wore a red muscle shirt, gray sweats, and black Reeboks. He had a Mohawk haircut. The tattoo on his right shoulder says, "How Do You Like Your Blue-Eyed Boy, Mr. Death?" If you ask him about it, Crews will reply: "Cummings just wrote it down on paper, but I got it on my body, and I'm going to take it to the grave with me."

D.A.: In two years you've published two novels and completed a third. How do you account for your productivity?

H.C.: I also during that time wrote a screenplay for Sean Penn—that was going to be his next project until *The Knockout Artist* became available and now he and I are working on that.

How do I account for the productivity? Well, apparently I have no alternative. People who think it takes a great deal of discipline on my part to work as I do don't understand what goes on in my head—have no conception of my emotional state, have no notion of how I view the world and the brutal, stupid hypocrisy that runs it, and how much I want to get away and not look at it. If they knew that, they would understand I go to my work as . . . almost as some kind of refuge.

And so when I say the brutal hypocrisy—the guilt and pride that run the world—I can't control any of that, but I can control the worlds I make in my fiction. I can control it to some extent. Anybody knows

From *Alumni* CLAS *Notes* (Summer 1992): 1+.

who has ever written anything that writing has a way of getting away from you. I would never be guilty of that old cliché of a book writing itself, but once that thing starts to live, and you feel a pulse and a heart beating, it takes enormous concentration and effort to keep that sucker from running off in all directions—or in directions you don't want it to go.

D.A.: What is your new book about?

H.C.: The working title is *Circus Act*—the book has nothing to do with the circus. It takes place in a trailer park in south Florida on the edge of a swamp—and nothing but very old people live in it. The guy who owns it is my age and comes from south Georgia. How the hell old would he be, and where the hell else would he come from but south Georgia? And his war was Korea, and that was my war. That's sort of it, if you talk about facts, the nuts and bolts.

What it's about is another thing. Our national shame of warehousing old people, who almost never live in families anymore. Almost no children are around old people, except their grandparents at Thanksgiving. It's just a waste—that the children are not there for the old and the old not there for the children. So that's what the book's about. Old people.

D.A.: Let me read you something I just recently came across. It's from Florence King, and it's about the South, and about that much-maligned figure called the good ol' boy: "He had a clearly defined fighting side and woe to anyone who walked on it. He was entirely capable of killing, in a mob or alone. The worst of the South? Yes, but also the best. There was no telling what he'd do if he got riled, yet he had an underlying sweetness, an almost female tenderness. . . . He said grace, he said ma'am, and he loved his countries—both of them."

H.C.: I have no quarrel with what that lady has written there. I would have said it in different ways, I guess. That he is reticent among strangers, generous to a fault, and very violent. He makes an enormous number of assumptions. He assumes you know what you must not speak about, what you must not bring up. He assumes you know that all kinds of behavior on your part will demand that he draw blood from you to satisfy his honor. It's a very dangerous place for an outsider to go into—it's a social structure where a great many things are in place and have been in place for as long as anybody living can remember. In the South, only blood satisfies blood insults—people think of it as a cliché, but it's only a cliché because it is true.

D.A.: And the female tenderness?

H.C.: I think it's there, though the male would die and go to hell before he admitted it was there, and does his best to put another face on it.

D.A.: How much do you plan ahead when you write? Do you know how your books are going to end when you start writing them? Do you make an outline?

H.C.: I have never made an outline in my life. It's from the images and the rhythm of the language that I discover what should come next. That is not to say that I don't make copious notes about my characters as I write about them—notes about where they went to school, how they felt about their mama—most of which never reach the book.

D.A.: You've been on the wagon now for two years. What caused you to go clean, and what's been the impact on your writing? Were drugs and alcohol necessary to the production of your works?

H.C.: I don't know if they were, but I felt like they were. My son—he's twenty-eight years old and we're very close—he knows he can talk to me about anything, and I can talk to him about anything. And we often talk about the time when I was laid up in bed. Whiskey and other things were involved, and he came in—and I said, "Without alcohol and drugs, life is unacceptable." That's what I said, and that's what I meant. I felt there were times it was absolutely mandatory that the world be skewed, that I could no longer bear it dead-on, that it had to be twisted.

I would like to say I just backed off and made up my mind to clean up my act. No, I'm afraid what happened was that my options were terribly limited. It became very obvious to me that I would die. And I didn't want to die. I wanted to stay alive and work.

It's easier to sit down and write now, but it's harder for the work to be of any consequence. I don't think it takes much perception, or very keen sensibilities, to see that it takes great courage—I know it's me saying this and what it makes me sound like, but I don't care—it takes great courage to look where you have to look, which is in yourself, in your experience, in your relationship with fellow beings, your relationship to the earth, to the spirit or to the first cause, or whatever—to look at them and make something out of them. Writers spend all their time preoccupied with just those things that their fellow men and women spend their time trying to avoid thinking about. The writer spends his time digging into that sore for whatever corruption will gush out.

D.A.: What do you want your work to do? Does art make nothing happen, is it simply a superior form of entertainment?

H.C.: If I were inclined to have it do anything at all, I would want for it to turn the reader back upon himself, to provoke him to examine himself. I am, however, not inclined to think that way. I am trying very selfishly to find out something about Harry Crews—I write because I don't understand or know myself, and not understanding or knowing myself is, among other things, very frightening. I do know that I am capable of bestial behavior, and I know that I am capable of rank cruelty—emotional cruelty and blood cruelty, too. And the more I can understand about that, the more I can live with it.

The poet Yevtushenko said that the most beautiful, aching work in the world is to be yourself. I suppose I write in order to live—in the best sense of that word—to find out what I am. That's a rambling, unsatisfying answer, but out of that kind of mulligan stew of fault and emotional reaction you make stuff. Out of that, you try to make something firm and beautiful and clean and sharp and focused and memorable and compelling.

D.A.: One final question. I have to ask—what's the deal with your hair?

H.C.: I got the 'do, and the 'too, in the same week, consciously and deliberately and with something very specific in mind. And that is to get back as close as I could and know again, deeply and personally, what it was to be an outsider, to be different in a way that brings pain and suffering and humiliation. You get a tattoo like this and a 'do like this, and wear a shirt where the tattoo shows, and you walk into a room of people and feel the animosity, the disapproval, the how-dare-you. You can feel it coming off of them like heat off a stove.

And the thing I want to ask them is, how have I deserved this, what have I done that so offends you? I have not asked you to cut your hair this way. I have not asked you what you thought of it, or to approve it. So why do you feel this way towards me?

And it's about the next thing I'm writing, called *Wire*, which is about a tightrope walker. Did you know that the steel wire the walkers use has a piece of hemp running through it, called "the soul of the rope"?

**TAMMY LYTAL AND
RICHARD R. RUSSELL**

Some of Us Do It Anyway:
An Interview with Harry Crews

This interview, part of the River City Writers Series directed by Gordon T. Osing, took place at Memphis State University in Memphis, Tennessee, on October 26–27, 1992. Other participants included Stacy Jones, Alex Adams, and Jason Smith.

T.L. & R.R.: All of us are interested in how you manage to capture so well the distinctive voices of the South. Is there a trick to writing the speech of a place?

H.C.: All right, first of all, no. No, there ain't no trick—or perhaps there is a trick, a bunch of tricks. But if there are, you only get them by paying a considerable price for them, the price coming out of your time, your energy, and the rest of it. When you're writing dialect, you're writing what people say in a certain way. There are all kinds of dialects, and I've come to grief over trying to write a couple of them.

When I wrote *The Knockout Artist*, I spent the whole year in Lafayette, Louisiana—in the heart of Cajun country—and recorded the language and found out ultimately I couldn't write it. *I couldn't write it.* I learned the idiom, and I listened—among other things the first thing you have to have to write effective dialogue and dialect, you

From *Georgia Review* 48 (1994): 537–53.

gotta have a good ear. Just like some people can't carry a tune, some people don't write very good dialogue; they don't write as people speak. By and large, people don't speak in long monologues. We just kinda fire bullets at each other—you get two or three words off and I interrupt you and put one back, and you back to me and me back to you.

Okay, now about the dialect. The first thing you wanna do is to get rid of what I call "Uncle Remus" dialect, gross misspelling or phonetically spelling everything. You know, "I'm gwine down to de ribber," and spell "river" r-i-b-b-e-r. I ain't even never heard nobody say "ribber," and I'm a sharecropper's son out of south Georgia. Most of what I see that passes for black dialect, I never heard, and I lived close with blacks all my life. Because I wanted to try to do it right, I went to some trouble to study it.

Here's what you do. You either do it with idiom—get a flavor of the speech, the dialect, like, "He'd rather climb a tree and tell a lie than stand on flat ground and tell the truth"—that's a pretty sorry fella.

So idiom will partly do it; the other way you do it is by syntax, the placing of the words, and by phonetically spelling a key word. Take an easy line: "There's enough business in this town for everybody." Where I come from, first we get rid of "there's," and we put "it's" in its place: "It's enough bidness (probably, spell it b-i-d-n-e-s-s) in this town for everybody." And I'd drop the "y" and spell it "ever" (run the "ever" right with the "body"), and I would not put one of those—if you drop a letter out of a word that you're writing, don't put one of those little apostrophe things.

T.L. & R.R.: Does the speech of a place, in real communities, create a bonding of the people in the community, so that someone is included or excluded because he or she can or cannot speak the language?

H.C.: Absolutely. Now, to what degree, I am not prepared to say. When I was in the Marine Corps, I brought a Spanish boy home with me on leave and introduced him to my mama—great lady. She did the thing all southern ladies do; she got out something to eat and made him feel at home—tried to. But the first time she got me off, she looked at me and said, "He ain't our kind of people, is he?" And she didn't say that in an ugly way. My mama hadn't been out of Bacon County,

Georgia, but about twice in her whole life, and she said, "He's not our kind of people." I said, "No ma'am, he's not."

Quickly, to show you where I come from: I was once in El Paso, Texas—I was gone a year and a half on a motorcycle when I got out of the Marine Corps—and I was going to Mexico and called my mom on the telephone. I said, "Darlin', I'm gonna go down into Mexico for a little while now." And she said, "Well, whatcha gonna do with the motorsickle?" And I said, "Well, darlin', I'm gonna take it with me." She says, "Put it right on the boat with ya?" You see, because my mama always talks about "across the water"—that phrase out of World War II—she doesn't know that you can drive out of the United States into Mexico or drive out of the United States into Canada. Hell no, it's an ocean there, man. Shit, we're an *island*.

So, speech—but you can include a lot of other things, like dress. You can get in serious trouble with your hair cut like this where I come from [*points to his Mohawk*]. I mean, you can lose blood. That's a fact. They don't mean nothing by it, except they think you're crazy. And I think they think they're probably protecting their own. "That fool has done something to his hair and it ain't safe to have him around here looking like that. So, you head him off if he goes that way and I get him this way. Bob, you get him over there by the tree and we'll fix that hair." They're liable to take it all off and then it'll look right.

T.L. & R.R.: In *Blood and Grits*, you often refer to certain characters who speak with grit; many times these characters are respected and loved more than those who don't. How would you define a person who speaks with "grit"?

H.C.: Well, you see, what the rest of the country call "rednecks" I call "Grits" with a capital *G*. They're people; they're my people; they're Grits. And in my lexicon, anyway, they have a great respect for values, for family, and for whatever other virtues you wish to name. I seem to admire them? Well yeah, I admire them because I'm one of them. They are my people; you're damned right I admire them.

There was a time when I went through an Atlanta airport line, and there was an agent there telling people which way to go. I'm next in line and I just walked up, and this guy stepped right in front of me and started talking. And I just took him by his nine-hundred-dollar jacket he was wearing and kinda turned him around and said, "You got to either be from New York City or California, because I know that if you was a southerner, you'd have better sense than to step in front of a grown man when he was trying to talk to somebody."

And then he's all like, "Well, I'm in a big hurry."

I said, "Buddy, we're *all* in a hurry; that's why we got a line here."

My mama would not have approved of my behavior. I should not have touched the guy, and I know that, because it's dangerous to touch a guy. You say something, that's one thing, but touch him, that's another thing. But anyway, in my mama's mind my behavior would have been unseemly. His would have been unseemly, too—unconscionable—but she would have just said he was sorry and let him go ahead and be sorry.

So yeah, we got ways of doing things, and we're not better than the folks in New York City, and we're not better than the folks that live in California or Nevada. We're just a little different: we talk different, we have different concerns; because the weather is different, we build different kinds of houses. Maybe we hold slightly different kinds of values for our children.

When I go to New York, women jump at my face for calling them "ma'am." If I say "Yes, ma'am" to a lady, she will say, "Pardon me? Don't be calling me *ma'am*." Apparently there is something derogatory about calling a woman "ma'am." I don't know what it is, but as soon as I say "lady," they jump. I'm supposed to say "person," when what I wanted to say was "lady." But what I tell them is that where I come from, when a female reaches puberty, she is "ma'am"; that's just the way it is. My mama told me that's the way it is, and since I have seen or heard nothing to change my mind or prove her wrong, I still say "ma'am." There's a lot of things you used to could do, you can't do anymore, except some of us do it anyway.

T.L. & R.R.: Do you see your knack for writing the spoken language of the South as the main reason your characters come alive?

H.C.: No. I would hope that it's a big part; I mean, it's important. Every little characteristic, every little idiosyncrasy—every little difference in the way they dress or walk, every difference in what they eat, and certainly differences in the way they talk—makes them different from other people. And therefore, they get substance. Because after all, that's just words on that piece of paper, man, that's not blood. Except the writer wants it to be blood.

T.L. & R.R.: Would you say that language is the core of a person's identity? Or is it more like the path down which a person can find out who he really is?

H.C.: Language as core of identity? Well, there's some work that's being done that makes us now begin to wonder if that's what separates us from the lower beings or animals: that we can speak and that we have language. But core of being, I wouldn't want to make it that, though maybe it is! I don't know. That's pretty strong: core of being. What's the second part of it? Down which he finds it? I like that.

T.L. & R.R.: The path down which people can find out who they are.

H.C.: Language you're talking about still, right?

T.L. & R.R.: Right.

H.C.: Find out who they are? No, no, no, no, no, no. I believe it's possible; I believe many people probably have done it. But no, champ, talk is cheap. No, that's why action and story line are so important in fiction. To hell with what you say—what did you *do*, Jack? What did you do? How did you act?

If a child was in a burning building that you could see was going to burn down with the child in it, and if it appeared that it was suicidal to go in there and attempt to rescue the child—who at this point hasn't even been burned, but the situation looks as though there's no way you gonna get him out—if you go in, you will both die. Do you go, or do you stand out here and watch him burn?

"No, I run right on in there with him, and I burn up too with him if that's what it takes."

Well, hell, that's easy. Doing it and saying it, that separates the sheep from the goats right there.

T.L. & R.R.: In *Body,* by the end of the book, Shereel moves from the language of the bodybuilders back to the language of her family, the Turnipseeds. Is this part of showing that she has finally come to terms with herself?

H.C.: No, I don't think so. If she'd come to terms with herself, she wouldn't have killed herself in the end of the book. But, no, here's what it comes out of. Her trainer Russell Muscle forces her to clean up her language, so she doesn't talk like a Grit, like a redneck hick out of Waycross, Georgia. But she does the same thing I do.

See, I speak two languages. I mean, I can go into the University of Florida president's office and talk to him and use standard English and standard pronunciation, but that is not the language that is native to me. When I am with my brothers and sisters out there who are part and parcel of my blood, then I just revert to the dialect and speak so-called substandard English. There's one good friend of mine from Auburn, Alabama—the two of us get together and, after we've been talking for about two hours, if you're not a southerner, you just about can't understand us. Because it gets so, so "back in the woods."

T.L. & R.R.: Is there always a character in your novels who is specifically you?

H.C.: Never. No, but there is a character in each book that has more of me in him than does any of the other characters. I identify with Joe Lon in *Feast of Snakes*—really, really identify with him. I identify with Easy Mac in *Car*, who's got two boys. But it isn't always the main character.

T.L. & R.R.: How much of yourself do you put into your novels—maybe not your own personality but your culture?

H.C.: I can truthfully say that just about every subject in my books comes from me. I got a book about karate, and I studied karate. I got a book about boxing, and I was in the ring when I was young. I wouldn't know any other way to do it. I have trouble with women and children; they are very difficult for men to do. This is not unique. If you notice, Hemingway didn't have any children in his books. Children have a way of screwing up the dialogue, getting in the way of the conversation so that it can't have the punch that it might otherwise have.

T.L. & R.R.: So many people suffer in your books. Do you see life as a continuous suffering? Is winning in this life nothing more than enduring through the suffering?

H.C.: Suffering is pretty much more or less with us in greater or lesser degrees. You grieve for your puppy, and you grieve for your dead son, but not in the same way. I mean, that's not even in the same world hardly, but it still can be grief. I got a thirteen-year-old golden retriever that I think more of than I think of most people I've ever known, but she's dying. She's on her last legs. I'm gonna have to kill her soon cause she's hurtin' too bad.

Suffering will be with us. And about the business of enduring it: you're gonna endure it whether you want to or not. The question is how, and what kind of face you're gonna put on it. For example, there was a very famous Roman general, and someone comes in and tells him his son has just been killed in battle. And hell, he's workin over a map, and he just goes right on with his business.

And the messenger says, "General, didn't you hear? I just told you your son was killed."

And he looks up right out of his eyes and says, "You did not think that I thought him immortal, did you?" And he went back to work. He's mortal; the son died.

Well, that's the natural order of things. So, we're gonna have to endure it, and it's just whether or not some people think it's very important not to show grief.

I think it's terribly important to really grieve. Really get down and gnash your teeth, pull your hair, beat your breast, claw your eyes, and get it all out. And then, straighten up, stand up, clean up, put that behind you, and go on with your life instead of dragging it out every Sunday. I buried a four-year-old son. I've never been back to the graveyard where they put him in the ground. Why? Cause the son that I had ain't in that ground, man. He returned to the nitrogen cycle. "Stars at elbow and foot"—a line out of somewhere, Dylan Thomas, I think. Yeah, so, when it happened, when he drowned, I thought I would never get over it. I wished I could've died at that moment. But we're talking about over a quarter of a century ago. Hey, I wish he could've stayed around and taken his licks like the rest of us are taking ours.

But no, there's awful good things, sweet things, wonderful things, moving things, uplifting things, things that make you whistle, sing, dance, hug your neighbor. So, it's not unrelieved suffering.

T.L. & R.R.: In *Karate Is a Thing of the Spirit*, why would a character like John Kaimon pursue the goal of karate, go through so much pain and rebirth, and then revolt against it for something he's not even sure he can have—the love of the girl?

H.C.: Well, in the first place, when we meet John Kaimon, he—as many young people are—is very much adrift. He doesn't quite know which path to take; he doesn't quite know who to believe, not to believe, what to do, what not to do. And he comes across these people who have a dedication, a focus, and a passion for something unlike any passion or dedication or focus he's ever heard of before. At first, he just wants to get close to it. Then, when he sees, he catches the bug and *he's* that way.

Why would he give that up to go with the girl, when he doesn't know for sure how that's gonna work out? He does that for the same reason you and I are in this room this morning. Most of us—all of us, I damn near suspect—are not in the world because men and women wanted children. We're in the world because men and women wanted each other. That's one of the ways the race keeps going.

And that's not to say anything ugly or nasty or unseemly about people either. They want each other because they love each other, flesh seeking flesh, two fleshes making one flesh, two beings making one being. Out of the one being another being is made: you or me. And so that last thing with the woman in the novel, that's the blood pull, that's the race-of-man pull. It will pull you away from anything; it will certainly pull you away from karate.

I mean, man, I'd probably leave karate for half the ladies in this room. See, now that's just telling the truth. You're saying, listen to that old man talking ugly. No, just telling the truth. Truth ain't always as pretty and nice as we'd like it to be. And God knows, we're not as pretty and nice as we'd like to be. I fall way short of my mark. I do. I'm not proud of that, but I do.

T.L. & R.R.: In your autobiography, *A Childhood,* you talk about your father and how tough it was for him—how he, as a sharecropper, worked day in and day out, and put in fifteen hours a day, with no real hope or no real reason for thinking anything was going to get any better. They just made payments and went on to the next year. I was wondering if you saw salvation in the cards for anyone and, if so, do you see it here or in an afterlife?

H.C.: Well now, you've got to ask somebody with a better mind and a better heart, and who knows things in a way that I don't know them, to get an answer to that. As a matter of fact, I am not interested in talking to you about what I believe or do not believe about God or the absence of God or heaven or hell or any of that. That's just a little too big for me. And I stand—if I stand any way before it—in fear and trembling.

My daddy literally worked himself to death, as a tenant farmer, as a great many men and women did. My ma says he worked himself to death and died at the age of thirty-one; his heart, his whole chest, blew out like a tire blows out. There doesn't appear to be any hope. There doesn't appear to be any way out. Yet we ourselves say, "Well, maybe nobody else made it out, but I'm gonna make it out. Maybe nobody else made it better, but I'm gonna make it better."

T.L. & R.R.: There was a time in your past where your behavior seemed pretty self-destructive. Where did that self-destruction come from? Is it a product of your southern culture?

H.C.: I don't know, and I wish I could say that my self-destructive behavior was behind me forever, but I can't say that. No, I don't think it's part of being a southerner. I quote Karl Wallenda in the front of *Body*. Wallenda, the great wire walker, always worked without a net. And he said walking the wire is living. Everything else is just a wait. There are some of us who really like to see how close to the edge of the abyss we can get and still get back.

It's like rock climbing. If you know anything about rock climbing—absolute vertical wall—the only thing you get is just a little bit of one finger in a crack and one toe. And you can't see where you're going. You can't find anything; you've got to go on up. Don't you know that when you finally get to the top or get off the wire, everything in the world is new again? You have reinvented the world. You're a miracle; that shoe is a miracle. The fact that breath is coming and going is a miracle. Everything is a miracle. Because you've been to the place where you almost weren't.

I never wanted to be well-rounded, and I do not admire well-rounded people nor their work. So far as I can see, nothing good in the world has ever been done by well-rounded people. The good work is done by people with jagged, broken edges, because those edges cut things and leave an imprint, a design.

T.L. & R.R.: Do you see southern culture in general as walking a tightrope, as being self-destructive? We're so enmeshed in our past, and yet we're trying to come out into the twentieth century.

H.C.: Well, we're not as enmeshed as we were, and we're getting more and more homogenized. That doesn't particularly please me, but it doesn't particularly displease me either. And statistically we are—southerners—a violent people.

T.L. & R.R.: Why is that, would you say?

H.C.: I've fasted and prayed, prayed and fasted about it. I've got a line where I say that there's more men in the South that's been killed over fence lines and bird dogs than anything else. I spent a year in various parts of Louisiana. There's parts of Louisiana where everybody is so courteous, and so nice, and so generous, but you get on the wrong side of them, man, and they won't hurt you, they'll kill you. A gun is always just within reaching distance.

I don't know; there's something about southerners. I sometimes think it's because we are a defeated people. Thank God we get farther and farther away from it, because you don't want to carry that stuff forever. God knows we've carried it too long already. As a general statement, I don't like Yankees. I'm as polite as I can be, but I don't like their behavior. I've had occasions to tell some Yankees that they wouldn't stay alive two days in the counties I come from, acting the way they act, talking the way they talk, shoving people out of the way. You can't do that. Because maybe this man won't do it, but sooner or later you're gonna push the wrong guy. And then he's probably gonna do the wrong thing. Manners are what protect us from ourselves and protect us from each other.

T.L. & R.R.: You speak often of your mother. What type of role does she play in your writings?

H.C.: Well, she's played a very strong role in my life because she raised my brother and me. And she's a good hard-working Christian lady that is very generous. See, much of the rest of the world seems to have a lot of trouble knowing what is right and what is wrong. My mama doesn't have any trouble with that. She knows what's right and what's wrong, and she'll be quick to tell you what's right and what's wrong, and what's discourteous and what's not. She's eighty-one years old.

T.L. & R.R.: Let's talk about some other women for a moment. Do you get a lot of flak from feminists?

H.C.: I did maybe the first three or five books. But *Body* is a book about a woman. Me, a man, having the nerve to say that when she gained more body fat, her period would return, and she would be glad because she strangely missed it. What right do I as a man have to make such a statement? How the hell do I know? I don't know; it just seemed like the right line. That book was on the front page of the *New York Times Book Review,* and it was reviewed by a woman novelist from Australia. She said that it was right on the money and righteously fine.

Some years back, I had a little press war with Gloria Steinem. She said something about me, and I wrote something somewhere answering it, and it got cranked up. But we met, and we found that we had much more we agreed about than disagreed about.

As a matter of fact, I was the rankest kind of feminist before I ever heard that word or before it was abroad in the land and everybody was talking about it. I know what a struggle women have had. Women couldn't own land, for God's sake, in this country. Women couldn't own property. And all the bullshit women had to go through to be able to vote. A woman went from being the property of her daddy to the property of her husband. Women had a hard time of it. It strikes me as ironic and really curious that they should have had such a hard time of it, when it is manifestly true, at least to me, that they are so much stronger than men are.

T.L. & R.R.: In what way?

H.C.: My belief and my feeling about women is all anecdotal, which doesn't do very well statistically in chalking up why this and not that. Here is a man going back to his mother. Why not? She was the strongest woman I ever knew.

I come to this conclusion because my own mother always had just enough—*just enough*—to *be* enough to get whatever job was at hand accomplished. I think of my mother—and all women—in childbirth. They have just enough strength to get through what—sometimes, not always—is the terror and the pain of labor. They have just enough, later on, to make the meal last out the number of people at the table. I probably sound like I'm talking about poor people, but for rich people, in other instances . . . the same thing is true. I think if I was going to write an essay about women, I'd call it "Just Enough."

T.L. & R.R.: Early in your career you wrote short stories, but now you're regarded mainly as a novelist and a nonfiction writer. How did you make the shift, and do you still write stories?

H.C.: Most answers writers give to questions about what they do turn out to be clichés, or seem to be clichés. Now if your question had been, "When did you stop writing short stories?" I'd have said, "I never stopped writing stories." A lot of times I do think I'm writing a story. It really has to do with conception, out entirely away from the paper. I'm out doing something—pushing a cart in the supermarket, for God's sake, or hunting on a trail, anything—and I just have that moment when I think, "God, yes, I've got to write about that." And I think it's a short story, but then it turns out that, no, it's another frigging novel.

So, I admire stories, but I don't write them now because, apparently, I can't. That's it. Now I *do* like novels, the whole business of writing them and the feel of them. I like the way the book feels in your hand, and for some screwy reason, that makes a difference—it really does. I like to smell it, hold onto it, look at it . . .

Listen, there are novels that are so personal that I just close the thing, mark it with my thumb, and look out the window to keep from crying. There are novels where I just can't bear . . . just can't bear the thing that only a god would ask you, the burden of it. I know that sounds precious, but so be it. I mean, just the other day I was thinking, damn, it's so expensive to stay alive, the burdens we're asked to bear to live: the death of a grandchild under the wheels of a truck, the sublime beauty of a woman bringing forth a little slimy-assed baby . . . and all those things are asked of us, and if we can't haul it and hack it and get it, and pay that rent, we can't live.

T.L. & R.R.: How do you feel about poetry?

H.C.: Only thing I've never written much of is poetry. I probably read as much poetry as I do fiction or anything else, probably read more. Because poetry by its very nature keeps you in touch with the possibilities of language. It is so compressed, so tight, that it teaches you a respect for language you would not otherwise have.

I agree with Robert Frost that there's no such thing as free verse. I don't believe there's free form in art, period. I think art by definition presupposes form of some kind. You might even have to go to Zen for a definition: the lack of form is also some form. In the same sense a Zen Buddhist would say the lack of style is also some style.

T.L. & R.R.: What are you working on now?

H.C.: What am I working on now? I'm working on something called *The Horsehog-Gator Connection*. See, I went over to see a fellow that had thirty-five hundred head of hogs and six thousand alligators. He had it all on about ten acres of land. And the damn entire process was like a perpetual motion machine. I mean, something came in at this end and went out at that end, and nothing was wasted. Even the hog manure solids were separated in a machine and fed back to the hogs, because they said solid manure is nothing but unused corn. And these hogs never see the sun, and they never stand on the ground. I haven't had much appetite for pork lately.

Everything about that operation . . . so much in there is, down deep, really, really small—and at the very same time, turned just so the light hits another way, it becomes unsayably huge. It turns into a great big thing, it's sweet and lovely, it's enormous and savage and full of blood, and it's got a sword in both hands. It's the equal and opposite of itself, in spades. And the metaphors just keep coming. I don't work for them; they're just *there*. Maybe that's what drives me crazy.

I've just got to write the novel. I'm right at about two hundred pages, enough to know that it's gonna be a book. But it's gonna have to shape up and get a good deal better than it is now, or it's gonna go in the stack that didn't make it.

T.L. & R.R.: I thought I heard you say the other day that the hog operation reminded you a little bit of Los Angeles.

H.C.: Yeah, well, when I actually saw the thing, it just seemed to me too good a metaphor for various places in the country and for what living has become for a great many people. For example, there are some professors at the University of Florida, where I teach, that haven't worked up a decent sweat in their whole life. They got hands soft as a woman's—which there's nothing wrong with, except I wouldn't want them. And they go from an air-conditioned house to an air-conditioned car to an air-conditioned office, and consequently, their body is never allowed to acclimate to the natural turning of the earth and the seasons. They've lost touch with something. This is not a condemnation of them; it's the state of the world I find myself in.

You have to go to considerable trouble to live differently from the way the world wants you to live. That's what I've discovered about writing. The world doesn't want you to do a damn thing. If you wait till you got time to write a novel or time to write a story or time to read the hundred thousands of books you should have already read—if you wait for the time, you'll never do it. 'Cause there ain't no time; world don't want you to do that. World wants you to go to the zoo and eat cotton candy, preferably seven days a week.

T.L. & R.R.: Often in your novels, heroes like Joe Lon and others develop as the story unfolds. How much of a plan do you start out with?

H.C.: I've never begun a novel that I knew how it ended. I just start and try to find out what it is I think about whatever it is I am writing about. Some people have made some noise about the fact that my recent endings, like in *All We Need of Hell*, are a much different kind—good, happy, or whatever—than the ending of *A Feast of Snakes*. I wasn't aware of it until they told me about it.

And then they said, "What does it all mean?"

And I said, "I don't know; I'll have to write another book to find out."

Look, I'm working on one book now that doesn't really even have a title. It happened because, just dicking around with the books in my house, as I am wont to do, I asked myself, "I wonder what the longest palindrome in the world is?" So I took down the *Guinness Book of World Records*, and there it was. I can't say it—it's Finnish, whatever language the Finns speak, and it's long—my God, it's long: it's about three shotgun shells end to end. And the word means "door-to-door soap salesman." And out of that process came a book that is now very close to going away from home and doing the best it can.

That's the way my books come about—I just wonder about the tiniest little stupid-assed thing, and I look at it and I think, "Hmmm, damn, why would people do that?" But they did.

T.L. & R.R.: How much time do you spend editing?

H.C.: I don't know that I ever think of myself as editing anything. I think of myself as rewriting. But I know what you're talking about. You see, I write through things, over and over and over and over again. It takes me the longest time to find out what I'm writing about, what the subject is. And you understand what I mean when I say "what the subject is." I don't mean if it's about hogs and cows, or if it's set in a farm or in the city. I mean is it about despair, or the healing nature of forgiveness and compassion, or somebody as flawed and failed as I am?

At the center of all books or poems or plays, there is a mystery, a mystery that cannot be solved or resolved or explained, but only kind of meditated upon and wondered at. And meditating upon that, and wondering about it, you inevitably have to wonder about yourself, and meditate upon yourself.

T.L. & R.R.: What do you do when you get mentally constipated and you just can't write? How do you work through it?

H.C.: Well, if you're a writer and you're not writing and you want to write, it really is a terrible and dreadful thing. I just make starts of any sort.

One time I was in that situation, and I wrote a sentence: "James Boatwright's son, who was also named James Boatwright, was coming at sundown tomorrow to kill him." See, I knew a whole bunch of Boatwrights from south Georgia, where I come from. A city man wouldn't have even said "sundown." He would have said, "it's kind of late in the afternoon," or "he's coming right about five," or "as soon as the traffic thins out." He wouldn't have said "sundown." I knew that. And then I built a little more and a little more, trying to keep it consistent with itself, trying to make it have some kind of integrity so that it was all of a piece. And it finally became a story. Because in writing if you get something going, if you get some people doing something, something's going to happen.

T.L. & R.R.: Do you have any other advice for those who wish to write?

H.C.: If you're gonna write, for God in heaven's sake, try to get naked. Try to write the truth. Try to get underneath all the sham, all the excuses, all the lies that you've been told. Sometimes the lies were told you by people who meant you well, and who meant the very best for you. Your mama might have. I know my mama told me some of them great lies. She didn't mean it. She didn't think they were lies. She didn't think they were lies then, don't think they're lies now. I know in fact they're lies. Don't make her bad, it's just the way we are. But if you're gonna write fiction, you have to get right on down to it.

Graham Greene has a book called *The Power and the Glory*. It's got a priest in it, in a state down in Mexico. And at this particular time, the church had been abolished; all the Catholic churches had been turned into banks or were deserted. All the priests had two choices. They could marry or they could die. But there was one priest that went underground. And he was totally flawed. He had a child out of wedlock, and he was a drunk. Everything was wrong with him, except he could intercede between man and God. With all the other stuff that he had done and was, that man was God's man in that place. He was God's representative. And God's representative was failed and flawed, as are all of God's representatives that it has been my good fortune to meet.

Listen, if you want to write about all sweetness and light and that stuff, go get a job at Hallmark. But if you're gonna write about human beings, you're getting down where it's quick. You know "quick"?—alive, bloody, bleeding, open, *quick*? Cut my finger in the quick.

I got nothing bad to say about almost any writer, because I got the feeling that a bad book is probably just as hard to write as a good book. I think people that write bad books are sweating just as much blood as I'm sweating. (You understand that, implicit in the remark I just made, is that I don't write bad books.)

And I'll tell you something else: when I write, when you read my stuff, I want to hurt'cha. I wanna hurt'cha by turning you back upon your own heart. I want to make you look into yourself, and to ask yourself, "Would I have done that?" or to think, "God, I done something just like that, and that's a damn sorry thing to do, but I did that too." In other words, I want you to make judgments about characters and actions. It's a psychological truism that you cannot make a judgment about somebody else until you first make a judgment about yourself.

If you can't get past my 'too—my tattoo—and my 'do—the way I got my hair cut—it's only because you have decided there are certain things that can be done with hair and certain things that cannot be done with hair. And certain of them are right and proper and decent, and the rest indicate a warped, degenerate nature; therefore, I am warped and degenerate. 'Cause I got my hair cut a different way, man? You gonna really live your life like that? What's wrong with you?

See, if I do my job right when I'm writing, I will really get you turned back on yourself, and on your own code of ethics or morality or vision of the world or sense of self or whatever. If I get you turned back on yourself, then I done my job. I've done what I set out to do.

RUTH ELLEN RASCHE

Blue-Eyed Boy

Harry Crews is tired. It's lunchtime, but it feels like midnight to him since he's been up all night writing. He's about fifty pages into his latest novel—his thirteenth—and things are going so well he's afraid to stop for something as trivial as sleep.

"Once I take hold of something, I work long, too long probably, and I never miss a day," says Crews. "I can't take a day off once I start something. I'm scared to. I'm always afraid that if I miss a day, I'll go back and I won't be able to find it, I'll lose the handle on the thing. That's why I was up all night last night, scribbling when I ought to be sleeping. At the moment, I'm right in the vein. When you're right on the money, and this happens some, thank God, you know you're right, it's strong and it's moving and it's almost like taking dictation.

"People talk about how hard writing is and how awful it is and how you got to fall down and chew the rug. Writing ought not to be like pulling teeth. Recently it's been going real nice, but talk to me the day after tomorrow and I might have lost my way."

Crews has earned some tangible rewards for his ongoing battle to put words on a page. He lives in a very secluded house in Gainesville and has accumulated enough dough at age fifty-seven to go into phased retirement; he teaches one semester a year and devotes the rest of his time to other projects.

From *University of Florida Today* 17 (November 1992): 10–13.

Fame for his work, dubbed "grit lit" for its earthy qualities, has resulted in media attention ranging from reviews of his books in the *New York Times* to an appearance earlier this year on *The Dennis Miller Show*. He made his acting debut with a small part in *The Indian Runner*, a movie directed by Sean Penn, and now is working with Penn on the film adaptation of Crews's 1988 novel, *The Knockout Artist*. But public acclaim isn't the reason Crews drives himself mercilessly to write.

"I've heard other writers say it, but it's true—whatever money comes from writing feels like found money. Faulkner said it's very difficult to imagine when you're writing a book that there are people out there who are actually going to read the damn thing," he says in his southern drawl. "So whatever acclaim comes, whatever money comes, it's not the kind of thing that sustains most writers."

The novel Crews is now working on is based on a guy he met in south Florida who raises giant pigs, called horsehogs, and thousands of gators. "What struck me was the madness of it," he says. "It came to me that this was self-contained, self-justifying madness. But then after I thought about it, I thought, well, so is everything else I know—the university, the government, Ollie North. I think that may be as much what makes a writer as anything else."

Even after writing a shelf full of books and an estimated half-million words for *Playboy, Esquire,* and other notable magazines (his record is twenty-one stories published in major magazines in one year), Crews still puzzles over the question of creativity.

"When I start writing, I rarely know what I'm writing about," he says. "Am I writing about all of those great abstract nouns that you've ever heard about—'love', 'integrity', 'honor', 'compassion', or whatever? The writer's job is to take those great abstract nouns and turn them into flesh and blood and bones. Then they are real. If they aren't flesh and blood, they're ciphers, just names on a page. If they're only names on a page, then you, the reader, will never make judgments about them.

"When I talk about judgments, I'm talking about moral judgments. Writing fiction is a moral occupation practiced by not necessarily moral men and women. I want you to make judgments. You know, your sympathies and your heart and even your hope will go out to this guy, who ain't a guy at all, he's scribbles on a piece of paper; but he is, you know him, you know what he wants and what he's willing to give up to get it. And then he starts to do something, and you say, 'Oh, man, c'mon, don't do that', and he does it anyway."

Lots of people over the years have felt the same way about Crews, especially in his hard-drinking days.

"I was drunk for about nine years," he says. "I mean I was always drunk. I haven't had a drink now for three years. I wish I could say I just put it down and walked away from it and there was nothing to it. Bull, it cost me a young fortune. To do it, I signed myself into the substance unit, a locked ward; man, you don't get off that sucker. And then I had relapses and had to go back in and had therapy. But now, here I am, I'm dry.

"I just squeaked through that phase, but I don't think you get a dime for refraining from doing something you were never tempted to do. All that drinking is a movie I wish I could have missed, I really do. But a lot of stuff happened that I never would've learned otherwise, because I was in places I'd never have been otherwise."

Crews still goes to some of those places, except now he's there for research instead of whiskey. He's always on the lookout for the guts and guise of a character.

"I keep a pool stick down on Fifth Avenue," he says. "You see a guy come in and he doesn't take a stick off the rack, he gets his stick from the man behind the bar, and he starts joining that thing together; well, hustlers come out of the woodwork and all kinds of things happen.

"When I'm bending over a table under a lamp, shooting pool with the brothers, it's important to me to know what's on their minds and what language they're using to express it. When I'm doing that, for what I do in the world, that's just as important as an eighteenth-century scholar poring over dusty, huge books in the stacks of the library in search of something he needs to know. You can't write dialect if you don't hear it."

Crews says some of his fellow professors don't appreciate that, but then again, they don't understand his Mohawk haircut or tattoos, either.

"It's a psychological truth that before you can make a judgment about somebody else, you have to make a judgment about yourself," he says. "People who can't get past my haircut are people who have already decided what can be done with hair and what cannot be done with hair. I designed this haircut myself, and I did it with malice and forethought.

Even his own mother isn't thrilled about the tattoo, which is a quote from an e. e. cummings poem. "I don't like tattoos at all, but what can I do about it?" says his eighty-year-old mother, Myrtice, who still lives in southern Georgia. "Harry's just always been such a brilliant person. He says he wants to give people something to look at, something to talk about. I guess he has."

Crews says writing is crazy and stressful at times, but he can't imagine doing anything else. "I was in a hang-dog, mope-around mood recently, and my son and I were talking about writing and stuff," he says. "Somehow the line came out of my mouth, 'What the hell's writing ever given me?'

"And my son said, 'It gave you a life, man, it gave you a life'. And so it has."

SUSAN KETCHIN

Interview with Harry Crews

Harry Crews stood on a busy sidewalk in downtown Raleigh, North Carolina, leaning against a brick wall outside Harry's Bar and Grill, a popular student hangout near North Carolina State University. He was talking to a group of students, filmmakers, reporters, the novelists Lee Smith and Tim McLaurin, my assistant, Hannah Byrum, and me. Crews was waiting for a ride to the university library, where he would see a preview for students and faculty of a Gary Hawkins documentary film about his life. Though it isn't far to walk, Crews welcomed the lift; his knees, injured a while back in a motorcycle accident, buckled slightly as he leaned against the building.

It was clear that he had lived life hard—his face showed a nose broken in nine places, a deeply creased forehead, a chiseled jaw, and uneven cheekbones (one, it is said, was flattened by a pool cue). Beneath craggy brows, his light blue eyes seemed to have a cast of sadness about them, even when he laughed. Once a middleweight boxer and brown belt in karate, Crews was heavier now, but still fearsome-looking.

A recovering alcoholic, Crews does not drink or smoke today, though his hoarse voice still holds the effects of years of hard use. As he spoke, his words fired out in rapid succession, in a tone that was sometimes sober, sometimes uproariously funny; his eyebrows alternately scowled and rose to punctuate his thoughts. As Lee Smith told Crews about my book and my hopes to interview him, he turned, focused intensely on my face for an instant, and gave me a bear hug. "It's great to be here. Look at all these pretty girls,"

From *The Christ-Haunted Landscape: Faith and Doubt in Southern Fiction,* by Susan Ketchin (Jackson: University Press of Mississippi, 1994), 335–51.

he said, laughing, releasing me and letting his eyes and huge, open arms embrace the crowd around him. "I'll be glad to let you ask me questions. I don't know if I have any answers, but I'll try." Then we were off to the preview in the small library theater where he would take questions from the audience after the showing.

As the lights went up after the film preview, Crews rose from his seat in the front row of the theater and made his way up three steps to the stage, talking to the audience of students and professors as he went. Though it was clearly painful for him to walk, he moved surprisingly quickly. When he reached the stage, he grabbed a molded plastic chair and sat down gingerly to face the audience in front of the blank screen. A portion of the question-and-answer session follows.

H.C.: I could, of course, give some sort of a lecture—but I'm not going to do it now and I'm not going to do it tonight—some sort of lecture about literature, or writing nonfiction, or writing autobiography—autobiography, or what this is really, is a memoir of my childhood—but I would much rather talk with you than at you. I would much rather you ask whatever question you may have brought here and have you know that I know that the question is important. For God in heaven's sakes, don't not ask it because you think it's, well, it's too obvious, it's too simple-minded, it's too unanswerable, or whatever. If you've got a question, it's important, and it's a good question.

I make no claims that I can answer those questions, but I can respond to them. Writing's the only thing that I've ever worked at consistently and as hard as I could work. I only teach four months out of the year now at the university, but since I started doing that, I work harder, harder than I ever worked when I was teaching full time. So. Take a minute.

Audience question: What kept you from giving up during the ten years you were trying to publish and weren't getting anywhere?

H.C.: As I said, questions one can't answer but only react to, or talk around. For whatever reason, I realized how unlettered I was—I'm not going to say dumb, but how unlettered I was, how much I did not know. How much I had to master before I could write something of value that somebody could pay money for and feel like they got something back for what they paid.

And, I simply could not think of myself then, nor can I think of myself now, as anything else but a writer. All the years I was at the university, I worked with young men and women who wanted to be fiction writers. Usually, I'd have two or three or four a year who really had the fire in their belly, who had already caught the disease for which there is no cure, and who were a great joy to work with. But I always told them, I told the institution, I told anybody that wanted to hear it, that I was a writer who taught, not a teacher who wrote.

Larry Brown, he's a helluva writer, stayed with me for a week not long ago at my house, we had a helluva time talking. When Larry Brown was talking about me staying there at the typewriter for three hours every day—I do that. I've been at a typewriter and I don't know what comes next. And what I say to myself is, I say okay, you don't have to write, just sit here three hours and you can leave, but you can't write letters, and you can't clean your fingernails, and you can't, obviously, look out a window. I always look at a wall when I write. And you know three hours is a long time to sit there like that, you can't read anything, and you'll eventually do something, even if it's wrong.

I really got that from something that Flannery O'Connor said which I think is just damn beautiful. You see, she said it much more elegantly than I just said it, and hers has got that element of mystery in it that I love, because where's all this stuff come from? You think I know? If I did I'd give it to you because some of you want it, you'd like to have it, and I'd give it to you. Share it. There's enough for everybody. I don't know where it comes from. She said, "I go to the typewriter every day for three hours so that if anything comes, I am prepared to receive it." To receive it, dig it? To receive it is the blossoming mystery. Receive it? Flannery O'Connor has an essay that begins "I am no vague believer." She was hard into Catholicism, God bless her heart, hey that's cool, I'm not a Catholic, but she was and—but—*receive* it.

I'm getting out of my depth here saying this, but I'm going to say it anyway. Anthropologists and others separate societies that are primitive from societies that are not primitive on the basis of whether or not they can leave a written record. If a society can leave a written record, it is not primitive. It can't leave a written record, it's primitive.

But if it can't leave a written record, the history of the tribe and the people and their gods and how their gods interact with one another and with man and how the seeds and animals came to flourish over the earth—they've got all that. Who carries those stories? Who carries the oral tradition? Without exception: the shamans. The medicine men. The, what we would call, preachers. I mean, the guy that goes up on the butte somewhere and fasts for four days, and has no water, and stares into the sun, and he finally has a vision, and I'm going to tell that guy that he didn't have a vision? I couldn't do what he did, it would scare me. I'd go blind, I'd die, you know, and a lot of other things. But he didn't.

I saw a documentary not long ago on television about an Indian, seventy years old, who wanted to go to the sweat lodge, or whatever kind of lodge it is where you sweat, a guy seventy years old, and they show him running down this road towards this other ritual that he was going to, and he looked like a young man. And he had all the world joined together. Everything was a part of everything else.

And when you write, what you are trying to do is to create a world that has integrity, and has coherence. It is all of a piece, every image or every action or every line of dialogue resonates against some other line of dialogue or image or metaphor, or whatever, and a lot of this resonates against a bunch of them. And of course it's all language, isn't it? It's so easy to see that with poetry and so damn hard to see it with fiction. But it works for fiction, too.

Audience question: You mentioned Flannery O'Connor's religious beliefs and the certainty that she had, and on the screen you talk about something like the same kind of certainty in sports. I noticed that every one of your books is organized around an activity like bodybuilding or football or karate, and I wonder if you think in terms of that analogy—are the people in those books looking for a kind of secular equivalent for what people used to get out of religion?

H.C.: I don't know if they're looking for it or not, but I am, and that's the way I think. That's the thing that fascinates me the most.

I'm thinking about the life of the greatest wire walker in the world now, his last name is D-e-t-i-t-e. It's French and I don't speak French. He's the guy that walked between the trade towers. He did it without anybody knowing it, until he was already up there and then they couldn't get him off the wire; he was fifty stories in the air. Never works with a net. He's alive. In one of my books, I quote Karl Wallenda. About six weeks before he died, in a conversation he said—he never worked with a net, never worked with a net, and he fell sixty feet to a concrete floor to his death in his seventies—and what I quote there is, "Walking the wire is living. Everything else is just waiting."

And if you care about fiction, or poetry, or music, or any of the arts—if you care about it enough, doing it is like walking the wire. Doing it is as dangerous in its own way. You either disappear into a bottle, or you stick your head in the oven, or cut your wrists. I mean, look at the lives of artists and their ends, or whatever. Dylan Thomas drank himself to death. My God, in the meantime while he was taking the very few years it took him to drink himself to death, his life was such a madhouse scramble. I believe it was his art that drove him to that kind of thing—I guess anything could drive him to that kind of thing. I'm just thinking out loud.

Audience question: Have you ever sat at the typewriter and nothing looks right, or do you think of something and write it out, or do you get an idea and decide to go out and do it, to live the experience and then write about it?

H.C.: I have to be honest and tell you just flat out "no." No, that's one of the things I've not done because, very early on, I was impressed by a number of writers—one of them is Robert Penn Warren—talking about that kind of thing.

I had a book called *Karate Is a Thing of the Spirit*, and I never would have written *Karate Is a Thing of the Spirit* if I hadn't just stumbled by a place—I'd never seen any karate—and it turned out there was a guy in there named Dirk Mosig, a German, raised in Argentina, and he was an eighth-degree black belt, and did all those things eighth-degree black belts do. Madness, madness, madness. And I wanted inside that madness. And I went inside. I had no notion of writing a book about karate. But if I hadn't studied with him for almost three years, I never would've written the book. I couldn't have written the book.

Let me just say this one last thing about that right there. There's a bunch of guys, men and women, seems like there's more men than women, who disappear into the library, and every six years or so they come out with a great big book. I'll give you two titles, both of them written by the same guy: *The Agony and the Ecstasy* and *Passions of the Mind*, the first about Michelangelo, the second about Freud. They're about that damn thick, and they make excellent doorstops.

Audience question: What was the cost to you to create a space for yourself, for your writing?

H.C.: Oh, God. Let me just answer you this day, this way. On most days, at my age, on most days, if I let myself think about it, I think the cost was much, *much* too heavy, too great, too great. I had to give up too many things. May have hurt too many people, maybe denied myself things that I shouldn't have denied myself. I'm not sure that I did any of those things, but I sometimes—if I get into one of those things, I think about it. Because that space you're talking about, if you really are successful about creating it, it does cost.

Strangely enough, Sean Penn—my last book was dedicated to him; he's become a great friend of mine 'cause we're making—he's not in an acting role, he's going to direct—and we're going to do *The Knockout Artist*—he talks about building that box for himself when it's time for the cameras to roll. And he's got to do it, he's got to have his space made already, before he moves, and really in a sense, you've either been there and know what a guy's talking about when he says, "My space, I've got to have it to do it," or it makes no sense. You can't explain it, somehow.

★ ★ ★

After the preview, Harry Crews and I arranged to meet in the lobby at the Crowne Park Hotel. When I arrived there, I called his room from the house phone near the front desk. The phone rang half a ring—"Harry Crews."

"Hello, Harry, this is the religion lady. Can you come down to the lobby?"

"Would you mind coming up here to my room to talk?" he asked. "I mean, I'm bushed. Don't worry. You've got the girl with you. If I get you into any trouble, you can both beat me up." With that, he hung up. Hannah ("the girl") and I grabbed Cokes and snacks from a vending machine downstairs and rode the elevator to Crews's room, not knowing quite what to expect. In fact, we encountered a polite and engaging man who addressed

each query with a searing intensity as if it were the most important question on earth.

S.K.: Okay, here's what I'm fascinated by, that I wanted you to react to: In his book *Flannery O'Connor's South,* Robert Coles writes about fundamentalism in the South and he quoted Flannery O'Connor. She wrote to John Hawkes, "I don't think you should write something as long as a novel around anything that is not of the greatest concern to you and everybody else, and for me this is always a conflict between an attraction for the holy and the disbelief in it that we breathe in with the air of the times."

H.C.: All right. I will tell you this—I don't think anybody in my house believes it much, but I have now for a long time, say, after about my seventh novel, I thought that everything I've written since that time, fiction anyway, was a search for faith. Or to say it another way . . . it's a search for the nature of belief.

I am a believer and I don't think a day passes that I don't think about it, dwell upon it. My brother, who is a very devout Baptist, is terribly displeased with the work I do (he's been in my house once in the last twenty years) because he finds it, as he says, pornographic, but then he took one look at one of Flannery O'Connor's books and found it pornographic, too, but that's all right, he's a good man. I am a believer, but not a—I don't consider myself affiliated with, or part of, or belonging to any institutionalized religion that I know of. I don't go to the Baptist church, although I've been to the Baptist church, I've been to the Methodist church, I've been to the Catholic church.

I spent a very long time going to church after church after church trying to find one I could go to because the thing I thought was, it came to me, that going to church, if it's nothing else, even if you can't believe that there's an everlasting life, that you have a soul that transcends the flesh, whatever—even if you don't believe that, you could go to a church one day a week, or more for that matter, you probably ought to go, most of us, certainly I should go more, and do this: meditate upon how we have failed ourselves, and failed our fellow man. I—now don't get me wrong, I don't think I'm the worst guy in the world. I think I'm immodest and bad enough to think I'm a pretty good guy. I try to—guy's in a ditch, I try to give him a hand. And I hope he'll pass it along if he can do it. But you can go there and think about your actions and how they are made manifest in the world that you happen to live in.

Because God is dead. He was dead a long time before Nietzsche said, "God is dead." God is dead because this is a secular world we live in. I mean, like it or not, deny it as you will, it is a secular world. That somehow offends me, really deeply offends me that it's a secular world. When I wrote *Karate Is a Thing of the Spirit*—that year—you can check me on this—that year, Buick, their advertising slogan that year was, "Buick: Something to Believe In." That was the slogan they had. Okay, I'm going to believe in a car. Well, wonderful. You'll pardon me if I find that obscene. I don't want to believe in a car. I would rather it run and not break down, but that's about as far as it goes.

Now that we have made religions of—we have made something that is very close to the framework of what religion used to be, once upon a time was, and belief in "a God" was. We've made it out of all things material, this materialistic world. The guy who dies with the highest score wins, the most toys, money in his bank account, you know.

I'm a sports fan, and I love boxing, and I recognize at the same time that it is totally indefensible. You can't defend boxing as anything but a brutal, terrible, barbaric act that is uncivilized, and if you happen to be a believer, unholy. That we would give millions of dollars to these two individuals, to hire this menagerie of trainers and dieticians, and lawyers, everything else, to make them as mean as they can make them and then put them in the ring, with the sole purpose of seeing which one can knock the other one senseless. . . .

So we've made a [religious] thing out of that and a whole bunch of other things we've named, like cars, and as we've already said, the material things. But then, I say, well, I apparently can't make that leap of faith. I can reason myself along for a certain distance towards something that's other than human, bigger than human, more mysterious than human, and the rest of it. But then I can't reason any farther. I can reason towards it, but I can't make that leap of faith.

What I can do is, I can contemplate the natural laws of the universe. I mean, rocks do not fall sideways if you turn them loose, they fall down, always. The mystery of a peanut putting the blossom on top of the ground and its fruit under the ground, the mystery of sap rising in pine trees at a certain time of the year, and those are just things everybody notices; it gets much more mysterious than that. I refuse to believe that I, or you, or any of my fellow beings, are an accident, or that we are some kind of a spark of electricity that happened back whenever.

And so, the characters in my books—in *The Gospel Singer,* in the karate book, in *The Knockout Artist,* certainly in the car book—my characters, not surprisingly, are doing essentially what I do much of. I writhe, and "suffer" is not too strong a word. I writhe and suffer in my unknowing. I don't know, and I want to know.

On the other hand, if I read the Koran, the Bhagavad Gita, the Old Testament, the New Testament, it isn't about knowing, it's about faith. And it may be that mankind has developed the physical world to such an incredible degree that it has simply overwhelmed his ability to have any faith. I mean, we got machines, Jack, that can do . . . I mean, *they're* almost godlike. I mean, I know that's blasphemous, but at least I said "almost."

I mean, I don't know if you've ever seen on television, or documentaries, or maybe in person, some factories that have . . . the automobile business has got it up for electronics. And it's all done by robotic maneuvers. These robots, they go zzzt-zzzt-zzzt, it's things moving down, and they've even got machines now that can reproduce themselves. Now think about that for a minute. Now that's like a human being reproducing another human being. The machine tears up, the machine knows it's torn up. If the part to fix it is available and the right program has been placed into the machine, then it takes out the broken part, gets the new part, puts it back in, and then works just like it ever did.

We've got machines now that we can talk to and the machine will type. It will transcribe; well, it doesn't type the way we normally think of it, but it does in fact transcribe the human voice. You just talk to it and it will put it on paper, and that can be taken off by another machine into regular English, and if you speak to it in French, it'll take it off in that, if it's got the right program built into it.

And most people save themselves a lot of pain or a lot of frustration by just refusing to think about the things that I've been talking about.

I'd give you this: that to be a fiction writer means you spend most of your time thinking about, meditating upon, trying to dissect and understand just those aspects of the human animal that other human beings try their damnedest never to think about. They don't want to think about that. I mean after all there it is, in *Oedipus the King*,—if you had a big auditorium full of men, and you looked out at them and you said, "Where is the man who has not dreamt of sleeping with his mother?" they would all say, "Not me." The line is in *Oedipus,* and it's as common as field peas, and it doesn't make anybody bad and it doesn't make anybody incestuous, it makes somebody human. There are mysteries we don't understand, and we are not going to understand them, I don't think. I know I won't, I don't believe anybody will.

Now, down there where I come from, those good folks have reduced—"reduced" is a bad choice of words—they have compressed and boiled down the religious experience to something that is hard and fast and simple in the best sense of the word. "Simple" doesn't mean simpleminded. An atom is simple. It doesn't mean it's easy or simplistic. They boil it down to something very, very simple. I leave to minds better than mine to judge them. If you're a snake handler and you pick up the snakes in a religious ecstasy and the snakes do not bite you because you are a believer, or nine of them bite you and you do not die because you are a believer, who am I, Harry Crews, to say that that is some kind of a charlatan, false, phony, accidental happenstance? I'm not prepared to say that and never will be.

And if you look at religions around the world, you see that all over the face of this earth, there are people whose religious experience and the way they worship things are every bit as, if you want to use the word "bizarre," as handling snakes or drinking a cup of arsenic. I can drink it and I won't die because I believe. And they drink it and they don't die. Well, in India there are holy men who live at the top of a mountain of solid ice, utterly naked, and why don't they die? They stick nails through their cheeks, and they do not bleed because they can control the capillaries in their body. That's the only possible explanation for why they are not bleeding; the capillaries do not rupture. Well, they say there's got to be some trick to it. Well, maybe so, maybe so. But you go take care of that. I don't know about those things. . . . But if I ever come to the place where *I* ought to be, and I don't think

I'm there yet, I think I'll come there through fiction because that's my work and that's my search. But if I don't, I don't.

Human beings are manifestly too hard on one another. Everybody wants everybody else to be better than they are. Hey, we're all flawed and faulted, and, I mean, we're all—maybe none of you've done it and maybe the next fifty people we've seen haven't done it, but good men and women have just slapped the hell out of a three-year-old baby—well, think: slapping a three-year-old baby? I mean, that's despicable and cruel and—yes it is, yes it is. It's also human. You're tired, your nerves are bad, money's short, you don't know what you're going to do with this, you're worried about that, and it happens.

And I'm sometimes talking to students outside of the classroom, at my house or something, and what I have been known to say is that I think the kindest and best thing you can do for yourself is to forgive yourself. There's no reason to continue to beat on yourself and hate yourself for a moment of fallibility, and let it turn into a cancer that you carry thirty years later. That's just a loser's way that accomplishes nothing. You admit you did it, you admit the wrongness of it, you try to make amends for it. Most times it's impossible to make amends for it. It's been done. It's like you say something to your wife, something really ugly, and then you didn't mean it, and then you say, "Let me take that back." Well, you know, I'm sorry. You can't take that back. The words have been said. And you may live together for, you know, fifty years happily after that, but those words are between you. It might conceivably make your marriage stronger.

So you can see that in my writing and in my life and belief (the things that make that writing), it's a very dicey situation. Sometimes it comes up seven, and sometimes it comes up snake eyes, and sometimes it comes up and there's nothing on it—it's a blank face, and all I know to do, until somebody somehow convinces me otherwise, is to continue to wrestle with it as best I can.

If you do manage to stay alive long enough, you begin to see more and more how much of the bad stuff that you do or have done—yeah, you shouldn't have done it, but it doesn't make you Satan, and it doesn't make you irrevocably horrible, in anybody's eyes—shouldn't, shouldn't. And whatever gods may be that look down, up, or wherever, I don't for a minute believe . . . By the very nature of being God, it would be impossible for it/him/her to condemn a man. We're too frail, we would be too frail no matter how many bombs we have. We make enough bombs to blow the whole place up, and we're still very, very frail. I mean, little tiny microorganisms that you can't even see without an electronic microscope can enter the pores of your skin and you'll be dead tomorrow. That isn't a very strong fortress for walking around in.

If you went to church, if anybody went to church once a week and got on his knees and simply thought about that, I don't think it would hurt him a hell of a lot. I think it'd make him probably sleep a little better.

S.K.: The epigraph in *Scar Lover* is "Guilt is magic."

H.C.: It's the last line of a poem by James Dickey. He, as best I can understand it (Jim's been my friend for many years, but I wouldn't ask him to explain a line to me), as best I can make out, having heard him really talk about it in all kinds of contexts, guilt is magic because we can't forgive or heal ourselves, so it can make us do just anything. It can make us do anything.

All those Japanese in the Second World War that were kamikaze pilots, and they didn't even have wheels once they took off in a plane loaded full of dynamite—they didn't even have wheels to land. They had to go down in a smokestack of a ship out there somewhere, and to do otherwise would dishonor them—not just them but their entire blood line—mama, daddy, and everybody else, and their ancestors, and being ancestor worshippers, they would be guilty of that, so *guilt* sends them down the smokestack. It's a powerful magic to send a man down a smokestack with a plane loaded with dynamite, I should think.

S.K.: In *Scar Lover,* Pete and Sarah fall in love with each other, and it seems that guilt becomes transformed into redemption.

H.C.: I hope so. I hope so. I wrote it out of the conviction that unqualified love can heal anything. It can heal emotional scars, physical scars, it can heal the crippled, it can—speaking here in metaphor—it can make the crippled man walk and the blind man see.

It occurred to me one day, like when I wrote that book or shortly before I wrote it, that you probably know that you really, really really love—let's talk about a man and a woman—you really know, if you're a man, you really know that you love a woman when you love her imperfections. She might have a—I don't know—a little funny twist to her nose or a little lobe of her ear, or whatever, an odd-shaped chin that maybe six years ago, when you first met her—you thought she was a great person, she made you feel good, and you liked her company, and she made you feel comfortable and safe, but you thought the chin was, well, you wished it was . . . But then one day you found that that was the very thing that you loved, you loved that little chin. Little chin's fine, and she's fine, and I'm hers and she's mine, and we're one flesh and that's where you are.

That is, of course, right out of the Bible, but most people get away from having to embarrass themselves in front of other people, embarrass themselves to themselves, by simply refusing to think about those things. Let's just not think about it, for God's sake. Let's not talk about it, certainly not in the family, where you know mama and daddy and little brother, and everybody's present.

S.K.: You talked at one time about writers who do go to the line, who do embarrass themselves and talk about these things, do probe when others look away, as being the shamans, the medicine men, of the community.

H.C.: Yes.

S.K.: Can you talk about that, about how that works?

H.C.: Well, they are the keepers of the oral tradition of the society since they can't write. Since they can't write, primitive societies have to keep their stories. But it's not just primitive societies. Galileo was driven to prove that Copernicus was wrong about the way the heavenly bodies moved about. He certainly could write. He was certainly not a part of a primitive society. He was part of a very sophisticated society. He searched nonetheless.

And people who can't write, so-called primitive, backwards societies, whatever, third-world peoples. Hey man, they've got to somehow come to some kind of understanding, some kind of grips with the fact that it rains, that lightning comes down and sets fire to those woods over there, and burns it off on the bottom and chars the trees, but then in about a month all these little green things start growing out, and it's this wonderful green grass comes where before it was black. And the sun coming up, and the sun going down, and all those things, the moon waxing and waning, all of those things they've got to understand—and they usually do it by making it into stories, giving those things personalities, even names. And they do what the rest of us do, they do the best they can.

CATHI UNSWORTH

Harry Crews: Literary Terminator

The words of Harry Crews do not just leave an imprint in your mind. Rather, they open up wild and, at times, magical worlds, inhabited by alcoholics, malcontents, white trash, black mystics, cripples, and desperados. The weight of truth and realism behind these people—losers all, to the great American Dream—lends them such reality that you can see them stepping off the page, hear their cursing speech, smell the trouble emanating from their skin. Crews's characters, born of rage, but also of rare insight and empathy, even love, are as large and real as the author himself—a great hunk of ex-Marine, professional light-heavyweight boxer, and karate brown belt. A man who makes sense of what others call insanity.

The events that shaped Crews's worldview all began in his tough passage to adolescence, which he chronicled in *A Childhood: The Biography of a Place*. The day Harry found out his friend Willalee "was a nigger" (the same day his aunt reprimanded him for referring to a black man as "mister"). His inclination to become a preacher at the same time that his stepfather's drinking and violence began to escalate: "And I heard Daddy come through the front gate, the plow points banging and his own drunk-heavy feet on the steps and the front door slamming, and then I heard, as I already knew I would, querulous voices as Mama and Daddy confronted each other there beyond the thin wall. . . . I could stand lying in my bed if I concentrated on hell and damnation. . . . With my whole self firmly immersed in hell, I could usually go back to sleep."

From *Purr* 4.4 (1995).

When Crews was older, he interrupted his university education to become a caller for the ten-in-one show at a traveling carnival, and he discovered he had a natural affinity and love for the freaks. He traveled America on a motorbike, got arrested, and met a range of real people that no academic mind could ever have created. As he wrote in his first novel, the classic *The Gospel Singer,* "Normal is for shit."

"A lot of people," growls Crews, on a phone line from his Florida home, "over the past twenty-five years, in newspapers and on the radio, public broadcasting companies and other places, have given me a good deal of grief, said stupid, unkind, and untrue things that didn't make me happy, over the fact that there are in my books so many of what they choose to call freaks. Which I prefer to call people with special considerations under the Lord."

As Crews's books vividly demonstrate, it is the surrounding characters who reveal themselves to be more corrupt and impaired than the physically different people they prey upon. Marvin Molar's girlfriend, for instance, in *The Gypsy's Curse,* and the repellent big businessman cum fetishist Oyster Boy from *The Knockout Artist.*

"That is absolutely right, and I think that's part of the reason that they are in the work I do," Crews expounds. "There is in a book I have just finished writing a person with a harelip, a cleft palate. And the way that they speak is perfectly understandable, but they don't speak the way you or I do because of the configuration of the mouth.

"I expect to catch all kinds of grief about that, including the charge that I am making fun of them, if you can believe that. That's been leveled against me, that I'm making fun of freaks and that I'm an anti-feminist, that I look down on women, whatever.

"I have been a feminist before feminists were invented. I have seen what women have been through, in this country anyway . . . . most anywhere you look, women doing the same work as men are doing, and often doing it better, are paid less. And that kind of thing just outrages me."

Rage is the fuel of Crews's literary furnace, the primal emotion that gives his writing such life. But this is not an incoherent fury; indeed, part of Crews's mastery rests upon just how well he observes human beings, their dialogue, thoughts, and actions, their hopes and nightmares.

"If that is true, and I hope it is, in my own case I would say that it is probably because I have never written about anything that I haven't been involved in personally, and know the smell and taste of it, the tactile surface of it, the sound of it. Which may or may not make sense to you, but what I mean is it's rather like an analogy. There is an experience in life, and you use the emotional and spiritual and financial and whatever else is at the core of it, and transfer it into different kinds of people and perhaps a different place.

"If what I write steps out of the page, it's because I, thank God, have never been silly enough to write about any place I've never been or write about the kind of people that I don't know. All my books are set in the South, 'cause that's where I come from, that's the idiom I know and the dialect I can write. And I know the kind of food they eat, their concerns, and the rest of it. So that's some of what makes my writing memorable, if it *is* memorable, and compelling, and I hope, significant.

"But also, I have never written anything that isn't screaming out of me or screaming to be written. Perhaps that sounds like hyperbole, but it's true. Apparently some writers have trouble finding subjects, or they go dry for long periods of time. That certainly isn't the case with me. There's far too many stories or novels or whatever in me than I'll ever live long enough to write."

In Crews's world, his literary creations seem always to be teetering on the brink, dealt a hand by fate that they strain to make the best of. I'm thinking of desperate men like *A Feast of Snakes*'s Joe Lon, ex–school football hero whose premature accolades and lack of anything after leave him frustrated to the point of homicide. Of Shereel Dupont, the female bodybuilder in *Body*, whose redneck family, the Turnipseeds, is a congregation from hell. And of the bulging-veined Duffy Deeter, who leaves his mark on *A Feast of Snakes* as well as fighting his savage way through *All We Need of Hell*. Despite the madness inside and out of these people, Crews fashions them as human beings, not as stereotypes.

"I hope they are," he affirms. "Many times they have to fight from the very beginning just to stay alive and keep things together.

"I don't now, but I have been teaching at the University of Florida, which is the ninth biggest university in the country, with, I think, thirty-eight thousand students. And I taught there thirty-four years. You know how many black students I had in thirty-four years? One.

Where I live in Florida . . . When people think of Florida, they think high-rise condos, and beaches, and a lot of traffic and palm trees. I'm up in the north, almost in Georgia, in Alabama, in Mississippi—there are a lot of black people.

"And here's the kicker. I don't think there is any conspiracy to keep them out of the university. But racism in this country was so terrible for so long, so blatant, so overt. And when the laws passed, when segregation 'ended', by then it was institutionalized. There is no one you can point to who is making this happen, but it is happening nonetheless. And I have written in an essay that if I had been born black in this country, I would be dead or I would be in jail.

"I mean, oftentimes, you run into a young black male, maybe, or female, and he's full of anger and outrage and resentment, and you don't really know why and you haven't done anything to him, but he's got that look in his eyes, that look of 'let's go to war' or something. And you're thinking, 'You're picking on the wrong guy here. I'm on your side', but he's been jacked around so long that all he sees is you're white, he's black, and he's been fucked over for too long. Now he's got the chance, he's gonna cut your goddamn throat. And I don't blame him. But that angers me."

America, as a whole, angers Crews. It has been suggested by one critic that he uses every month as Freak the Citizens month. "I think probably that's why a good many people are put off by what I write," he says. "They just don't really want to read it. They don't like having to face up to things the way they really are. It doesn't conform to their notion of the world.

"This is a terribly arguable and terribly controversial point, but it seems to me that most people carry around an enormous number of lies in their heads, in their hearts. It's so much easier, in a way, to pass through the world full of lies, than it is to pass through the world seeing things how they truly are. Rather than the kind of bullshit that most mamas and daddies tell their children: 'Work hard and you'll be president', or 'See that feller lying there on the sidewalk—well, if he wanted to succeed and join the rest of us in society, then he'd get up and scrub up and get a job'. Bullshit. They don't walk in his shoes, they don't know what he's carrying on his back or in his heart, and they make their judgment and pass it on to their child.

"The most stupid goddamn thing I ever heard was 'If you don't like to live in the ghetto, then simply work harder'. These people are poor, these people are uneducated, but the people in the ghetto are the hardest goddamn working people that I know. It's the people who don't work, I mean don't *really* work, that make all the money.

"I've worked with movie directors in pre-production in films who work for maybe three or four hours and then say, 'Wow, that was a good day's work. Let's go shoot a round of golf'.

"Well, I can play golf, but I didn't. I passed. I said, 'No, I don't think so. If you're through with me, then I gotta go see a man about a dog' or something."

Crews has cataloged America's decay, so how does he see the future of his country?

"For a country as rich as this country, and it was all an accident ...When we took possession of this country, we literally killed nations. We killed the Navajo Nation, the Arapaho Nation, the Apache Nation, the Mohawk Nation; after we killed all those nations, we found ourselves in possession of a land with unlimited resources, enough timber to build houses for everyone in the friggin' world, and gold and silver and iron and minerals—you name it—and water power, and all of that stuff. All of that stuff we have consistently wasted, and, in terms of your country [*Unsworth is British*], this country is a child, and that's the way we've acted. We're still a child, we haven't even reached adolescence yet, and we have, willy-nilly, for nothing more significant than a goddamn dollar bill, ruined the friggin' country.

"But not many people seem to notice it, you know. They just get their little house and build a fence around it, and get a job and send their children to college to get a valuable degree, and they've got a lot of insurance, and they associate with their own kind. So if you start talking to them about poverty and homelessness, hell, they've never seen it. And they will argue with you: 'Sure, there are a few homeless, and the poor will always be the poor, and there are a few people hungry, but that's their own fault—they don't work'.

"I fought for this goddamn country in a time of war," he seethes. "I volunteered, they didn't even have to come and get me. My brother was already out there in Korea, and I went down in the goddamn Marine Corps. I didn't join the Air Force or some wimpshit, bullshit thing so I could stay in the background in supply units and send shit up to the fighting guys. I did that, and I suppose I would do it again, but it doesn't mean that I have to love everything that's going on in this country. I know I have been awfully negative about this country, but that's how I feel most of the time."

If Harry were to see active service ever again, he certainly has his target chosen. "I don't know how many goddamn things we have amassed around Iraq," he ponders, "but that goddamn madman running that fucking country . . . I don't know. I'm not a terrorist, but I could happily assassinate that little son of a bitch. He's not a madman, he's an evil man, a very, very evil man.

"But it's important for me to say that all of what I have been talking about could be construed as saying that I, Harry Crews, am above all that, and that I'm innocent of all that kind of behavior. No, no, no! I have my share of madness and bloody slaughter in me, simply because I'm a human being, and human beings are fatal, flawed, fucked-up creatures, and they do that kind of thing. And that's why I insist on showing, dramatizing, trying to set down on paper in my books in such a way that if I can find a reader that can get through the whole book, the least he will have to do is reexamine his own values. Because it's a psychological truism that before you can judge anybody else, you've got to first judge yourself.

"As a matter of fact, I have often said that all my fiction is about the same thing," he concludes. "People doing the best they can with what they've got to deal with. And that means the kind of clothes, the kind of house, the kind of physical possessions, but more than that, it's the kind of heart they have, the kind of compassion, the kind of quality of mercy they have, the ability to sympathize with other people's predicaments. And that's what I try to do.

"I've been involved with a black writer who died far too young, James Baldwin, who wrote *The Fire Next Time* and a play called *Blues for Mister Charlie*. In the introduction of *Blues for Mister Charlie* (Charlie being the white man), he said, 'No man is a villain in his own heart'. People do the most dreadful things without feeling bad about it, because they manage to make excuses, reasons, or whatever, for what they've done. What I want to do is strip away that mask, take off the rose-colored glasses, and see the world and what's in it for what it really is."

DAMON SAUVE

Everything Is Optimism, Beautiful and Painless: A Conversation with Harry Crews

In mid-February 1996, a few years after I graduated from the University of Florida, I returned to Gainesville to interview Harry Crews, with whom I had studied creative writing as an undergraduate. At the time, I was working on a comprehensive bibliography of Crews's work. My desk was populated with piles of photocopied interviews, book reviews, and critical articles. Besides the research, I had been rereading his novels and nonfiction. My head was full of the sound and cadence of his voice. I was eager to interview him myself, despite whatever trepidation I had about disturbing his privacy.

As a teacher and writer, Crews had had considerable influence on his students, including me. Each semester, we lined up down the hall to register for his fiction classes, which inevitably filled quickly. Many of the students at the front of the line were, like me, repeats, people who had already taken a class with him. Although I had not read one word of his prior to the first class, by the end of four semesters I had read everything. I also read the novels and authors he recommended in lecture. A few years after college, I started a literary magazine called Oyster Boy Review, named after a character in The Knockout Artist. When Crews received his copy of each issue, he would often respond with an encouraging note or a phone call.

My girlfriend and I visited with Crews on a Saturday morning at his house, which is secluded by trees from the busy street. Crews sat in a stuffed chair, the same chair pictured in many of his other interviews, and we sat

This interview is published here for the first time.

across from him. He had been at work on his next book, an autobiography, and offered to read from it. We listened intently as he read for twenty minutes. The chapter was, as one would expect, painfully vivid, and the image of his dead mother's opened, black mouth was difficult to dispel from my mind.

Knowing that any question I could frame would have already been asked and answered in nearly twenty-five years of interviews, I didn't bother with the notes I had made about what I wanted to ask him. I set up my tape recorder near his chair, and our conversation continued for several hours, interrupted by a run to the truck to retrieve my bottle of bourbon.

D.S.: You said once in an interview that you bought an expensive microphone setup here in town, and you used that for some of the interviews you've done.

H.C.: I mean, I used to when I did so much of it. I used a tape recorder *and* a legal pad, but then I bought myself a wire, because—and I would tell people I was wired—they see things and get intimidated. Certainly they see a mike and they get intimidated. Some people do. If you're interviewing people who make films or who are very public people, they don't get intimidated. A truck driver or a whatever, he looks at that thing, and keeps looking at it, and his speech becomes stilted, he's careful about what he says, and the rest of it.

If you do a lot of it, and God knows I did a lot of it for a time. I don't know how the hell I did it. Hundreds and hundreds of hours. All across the country.

I wrote a piece on Madonna. I wrote the piece on Sean Penn. They could give a shit about a microphone. They didn't care. But I tell people, I just write off the ends of my fingers. If they're working, I stay out of their way.

D.S.: I remember you talked about writing a script for Sean Penn. Did that ever work out?

H.C.: I wrote the screenplay for Sean Penn and was paid for it. Sean's been very good to me. He gave me a lot of work. For which I was paid. Well, everybody in show business is paid ten times as much as they're worth. No, he just could never raise the money to make the film.

D.S.: I guess that happens a lot.

H.C.: Yeah, it does. I don't know if you heard, but *The Knockout Artist* is being made into a film. The director, producer, and the screenwriter were here two weeks ago for a few days. They consulted on the film because they don't—it's set in New Orleans, as you may know. They know about New Orleans what a tourist would know about New Orleans, which is not what I wrote about. And they simply don't know where to find anything.

Some years ago, they had—I believe it was a Democratic convention in New Orleans—and they cleaned out. They took all the porn film houses, the live sex shows, and the snuff films—all that bullshit—and they took it out of New Orleans and put it across the river in the so-called West Bank. It's across the Mississippi. And if you don't know where to look, you just go to Bourbon Street. Everybody goes to Bourbon Street. The Quarter's all right. Jackson Square's nice. I like when it's open to sit on a bench, watch kids play music, guys juggle and do whatever they do. And there's a ferry right down in Jackson Square. And if you're on your feet, you don't have a car, it's free to go across the river. There's a great restaurant just directly across the river from the ferry. Every thirty minutes one goes across. If you got a car, it costs a buck. Best deal in town.

★ ★ ★

H.C.: A writer friend of mine had a cabin up in the northeast of Louisiana. I stayed up there to write [*The Knockout Artist*]. It was a good tight cabin.

I didn't have a phone. I didn't have a radio. I didn't have a television set. I had an iron stove to cook on. Wood-burning. Four eyes on top. A reservoir. But no running water. I had to get water out of a jerry can. It had an outhouse. The cabin was just one huge room. Huge. *Huge.* And every wall was filled from top to the floor with books. And I had my dog with me. It was one of the best years I ever had. Great.

Because, twelve miles out of the swamp where I was, there was Winnsboro. A little town. About like Waldo [*a small, one-light town near Gainesville*]. And curiously enough, they had a gym. And so six days a week I got a hot shower and a shave, and a work-out, and on the seventh day, my dog and God and I rested. I got up every morning at four o'clock to work. By the time the gym opened, I was finished writing for the day. Read a whole bunch of books. Had a lot of time to read.

★ ★ ★

H.C.: I have a computer, printer, and stuff like that, but I don't think I'm ever going to—I'm through with computers.

Did you know that Shelby Foote's three-volume history of the Civil War, he wrote with a *dip* pen? One of those little inkwells and you just—you don't even fill the pen with ink. You just dip it and write.

And that Graham Greene—and if you look at the list of books that Graham Greene wrote, I mean, it's mind-boggling that anybody could write that much—all in longhand. His line was "I never mastered the machine."

My feeling about a computer, now—if I write it in longhand and then I type it into the computer and revise it a little bit as you type it in, or *a lot,* and then use a computer to revise—a computer's a marvelous instrument to revise on. I don't even remember—I can't imagine how in the hell we used to do it. I seem to remember a lot of scissors and tape and paste and stuff before computers.

But as far as composing on a typewriter, nobody needs to go faster. I, first among them. Everybody needs to go slower. Since, max, five hundred words a day is a good day's work. Particularly if you can keep the five hundred, which many times you can't. I just threw away a hundred pages of that thing I read down there [*the autobiography in progress Crews had read from earlier*]. It was good shit, but it just didn't belong in the book. That's the trick of it.

I don't know. But I was *never* able to write on an electronic typewriter. Those things talk back to you. Computers don't do that.

But, no. I say that. I may do it. I don't know. It doesn't really matter pretty much how you do it just as long as you do it. Get the work done.

★ ★ ★

H.C.: It seems that everybody wants to be saved for the chair. You know, you see these old guys about eighty years old, they're [sitting in] the chair. And modern medicine has just kept them alive. I have a good friend who's my age who's just had his . . . First, he got his liver cut out 'cause he drank. Well, he didn't drink any heavier than I did, but his liver didn't hold up. Cut it out. Immediately after that, they had to cut part of his lung off 'cause he had cancer there. He's still alive. Looks good.

I don't know. We'll see when it comes down to it. But I have an elaborate will that contains how I'm supposed to be buried and burned up. And no memorial service. No words said. No cards. No flowers or nothing. No marker. But also, you know, everybody knows many wills don't have a whole list of the actual machines—well, George [*Crews's girlfriend for the last several years*], being a nurse, knows all about those. She has the same thing. About shit you can do and you can't do.

I am sixty-two years old in June, and eight more years is three-score and ten. Not bad, if it matters, but what the hell. But sixty-one's a pretty good ride. That's a pretty busy ride. I hope to die falling face forward and dead, which is the way I hope—I hope when I go that my whole chest blows out, my heart slams against a wall in the end. That's the—that's the—wonderful. But if it doesn't, it doesn't. Make the motherfuckers send you home, and just get yourself some good dope and stay doped for as long as it feels good and when it don't feel good anymore, load that goddamned syringe up and nod out on the final ride.

But I've never had any notion of shooting myself. You know how they put that—*eat the gun.* Put that son of a bitch in there and pull the trigger. Well, yeah, you put brains on the ceiling. But it also— the blow-back—you got brains come out of your nose, out of your fucking ears. Out of your *mouth.* I mean, you'd think it would blow, but it's like a blow-back in a fire. And I just—nah. I don't think so.

And over and above that, I wonder if, by some chance that—course you get a physical every six months, you get your prostate every whatever—stick a garden hose up your ass and all that stuff. Idiot bullshit. No, if I ever have cancer, why would I let them cut in there and fuck with my bypass, you know, my quadruple bypass? Why would I do that? At my age? I mean, or cut in there and take a lung out and leave me with one? Which you can get along with, I know. I have friends with one lung. But to what point?

I am not a religious man, but all that shit seems highly immoral to me. I bought this place because of the trees, and my lawn out there. Nothing growing in that lawn ain't supposed to be growing in that lawn. What's growing out there is supposed to be growing there. A tree grows old, it's supposed to fall down and rot. I've got a—I've got a three-year-old grandson, and he's got to have some room to grow up. And for him to have some room, some of us old fuckers have got to go on across the river. A great line by Dylan Thomas, "I shall have star at elbow and foot." Meaning, simply, that you return to the nitrogen cycle. Go up there and come down as rain or something.

But, you know, I say that sitting here, doped and smoking is one thing. It's another thing to be . . .

But you know, the trick is not to get in the hospital just to get—I know from having been hurt so much in my life that if the pain gets right, and you can't score something on the street to stop it, you do what you can. You *will* go to a doctor or to a hospital to stop the pain if it gets bad enough. I don't give a shit who you are.

I mean, there's a certain proportion to everything, which, if one goes beyond that—I've said it already—or distorts that proportion—then you distort the whole experience of having been alive, and never mind living or any of that. Check that at the door. . . .

Here is the thing. I won't mind leaving all the steaks I haven't eaten, and the cobalt skies I won't look at. The thing I will mind leaving—it terrorizes my *soul*—is the flesh of a woman. I cannot—I am temperamentally incapable . . . Man, I can walk by a . . . I mean, it just reminds me of when you were like fourteen, or whenever you started dating—how you put your arm around a girl? You know, in a movie or a car. . . .

But it's curious. Life, apparently—you get right down to the wire, and I guess every day becomes—you don't want to die. You don't want to go. You want to stay, man, just to . . .

Talk's cheap. We'll see what happens when it comes time.

★ ★ ★

D.S.: That piece that you were reading earlier, that's . . .

H.C.: It's just like *A Childhood*, only it's later.

D.S.: Writing about your family like that, do you feel—it would be difficult for me to write about my family that way.

H.C.: Well, it's difficult for me. *A Childhood* almost killed me. And that one *will*.

I think you have an obligation—there are all kinds of obligations you have as a writer. You know them, so no use in boring both of us by going through obligations that you know we have. But if whatever the subject is, or whatever any subject is that you are writing about, and if it's important and significant in a sense larger than itself—you're not just writing this to hurt somebody or writing this to get back at somebody or writing this to libel. God forbid.

But libel is almost impossible to prove. And even if they prove libel, then there is—almost always they inevitably ask for a judgment against you for having libeled them. But say they ask for a hundred thousand dollars. The burden of proof is on them that you hurt them a hundred thousand dollars' worth. Kept them from working. Kept them from getting a job. Made them lose a job. Made them nuts and they had to go to the crazy house. How the hell you going to prove that?

So, and I don't know, it's not that *that's* true . . . that I do it without . . . I mean, I'm a writer, and that's what I do. If there's something that I think is of significance and ought to be put down and has value larger than its immediate confined context of the moment—it has ramifications beyond that—then I don't have any feelings one way or the other. . . . The pain comes not because I might hurt somebody. The pain comes from just having relived the shit. Because when I write stuff, everything I write, I'm in. And I mean fiction, too.

If you're crazy enough to read yourself—and almost no writer reads his own novel once he finishes it. He never looks at it again. I've never read a novel of mine, a whole novel that I did, after it's published. Never. Why would you? But you look in them sometimes. Usually, I find myself looking in them 'cause I'm stuck and feel totally incompetent and burned out and think, "Well, it's over, I can't write anything else." And then I go to a book like that one up there [*points to the book jacket of* Naked in Garden Hills *framed on the living room wall*], which I'm very proud of, and I look at places in it, and I see what I did, and I think, hey man, if you did it there, you can do it again. Just goddammit go back and sit there till it comes.

Did you ever see the stuff that's written on the back of that book? Let me read that shit. Absolutely amazing reception it had. This is from the review in *Harper's* magazine [*reads from the blurb on the book jacket*]: "Ruthless, cruel, and blackly beautiful." That's one of the reviews on the back of the book. So, yeah, shit like that keeps me alive.

Graham Greene—you've probably heard me quote before, because, God knows, it's true—"The writer is doomed to live in an atmosphere of perpetual failure." There it is. There it is. Nah, you write things and write things—write a book for instance—and write and write and write and write and write, and you know, it's not—every writer writes with the knowledge that nothing he writes is as good as it could be. Paul Valéry: "A poem's never finished, only abandoned." The same thing with a novel. I've had any number of novels where I've just at some point said to myself, well, unless you're going to make the career out of this book—spend the rest of your goddamn life chewing on it—you might as well just package it up and send it on to New York. Go on to something else. Because between conception and execution there is a void, an abyss, that inevitably fucks up the conception. The conception never gets translated to the page. It just doesn't. I don't think it ever does.

I think Flaubert kept *Madame Bovary* for nine years. Took him nine years to write it—well, he didn't write it all in nine years. He could have written it in *nineteen* years, and he would still have felt the way he felt, and that was that it was a fine piece of work, but it was not as good as it could be. Same old, same old.

★   ★   ★

D.S.: Gorse republished *The Gospel Singer* in 1995 in the U.K. along with the companion novel *Where Does One Go When There's No Place Left to Go?*

H.C.: Yeah.

D.S.: It's pretty strange.

H.C.: Isn't that pretty strange? Yeah.

D.S.: Where do you place yourself in there? Or do you?

H.C.: I place myself. I'm in there. *My name.* And *me.* I lived in that place. I lived in that shack. And they came. And they arrived. When

I lived on Swan, the lake out there, I had a shack, and my head *was* shaved at that time. And why did I write it? How did I happen to write it? Why did I want to write it? I don't have the foggiest notion.

D.S.: But you spent time writing that.

H.C.: Yes, I did.

D.S.: Did you expect that to be publishable?

H.C.: Of course. Of course I did. I wrote it to be published. Sure I did. Damn straight I did. It saddens me to say it, but it is a kind of postmodernist piece of work, the only such piece I have. I don't admire that shit.

The subject of that novel is the novel. The subject of that writing is writing. And the people I've created, much of the time, have greater substance than anybody that I know who's alive, and are, to me, more memorable. And in some instances, I can even say I care more about. Which is a rather dreadful thing to say. But nobody ever accused artists of being anything but dreadful. They commit all kinds of larceny and betrayal and—you have to be careful about what you say around a writer. Shit'll turn up in a book. May turn up in such a way that you'll be identifiable.

And the writer, in almost every instance—except hacks and people with really bad hearts—the writer doesn't mean to do that. He just does it. Doesn't realize he's done it. And the editor doesn't know. Nobody knows. Except you and the guy you're fucking with. And you don't understand that.

The guy Poncy in *A Feast of Snakes* is based absolutely—I mean from start to finish—on a guy that I considered to be my best friend. And I didn't really realize it until he said something—he's much older than I was. Old guy. And he had a Porsche. And he was of Latin descent. From Cuba. And had worked in Latin America. And is dead now. Been dead long now. Died in his sleep.

★ ★ ★

H.C.: My stepfather, Mr. Turner, he saw one doctor in his entire life, when he went in World War I. Had to get a physical. Saw two. Right there at the end of his life, he fell in the back yard. They wanted to take him down to the doctor, and goddamn he fought tooth and nail and cussed everybody for fucking with him, and he didn't want to go to the doctor. And they took him down there, and the doctor x-rayed him and said he was going to die of lung cancer. He'd been smoking unfiltered Camels since he was nine years old. He's eighty-three.

And [the doctor] says, "Well, we can take you up to that big hospital in Atlanta, and you know, operate."

And he said no. "No, no, no, no. They're not going to do any of that."

Never saw him take a pill. Wouldn't take an aspirin. Took nothing. I know he had to be in pain sometimes, but he just never—you didn't know it if he was.

And he said, "I'm going back home."

And, as soon as he stepped out of the doctor's office, he reached for his Camels, lit one up, gone on back home.

And the old doctor said, "Well, Mr. Turner, if I was you, I think I might do the same thing." He said, "You don't want to go up there. You want to go back home. Go back home, and if you have any pain, I'll give you something for it."

About four weeks later, he sat up on the side of the bed one morning—and my mama's name was Myrtice—sat up on the side of the bed one morning and said, "Myrtice, I don't feel just right." And lay back and was dead.

What the fuck you want? That's *righteous*.

And that's also great luck. Sad to say, but the chances of even any of the three of us having that kind of quick, painless demise is remote. That's not the nature of death.

Well, Ma went fine. She pitched forward in her living room onto her face, and had had a massive stroke and massive brain damage. Had always wanted to die in her own house. And so we kept her in her own house. And that's where she died. Back in her own bed.

My brother and I were there, and Eugenia came in—Eugenia was right by her bed the whole—took her, took her twelve days to die, but she never opened her eyes. She never said a word. Didn't do anything but just—her face was *aarrrr* [*makes a forced expression*]—her mouth was open, and she had no swallowing reflex, et cetera, et cetera, et cetera. But she didn't know anything about it. Nothing. Zip.

She did suffer pain, the doctor said. The heart blew from ministrokes there toward the end. And they had Dilaudid suppositories.

I don't know if you know what Dilaudid suppositories are, but if anybody ever offers you one, don't turn it down. Take it and run. It's not as good as mainlining it, but it's not bad.

Dilaudid is a sweet drug. Doesn't last quite as long as heroin. It's got a better rush.

Dilaudid—if you never shot Dilaudid in your whole life, and you took a Dilaudid 4, a pill about as big as an aspirin, and crushed it up in a spoon—actually, what you do is take one of these things [*picks up a matchbook*], take the matches out of it, put the pill between there, and you just put it down on a hard surface, you take a spoon and tap it until it gets all crushed, and then you pour it into the spoon, and then you take your U-40—used to be called a U-40, a kind of disposable diabetic syringe—I don't know what the hell they call it now. You pull up enough water—however the much water you're going to use—and you squirt it into the spoon. And take a cigarette lighter or a match and put it under the spoon until you just get just the tiniest starting of bubbles around the edge, and blow out the light. And then you take a tiny, tiny little piece of cotton and put it in the spoon, put the point of the spike right in the cotton and draw it up—and there will be some yellow residue left in the spoon.

And when I knew about Dilaudid, Dilaudid's form on the street cost twenty-five dollars—it probably costs sixty now. God knows. And you start shooting one, and . . . when you just *touch* that syringe—I mean, an enormous yellow pumpkin explodes behind your eyes. You look bigger and better than God. I mean everything is optimism, beautiful and painless and wonderful. And then you're on the nod. And a Dilaudid 4—if you're as big as I am, and you never shot one—would probably last you about five hours. Four or five hours. Heroin lasts twelve.

You know what you got if you got Dilaudid in your hand. You don't know what the fuck you got if you got a bag of heroin. I mean, if you got five percent heroin in a bag, you got a fairly good bag of shit. The rest of it's cut with whatever—cocaine or whatever it is they use to cut coke with—but whatever it's cut with.

Ah, no. The dose that killed Sid Vicious, his mama went out in the streets of New York and bought the bag that killed him. And it just happened that whoever cut it didn't cut it very much. And he put in the spoon about what he normally shot and never got, never got the syringe out of his arm, as—most people don't know—neither did Sonny Liston. Died in Las Vegas. Still had a spike in his arm. A guy that big. And you *know* he had some good shit, Jack. I mean, because, you know, you're using a teaspoon. We ain't talking a tablespoon. A teaspoon will do it.

But it's just one more extreme that—human beings being what they are—I suppose I wish I could've missed a whole bunch of things. But I didn't. And, I know what people—some people, many people, most people—would say and think about such a statement. I'm not proud of any of it, but I'm damn sure not ashamed of it, and I can't say with a good heart that I'm sorry I did any of it. I did what I did. Seemed like a good idea at the time.

And, you know, I certainly don't . . . I never encouraged anybody or sold any. If anybody asks me about whether they ought to or maybe try it, I say, "Well, you know, you're a free agent in the world. I have nothing to say about it. I'm not you. But if I *were* you, I think I'd just slide on past that. Probably be all right without it. Don't need it."

Well, those who like to think there's a white-gowned, long-bearded old guy up in the sky, keeping score on what we're doing—if there is such a being, he knows. You sure as shit don't know what I need, the shrink doesn't know what I need, the neurologist doesn't know what I need.

Nobody that I've ever respected or thought anything of pretended to know what, for the lack of a better phrase, your psyche needs. Or that your brain is you any more than your hand is you. Or your foot is you. Or the hair on your head is you. It's been known since the Greeks that the whole notion of this duality between the mind and the body is some kind of rank horseshit that doesn't work.

I'm told that I think with something that's locked into a bone box called my skull—that I think with that. I'd just as soon believe that it's in my big toe. I mean, I don't know where the hell it is. I didn't go to school for that, and it never interested me.

And I happen to know a very famous neurologist and a very famous neurosurgeon, and both of them are about as fucked up as you want to get. This one neurologist—heart attacks run in his family, and he drinks like a fish, and he's in the office every day. You think that sumbitch don't feel bad when he wakes up in the morning? That he's immune to hangovers and trembles and shakes and whatnot? Well, sweetheart, he's got a whole goddamn box full of shit.

And the best connections I've ever had—and the most rabid junkies I've ever known—have all been doctors. Every last fucking one of them. I've known some pretty rabid junkies that weren't doctors, but . . . And doctors don't have unlimited access to, I guess, Class I drugs? I guess it was Class I. Threes are down there—and Class I—the class that Dilaudid is in, and I guess Percodan and Seconal, Nembutal, Tuinal, all that. That shit is so highly controlled, man, that even the doctor can't get it.

There's a doctor, well, in a town not far from where we sit, there's a doctor who got nailed not too many years ago, short enough ago that one can say "recent," and he was simply writing scripts for people that worked for him. And they had to bring back the dope to him, or most of it.

★ ★ ★

D.S.: Did you write the story called "Becky Lives" for *Little Deaths*,[1] the horror anthology, or did you have that in mind for somewhere else?

H.C.: I wrote that story because another writer—whose name you'd recognize if I told it, but I won't tell it—I know the woman who edited that, and she'd asked writers to do it, and she asked me to write, you know, a story for that thing. And she told me what the story's to [be], and I said, "No, I don't do that type of shit."

And so, this writer called me and said, "Well, the reason you said no is you can't do it."

And I said, "Bullshit. Of course I can do it."

And so I wrote the story, and I got that certificate in the back there—they give a prize, the Horror Writers' Association of America gives a prize for the best one of those stories of the year. The Bram Stoker Award. I got a fucking thing back there in the study.

D.S.: Did you win it?

H.C.: Well, I was a finalist. Harlan Ellison won it. And I was second.

D.S.: There you go. He had good company.

H.C.: No, I'm not good company. It was a piece of shit. I wrote it in one afternoon. I just sat down and wrote the goddamn thing.

D.S.: I was surprised to see your work in that anthology. I thought it was great.

H.C.: Well, writers write, and writers write things for the most curious reasons.

★ ★ ★

H.C.: Damn, man. Boy, did that whiskey feel good.

D.S.: There's more over there.

H.C.: Well, I might have just another. You know, I have to be very careful with the shit. Really have to be careful. Like yesterday. I bought a four-pack, each bottle is a pint. Two quarts of beer. And it just made the afternoon a little better than it otherwise would've been.

So. But I never let myself get shit-faced anymore. . . . The way I like to drink whiskey—I haven't eaten anything today. And if I was going to drink, I wouldn't eat anything because the rest of the day I would have been drunk. What amounts to a coma. Get up the first thing in the morning and take another drink. I wouldn't eat *then*. I wouldn't eat till I got through drinking. If it was four days I wouldn't, because, as old drunks will tell you, you can ruin a fifty-dollar drunk with a fifty-cent hamburger. And that's the damn truth. Who the hell wants to drink on top of food?

An old guy told me about putting ice in whiskey. He said [*in a heavy Georgia drawl*], "Now, son, that whiskey—that whiskey has to get to the temperature of your guts before it can make the jump to your blood." Which happens to be the truth. And that ice just makes it wait.

And I do have to confess. I did knock back a couple shots. It's like water. Whatever it was, it seemed to be just about right.

★ ★ ★

D.S.: I feel like sometimes I cross—without having any intention—I cross this boundary between . . . I'm not obsessed, I'm not compulsive about your writing, but I've been living with Harry Crews for the last eight months solid since I started research for this bibliography.

H.C.: What the fuck's wrong with that, man? I mean, what's strange about it and what's unique about it? Don't you think that Lytle was *god* to me and that I went to see him and—in Lytle's case, you walk in his house, and the first thing he does—in a solid silver cup he pours you a dollop of whiskey, and he says, "Anything but silver chaps our lips."

And right after the time he died in '95, everybody else I knew that ever studied with him, called him "Andrew." I didn't call him "Andrew" my whole fucking life. Any more than I would call God "Jerry" or something. No. He's my man.

★ ★ ★

H.C.: Everybody comes to grief over endings. Closures, as they like to say. I love what E. M. Forster said. "No writer should be expected to write an ending because nothing ever ends." The problem with that is, the convention of the form is, it does end.

The reader doesn't want to feel cheated. The reader just wants to feel good. And I swear to God, after all these decades at it, that's as close as I can get to it. That it feels good.

I have a feeling a lot of times, when writers come to see me, they think that I got this secret, that sometimes, somehow, I keep it from them. That if I would just open up, be honest, and give it to them, then they'd be all right, and everything would be fine. I *don't*. It's as much a mystery to me today as it was when I started. Except that in matters of—ah, forgive the phrase—craft, and technique and that stuff, I—yeah, I know some things about writing transitions. But that's not what we're talking about. Not really. Ultimately. Or maybe we are. I don't know what the fuck we're talking about. We're talking about making the thing whole. How do you make it *whole?* How do you make it get up and walk?

D.S.: What was it like when you finally got things published, after you got involved with Bread Loaf and you got your start . . . it seems that you enjoyed yourself.

H.C.: I've never enjoyed myself. I'm incapable of enjoying myself. There's just some people who don't enjoy themselves very much.

Note

1. "Becky Lives," *Little Deaths: An Anthology of Erotic Horror*, ed. Ellen Datlow (New York: Dell, 1995), 35–63.

ERIK BLEDSOE

An Interview with Harry Crews

The following interview was conducted on July 26, 1997, at Harry Crews's home in Gainesville, Florida. Like many writers who have been interviewed repeatedly, Crews has stock answers that he gives to frequently asked questions. I wanted to avoid asking the usual questions. In particular, I vowed not to ask him about the so-called freaks that populate his fiction. Entirely accustomed to the interview process, Crews did not wait for me to begin taping or even to ask a question before he launched into an "answer" about his writing habits. The interview begins as he discusses his efforts to maintain both his productive work habits and the physical condition of his body, weakened by years of hard living and age.

H.C.: So I said, "Good Lord, let me see what kind of shape I can get into one more time before I die," so my normal routine is I get up at 4:00 and start to work, and work until 8:30, when my gym opens. And then I go to the gym. Whatever isn't written between 4:00 and 8:30 doesn't get written. And then I come back and do all those things you have to do around the house and then I revise. I have to revise. Whatever I wrote in the morning doesn't even look like it did.

E.B.: So, you revise in the afternoon what you wrote that morning?

H.C.: Yeah. But of course you understand that it's just the way I happen to work. Some guys write the book, trying to find a narrative line

From *Southern Quarterly* 37.1 (1998): 97–117.

of a story in any language. But I can't do that. I find the story out of the language that I use.

I recently threw away a hundred pages. It was a bus trip, and I have to say I liked the writing, and I sort of liked what went on on the bus, except it just didn't belong in the book. And I didn't know it until George [*his longtime girlfriend*] read it. And she just made a couple of low-key observations, she wouldn't go and tell me how to write it or something. And as soon as she said it, I thought, "Oh man, that won't do." So, I threw it away.

I do a lot of things that are not, I think, the best way to go about it. But as you know, every writer works a different way. Some writers can't work any way except starting to work when it starts to get dark. Work all night, sleep all day. I don't trust anything I write at night. I did when I was young. Because I had to. I had to go out and make a living. I worked ten years, writing as hard as I knew how to write, and I made one hundred dollars. Sold a story to *Sewanee Review*. Then I published *The Gospel Singer* in 1968. And I pretty much published everything I've written since then. I don't understand. I turned the corner. I'd also had migraine headaches, bad ones, up to that time. Published *The Gospel Singer* and never had another one.

E.B.: How did you find a publisher for *The Gospel Singer*?

H.C.: Oh, God, oh God. Well, fasting and praying and watching small drops of blood break out on sundry parts of my body. I sent it to World Publishing Company because I saw that they—this is how innocent I was—they were having a, quote, novel contest for unpublished writers, unquote, and Herbert Gold, who later I got to know, was the judge. So I sent it up there, and in about a month I got this letter that said, "We're gonna publish your novel." And, God, I was overjoyed. To make it short, they kept it a year and a half. No contract. No money had changed hands.

And Donn Pearce, who wrote *Cool Hand Luke*, happened to live in the same town, Fort Lauderdale. I told him that and he said, "You're fucking crazy! What are you doing that for? Get your book."

I said, "No, no. They said they were gonna publish it. I can't."

And then he got me an agent in New York. And the agent wrote back and said, "This is crazy. You're crazy. Write me a letter. Give me authorization. Let me go and get your damned book back."

He did. In five days I had a contract from William Morrow, who published the first five books I wrote. That's the way it was.

And then I left that agent after that book and went with John Hawkins and Associates, John Hawkins. He's been my agent ever since. Thirty years.

E.B.: You left the first agent after *The Gospel Singer?* Or after the first five novels?

H.C.: No. The first five books were published by William Morrow, but I got a new agent for *Naked in Garden Hills,* John Hawkins.

And one day Hawkins called me—I think it's probably one of the really bad moves I ever made—John Hawkins called me and he said, "I was at a party last night and the guy that runs Knopf came up and said, 'I want to whisper something in your ear'."

And he said, "What?"

And he said, "Harry Crews."

He said, "I'll give you some money"—it wasn't much, a little bit of money—"just for switching publishers, and we'll get the next book." And I had a book done.

And so I published two books with that publisher. The first book they took of mine was *The Hawk Is Dying.* Couldn't get along with that editor, though.

E.B.: You've talked about growing up and you've told the story about the Sears, Roebuck catalog a lot. But making up stories about the Sears, Roebuck catalog is a world away from imagining that you can actually make a living writing stories.

H.C.: I didn't, I didn't, I never thought of it as making a living at it. Certainly back then I was just a little kid.

I'm a storyteller, that's what I do. I just imagine that I'm back in the Stone Age and I'm squatting in front of the cave, and all my buddies with loincloths and wives and children and all are standing around, and we're eating saber-tooth tiger. And I killed that saber-tooth tiger that day.

And I'm squatting there, and I say to them, "That tiger, when I first saw it, he come charging and got me up a little spindly tree, so spindly that he couldn't climb it. So I was at the top of it."

Well, the obvious question the reader always asks is "What then?

Why do we have the tiger on the fire and you're not eaten up?" So I gotta get out of that somehow; I've got to tell the story. And you don't tell stories by, oh God, making the novel the subject of the novel. Or whatever.

E.B.: You've expressed your disdain for postmodernism before.

H.C.: I was gonna use that word, but I decided I wouldn't. But no, "disdain" is probably not too strong a word. It probably is not too strong a word, but I don't know. Disdain? It's just not my bag, man. It's just not.

E.B.: How do you handle students in your classes who come in and that's what they want to do?

H.C.: Well, I don't teach anymore. Haven't taught for a while now. But there were never any "thou shall nots" in a writing class. You and I both know—hardly new to anybody—that you can't teach writing novels or stories. Maybe you can teach writing essays, but I doubt that too, [not] very good essays. You can teach form, but there won't be very much inside the form. There were no "thou shall nots," except you couldn't write horror stories, science fiction, or detective shit. You couldn't do that. But outside that, you could write anything you wanted to.

A writer can't be taught, but he can be coached. And we would have a conversation. Criticism should never be a monologue. It ought to be a dialogue. Mainly because you're trying to get a young writer—and sometimes an old, established writer—to see what he has done. He is so damn close to it, has lived with it for so long, that he can't see it anymore. And if nothing else, a good editor—and there are damn few of them left—he can get you to see what you've done, and sometimes in seeing that he doesn't even have to tell you. You see where you went wrong.

E.B.: You've written that "A teacher must hold up a standard of excellence to his student and demand that he at least make every effort to meet the standard. But it has to be done in such a way that his spirit, his desire to excel, is not killed." How do you walk that line?

H.C.: Not easily. Not easily. And I know, as does every other teacher who will admit it, I know that I've hurt a great many students without meaning to. You don't want to take everything from the writer. Among other things, you want to give him a place to go back and work. A good class is where the writers can't wait to get home to their typewriters, and, as a matter of fact, about half the classes, they don't want to come to. They want to stay home and write. If you turn them into somebody who doesn't want to write, then you've just failed and hurt them.

I try as best I can to see what they've done, and understand what they're trying to do. And that can only come out of them; it can't come out of me. I help them to do that by talking to them. Talking about language. Writing is good to the degree that it is concrete and specific. And bad to the degree that it is abstract and vague. You know. I don't know what a soul is. I don't know what a spirit is. I don't know what your, your—my endeavor to soar among the—all that kind of writing. I don't know what any of that is. I know what a brick is. I know what steps are. Shoes. And, God bless me, ladies' panties. I know what they are. They're the stuff of the world; they're what makes our heart sing. A brick can make your heart sing. You know?

E.B.: Out of any given class, how many students in there can really write?

H.C.: Man, I'll tell you, the last class—the last few classes—I taught, every one of them wrote really, really well. They *wrote* well. The problem was that—I'll just go ahead and say it—they didn't have anything to write about. I go to great pains to tell them that it was a great shock to me to learn that writing well was not enough. God knows, that's hard enough, but learning to write well is not enough.

You know, when the thing is put together in four or five hundred pages, it ought to mean something, it ought to be memorable, it ought to feel inevitable. The reason the stuff happens in the book the way it does is because it couldn't happen any other way. It ought to have that feeling. And it ought to hurt your heart. It ought to crush your heart with a living memory. And then you do remember it. Try to remember an episode of *Perry Mason*. Or any other of those things that purport to be drama on television. You can't. You can't. Not a single one can you remember. The highest rated thing on television is *Seinfeld*. Now, try to remember one episode. You can't. But books!

E.B.: You said earlier that you thought that leaving Morrow was a mistake.

H.C.: Yeah, I do.

E.B.: Why?

H.C.: Because I had a great editor there who—he had just started, he was younger than I was, and I wasn't very old when I published *The Gospel Singer*, but he was a *great* editor. The best editor I've ever had, Jim Landis. Who's no longer at Morrow. No longer in publishing. He's writing. Novels. That fool. [*Laughs.*] But anyway, I like Jim Landis a lot, and it genuinely hurt him when I left. I wrote him a letter, the kindest letter I could write. I said, "Hey listen, bud, when my work is in with me and the legal pad and the pencil in the room where I write, it's—I hope—art. Or at least I have pretensions to art. When it gets outside that room, it's a business. The guy offered me money, I need money. I got a wife and a kid, and I don't make much where I work."

E.B.: Erskine Caldwell's widow once told me that she thought the greatest mistake Caldwell had made was switching publishers, because he didn't stay and develop a career with Scribner's, particularly with Max Perkins. Reynolds Price has told me that he was very conscious of staying with the same publisher throughout his career.

H.C.: Well, good for him. He's smarter than I was, that's all. I just thought that's what you did—you do what your agent tells you to do. That's why he's a ten-percenter; he's got ten percent of your life. And so he said it was a good idea, and I knew Knopf, I mean, damn, I thought they had—and they may have had at this time, they may have now—the best list in the country. I did what I thought was right and it wasn't.

E.B.: I want to go back a ways to your story "The Player Piano."

H.C.: Way back.

E.B.: That reminds me of Caldwell. It's got that same kind of sexual tension going on with one character not really being aware of the overtones that are being made. Were you reading a lot of Caldwell at the time?

H.C.: Yeah, and since you . . . you ever read a story of Caldwell's called "A Knife to Cut the Cornbread With"?

E.B.: Yeah.

H.C.: You know, there it is. The guy's paralyzed and his wife is out picking cotton, and he's in there paralyzed in the bed. They don't have any meat to eat. Well, you don't have to go any further than that. He wisely left that off stage.

Here's sorta the way it went. The first writer I read all of was Mickey Spillane. *I, the Jury; My Gun Is Quick; Kiss Me, Deadly*—I could name them all. Well, I can't name them all because I stopped, and he's written some more, but reading, like water, seeks its own level. You get tired of that after a while. You run into something else. And, I admit it, I was in my early teens, and I just liked all those naked ladies and stuff.

And then, curiously enough, I went to Caldwell. I didn't read him all then. But I read a lot of it. And then I went to Somerset Maugham. Read all of him. I really did. And then I read all of Ayn Rand, *The Fountainhead* and so on. Well, Somerset Maugham's got one book. Well, you can give him more than that. *Of Human Bondage* is a fine book. The rest . . . He's an expert at cheating, particularly in short stories. The guy I studied with, Andrew Lytle, used to call him "that old whore of literature." Ayn Rand, of course, doesn't write as well as Maugham does, and she writes thesis literature, which I've been accused of writing. I don't care. I don't believe I do or did. And a lot worse things have been said about me than that. But then somewhere after Maugham I went to Greene. And when I went to Greene, man, I *did* read all of him. And I read him again.

I read a lot of stuff that's just coming out, but I also read a lot of things like—well, William Faulkner said he read *Madame Bovary* once a year. I don't do that, but I read a lot of stuff back there. I read to steal. I read—if not to steal, you can say it a better way—to learn. It's not as though I go through there with a pencil trying to pick up lines. I don't. You get it through your skin. It's osmosis or something.

E.B.: Your first published story, "The Unattached Smile," appeared in *Sewanee Review* . . .

H.C.: Yeah.

E.B.: Lytle was the editor at the time?

H.C.: Yeah, he was.

E.B.: Did he help you get that published? Did it come up in a workshop and he said, "I want this"?

H.C.: No, no. Mr. Lytle had left here and gone back up there to Sewanee to be editor of the *Sewanee Review* and other things, and I was here working with another guy, Smith Kirkpatrick, to whom *Naked in Garden Hills* is dedicated, probably a mistake, probably should have dedicated . . . I never dedicated a book to Mr. Lytle because I never thought I wrote anything he would want his name on. Mr. Lytle wanted nothing but perfection, in his work as well as yours, which he knew he couldn't have. But he wanted it anyway. But no, Mr. Lytle never saw that in workshop or in draft.

But once he accepted it at the *Review*, I went through about ten different revisions. He would just say little things, and you could see right off that he was right. And the little things would lead to other things. God, he would have made a great editor. If he had wanted to go to a house, I really do believe that he could have had the reputation of a Maxwell Perkins, or somebody like that. Man, when he read something of yours, the words were read right off the page. He didn't even have to look at the story when he was talking to you about it. He never looked at the story.

E.B.: He died just over a year ago. How did that affect you?

H.C.: As though some rent had been made in my life or a big hole jerked in it that can never be replaced. Although he was no longer reading for me or . . . I still enjoyed . . . Mr. Lytle always . . . I enjoyed talking to him. Mr. Lytle tended to talk in essays. I mean, you'd ask him a question, and he would give you an essay back. And I certainly don't mean that in any pejorative sense. But he would.

But we were from very different Souths, and I don't think he ever realized that. His daddy sent him to France to study. His daddy was a planter that never touched a plow, never had his hands on a plow or stock. My family was the white trash way down at the end of the road from the big house. And, you know, he never understood that.

I remember one time we were driving somewhere, and I brought up the white/black business. Well, anyway, I don't want to talk about . . . but what he gave me was an essay, essentially, out of the Middle Ages, where every man had his man, and God had the king, and, obviously, the poor shall always be with us there on the bottom rung. But somebody's got to . . . I don't know. I'm doing him an injustice, but I did get an essay back. And I thought to myself, "I love you, I love you, but that's all bullshit." I mean, it ain't right. It ain't never been right. And it won't ever be right. But it's probably always going to be with us.

E.B.: *The Gospel Singer* is one of the few books, maybe even your only book, where racial tensions are at the surface, or one of the primary themes. Does that subject just not interest you as something to write about?

H.C.: Oh, it interests me, but the only thing I can say is that I'm scared of it. Because it's so old, and by that I mean the issues involved are so old and they have been debated so long, it's very difficult not to fall into X number of clichés. What the hell can I say about it? Well, you can say a lot of things about it, and a lot of good novels can be written about it and will. But I don't write novels hoping to cure the sins of the world. I don't think novels cause things to happen. Maybe *The Jungle* caused something to happen, the meat industry and all that, passing legislation, but other than that, I mean, I don't know. You name one; maybe you can, I can't.

E.B.: As far as I've been able to find out, you only published three short stories before *The Gospel Singer,* and I think you've published one more since then in a recent anthology called *Little Deaths.*

H.C.: I'll tell you about short stories. This may be a very bad reason not to write short stories, but here it is. Okay, you write a short story. How many places are there to publish it? I mean, nationally. *Playboy* and *Harper's* and *Atlantic* and whatever. But you can name them all with two hands. And, okay, on top of that, how many people are gonna read it? Even when you look at Raymond Carver's short stories, you look in the front of a collection, half of them were published in little magazines that maybe two thousand people read. All right, a lot of people read Raymond Carver short stories. Well, that was

Raymond Carver. How many people are gonna read a book of short stories by Harry Crews? I don't think many people. Because I'll tell you something else, I don't think I've ever sold ten thousand copies of a hardcover book in my life. I finally found an audience. France. France. The French love me.

E.B.: Same with Caldwell.

H.C.: I just said, "Well, if you're gonna read anything, you read novels." Short stories, they're too hard to write to not have anybody read them.

E.B.: You joined the Marines at seventeen.

H.C.: Yeah, well, just before my eighteenth birthday, but yeah, I was seventeen.

E.B.: Okay, so, about 1953?

H.C.: Yeah.

E.B.: That was during the Korean War.

H.C.: Yes it was.

E.B.: Did you serve in Korea?

H.C.: No. My brother was fighting in Korea at the time I joined. It ended while I was on Parris Island. And we were, of course, all extremely disappointed. There's something—and this may be a lie, or a myth, or whatever—but it seems to me that when a war breaks out, all the southern boys run down as quick as they can. Probably out of ignorance. And also because, in many instances—as was true in my case—there's no jobs, and I had no skills. And my brother was in Korea, you know, so you run down and join up.

I joined the Marine Corps for two reasons. I thought if you were gonna go, that you might as well try yourself. And the other reason, I frankly admit, was to see if I could do it. I had polio when I was a kid, or something. They think now it wasn't polio. That was the only thing I was worried about was my legs, whether or not they were strong enough. And I got through, you know.

E.B.: After the Marines you came back and attended the University of Florida.

H.C.: Straight in there. Well, not straight in there; I went to Jacksonville and worked that summer in a pulp mill. Then I went to the University of Florida. And why I went to the University of Florida instead of the University of Georgia, God only knows. If I hadn't been a vet, they would have never let me in. I was a very bad student in high school because I wasn't there most of the time. If I could, I read all night long, and then I slept through the day. That was when we were at Jacksonville. My mom had to go to the King Edward cigar factory and work, so there was nobody there to make me go, so I just slept. I never failed a course, but I made a lot of D's. I didn't take any science, I didn't take any math, I didn't take any languages.

The university to me was really easy. I was there about a week or two weeks, we had to take a test of some sort, and a guy called me over to the administration and he said, "Look, on the basis of these here scores on these tests, what you ought to do is drop out and apprentice yourself to a cabinetmaker or a plumber or something, because you're gonna fail here. Then you're gonna think of yourself as a failure."

And he was a good guy, he meant well. And I said, "Does that mean I have to leave?"

And he said, "No, no, you can stay if you want to."

And I said, "I think I'll stay. Just let me give it a shot."

I made the dean's list the first semester, and with the exception of Shakespeare and a little geology, and a little history, I was never assigned a book I hadn't already read.

When I was in Jacksonville, of course, I had access to libraries. In Georgia I never did. And, it was very hard getting old books. When I went to my first duty station, I found out there was a library, there was a library on every station. And if they didn't have the book, they'd get it for you. So I spent my time in the Marine Corps with a rifle in one hand and a book in the other.

E.B.: You left Florida after two years and took the eighteen-month motorcycle trip.

H.C.: Yeah, at the end of my sophomore year. I couldn't take it. I had a brand new motorcycle and I left here with less than a hundred dollars in my pocket. Didn't know where I was going or how long I was staying. And I went from, to make it quick, here to Wyoming, up through Montana to Canada, from Canada back across to Salt Lake City, Salt Lake City to San Francisco, San Francisco back across over Monarch Pass—the highest pass in the Rockies—to Colorado Springs, from Colorado Springs west over Rathhome Pass in New Mexico down to El Paso, down through the desert to the state of Chihuahua and the city of Chihuahua, back up to El Paso. And then the longest trip I ever expect to make, from El Paso to New Orleans. Across the longest part of Texas. I thought I would *never* get out of Texas. And from New Orleans back into Gainesville.

How'd I do it on a hundred dollars? I'll tell you. And I think it is true to this day, although people may tell me otherwise. If you can cook or tend bar, you can work in any city in this country. It ought to take you about two days to find a job. I'm not saying you'll make much money, maybe a lousy bar, maybe a neighborhood bar, maybe whatever. It may be turning hamburgers. So that's what I did. I did other jobs too, cut straw, worked in a salt mine where they let the ocean in and let it evaporate. I worked in a lot of places.

E.B.: You've called *Naked in Garden Hills* your best book.

H.C.: I think it is and I think it would run even a good critic, a critic's critic, the guys who do this for a living, I think it would run the best of them crazy trying to figure out the time sequence, which I think makes sense and works. I like the people in it. I just like what I did in it.

Two books, *Naked in Garden Hills* and *Car,* both of them I wrote in six weeks. But in those days I was young. I pretty much lived on amphetamines and when I got too wired, there was always the bottle. I had a Mason fruit jar full of amphetamines and a bottle of Wild Turkey, and if you get too wired, you just take a hit. I'd bubble the bottle a couple of times and be ready to work. Stay up, it's amazing how long you can stay up when you are young. I was real healthy.

E.B.: Most of the characters in that book are called something other than their given names.

H.C.: Well, if you look through all of my work, I've got a screwy thing about names.

E.B.: What's up with that?

H.C.: I don't know. I really don't know. It might be somehow connected with the fact that I consciously change the way I look, pretty much every day. People have made a lot out of this, and it was all making fun of me or saying something bad about me, but that's all right, I don't mind that a bit. That's fine, doesn't hurt my feelings.

If you look at that picture back there, the documentary *Guilty as Charged*. Now that picture was made ten years ago, eleven years ago, and I had that mustache for twenty years, and it really is that white. I've had a Mohawk haircut; I had my head shaved for about three years.

It was down to my shoulders, and I was living out of town on a lake, and I got drunk one night, and I had a girl there with me, and I said, "I wonder what I'd look like bald."

And she said, "I don't know. Let's," she was drunk too, she said, "Let's shave your head."

And I said, "Fine, let's do it."

I forgot I had to go to the university the next morning. So I walk into the English Department. Then I thought you've got to have the courage of your madness, so I kept it shaved three years. I don't know. Maybe it has something to do with that.

Maybe it has something to do with this, and this will blow you away and you'll think "Oh, you've got to be kidding because it's not true." Well, maybe, maybe not. I think that all of my books, everything I've written as a matter of fact, including the journalism, in one way or another is either about people searching for something to believe in, something that has to do with faith, or the nature of faith. And hooked, it seems inevitably, with that is identity, because after all, monks—that's one extreme end—have an identity, but then so do the churches devoted to worshipping Satan in the hills of California. Those guys have an identity.

E.B.: So in order to have something that you believe in, you must first know who you are? And tied up in that is naming?

H.C.: Yeah, I would agree with that. And connected to that—I've said this before, but I don't think I've ever written it—yeah, I have; I wrote it in the *Childhood* book in the front where I've got all those disclaimers. But I have never been sure of who I am.

I was in the university my whole working life; I was *in* it, but not *of* it. I wrote that somewhere; I've written everything I know somewhere. So somebody calling me "professor"—I don't have a Ph.D. I don't even have a master's, really. The English Department I taught in turned me down to work for an English master's degree, and I got a master's degree in education, which is no master's degree at all. I never even bought any of their books. You don't have to buy their books. I made up the bibliographies for papers I wrote. I made up the footnotes. I made up the authors. Nobody ever knew, nobody ever cared. I got a master's degree in nine months and didn't write a thesis, had no language. You figure it out. But it allowed me to teach in a junior college. The year previous to that I met a hundred and eighty kids every day.

E.B.: Teaching in junior high?

H.C.: Yeah, and taught five different classes in five different buildings. And wrote a book that year. It's called *This World Uncommitted,* and you can tell from the title what it might have been like. It's a very bad book.

E.B.: You called *Naked in Garden Hills* your best book; you've also referred to *This Thing Don't Lead to Heaven* as being the book you are the least satisfied with.

H.C.: You know, I did say that, and I've changed my mind.

E.B.: Okay, why?

H.C.: I changed my mind because it was the third book I wrote, and it is dedicated to my dead son. James Boatwright, who was then and perhaps is now, was until very recently if he's not still down there, the editor of the *Shenandoah Review,* he reviewed it in the *New York Times*. Half a page review. Big, big review. He was not just unhappy with the book. He was unhappy that I was alive. About halfway through the review it just switched from the book to me. I just believed the guy.

It was an early book and I believed the guy. I caught the virus. I got down on it.

Later, when he was on sabbatical and a poet was the guest editor, I published a piece in his journal, the *Shenandoah Review*, that won the Coordinating Council of Literary Magazines in America's award for the best nonfiction piece published in any literary magazine in the whole country that year.

E.B.: What was that piece?

H.C.: It was a piece out of the *Childhood* book. It was the piece dealing with the scalding.

E.B.: Okay.

H.C.: About that, let me just tell you this. Most people don't notice this stuff, some do, some don't. I'd been writing really regularly a book a year almost, and then I got into dope and stuff and it was a book every two years, but the *Childhood* book . . . I wrote the *Childhood* book, and then after that I published *Blood and Grits*, but that book was already written, so you can't count that. So I wrote the *Childhood* book, and then there was a nine-year yawning silence. And it was simply because the *Childhood* book damn near killed me. I don't want to make too much out of it. But I thought, and maybe I've written this somewhere, but I thought that living through it again, remembering it all and writing it down in the most concrete, specific language I could summon, would be cathartic and I would no longer be plagued with the memories. Didn't work at all. So much for that.

I'm writing now, or I have a contract with Simon and Schuster to write, a book called *Assault of Memory*, which is another memoir after the fashion of *A Childhood*, but in this one I am starting out when I'm ten, my brother is fourteen, my mother is just going into a body cast.

E.B.: Has this one been as difficult to work on?

H.C.: I've quit working on it. I wrote my agent and said I'm happy with what I've got. I've got about, I don't know, a hundred and eighty manuscript pages, but I just couldn't go on with it.

And I had a novel with me that I'd been working on for a long time; it was called *The Horsehog-Gator Connection* and then it was called a whole bunch of things. It was called just *Horse*, now it's called this, and it'll probably be called something else finally. But I've had it with me a long time, and I like it. So I said I'll just finish this novel.

I do think that if I live, and assuming they don't blow the frigging world up, that I'll finish *Assault of Memory* because I really want to write it, but, damn, it's ugly. And I just, you know . . . I'd much rather sit here and look at the trees—and just beyond, just right out where the trees start is a little creek. And it is clear, a really clear little creek. Poison, of course.

E.B.: I know that you worked on several screenplays in the early eighties . . .

H.C.: Yeah, earlier than that . . .

E.B.: Has anything ever come out of any of the screenplays that you've done?

H.C.: Money! I got paid for them. Larry McMurtry's told me he'd written, at that time, and this was a couple of years ago, that he's written twenty-seven screenplays, and I think he said three or maybe four had been made into films. That's generally the way it works.

I wrote a screenplay for *The Gospel Singer*. See, I sold *The Gospel Singer* outright to Larry Spangler. I'd already found the location to shoot the film, Tallahassee, Alabama. It looked just like the town I had described in Enigma, Georgia. But he got into some legal trouble, and he sold my screenplay to Tom Jones. I went to see Tom Jones, and he hit on my wife. That was fun, hit on her while I was sitting there. Sally was beautiful though; she's a very beautiful woman. Tom Jones hit on everything that moved. I'm surprised that he didn't hit on me. But he was on tour, and we went to see him on tour. Anyway, it got locked up in courts, between the two of them, and now it's tied up and nobody will ever make it, but I wrote the screenplay for it and got paid for that.

I wrote a screenplay for *Naked in Garden Hills* for Frank Perry. I learned what I know from him. And then I wrote a screenplay for *The Hawk Is Dying*. That fell through. Couldn't find the money. I wrote an original screenplay for Sean Penn. He took me out to his house in Hollywood for a week and introduced me to Ed Harris and some of his other friends. I was supposed to write a screenplay for those people to be in. Ed Harris is one of my favorite movie guys anyway. So, yeah, I've written some screenplays. I wrote a screenplay for Michael Cimino right after *Heaven's Gate* came out.

E.B.: Who's doing *The Knockout Artist*? And is it far enough along now that it will be made?

H.C.: Francis Ford Coppola is the moving force behind it. A guy named Don Was, if you know anything about music, he's the guy that is directing it. Coppola was the guy that talked him into getting out of making videos and other things and into big screen. Coppola's company is doing the money part of it.

Francis Ford Coppola put in for me to write the screenplay for Kerouac's *On the Road,* which he's got the rights to. I didn't tell him yes; I didn't tell him no. I went down to the end of the street and bought the damn book and read it again, and said, "I don't want to write this." And I didn't. And I called him, and I said, "No, I don't think I want to write it."

And he said, "What do you want, more money?"

And I said, "That's not the issue. You know, you travel all the hell over in the book," and I named the city, and I said, "You know, I don't know the city, I don't know what it looks like this time of year, and I'd just be, I . . ."

He said, "Hey, you rent yourself a big coach, get a couple of friends, put one in the driver's seat, just go, follow the route, whatever, do it that way."

I said, "Man, you know how long you're talking about taking out of my life? I mean, I'd be on the road for X number of weeks, then I'd be on the set."

See, I wrote a screenplay called *The New Kids,* about a boy and girl whose daddy was a colonel, and a big hero, and they lived up north. They'd lived all over, been overseas, army brats. Their daddy was flying to Washington for the President to pin a medal on him and the plane went down and crashed, and he and the mama died. Left the two kids. One's in the eleventh grade, and one's in the twelfth grade. And the only relative they've got is an uncle, lives in Homestead, Florida, a cracker, and so they have to move down there to live with him. So, they've got to go, these two Yankee kids, into a redneck school.

The guy that made it, Sean Cunningham, his claim to fame is he made the first *Friday the 13th,* and got rich off it, and he's been making shitty pictures since. I was on the set of that film. I spent two days and two nights in a room with James Spader trying to teach him how to talk southern, because he was supposed to be a southern redneck. But he'd already had voice lessons in New York. I'd talk southern, and they only teach one dialect, the Delta dialect . . . "cah," you know, they call car "cah" . . . well, they don't call it "cah" down there, they call it "car," with a hard "rrrr," "carrrr." And he never could do that. But, we made the film.

All I can say is the money's good. And it was shitty work, but I liked Cunningham, I like his wife, they were down there, so it was all right. So, I've done a lot of that, and I've had the chance to do more. Had a guy that said, "Move to Los Angeles, I'll put you on salary and give you a great place to stay, and then when I got a project, then I'll pay you scale." I belong to the Screenwriters Guild, and—actually, it's the Writers Guild West, is what they call it. The least you can make for writing a screenplay is something like sixty thousand dollars; it goes up quickly from there. And it was really easy to say "no."

I'm gonna leave this? I ain't a screenwriter. I didn't start out to be a screenwriter; I didn't start out to work for *Playboy* either. I did it because my salary from the university went for alimony, so I had to make a nickel somewhere. And, so, that's what I did. I couldn't do it today. When I was younger, I stayed on the damn airplane, and in hotels, and dancing with people, you know.

E.B.: During an interview while you were working on *Scar Lover,* you called it "the darkest, blackest book I've written." Yet many, most, reviewers have seen the ending as being kind of upbeat and affirming the possibility of love and family.

H.C.: Well, I guess I called it that. Naw. Obviously I think that if we polled a whole bunch of people who read this stuff, if we could find them, they'd say *Feast of Snakes* would be the blackest. But I don't know. I love the business of loving a scar because once it scars, it don't hurt no more. That's cool. You'd be hard pressed to name something on me that hadn't been broke, including my neck and my cheeks crushed, my nose broken. Anyway, so scars, I loved that.

But burning that guy, going in the freezer. I mean, I don't even know. Going in the cold storage and looking for the tag on his toe. Said, "The hell with the tag, look for one with four toes, cut one off in the chopping block" [*laughing*]. And the woman picking up the skull after it cools. She had her fingers in his eye sockets; it was like a bowling ball, and I wrote that and I thought, "man, damn, this is . . . where is this shit coming from? This is terrible."

E.B.: *Scar Lover* and *The Mulching of America* seem to me to be a little bit different than your previous works in that . . .

H.C.: Outside the corpus . . . is that what they call it? Or whatever, oeuvre, or however you say that word. Yep, they seem to be outside and they are.

E.B.: They are almost surreal.

H.C.: They are, they are. God knows, anybody with any sense of fair play knows that I am not full of myself; you can't mention Faulkner in the same breath with me, but it is a little like *A Fable* with Faulkner. Somebody gave him that idea; you know that. It's got it right in the book. "I'm indebted to so and so for this idea." Well, he should have gone and shot the guy who gave him the idea. I think, that's just my own opinion.

And truthfully, *Mulching of America* . . . um [*sighs*], *Mulching of America* just got away from me. It got away from me and I never could get it back. It has about it, certainly in the ending and in other places, the cardinal sin of any drama or novel; it is just totally unbelievable. It is painful to say these things, but, if it is the truth . . . It's like my ma said about the *Childhood* book, "If it's the truth, write it." So, the truth is that I wish I had the *Mulching* book back, and I would burn it. Although the French just bought it for, God bless them, I mean, I can keep my head above water for a while on what they paid for it. I don't know why. The French are curious people.

E.B.: You've talked a lot in the past about writers that you've read that influenced you, who you think are good. What about the current crop of writers? Who do you think is out there writing right now that you think is good?

H.C.: Curiously enough, I think that Barry Hannah has the most distinctive voice maybe in the whole damn country. He does things with sentences that I look at them and try to see what the hell he did with them to make them sound so memorable, so uniquely his own. I never can see. So I like his work a lot. One of the really new ones—well, he's been at it a while now, but it hasn't been too terribly long—Larry Brown is right up there. He lives right there by Barry Hannah. I don't know; people ask me questions like that and it's like asking "What books have you read recently?" and I can't name any despite the fact that I read constantly.

E.B.: You've said before that "I'm a believer with nothing to believe." Could you elaborate on that a little bit?

H.C.: I am a believer. Natural laws just put you into a bind. Why does everything fall down instead of sideways? And why does sap rise at a certain time? And all that kind of thing. I mean, it just blows me away. And one famous theologian, whose name I can't recall, said the ultimate question to ask an atheist is "Why is there something instead of nothing?" And then you think about first cause. All right, some proteins came together and crawled up out of the sea, all right, but anyway, you know what I mean.

But number one, I have never . . . and I've tried, I really gave it a shot. I went to all of them practically that I could find, churches, organized religions, trying to find one that I could just . . . 'cause I think church is a really good . . . Going to church is really good for one reason: it is a place to go and sit down and contemplate the inadequacies of your own heart and just leave it there. But you could do that anywhere. But I couldn't find anything like that.

And then secondly the whole business of—I mean, we've got Bangladesh and Bosnia, and there is supposed to be somebody or something somewhere that knows Harry Crews—Harry Crews?—and some kind of record is being kept? And we got mansions and streets of gold and, hell, I mean, really. Oliver Wendell Holmes, a confirmed atheist, said, "You'll have to forgive me if I cannot believe in your fairy tales."

But it's not so much believing. The Bible is a great book to read because there is just so much in it that is patently true. You can't go around coveting your neighbor's wife. It won't work. You don't necessarily need the Bible for that. But we live in a totally secular world. I mean the "God is dead" thing; of course, that goes back a long time, Nietzsche, even earlier.

But wouldn't it be wonderful, and I'm talking about me now, wouldn't it be wonderful for me if I did have something immutable, omnipotent, ubiquitous—all those other English teacher words—and that I could put myself into the keeping of that kind of power and knowledge. And He will, or She. . . It will provide. So, no, I believe, but there ain't nothing to believe. Said another way, the culture and, God help us, the economic system I live in has killed any semblance of anything that resembles or could resemble a godhead or first cause or anything like that.

If communism worked, if we really could "from each according to . . . , to each according to," if it really worked . . . Property is theft. I really believe that. What am I doing in this house? Please tell me. When there are people sleeping in refrigerator cartons, boxes, pasteboard boxes, and starving to death, and my stomach is full. And I still got some money left. What the hell is that all about?

So, but for communism as Lenin and Marx and Engels, the stuff that all three of those guys wrote, for that to work you'd have to have an entire population of what Jesus is reported to have been. If you had everybody like that, then you could do it—somebody who would ride a donkey when he could get into a Cadillac. After all, if you can change water into wine, why not change water into Cadillac even back then? He could have just gotten himself some gas and tooled around. But he didn't do that.

E.B.: Your comment about church being a good place to contemplate the inadequacies of your own heart actually sounds very familiar, very similar to some of the comments you've made about what effect you want to have on your readers. That you want them to look . . .

H.C.: I want my work to turn them back upon themselves and force them to look into their own hearts. And I think that if you can really get them so that they are so involved with, so enamored of, so outraged by these people that never existed—they don't exist, just little scratches on a piece of paper—if you can get them so enamored that they begin to make judgments, every effort of the writer is to make the reader make the judgments, the big judgments. You make the little ones—he was a little man—well, how little is little? What the hell does that mean? Well, let it go, you know, he was a little guy. Not those judgments. To make him make the big judgments.

The greatest of that kind of literature will change you, make you weep. Faulkner's short story "Two Soldiers"—if I want to tear up, I can just go read that. World War II has just started, and this guy says to his younger brother, "Well, I gotta go down and join up."

And his little brother says, "Yeah, we'll just have to go on down there and join up."

And he says, "Well, you can't go. You're too little."

And the little brother says, "Well, they'll have to have somebody to cut the wood and tote the water. I can go do that." And he follows his brother up to the recruiting station and pulls his knife—he's just a little boy—pulls his knife on the recruiting sergeant, but they finally sent him back home.

But there's a lot of places like that. Hemingway, as melodramatic and operatic as he can sometimes be, when Robert Jordan has broken his leg, right at the end of the book [*For Whom the Bell Tolls*], and he's running from the guys coming up the hill, and he's off his horse, he can't ride. Maria's still on the horse, and he says, "We can never go to Madrid together." And he's asking for a gun to hold them off as long as he can. And he and Maria are talking and she's got his baby, and interspersed all between this, which is just a stroke of genius, interlaced between this terribly touching thing between him and Maria, this fucking gypsy keeps saying, "Do you want me to shoot you, *Inglés*? It is nothing, *Inglés*. I could shoot you." He's not an Englishman, he's a goddamn American, but he calls him *"Inglés"* all through. You know, that's just a moment.

And that turns you always; it always comes back here [*pointing to himself*].

E.B.: What was the last book that you read that had one of those moments that made you turn back in upon yourself?

H.C.: Well, I just got through with a book called *Suicide Blonde*—I wish they hadn't called it that—by Darcy Steinke. God, the paperback's got a naked lady lying on a bed lighting a cigarette—I wish that weren't there too—and it is, as George Garrett says on the back of the thing, aflame with sex. But it also deals with lust and love, and deals with how the promise of Eden can turn into a nightmare. It is beautifully written. It's about this girl that's living on the edge where there is no edge. She's looking right into the abyss. And she's not doing it to make a lot of money, she's not doing it to be famous, not for game, but really for the most ordinary human reasons. What kind of human reasons? Because she is lonely. Because she wants to be loved. Because she wants to save certain people she cares about from themselves. Just the kind of shit we all get caught in.

E.B.: In *The Hawk Is Dying* you begin with an epigraph from Flaubert that I'll read . . .

H.C.: I can quote it.

E.B.: Okay, go ahead.

H.C.: "Human language is" —I may get some words wrong, just let me say it— "Human language is a cracked bell on which we beat out tunes for bears to dance to while—while all the—something—we are longing to move the stars to pity." Which is just a long way around of saying that . . . anybody that writes a book and doesn't feel that it is a failure I am suspect of. It took Flaubert nine years to write *Madame Bovary*, but that don't mean nothing necessarily. The guy who wrote *Look Homeward, Angel*—see, I can't get these names. I know where the guy comes from and everything else.

E.B.: Thomas Wolfe.

H.C.: Yeah. Thomas Wolfe's *Look Homeward, Angel* never would have been published if it had been left up to him. They gave him a little spot up in the Scribner's building and he was up there, goddamnit, rewriting the galleys, which you can't do. Jesus, it would cost a fortune to rewrite those sons-of-bitches. But he was. One time Maxwell Perkins sent him home to cut this piece, and he came back the next day and it was ten thousand words longer. Maxwell Perkins without his knowledge just sent the son of a bitch right on to the printer. Because, you know, he just couldn't get it right.

And all those times that Hemingway rewrote the ending to *A Farewell to Arms*. He rewrote it fifty-some-odd times.

They said, "What were you trying to do?"

He said, "Get the words right."

I always love answers like that. I mean, hey, don't ask me stupid questions. If I'd figured it out, I wouldn't have had to rewrite it fifty-three times, or forty-two, or nineteen, or whatever it was.

E.B.: While you were working on *All We Need of Hell*, two excerpts appeared, both called "The Enthusiast," which was the novel's working title. One of those excerpts was in *Black Warrior Review*, but it is a very different-feeling piece than the published novel. It's about a writer named Harry Crews . . .

H.C.: Oh yeah, well, that now has become *Where Do You Go When There's No Place Left to Go?* Harry Crews is in that novel. And Belt is in it from the karate book. Margo the hotel whore is in it from *Car*, as is the boy that eats the car. Fat Man is in it from *Naked in Garden Hills*. The Gospel Singer is in it. He didn't die. He's got this purple scar around his neck. He can't sing anymore, but people can come up after he gets through preaching and they can hold his throat, and many times they are healed. But his voice is ruined from hanging on the rope all night. He can't sing anymore. And Didymus says that it's a miracle, but Harry Crews doesn't understand, because what would he know about miracles.

And it turns out, someplace in the book, Margo asks him, "Did you ever think about healing yourself or your ruined voice by holding your own throat?" And of course he holds his own throat, but he holds it so tight he ends up strangling himself to death.

It is a curious book. Those were curious times. I was starting things and not finishing them. And I was confused.

E.B.: That's also about the same time that you started *Blood Issue*.

H.C.: Yeah, yeah, yeah, that was about that time. It's true.

E.B.: But you didn't finish that until 1989 or so?

H.C.: Well, it was after I came back from Louisiana and I'd just sold *The Knockout Artist* for way and again more money than I'd ever sold any novel for. I sold it for more than I'd ever sold four novels for. And the Actor's Theatre of Louisville asked me if I'd take fifteen thousand dollars' commission to write a play, a full-length play. And since I'd never written a play, didn't know the first thing about it, I said yes, just to see if I could.

The play got a standing ovation. There were seven new plays done there, and I got a standing ovation. It's been performed at several local places since then. I always threatened to keep working on it until I got it down; it's too damn long. I know now why playwrights are thought of as poets and why poets have been playwrights. Man, language—language is the gig. I mean, if Tennessee Williams wasn't a poet, what the hell was he? As a matter of fact, can I tell you this thing about Tennessee Williams?

E.B.: Sure.

H.C.: I knew Tennessee Williams off and on and saw him here and yonder for many, many years. And Tennessee was down at this time in Key West, and the university was forever trying to get him to come up here and do something, anything. So finally he wrote and said, "Yeah, I'll come up if you let Harry Crews introduce me." They never let me introduce anybody because they were afraid of what I'd do. And so Tennessee and I were supposed to go to dinner, and we did go to dinner, but we didn't eat, we drank it. So we're both pretty well lit, and we are going back to the Reitz Union, that seats six hundred people. There were people sitting in the aisles and all the seats are full. And right in the front were the president of the school and all the bald-headed deans and vice presidents, all that bullshit.

Somebody introduced me, and it was long and terrible. And I said, "Thank you very much for that warm and generous introduction."

And then here is the introduction I gave for Tennessee, verbatim. I said, "Ladies and gentlemen, it is customary on these occasions to say where the writer went to school and where he was born, and the honors he has won. But who gives a shit?" You hear this collective gasp. "But who gives"—I'm staring right at the power structure of the school—"who gives a shit? If Tennessee Williams had not written anything other than the long lyrical poem that is *The Glass Menagerie*, it would be enough for us to come here and pay him homage. Ladies and gentlemen, America's greatest living playwright, Tennessee Williams."

And he made his way to the podium, and he just was kind of blinking and shaking his head, and in that lovely accent of his he said, "That's rather the nicest introduction I've ever had." And only because he said that I didn't hear a word from anybody about what I had said. If he hadn't said that, I would have been, first, in the chairman's office the next morning, and after that I would have been in the dean's office.

E.B.: You begin *A Childhood* with "My first memory is of a period ten years before I was born..."

H.C.: I can quote that sentence, too. Sentences like that don't just pop out of your head. "My first"—let's see if I can—"My first memory is of a time before I was born and takes place where I have never been and involves my father, whom I never knew." It's not antithetical, but it is classically balanced. I'm proud of the sentence. I was proud of the sentence when I finally got it.

I'll tell you, for whatever it is worth, and worth very little, I suspect, but I consciously try to write the strongest beginning, whether it is an essay or a novel or anything. I try to write the strongest beginning I can write and try to live up to it. You know, say, "All right, boy, that fucking beginning sings, Jack. You're from the Hell's-a-Poppin' School of Literature and that motherfucker is exploding there." I say that to myself whether it is or not. A writer's the worst judge of his work. The worst person in the world to ask about a book is the guy that wrote it. But then I try, as I say, *try* to live up to it. That's how that sentence came to be.

E.B.: One of your favorite techniques is to bring characters from one novel to another one.

H.C.: Yeah, well, it's not so much as I bring them, as the sons-of-bitches turn up. I think it's because I already know them. I'll tell you, Tote Walker, in *All We Need of Hell*, he really deserves a novel that's all his own. I think he's got one of the best hearts of any guy I ever met, the way he deals with the kid, the way he deals with the cops, the way he deals with Duffy. Know when to use it, and know when to lose it. It doesn't matter, that coke and shit; he shouldn't be doing it, but he does it. He deserves his own novel.

Do you know the book *Edisto*? Padgett Powell just wrote a sequel to that novel. If I'm going to write a sequel about anything, it would be *The Knockout Artist*, when the guy looks up and he says, "You want me? I got nothin', we got nothin'—we got nothin'."

And the Cajun kid holds up his fists, and he says, "We got dese."

And they're going away in a pickup truck, they're leaving New Orleans and they're getting away from Oyster Boy and all that stuff. And, you know, I wonder where they went and I wonder what they're doing. I don't know, but I can find out.

E.B.: Like many writers, you speak as though your characters are a separate thing.

H.C.: I'll tell you something, man, the reason I gotta go back in there every morning is I leave my characters. Sometimes they are about to eat a meal, or sometimes they're coming down a ladder, and I've left them there. Jesus . . . that's no way to do! I mean, you gotta go get them down off the ladder, or you gotta feed them, or the guy has just cut himself bad, and nobody's even picked him up, he's gotta get to a hospital. And that bothers me. But, hell, if he's in a really good place, I want to know how much he's gonna enjoy it.

At first, you only have a name, Jim or John, or whatever, and then he's a cipher. It's nothing. But gradually that thing begins to get blood and bone and hair and bad breath and history and children and a mother, and he feels like however he feels toward his mother and where he's born and how he is and how he talks, and what he wants and what he is willing to give up to get it, and all of these things. It's impossible, it seems to me, that if you are writing honestly and hard, not to come to think of them as living, breathing beings. And so that's the way that is. You're absolutely right. I talk about them that way; I think about them that way.

E.B.: The character of Russell Morgan, Russell Muscle, seems to be one of your favorites. He's been in four novels now.

H.C.: Yeah, well, he just keeps popping up. He's just got bit parts, cameo roles in the others. In *Knockout Artist*, he just introduces the fighters. But I know Lee Haney, who's won Mr. Olympia more times than Schwarzenegger won it. I have talked at great length to Schwarzenegger, out in California, at Gold's Gym. I know the Golden Eagle, and I know Franco Columbo, who won Mr. Olympia, too, and who's a chiropractor, and Sylvester Stallone's trainer. I've known those guys, and Russell Morgan just so reminded me of them. He works out like a house afire, and then he lies in a dark room and plies himself with these supplements and all kinds of other things. I am convinced that a lot of the top body builders in this country are on steroids.

Russell Morgan is just sweet and tragic at the same time. That business of his wife, his poor little wife and his little children, how beat down and brutalized they are. A guy that wants to do something that bad is willing to sacrifice anybody, including his mother. It's just the way they are, and it's the thing they make themselves. And you can't do it any other way than to do it that way.

There's an overwhelming fascination for me with people who are willing to pay the price, whatever the price is, to do what's in them to do. A twenty-eight-year-old Mr. America dropped dead of a heart attack from steroids. And you get into roaring rages. They pump enough testosterone in you and you'll attack an elephant.

So you say, "Well, why are these guys doing this?" Well, let me tell you something. When I was twenty-eight or twenty-nine years old, I'd been struggling all this time and losing, if somebody had come to me and said, "Harry, I've got a needle with some stuff in it, that I can just hit you in the ass with, but I gotta keep hitting you with it for a while, a month, or two, or three, and then you'll have a novel, and it'll be a fine novel." I would be to a novel what Lyle Alzado was to his position.

"But," the guy would tell me, "you might, you might not, but there's a fair chance that you will die early, or have some side effects that are rather dreadful."

I wouldn't have hesitated a second. I would have said, "Where is the needle?" That's how bad I wanted it, and those guys want it that bad.

E.B.: Gaye Nell O'Dell was first in *Karate,* but then also in *Mulching of America.* But she seems like a very different character. Is it the same person?

H.C.: No, no, no, no. She's named after a girl I knew who . . . I'm not prepared to say that she was a bad human being, or worse than most of us, or anything else. But, I am prepared to say that she ruined my best friend's frigging life, and, as far as I am concerned, caused him to do time. Fairly serious time. In that serious jail they got up here at Starke, or Raiford, or wherever the hell it is. That's the only person I've ever used a real name like that, that's still alive. I used a lot of the characteristics she had. I've used some names of people that were dead. Hickum Looney was a real guy.

E.B.: Really?

H.C.: Yeah. Tennessee . . . East Tennessee. But, long time ago. He's been dead for twenty years.

E.B.: You've used just the names of some people, like your childhood playmate Willalee, who . . .

H.C.: Willalee Bookatee was . . . Now, we know what "Bookatee" would have come from. That's Booker T. Washington. Willalee? I don't know what that's all about, but he was just called Willalee Bookatee. Little black boy, about the same age as me.

E.B.: But I'm not just talking about in *A Childhood*. In *The Gospel Singer*, you have a character with that same name. He ends up being lynched at the end, and then Willalee's real sister was named Lottie Mae, right? And you have a character named Lottie Mae in *Feast*, and she's the one who is raped by the sheriff. That seems like a strange thing to do to your childhood friends—to use them to name your characters who suffer such horrendous ends.

H.C.: [*pauses*] I didn't even know I'd done that, until you just told me . . .

E.B.: Really?

H.C.: No. Uh-uh . . . oh God. Well . . . well, I'm just glad that I won't be around . . . well, ain't anybody gonna pick over my work anyway. And if they do, I . . . I hope I'm not around to see it, or . . . I never read any reviews or stuff, and certainly I don't read interviews because I always sound like such a fool, and I get stuff wrong. When it's wrong, I say to myself, "I couldn't possibly have said that."

E.B.: Were you hurt or angered by Sterling Watson's fictionalized portrayal of you in *The Calling*?

H.C.: He sent me the book, and he said something to the effect that he meant it as a tribute, or something, whatever. You know, Sterling Watson... I didn't do anything for Sterling Watson but buy his food half the time, buy him his whiskey, help him with his family—he had a wife and kid, he was a student of mine—and I taught him everything I could teach him. Hung out with him. Back in those days, we ran together, every evening and all that.

And he's not only got me in there, he's got my wife in there. My son was receiving death threats, not delivered with a stamp on it from the postman, but in an envelope in my mailbox. I never could find out who was doing it. But he's got that in there. He's got my dog in there, and there's just a lot of things he's got in there that are just... true. And the guy that reviewed it in the *New York Times* said, "This is supposed to be a roman à clef, but you don't need a key. Anybody that knows anything about American literature knows that this is patterned after Harry Crews."

Sterling called me one time, and I said, "The only thing I've got to say is that this is a blood offense. And the only thing that satisfies a blood offense is blood." And that's where the matter stands.

I haven't seen him. There was a big literary fair down there at the school where he is, and every writer in the country was there. But he didn't show up anywhere around there. I didn't know quite how it would be if he did. It didn't bother me that much of what he wrote was true. What bothered me was the tone of it. The stance that was taken on it. How this was a guy that hurts people, that fucks over people, that doesn't care about people, that is a slobbering drunk that doesn't do anything but drink.

People say, "Well, you've stayed drunk and done all this your whole life?"

I just say, "Look at the work, man, you can't do that drunk, or any other way. You gotta be straight to do that. And, you can't do it with your head on the curb, or anything else."

So there's this perception of me, and I wish it weren't true. The word in the street and in the writing community, such as I am in the writing community—it's just all wrong. The guy in the *Tampa Tribune*, when he did that article, up at the top, it had "Tough Guy." Going way back, yeah, it's true, I hung out in bars, and you hang out in certain places, well, you ain't gonna fall off a ten-thousand-foot rock face unless you put yourself up there. If you put yourself in the right place, things happen.

But, going way back, when I was healthy and young, and a lot stronger than I am now, guys would walk up to me and tell me things I was supposed to be involved in, and I'd say, "No, man, no . . . whoever told you that, I wouldn't have been nowhere around that."

And guys would walk up to me and say, "Oh, you're so and so," and "You're the guy that thinks he's so bad."

And I'd say, "No, no, wait a minute. I don't think I am." And he'd be talking so loud, and I'd say, "Now wait a minute, man, I don't know you; you don't know me. We got nothing to say to each other. See that door over there?" I mean, I'm in the corner, the bar is here, the wall's there, and I got no place to go and he's between me and the door. I'd say, "You see the door over there? If you'll just let me get to the door, and walk out of here, then you won't have to bother with me any more, because I don't want it this way." But that's the wrong thing to say, too, because that just makes the guy think you're playing with him or something.

I wish that perception wasn't there. I think it comes from the subject matter of my books, and I think it comes from my mugging for cameras, which I do because it's the only way I can stand to look at a camera. I just can't do it. I feel so weird, and particularly if you've got six or seven guys with cameras, you feel like something in a zoo. So, you want something in a zoo, I'll show you something in a zoo.

It's a mistake I started making early, and I never knew it was a mistake until it was too late. So now it's stuck, and that's the label that's on me. Back when I drank so bad, when I went anywhere to lecture, or do something at a university, first thing that happened when I get off the plane is some guy handed me a glass. And the game was "Let's give Crews all the alcohol he'll take in his hand, and watch him get totally out of it and be a fool." Which is what all stone drunks end up doing 'cause they don't know what they're doing.

So that's part of it. But I suspect that it's not just writers. It's not unique to any given profession or avocation or anything else. Everybody's got a whole bunch of stuff that they think, "Gee, I know if I could have cut that out, or if I could edit this life, I would snip that out." Of course that really doesn't work.

E.B.: Nearly everyone I told that I was coming down here to interview you had a Harry Crews story to share. Do you worry that "Harry Crews: The Legend" threatens to overshadow "Harry Crews: The Work"?

H.C.: Well, as far as that goes, I already do. I mean, more people are more interested, it seems, in talking about what I'm supposed to have done and what I still do than they are interested in my books. They read one book and they've read me or something. Hey, if you like my work and you read a lot of it . . . well, of course I'm glad. I mean, that's what I wrote it for. But if you don't, I'm not angry, I'm not sad, I'm not anything. Nobody's under any obligation to read any more than you want to read, or read any at all. It certainly doesn't worry me.

I worry a lot, but about the only thing I ever worry about is the next five hundred words. Because, I'll tell you, I can't understand anybody who tells me that they enjoy writing, that it's fun. Frankly, I don't believe them. It's certainly never been fun for me. What *is a real rush, for me, is after you've done it, before you even send it to New York, and that's it. I know this is strange, but when you look at it, and you think, "Before me, this was not. Because of me, this is." Now that's a rush.*

CREDITS

"Interview with Harry Crews," by Anne Foata, from *Recherches Anglaises et Americaines*. Reprinted by permission of *Recherches Anglaises et Americaines*. Copyright 1972.

"Arguments over an Open Wound: An Interview with Harry Crews," by Sterling Watson, from *Prairie Schooner*. Reprinted by permission of the author and the University of Nebraska Press. Copyright 1974 by the University of Nebraska Press.

"Harry Crews: An Interview," by Joe David Bellamy, from *Fiction International*. Reprinted by permission of the author and the San Diego State University Press. Copyright 1976.

"Harry Crews: Working the Kinks Out," by Al Burt, from the *Miami Herald*. Reprinted by permission of the *Miami Herald*. Copyright 1974.

"Harry Crews Is a Stomp-Down Hard-Core Moralist," by Steve Oney, from *Atlanta Journal and Constitution Magazine*. Reprinted by permission of the *Atlanta Journal and Constitution*. Copyright 1977.

"Harry Crews: Part of an Interview," by David K. Jeffrey and Donald R. Noble, from the *Black Warrior Review*. Reprinted by permission of the authors and the *Black Warrior Review*. Copyright 1979.

"Harry Crews: An Interview," by David K. Jeffrey and Donald R. Noble, from *A Grit's Triumph: Essays on the Works of Harry Crews*. Reprinted by permission of the authors. Copyright 1983.

"The Troubles with Harry," by Al Burt, from the *Miami Herald*. Reprinted by permission of the *Miami Herald*. Copyright 1978.

"Harry Crews," by Tom Graves. Portions appeared in *Southern Exposure*, *Chouteau Review*, and the *Memphis Flyer*. It appears here in a more complete version by permission of the author. Copyright 1998.

"An Interview with Harry Crews," by Kay Bonetti, from the *Missouri Review*. Reprinted by permission of American Audio Prose Library. Copyright 1983. This interview is available on audiocassette from the American Audio Prose Library (AAPL, P.O. Box 842, Columbia, MO 65205, [800] 447-2275, www.americanaudioprose.com).

"The Freedom to Act: An Interview with Harry Crews," by Rodney Elrod, from *New Letters*. Reprinted by permission of *New Letters*, the curators of the University of Missouri–Kansas City, and the author. Copyright 1989.

"Harry Crews," by A. B. Crowder, from *Writing in the Southern Tradition: Interviews with Five Contemporary Authors*. Reprinted by permission of Rodopi Publishing. Copyright 1990.

"The Writer Who Plays with Pain: Harry Crews," by Hank Nuwer, from *Rendezvous with Contemporary Writers*. Reprinted by permission of the author. Copyright 1988.

"Still in the Game: On the Straight and Narrow with Writer Harry Crews," by Mary T. Schmich, from the *Atlanta Journal and Constitution*. Reprinted by permission of the *Orlando Sentinel*. Copyright 1985.

"Harry Goes Cruising for a Bruising," by Mary Voboril, from the *Miami Herald*. Reprinted by permission of the *Miami Herald*. Copyright 1987.

"Harry Crews," by William Walsh, from *Speak So I Shall Know Thee: Interviews with Southern Writers*. Reprinted by permission of McFarland and Company. Copyright 1990 by William Walsh.

"Harry Crews: Pen-Packin' Old Boy," by Rob Michaels, from *Motorbooty*. Reprinted by permission of the author and *Motorbooty* (Box 02007, Detroit, MI 48202, www.motorbooty.com). Copyright 1990.

"An Interview with Harry Crews," by Dinty W. Moore, from *Associated Writing Programs Chronicle*. Reprinted by permission of the author. Copyright 1992.

"Still Macho after All These Years," by Joann Biondi, from *Sunshine: The Magazine of South Florida*. Reprinted by permission of the author. Copyright 1991.

"Writing Is an Act of Discovery: Harry Crews," by David Aronson, from *Alumni clas Notes*, University of Florida. Reprinted by permission of *Alumni clas Notes*. Copyright 1992.

"Some of Us Do It Anyway: An Interview with Harry Crews," by Tammy Lytal and Richard R. Russell, from *Georgia Review*. Reprinted by permission of the authors. Copyright 1994.

"Blue-Eyed Boy," by Ruth Ellen Rasche, from *University of Florida Today*. Reprinted by permission of *University of Florida Today*. Copyright 1992.

"Interview with Harry Crews," by Susan Ketchin, from *The Christ-Haunted Landscape: Faith and Doubt in Southern Fiction*. Reprinted by permission of the University Press of Mississippi. Copyright 1994.

"Harry Crews: Literary Terminator," by Cathi Unsworth, from *Purr*. Reprinted by permission of the author. Copyright 1995.

"Everything Is Optimism, Beautiful and Painless: A Conversation with Harry

Crews," by Damon Sauve. Published here for the first time by permission of the author. Copyright 1998.

"An Interview with Harry Crews," by Erik Bledsoe, from the *Southern Quarterly*. Reprinted by permission of the *Southern Quarterly*. Copyright 1998.